THE ILLUSTRATED ENCYCLOPEDIA OF

BIRDS OF AMERICA

THE ILLUSTRATED ENCYCLOPEDIA OF
BIRDS OF AMERICA

DAVID ALDERTON

with illustrations by Peter Barrett

LORENZ BOOKS

This edition is published by Lorenz Books

Lorenz Books is an imprint of Anness Publishing Ltd
Hermes House, 88–89 Blackfriars Road, London SE1 8HA
tel. 020 7401 2077; fax 020 7633 9499
www.lorenzbooks.com; info@anness.com

© Anness Publishing Ltd 2004

UK agent: The Manning Partnership Ltd, 6 The Old Dairy, Melcombe Road, Bath BA2 3LR
tel. 01225 478444; fax 01225 478440; sales@manning-partnership.co.uk

UK distributor: Grantham Book Services Ltd, Isaac Newton Way, Alma Park Industrial
Estate, Grantham, Lincs NG31 9SD
tel. 01476 541080; fax 01476 541061; orders@gbs.tbs-ltd.co.uk

North American agent/distributor: National Book Network
4501 Forbes Boulevard, Suite 200, Lanham, MD 20706
tel. 301 459 3366; fax 301 429 5746; www.nbnbooks.com

Australian agent/distributor: Pan Macmillan Australia
Level 18, St Martins Tower, 31 Market St, Sydney, NSW 2000
tel. 1300 135 113; fax 1300 135 103; customer.service@macmillan.com.au

New Zealand agent/distributor: David Bateman Ltd
30 Tarndale Grove, Off Bush Road, Albany, Auckland
tel. (09) 415 7664; fax (09) 415 8892

Publisher: Joanna Lorenz
Editorial Director: Helen Sudell
Project Editor: Catherine Stuart
Text Editors: Ian Woodward and Jen Green
Design: Nigel Partridge
Chief Illustrator: Peter Barrett
Additional Illustrations: see Picture Acknowledgements
Editorial Readers: Lindsay Zamponi and Jay Thundercliffe
Production Controller: Pedro Nelson

1 3 5 7 9 10 8 6 4 2

Pictures: endpapers: Flamingos (Phoenicopteridae); *page 1: red-breasted sapsuckers* (Sphyrapicus
rubber); *page 2: gila woodpecker* (Melanerpes uropygialis); *page 3: ringed kingfisher pair*
(Megaceryle torquata); *page 4: greater sage grouse displaying, and pair* (Centrocercus urophasianus);
page 5, top: bananaquit (Coereba flaveloa); *bottom: red phalarope pair* (Phalaropus fulicaria)
Jacket pictures: All photographs on jacket front supplied by Ardea; all artwork by Peter Barrett

CONTENTS

INTRODUCTION

Birds have been a source of fascination and inspiration to people since the dawn of history. Birds' mastery of the skies not only inspired humans to invent flying machines but also helped facilitate the development of modern aircraft, since airplane designers borrowed the aerodynamic features of birds to revolutionize aircraft used in intercontinental travel.

Birds have also influenced our cultures in a spiritual sense, as indicated, for example, by the thunderbird legends of the native North Americans. The feathers of various parrots, especially the majestic multi-colored macaws, continue to adorn ceremonial head-dresses and other garments, as part of the traditions of various Central American tribal people. Other occurrences reflect the role of birds as harbingers of the seasons. The reappearance of migrants from southern wintering grounds, such as the scarlet tanager (*Piranga olivacea*), is eagerly anticipated every North American springtime, as a sign of the approaching warmer weather.

It may seem surprising, but there are still new species of birds being discovered every year. Among the most recent is a new bald-headed parrot from the Mato Grosso region of Brazil, reported for the first time

Below: Birds have adapted to live, feed and breed in a wide range of different habitats. Here a puffin (Fratercula arctica) *is returning from a successful fishing trip at sea.*

Above: Rheas are the largest birds found in America today, and are confined to the southern continent where they roam the grassland areas. They stand about as tall as an adult person.

in July 2002. As an approximate guide, there are over 9,000 avian species present on Earth—a total far in excess of the number of mammals. There is virtually no environment on the planet where birds are not to be seen, even in the freezing wasteland of Antarctica, where penguins maintain a remarkable vigil to breed in one of the most inhospitable environments to be found anywhere on Earth.

Birds have spread so widely over the planet's surface not only because of their ability to fly, but also because they are highly adaptable in their feeding habits. Birds eat a wide variety of foods, ranging from microscopic plankton to the carcasses of large mammals, as well as all types of vegetable matter and numerous invertebrates.

In recent years, human activities have had an increasingly harmful impact on numerous avian populations around the world, and are now threatening the very survival of many species. On the bright side, however, technology is being applied as never before to assist the survival of critically endangered species such as the Californian condor (*Gymnogyps californianus*), giving real hope for such birds' survival in what may hopefully become a more enlightened era of human activity.

Birdwatching has also benefited from technological advances, such as the Internet, which enables information about new sightings to be relayed instantly to

enthusiasts. Undoubtedly, webcam opportunities to observe bird sites even on the other side of the world will increase in the years ahead. Yet one of the reasons why birdwatching has become such a popular pastime is that it can be carried out basically anywhere. No special equipment is necessarily required, although binoculars, sketchpads and similar items can add greatly to your enjoyment and understanding of avian life.

This book is a celebration of birds that sets out to reveal the diversity that exists in both their form and lifestyles. The second part features species that can be observed throughout America, and off the shores of these two continents. Each bird is placed within the geographical context in which it is most likely to be seen. Even if you do not have the opportunity to visit the lush rainforests of the Amazon basin, or the Alaskan tundra, you will still be able to marvel at the diversity of American avian life, as portrayed in these pages.

Below: Secure nesting sites are important for the survival of all birds. This Harris's hawk (Parabuteo unicinctus) *has bred successfully, with its nest being protected by a thorny cactus.*

HOW BIRDS LIVE

The most obvious thing that distinguishes all birds, from the tiniest hummingbirds (Trochilidae) to the gigantic Californian condor (*Gymnogyps californianus*), is the presence of feathers on their bodies. The need for birds to be lightweight, in order to fly with minimum effort, has led to significant changes within their bodies as well, and yet the basic skeletal structure of all birds is remarkably similar, irrespective of their size. In other words, birds are unmistakable. It is instantly clear that even the few groups of flightless birds, such as penguins (Spheniscidae), are descended from ancestors that possessed the power of flight, although these birds have since evolved along different lines to suit their habitat.

The other feature unique to birds is that all species reproduce by means of calcareous eggs. Birds' breeding habits are very diverse, however. Some birds even transfer the task of incubation to other species, by laying eggs in their nests, while others create natural incubators that serve to hatch their chicks and carefully regulate the temperature inside.

There is even greater diversity in the feeding habits of birds, as reflected by differences in their bill structures, and also in their digestive tracts. Birds' dietary preferences play a critical part in the environment as well. For example, in tropical rainforests, many fruit-eating species help to disperse indigestible seeds through the forest, thus helping to ensure the natural regeneration of the vegetation.

The birds of tropical rainforests are often surprisingly hard to observe, betraying their presence more by their calls than by their bright colors. However, birds can be easily observed in many other localities. Birdwatching itself can develop into an absorbing pastime offering an unparalleled insight into the natural world. Many practical tips to help you enjoy this activity are included in the following pages.

Left: Many seabirds, such as these common terns (Sterna hirundo), *are highly social by nature, and congregate in large, open-air colonies during the breeding season. They are also relatively slow to mature, and long-lived, with a life expectancy of more than a decade.*

THE ORIGINS OF BIRDS

Vertebrates—first flying reptiles called pterosaurs, and later birds—took to the air about 190 million years ago. Adapting to an aerial existence marked a very significant step in vertebrate development, because of the need for a new method of locomotion, and a radically different body design.

The age of *Archaeopteryx*

Back in 1861, workers in a limestone quarry in Bavaria, southern Germany, unearthed a strange fossil that resembled a bird in appearance and was about the size of a modern crow, but also had teeth. The idea that the fossil was a bird was confirmed by the clear evidence of feathers impressed into the stone, as the presence of plumage is one of the characteristic distinguishing features of all birds. The 1860s were a time when the debate surrounding evolution was becoming fierce, and the discovery created huge interest, partly because it suggested that birds may have evolved from dinosaurs. It confirmed that birds had lived on Earth for at least 145 million years, existing even before the age of the dinosaurs came to a close in the Cretaceous period, about 65 million years ago. As the oldest-known bird, it became known as *Archaeopteryx*, meaning "ancient wings."

Pterosaurs

A study of the anatomy of *Archaeopteryx*'s wings revealed that these early birds did not just glide but were capable of using their wings for active flight. Yet they were not the first vertebrate creatures to have taken to the skies. The pterosaurs had already successfully developed approximately 190 million years ago, during the Jurassic period, and they even shared the skies with birds for a time. In fact, remains of one of the later pterosaurs, called *Rhamphorhynchus*, have been found in the same limestone deposits in southern Germany where *Archaeopteryx* was discovered. The pterosaur's wings more closely resembled those of a bat than a bird, consisting simply of a membrane supported by a bony framework, rather than feathers overlying the skin.

Some types of pterosaurs developed huge wingspans, in excess of 23ft (7m), which enabled them to glide almost effortlessly over the surface of the world's oceans, much like albatrosses do today. It appears that they fed primarily on fish and other marine life, scooping their food out of the water in flight. Changes in climate probably doomed the pterosaurs, however, since increasingly turbulent weather patterns meant that gliding became difficult, and they could no longer fly with ease.

Avian giants

In the period immediately after the extinction of the dinosaurs, some groups of birds increased rapidly in physical size, and in so doing, lost the ability to fly. Since their increased size meant that they could cover large distances on foot, and as they faced no predators, because large hunting mammals had not yet evolved, these tall birds were relatively safe. In New Zealand, home of the large flightless moas, such giants thrived until the start of human settlement about a millennium ago. The exact date of the final extinction of the moas is not recorded, but the group had probably died out entirely by the middle of the nineteenth century.

Below: The largest species of moa would have dwarfed a man.

Above: An impression of how Archaeopteryx *may have looked. It is impossible to be sure of its coloration from its fossilized remains.*

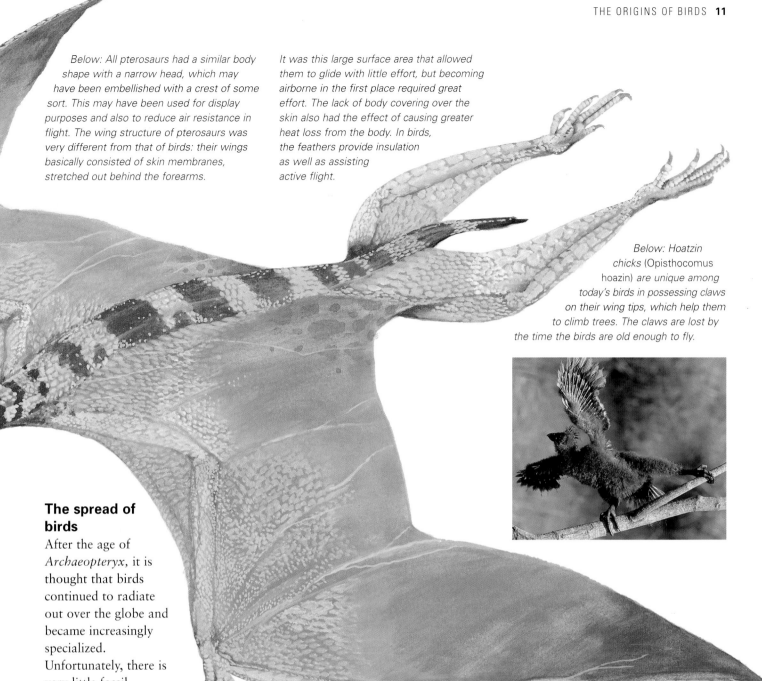

Below: All pterosaurs had a similar body shape with a narrow head, which may have been embellished with a crest of some sort. This may have been used for display purposes and also to reduce air resistance in flight. The wing structure of pterosaurs was very different from that of birds: their wings basically consisted of skin membranes, stretched out behind the forearms.

It was this large surface area that allowed them to glide with little effort, but becoming airborne in the first place required great effort. The lack of body covering over the skin also had the effect of causing greater heat loss from the body. In birds, the feathers provide insulation as well as assisting active flight.

Below: Hoatzin chicks (Opisthocomus hoazin) are unique among today's birds in possessing claws on their wing tips, which help them to climb trees. The claws are lost by the time the birds are old enough to fly.

The spread of birds

After the age of *Archaeopteryx*, it is thought that birds continued to radiate out over the globe and became increasingly specialized. Unfortunately, there is very little fossil evidence to help us understand their early history. This lack of fossils is partly due to the fact that the small carcasses of birds would have been eaten whole by scavengers, and partly because their lightweight, fragile skeletons would not have fossilized easily. In addition, most birds would not have been trapped and died under conditions that were favorable for fossilization.

By the end of the age of the dinosaurs, birds had become far more numerous. Many seabirds still possessed teeth in their jaws, reflecting their reptilian origins. These probably assisted them in catching fish and other aquatic creatures. It was at this stage that the ancestors of contemporary bird groups such as waterfowl and gulls started to emerge. Most of the forerunners of today's birds had evolved by the Oligocene epoch, some 38 million years ago.

Some groups of birds that existed in these times have since disappeared, notably the phororhacids, which ranged widely over South America and even into parts of the southern United States. These birds were fearsome predators, capable of growing to nearly 10ft (3m) in height. They were equipped with deadly beaks and talons, and probably hunted together in groups.

Recent finds

During the mid-1990s, the discovery of avian fossils in China that were apparently contemporary with those of *Archaeopteryx* aroused considerable interest. Like its German relative, *Confuciusornis* possessed claws on the tips of its wings, which probably helped these early birds to move around. Similar claws are seen today in hoatzin chicks. *Confuciusornis* resembled modern birds more closely than *Archaeopteryx* in one significant respect: it lacked teeth in its jaws. Further study of the recent fossil finds from this part of the world is required however, as some may not be genuine.

THE SKELETON AND PARTS OF A BIRD

The bird's skeleton has evolved to be light yet robust, both characteristics that help with flight. To this end, certain bones, particularly in the skull, have become fused, while others are absent, along with the teeth. The result is that birds' bodies are lightweight compared to those of other vertebrates.

In order to be able to fly, a bird needs a lightweight body so that it can become airborne with minimal difficulty. It is not just teeth that are missing from the bird's skull, but the associated heavy jaw muscles as well. These have been replaced by a light, horn-covered bill that is adapted in shape to the bird's feeding habits. Some of the limb bones, such as the humerus in the shoulder, are hollow, which also cuts down on weight. At the rear of the body, the bones in the vertebral column have become fused, which gives greater stability as well as support for the tail feathers.

The avian skeleton

In birds, the greatest degree of specialization is evident in the legs. Their location is critical to enable a bird to maintain its balance. The legs are found close to the midline, set slightly back near the bird's center of gravity. The legs are powerful, helping to provide lift at take-off and absorb the impact of landing. Strong legs also allow most birds to hop over the ground with relative ease.

There are some differences in the skeleton between different groups of birds. The atlas and axis bones at the start of the vertebral column are fused in the case of hornbills, for example, but in no other family.

Feet and toes

Birds' feet vary in length, and are noticeably extended in waders, which helps them to distribute their weight more evenly. The four toes may be arranged either in a typical 3:1 perching grip, with three toes gripping the front of the perch and one behind, or in a 2:2 configuration, known as zygodactyl, which gives a surer grip. The zygodactyl grip is seen in relatively few groups of birds, notably parrots and toucans. African touracos have flexible toes so they can swap back and forth between these two options.

The zygodactyl arrangement of their toes helps some parrots to use their feet like hands for holding food. Birds generally have claws at the ends of their toes, which have developed into sharp talons in the case of birds of prey, helping them to catch their quarry even in flight. Many birds also use their claws for preening, and they can provide balance for birds that run or climb.

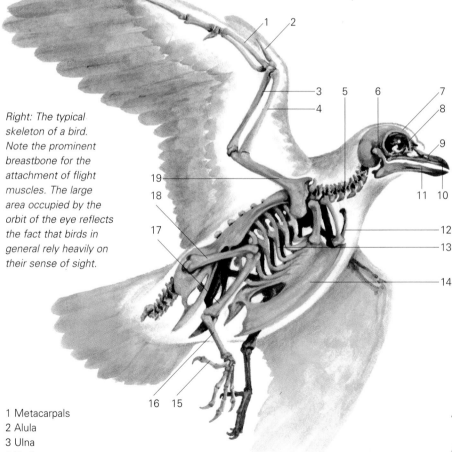

Right: The typical skeleton of a bird. Note the prominent breastbone for the attachment of flight muscles. The large area occupied by the orbit of the eye reflects the fact that birds in general rely heavily on their sense of sight.

Parrot

Above: Parrots use their feet to hold food, in a similar way to human hands.

Bird of prey

Above: In birds of prey, the claws have become talons for grasping prey.

Wader

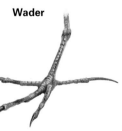

Above: Long toes make it easier for waders to walk over muddy ground or water plants.

Duck

Above: The webbed feet of ducks provide propulsion in water.

1 Metacarpals
2 Alula
3 Ulna
4 Radius
5 Cervical vertebrae
6 Ear
7 Cranium
8 Eye socket
9 Nostril
10 Bill (upper mandible)
11 Bill (lower mandible)
12 Clavicle (wishbone)
13 Ribs
14 Sternum (breastbone)
15 Metatarsals
16 Tarsus
17 Tibia and Fibula
18 Femur
19 Humerus

Above: The narrow bill of waders such as this whimbrel (Numenius phaeopus) *enables these birds to probe for food in sand or mud.*

Above: Birds of prey such as the golden eagle (Aquila chrysaetos) *rely on a sharp bill with a hooked tip to tear their prey apart.*

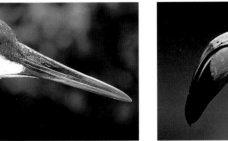

Above: Cranes have strong, pointed bills, which they use like daggers to seize prey such as frogs between the upper and lower parts.

Above: Flamingos have bills that enable them to feed with their heads trailing backwards in the water.

Above: The hyacinthine macaw (Anodorhynchus hyacinthinus) *has one of the most powerful bills of any bird.*

Above: The curved, twisted bill of the red crossbill (Loxia curvirostra) *allows these birds to extract seeds easily from pine cones.*

Bills

The bills of birds vary quite widely in shape and size, and reflect their feeding habits. The design of the bill also has an impact on the force that it can generate. The bills of many larger parrots are especially strong, allowing them to crack hard nut shells. In addition, they can move their upper and lower bill independently, which produces a wider gape and, in turn, allows more pressure to be exerted.

Wings

A bird's wing is built around just three digits, which correspond to human fingers. In comparison, bats have five digits supporting their fleshy

membranes. The three digits of birds provide a robust structure. The power of the wings is further enhanced by the fusion of the wrist bones and the carpals to create the single bone known as the carpometacarpus, which runs along the rear of the wing.

At the front of the chest, the clavicles are joined together to form what in chickens is called the wishbone. The large, keel-shaped breastbone, or sternum, runs along the underside of the body. It is bound by the ribs to the backbone, which provides stability, especially during flight. In addition, the major flight muscles are located in the lower body when the bird is airborne.

Darwin's finches

In the 1830s, a voyage to the remote Galapagos Islands, off the northwest coast of South America, helped the British naturalist Charles Darwin to formulate his theory of evolution. The finches present on the Galapagos Islands today are all believed to be descended from a single ancestor, but they have evolved in a number of different ways. The changes are most obvious in their bill shapes. For example, some species have stout, crushing beaks for cracking seeds, while others have long, slender beaks to probe for insects. These adaptations have arisen to take full advantage of the range of edible items available on the islands, where food is generally scarce. Some species have even developed the ability to use cactus spines and similar items as tools to extract seeds and invertebrates. In total, there are now 12 recognized species found on these islands, and nowhere else in the world.

Below: The finches of the Galapagos Islands helped to inspire Charles Darwin's theory of evolution. They are thought to be descended from a common ancestor, and have diverged significantly to avoid competing with each other for food. This is reflected by their bill shapes. The woodpecker finch (Camarhynchus palidus) *has even acquired the ability to use a tool, in this case a cactus spine, to winkle out grubs hiding in tree bark.*

FEATHERS

The presence of feathers is one of the main distinguishing characteristics that set birds apart from other groups of creatures on the planet. The number of feathers on a bird's body varies considerably—a swan may have as many as 25,000 feathers, for instance, while a tiny hummingbird has just 1,000 in all.

Aside from the bill, legs and feet, the entire body of the bird is covered in feathers. The plumage does not grow randomly over the bird's body, but develops along lines of so-called feather tracts, or pterylae. These are separated by bald areas known as apteria. The apteria are not conspicuous under normal circumstances, because the contour feathers overlap to cover the entire surface of the body. Plumage may also sometimes extend down over the legs and feet as well, in the case of birds from cold climates, providing extra insulation here.

Feathers are made of a tough protein called keratin, which is also found in our hair and nails. Birds have three main types of feathers: the body, or contour, feathers; the strong, elongated flight feathers on the wings; and the warm, wispy down feathers next to the bird's skin.

A diet deficient in sulphur-containing amino acids, which are the basic building blocks of protein, will result in poor feathering, creating "nutritional barring" across the flight and tail feathers. Abnormal plumage coloration can also have nutritional causes in some cases. These changes are usually reversible if more favorable environmental conditions precede the next molt.

The functions of feathers

Plumage has a number of functions, not just relating to flight. It provides a barrier that retains warm air close to the bird's body and helps to maintain body temperature, which is higher in birds than mammals—typically between 106 and 110°F (41 and 43.5°C). The down feathering that lies close to the skin, and the overlying contour plumage, are vital for maintaining body warmth. Most birds have a small volume relative to their surface area, which can leave them vulnerable to hypothermia.

A special oil produced by the preen gland, located at the base of the tail, waterproofs the plumage. This oil, which is spread over the feathers as the bird preens itself, prevents water penetrating the feathers, which would make the bird so waterlogged that it

Below: Feathering is not only necessary for flight and insulation, it is also used for display purposes. This orange cock of the rock (Rupicola rupicola) *relies on its colorful appearance to attract a mate at a communal display ground, or "lek."*

Above: A bird's flight feathers are longer and more rigid than the contour feathers that cover the body, or the fluffy down feathers that lie next to the skin. The longest, or primary, flight feathers, which generate the most thrust, are located along the outer rear edges of the wings. The tail feathers are often similar in shape to the flight feathers, with the longest being found in the center. Splaying the tail feathers increases drag and so slows the bird down.

1 Primaries
2 Secondaries
3 Axillaries
4 Rump
5 Lateral tail feathers
6 Central tail feathers
7 Breast
8 Cere
9 Auricular region (ear)
10 Nape
11 Back
12 Greater under-wing coverts
13 Lesser under-wing coverts

Above: The absence of feathers on the head means that carnivorous birds, such as the turkey vulture (Cathartes aura), *can feed on offal inside large carcasses without staining its plumage with blood.*

could no longer fly. The contour feathers that cover the body are also important for camouflage. Barring, in particular, breaks up the outline of the bird's body, helping to conceal it in its natural habitat.

The plumage has become modified in some cases, reflecting the individual lifestyle of the species concerned. Woodpeckers, for example, have tail feathers that are short and rather sharp at their tips, providing additional support for gripping onto the sides of trees. Vultures, on the other hand, have bare heads because plumage here would soon become stained and matted with blood when these birds fed on a carcass.

Social significance of plumage

Plumage can also be important in social interactions between birds. Many species have differences in their feathering that separate males from females, and often juveniles can also be distinguished by their plumage. Cock birds are usually more brightly colored, which helps them to attract their mates, but this does not apply in every case. The difference between the sexes in terms of their plumage can be quite marked. Cock birds of a number

of species have feathers forming crests, and others have magnificent tail plumes, such as the booted racquet-tail hummingbird (*Ocreatus underwoodii*), whose display is one of the most remarkable sights in the avian world.

Recent studies have confirmed that birds that appear relatively dull to our eyes, such as the cowbird (*Molothrus*), with its blackish plumage, are seen literally in a different light by other birds. They can visually perceive the ultraviolet component of light, usually invisible to us, making these seemingly dull birds appear greener. Ultraviolet coloration may also be significant in helping birds to choose their mates.

Molting

Birds' feathering is maintained by preening, but it becomes frayed and worn over time. It is therefore replaced by new plumage during the process of molting, when the old feathers are shed. Molting is most often an annual event. However, many young birds shed their nest feathers before they are a year old.

Molting may also be triggered by the onset of the breeding season in some species, as is the case with many finches. Cock finches usually have significantly duller plumage for much of the year, which undergoes a dramatic transformation when they are ready to breed. After losing their original feathers, they develop a new, more colorful and attractive plumage. Hormonal alterations in the body are important in triggering this process, with external factors, such as increased daylight hours, playing a part in prompting breeding behavior.

Iridescence

Some birds are not brightly colored, but their plumage literally sparkles in the light, thanks to its structure, which creates an iridescent effect. One of the particular features of iridescence is that the color of plumage alters, depending on the angle at which it is viewed, often appearing quite dark, almost black, from a side view. This phenomenon is particularly common in some groups of birds, notably members of the starling family (Sturnidae), and hummingbirds (Trochilidae), which are sometimes described as having metallic feathers because of the shimmering effect they create.

In some cases, the iridescent feathering is localized, while in others, it is widespread over most of the body. Green and blue iridescence is common, with reddish sheens being seen less often. Iridescence is especially common in cock birds, helping them to attract mates. In some cases, therefore, it is seen only in the breeding plumage, notably on the upperparts of the body and the wings rather than the underparts.

Below: A blue-chinned sapphire hummingbird (Chlorestes notatus) *displays its iridescent plumage.*

Right: The feather shaft holds the feather in place in the skin. Barbs run off the shaft at regular intervals, rather like the branches of a tree, and divide into smaller branches called barbules. Tiny hooks are attached to these, that reinforce the structure of each flight feather, making them more rigid.

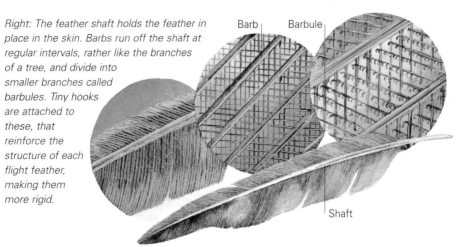

Barb Barbule

Shaft

FLIGHT

Some birds spend much of their lives in the air, whereas others will only fly as a last resort if threatened. A few species are too heavy to take off at all. The mechanics of flight are similar in all birds, but flight patterns vary significantly, which can help to identify the various groups in the air.

In most cases, the whole structure of the bird's body has evolved to facilitate flight. It is important for a bird's body weight to be relatively light, because this lessens the muscular effort required to keep it airborne. The powerful flight muscles, which provide the necessary lift, can account for up to a third of the bird's total body weight. They are attached to the breastbone, or sternum, in the midline of the body, and run along the sides of the body from the clavicle along the breastbone to the top of the legs.

Weight and flight

There is an upper weight limit of just over 40lb (18kg), above which birds would not be able to take off successfully. Some larger birds, notably pelicans and swans, need a run-up in order to gain sufficient momentum to lift off, particularly from water. Smaller birds can dart straight off a perch. Close to the critical weight limit for flight, the male Kori bustard (*Ardeotis kori*) from Asia is the world's heaviest flying bird, although it prefers to run rather than fly because of the effort involved in becoming airborne.

Below: A typical take-off, as shown by a Harris's hawk (Parabuteo unicinctus).

Above: Birds such as the Andean condor (Vultur gryphus) can remain airborne with minimum expenditure of energy, by gliding rather than flying.

Wing shape and beat

The shape of the wing is important for a bird's flying ability. Birds that remain airborne for much of their lives, such as albatrosses, have relatively long wings that allow them to glide with little effort. The wandering albatross (*Diomedea exulans*) has the largest wingspan of any bird, measuring about 11ft (3.4m) from one wing tip to the other. Large, heavy birds such as Andean condors (*Vultur gryphus*) may have difficulty in flying early in the day, before the land has warmed up. This is because at this stage, there is insufficient heat coming up from the

ground to create the thermal air currents that help to keep them airborne. In common with other large birds of prey, Andean condors seek out these rising columns of air, which provide uplift, and then circle around in them.

The number of wing beats varies dramatically between different species. Hummingbirds, for example, beat their wings more frequently than any other bird as they hover in front of flowers to harvest their nectar. Their wings move so fast—sometimes at over 200 beats per minute—that they appear as a blur to our eyes. At the other extreme, heavy birds such as swans fly with slow, deliberate wing beats.

Lightening the load

It is not just the lightness of the bird's skeleton that helps it to fly. There have been evolutionary changes in the body organs too, most noticeably in the urinary system. Unlike mammals, birds do not have a bladder that fills with urine. Instead, their urine is greatly concentrated, in the form of uric acid, and passes out of the body with their faeces, appearing as a creamy-white, semi-solid component.

1. When resting, a bird typically has a relatively upright stance.

2. As it leans forwards for take-off, it raises its wings and starts to lift its legs.

3. Leaving its perch, the bird pushes off into the air, and opens its wings.

Above: Hummingbirds such as this broadtail (Selasphorus platycercus) have unparalleled aerial maneuverability, thanks to their rapid wing movements.

Below: The black-browed albatross (Diomedea melanophris) and its relatives often skim just above the waves.

The aerofoil principle

Once in flight, the shape of the wing is crucial in keeping the bird airborne. Viewed in cross-section from the side, a bird's wing resembles an airplane's wing, called an aerofoil, and, in fact, airplanes use the same technique as birds to fly.

The wing is curved across the top, so the movement of air is faster over this part of the wing compared with the lower surface. This produces reduced air pressure on top of the wing, which provides lift and makes it easier for the bird to stay in the air.

The long flight feathers at the rear edge of the wings help to provide the thrust and lift for flight. The tail feathers, too, can help the bird remain airborne. The kestrel (*Falco tinnunculus*), for example, having spotted prey on the ground, spreads its tail feathers to help it remain aloft while it hovers to target its prey.

A bird's wings move in a regular figure-eight movement while it is in flight. During the downstroke, the flight feathers join together to push powerfully against the air. The primary flight feathers bend backward, which propels the bird forward. As the wing moves upward, the longer primary flight feathers move apart, which reduces air resistance. The secondary feathers farther along the wing provide some slight propulsion. After that, the cycle simply repeats itself.

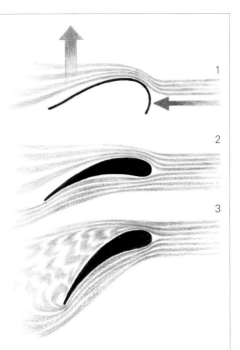

Above: The flow of air over a bird's wing varies according to the wing's position.
1. When the wing is stretched out horizontally, an area of low pressure is created above the wing, causing lift.
2. As the wing is tilted downward, the flow of the air is disrupted, causing turbulence and loss of lift.
3. When the wing is angled downward, lift slows, which results in stalling. The bird's speed slows as a consequence.

Flight patterns and formations

Different species of birds have various ways of flying, which can actually aid the birdwatcher in helping to identify them. For example, small birds such as tits (Paridae) and finches (Fringillidae) alternately flap their wings and fold them at their sides, adopting a streamlined shape, which helps to save energy. This produces a characteristic dipping flight. Large birds such as ducks and geese maintain a straighter course at an even height.

In some cases, it is not just the individual flying skills of a bird that can help it to stay airborne, but those of its fellows nearby. Birds flying in formation create a slipstream, which makes flying less effort for all the birds behind the leader. This is why birds often fly in formation, especially when covering large distances on migration.

4. Powerful upward and downward sweeps of the wings propel the bird forwards.

5. When coming in to land, a bird lowers its legs and slows its wing movements.

6. Braking is achieved by a vertical landing posture, with the tail feathers spread.

LOCOMOTION

For most birds, flight is the main means of locomotion. However, the ability to move on the ground or in water can be vital, particularly when it comes to obtaining food. Some birds have even lost the ability to fly, relying instead on their swimming or running skills to escape predators and find food.

Not all birds possess the ability to fly, but this does not mean they are handicapped in their natural environment. Penguins may appear to be rather clumsy shuffling around on land, but they are extremely well adapted to life in the water. Like other primarily aquatic birds, their webbed feet enable them to swim very effectively. Webbing is a common feature seen in aquatic birds. The skin folds linking the toes turn the foot into an effective paddle, allowing the bird to maximize its propulsive forward thrust by pushing against the water. On land, however, webbed feet do impose certain restrictions, because being linked together in this way means that the individual toes are not as flexible.

Aquatic locomotion
When penguins dive, their sleek, torpedo-shaped bodies allow them to swim fast underwater, reaching speeds equivalent to 25mph (40km/h). Their flippers, which evolved from wings,

Below: A group of king penguins (Aptenodytes patagonicus) *leap in and out of the water as they swim along, in a form of movement known as porpoising.*

help them to steer very effectively as they pursue fish, which form the basis of their diet. Like flying birds, penguins need effective wing muscles to control their movements, so their skeletal structure bears a close similarity to that of flying birds.

Flightless ducks and other aquatic birds, such as the Galapagos Island cormorant (*Nannopterum harrisi*), use a different method of locomotion: they rely entirely on their feet rather than their wings for propulsive power. Their skeletons differ from those of flying birds in that they lack the prominent keel on the sternum for the attachment of flight muscles.

Flightless land birds
A number of land birds have lost the ability to fly. Typically, they are birds that inhabit islands where, until the arrival of cats and rats brought by ships from Europe, they faced few if any predators. The arrival of predators has left them vulnerable, and many have since become extinct, including the dodo (*Raphus cucullatus*), a large, flightless pigeon from the island of Mauritius in the Indian Ocean. A high percentage of flightless birds evolved

Above: Penguins such as the chinstrap (Pygoscelis antarctica) *are less agile on land than they are in the sea, where their body shape lessens water resistance.*

on the islands of New Zealand, but many have since vanished, including all species of moa (*Dinornis* and related forms). Moas represent the most diverse group of flightless birds ever recorded. The last examples probably died out at the time of European settlement of these islands in the nineteenth century.

The giant moa (*Dinornis maximus*) was the largest member of the group and, indeed, the tallest bird ever to have existed. It would have dwarfed today's ostriches, standing up to 11½ft (3.5m) high. There may have been as many as a dozen or more different types of moa, which filled the same sort of niche as grazing mammals, which were absent from New Zealand.

In the absence of predatory mammals, the moas faced no significant threats to their survival until the first human settlers reached New Zealand and started to hunt them. Their large size made them conspicuous, and, having evolved in an environment where they had been safe from persecution, they had lost their ability to fly. Moas were not even able to run fast, in contrast to modern flightless birds such as ostriches. These defenseless giants were soon driven to extinction.

Circulation

The circulatory system is vital in supporting the activities of both flighted and flightless birds, ensuring that their muscles are well supplied with oxygen. The heart acts as the pump, driving the blood around the body. The basic design of the heart is similar to that of a mammal, with the left side being highly developed because it does more work. Overall, the heart rate of birds is much more rapid than mammals of similar size, having been measured at 1,000 beats per minute in the case of canaries at rest. The heart beat rises dramatically during flight, but soon returns to normal when the bird touches down.

The respiratory system

Birds have lungs, located close to the vertebral column, but these do not expand and contract in the same way as those of mammals. Instead, birds rely on a series of air sacs that act rather like bellows, to suck

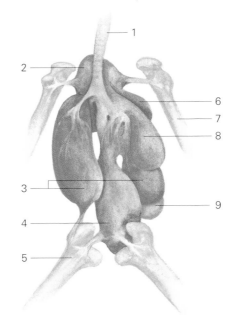

air through their respiratory system. In some cases, these link with the hollow limb bones, and thus help to meet the bird's high requirement for oxygen when flying. A bird's respiratory rate is a reflection of its body size, as well as its level of activity and lifestyle. Common starlings (*Sturnus vulgaris*), for example, typically breathe about 85 times every minute, whereas domestic chickens, which are more sedentary, have an equivalent respiratory rate of only about 20 breaths per minute.

1 Trachea
2 Interclavicular air sac
3 Lungs
4 Abdominal air sac
5 Femur (leg bone)
6 Cervical air sac
7 Humerus (wing bone)
8 Anterior thoracic air sac
9 Posterior thoracic air sac

*Above: The roadrunner (*Geococcyx californianus*) is a fleet-footed member of the cuckoo family. It has adapted to hunting on the ground, but can fly if necessary.*

Ratites

Not all flightless birds are helpless in the face of danger, however. The large, flightless birds known as ratites, including cassowaries, ostriches, emus and rheas, are particularly well able to defend themselves. Their strong legs are quite capable of inflicting lethal blows, especially in the case of the cassowaries (Casuariidae), found in parts of northern Australia, New Guinea and neighboring islands. These birds have an elongated and deadly sharp claw on their innermost toe. If the cassowary is cornered and unable to run away, it lashes out with its legs and is quite capable of disembowelling a person with its sharp claws. The bird

also has an elongated, hard, bony crest called a casque, which protects the top of its head.

The large ratites all share a similar shape, having bulky bodies, long legs and long, slender necks. Like all flightless birds, they do possess wings, which assist them in keeping their balance and may also be used for display purposes. Most birds have four toes on each foot, but ratites have no more than three toes, and less in some cases. Ostriches have just two toes on each foot. The fastest birds on land, they can run at speeds equivalent to 31mph (50km/h). The reduction in the number of toes may help these birds to run faster.

Emus (*Dromaius novaehollandiae*) have the most rudimentary wings of all ratites, which are not even used for display purposes. The rheas (Rheidae) of South America have the most prominent wings of the ratites. They cover the rump, but they do not enable these birds to fly, even when they are young. Rheas can run if necessary immediately after hatching.

Kiwis (Apterygidae) are also ratites, but they are much smaller birds with shorter legs. Unlike other ratites, they are not fast runners, but rely on camouflage and their nocturnal habits to conceal their presence from predators, rather than speed to escape.

Running in flighted birds

Some birds that are able to fly still prefer to use their running abilities to obtain food and escape danger. They include the roadrunners (*Geococcyx californianus*) of North America. With their short wings, these birds can fly clumsily, but prefer to use their strong legs to overtake and pounce on prey. In general, flying uses considerable energy compared to running or hopping. Many birds will elect to move swiftly over the ground in order to pounce on a food item or avoid an enemy if they judge that the situation does not warrant flight.

Below: The height and keen eyesight of rheas (Rheidae) means that they are hard to ambush in open country. Their pace allows them to escape an enemy, while their long stride length enables them to cover large amounts of ground in a single step.

AVIAN SENSES

The keen senses of birds are vital to their survival, in particular helping them to find food, escape from enemies and find mates in the breeding season. Sight is the primary sense for most birds, but some species rely heavily on other senses to thrive in particular habitats.

Birds' senses have evolved as a result of their environment, and the shape of their bodies can help to reflect which senses are most significant to them.

Sight and lifestyle
Most birds rely on their sense of sight to avoid danger, hunt for food and locate familiar surroundings. The importance of this sense is reflected by the size of their eyes, with those of

starlings (*Sturnus vulgaris*), for example, making up 15 per cent of the total head weight. The enlargement of the eyeballs and associated structures, notably the eye sockets in the skull, has altered the shape of the brain. In addition, the optic lobes in the brain, which are concerned with vision, are also enlarged, whereas the olfactory counterparts, responsible for smell, are poorly developed.

The structure of the eye also reveals much about a bird's habits. Birds of prey have large eyes in proportion to their head, and have correspondingly keen eyesight. Species that regularly hunt for prey underwater, such as penguins, can see well in the water. They have a muscle in each eye that reduces the diameter of the lens and increases its thickness on entering water, so that their eyes can adjust easily to seeing underwater. In addition, certain diving birds such as little auks (*Alle alle*) use a lens that forms part of the nictitating membrane, or third eyelid, which is normally hidden from sight. Underwater, when this membrane covers the eye, its convex shape serves as a lens, helping the bird to see in these surroundings.

Eye position
The positioning of the eyes on the head gives important clues to a bird's lifestyle. Most birds' eyes are set on the sides of the head. Owls, however, have flattened faces and forward-facing eyes that are critical to their hunting abilities. These features allow owls to target their prey.

There are disadvantages, though—owls' eyes do not give a rounded view of the world, so they must turn their heads to see around them. It is not just the positioning of owls' eyes that is unusual. They are also able to hunt effectively in almost complete darkness. This is made possible in two

Above: Vultures such as the Andean condor (Vultur gryphus) rely on their keen eyesight and sense of smell to pick up powerful odors arising from carcasses on the ground.

ways. First, their pupils are large, which maximizes the amount of light passing through to the retina behind the lens, where the image is formed. Second, the cells here consist mainly of rods rather than cones. While cones give good color vision, rods function to create images when background illumination is low.

The positioning of the eyes of game birds such as woodcocks (*Scolopax rusticola*) allows them to spot danger from almost any angle. It is even possible for them to see a predator sneaking up from behind. Their only blind spot is just behind the head.

Smell
Very few birds have a sense of smell, but kiwis (Apterygidae) and vultures (forming part of the order Falciformes) are notable exceptions. Birds' nostrils are normally located above the bill, opening directly into the skull, but kiwis' nostrils are positioned right at the end of the long bill. They probably help these New Zealand birds to locate

Field of vision
The positioning of a bird's eyes on its head affects its field of vision. The eyes of owls are positioned to face forward, producing an overlapping image of the area in front known as binocular vision. This allows the owl to pinpoint its prey exactly, so that it can strike. In contrast, the eyes of birds that are likely to be preyed upon, such as woodcocks, are positioned on the sides of the head. This eye position gives a greatly reduced area of binocular vision, but it does give these birds practically all-round vision, enabling them to spot danger from all sides.

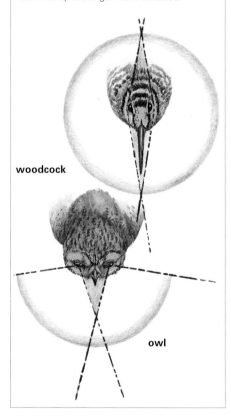

woodcock

owl

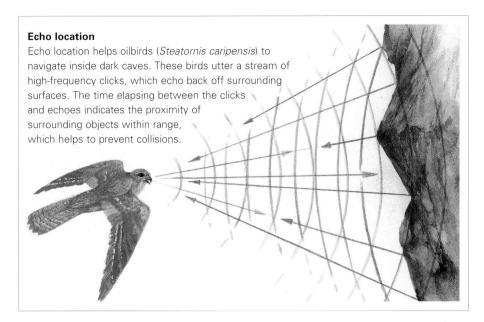

Echo location

Echo location helps oilbirds (*Steatornis caripensis*) to navigate inside dark caves. These birds utter a stream of high-frequency clicks, which echo back off surrounding surfaces. The time elapsing between the clicks and echoes indicates the proximity of surrounding objects within range, which helps to prevent collisions.

earthworms in the soil. Vultures have very keen eyesight, which helps them to spot dead animals on the ground from the air, but they also have a strong sense of smell, which helps when homing in on a distant carcass.

Taste

The senses of smell and taste are linked, and most birds also have correspondingly few taste buds in their mouths. The number of taste buds varies, with significant differences between groups of birds. Pigeons may have as few as 50 taste buds in their mouths, parrots as many as 400.

Birds' taste buds are located all around the mouth, rather than just on the tongue, as in mammals. The close

Below: Birds have good color vision. It is this sense that encourages hummingbirds, such as this long-billed starthroat (Heliomaster longirostris), to home in on red flowers.

links between smell and taste can lead vultures, which feed only on fresh carcasses, to reject decomposing meat. They may start to eat it, but then spit it out once it is in their mouths, probably because of a combination of bad odor and taste.

Hearing

Birds generally do not have a highly developed sense of hearing. They lack any external ear flaps that would help to pinpoint sources of sound. The openings to their hearing system are located on the sides of the head, back from the eyes.

Hearing is of particular significance for nocturnal species, such as owls, which find their food in darkness. These birds are highly attuned to the calls made by rodents. The broad shape of their skull has the additional advantage of spacing the ear openings more widely, which helps them to localize the source of the sounds with greater accuracy.

Hearing is also important to birds during the breeding season. Birds show particular sensitivity to sounds falling within the vocal range of their chicks, which helps them to locate their offspring easily in the critical early days after fledging.

The oilbird (*Steatornis caripensis*), which inhabits parts of northern South America, uses echo location to find its way around in the dark, rather like bats do. Unlike the sounds bats make,

however, the clicking sounds of the oilbird's calls—up to 20 a second in darkness—are clearly audible to humans. The bird interprets the echoes of its call to avoid colliding with objects in its path, although it also uses its eyesight when flying. Cave swiftlets (*Aerodramus*) from Asia, which also inhabit a dark environment, use echo location in a similar way to fly.

Touch

The sense of touch is more developed in some birds than others. Those such as snipe (*Gallinago*), which have long bills for seeking food, have sensitive nerve endings called corpuscles in their bills that pick up tiny vibrations caused by their prey. Vibrations that could suggest approaching danger can also register via other corpuscles located particularly in the legs, so that the bird has a sensory awareness even when it is resting on a branch.

Wind-borne sensing

Tubenoses such as albatrosses and petrels (Procellariiformes) have a valve in each nostril that fills with air as the bird flies. These are affected by both the bird's speed and the wind strength. The valves almost certainly act as a type of wind gauge, allowing these birds to detect changes in wind strength and patterns. This information helps to keep them airborne, as they skim over the waves with minimal effort.

Below: A combination of senses, especially touch, helps American oystercatchers (Haematopus palliatus) to detect their prey, which is normally hidden from view.

PLANT-EATERS

All over the world, many birds depend on plant matter as part of their diet, with seeds and nuts in particular providing nourishment. A close relationship between plants and birds exists in many cases. Birds fertilize flowers when feeding on nectar, and help to spread their seeds when eating fruit.

Many different types of birds are primarily plant-eaters, whether feeding on flowers, fruit, nuts and seeds, or other plant matter. Plant-eating species have to eat a large volume of food compared to meat-eating species, because of the low nutritional value of plants compared with that of prey such as invertebrates.

In the last century or so, many species have benefited from the spread of agriculture, which now provides them with large acreages of suitable crop plants to eat. These birds' feeding habits bring them into conflict with farmers when they breed rapidly in response to a swift expansion in their food supply. For example, populations of *Brotogeris* parakeets have grown significantly in certain parts of Central and South America, thanks largely to the spread of arable agriculture,

Below: Birds such as the cactus wren (Campylorhynchus brunneicapillus) *have a close association with particular plants. This wren not only feeds on the plants after which it is named, but also takes advantage of their protective thorns when nesting.*

especially fruit-growing, in these regions. As feeding opportunities have increased, these small members of the parrot family have bred rapidly, and flocks are capable of wreaking havoc on crops. The birds are now considered to be pests in some areas.

Adapting to changing seasons

Birds from temperate areas exist on a varied diet that is related to the seasons. In the far north, where a blanket of snow conceals food on the ground during the winter months, willow ptarmigans (*Lagopus lagopus*) survive by feeding on buds and even the bark of dwarf willow bushes that grow in the region. During the brief northern summer, when the ground is again uncovered, they feed on flowers and other vegetation.

Some birds store plant food when it is plentiful, to sustain them through the winter. Nutcrackers (*Nucifraga*) collect hazel nuts, which they feed on in winter until the following year. Acorn woodpeckers (*Melanerpes formicivorus*) drill holes in trees that they fill with acorns, creating an easily accessible larder for the winter.

Flowers

A number of birds rely on flowers rather than the whole plant as a source of food. Pollen is a valuable source of protein, while nectar provides sugars. Not surprisingly, flower-feeders tend to be confined to mainly tropical areas, where flowers are in bloom throughout the year. Hummingbirds (Trochilidae), for instance, use their narrow bills to probe into flowers to obtain nectar. Some hummingbirds have developed especially curved or elongated bills, which allow them to feed on particular flowers. These birds help to pollinate the plants on which they feed by transferring pollen from flower to flower on their bills or even on plumage.

The digestive system

Birds lack teeth, so their food must be swallowed whole. Birds have a storage organ known as the crop, which is located at the base of the neck. From here, food passes down into the proventriculus, where the digestive process starts, before entering the gizzard, which is equivalent to the mammalian stomach. Nutrients are then absorbed through the wall of the small intestine.

The digestive system of plant-eaters differs in various respects from that of predatory species. Vegetable matter is less nourishing than meat, so plant-eaters generally need longer digestive tracts to process the large quantities of food they must consume in order to obtain enough nourishment. In addition, digesting plant matter poses certain difficulties. The gizzards of seed-eating species such as many finches (Fringillidae) have especially thick muscular walls, which serve to grind up the seeds.

1 Esophagus   6 Large intestine
2 Crop   7 Liver
3 Proventriculus   8 Spleen
4 Pancreas   9 Small intestine
5 Gizzard

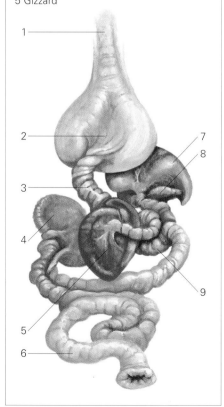

Above: Feeding on plants comes at a price, as many contain potentially harmful chemicals. Various parrots, such as these macaws (Ara species), make daily visits to cliffs to eat clay, which is believed to have a detoxifying effect on their digestive systems.

Honeycreepers, who belong to the tanager family (Thraupidae) of Central America, fill a similar evolutionary role to hummingbirds, with whom they share their small size and bright color. Unlike hummingbirds, however, they are unable to feed in flight, but have to perch within reach of the flower, sometimes pecking at the base to obtain nectar. Flowers are also a dietary favorite of some American members of the parrot family, such as the small *Touit* parrotlets, who may choose to eat them whole.

Fruit

Exclusively frugivorous (fruit-eating) birds such as fruit doves (*Ptilinopus*) are found only in the tropics, where fruit is available throughout the year. These species usually dwell in tropical rainforests, where they have a valuable role to play in protecting the biodiversity of the forest. The seeds of the fruits they eat pass right through their digestive tracts, unharmed, to be deposited far from the parent plant, which helps the plants to spread.

Plant matter

Relatively few birds feed almost entirely on herbage, although the bizarre hoatzin (*Opisthocomus hoazin*) from the rainforest of South America is one example. Its gut can become so distended with leaves that it has difficulty flying. Vegetation tends to feature quite prominently in the diets of many waterfowl too—the floating plant duckweed (*Lemna*) is so-called because of its attraction to these birds.

The breakdown of vegetation presents considerable difficulty, since birds do not possess the necessary enzymes to digest the cellulose in plants. Birds such as grouse (Tetraoninae), which feed regularly on plant matter, have evolved long, blind-ending tubes known as caeca. These contain beneficial microbes that can break down cellulose.

Nuts and seeds

These dry foods are a valuable resource to many different types of birds. However, cracking the tough outer shell or husk can present a problem. Finches such as grosbeaks have evolved a particularly strong bill, and often succeed in cracking the pit (stone) of a fruit to extract the edible kernel within. The hyacinthine macaw (*Anodorhynchus hyacinthinus*) has a bill strong enough to crack Brazil nuts.

Above: Willow ptarmigans (Lagopus lagopus) have to be versatile in their feeding habits, because of the marked climatic change that takes place in their habitat between summer and winter. Their white plumage disguises their presence when snow is on the ground.

The most bizarre example of bill adaption for eating seeds is seen in the crossbills (*Loxia*) of northern coniferous forests. These birds have literally twisted upper and lower mandibles, which help them to crack open the seeds inside the larch cones, which they eat. Some cockatoos such as the Moluccan (*Cacatua moluccensis*) have bills that are even strong enough to open coconuts.

Below: Canadian geese (Branta canadensis) can be a problem in agricultural areas, since they will sometimes descend in large numbers to graze on young cereal crops.

PREDATORS AND SCAVENGERS

Just as with other vertebrates, there is a food chain within the avian kingdom. Some species hunt only other birds, while others seek a more varied range of prey, including, commonly, invertebrates. Even birds that feed mainly on seeds catch protein-rich insects to feed their chicks in the nest.

Some avian predators feed mainly on other birds, as typified by the merlin or pigeon hawk (*Falco columbarius*) which preys on small coastline waders. Many predatory birds hunt when food is plentiful but scavenge when their prey becomes scarce. Both hunters and scavengers have evolved to live in a wide range of environments, and display correspondingly diverse hunting skills to obtain their food.

Birds of prey have sharp bills that enable them to tear the flesh of their prey into strips small enough to swallow. Eating whole animals can potentially cause digestive problems for these birds because of the bones, skin, feathers and other relatively indigestible body parts. Owls overcome this problem by regurgitating pellets composed of the indigestible remains of their prey. Kingfishers produce similar pellets of fish bones and scales. These are of value to zoologists studying the feeding habits of such birds.

Below: Peregrine falcons (Falco peregrinus) are adept aerial hunters, with pigeons—including homing pigeons—featuring prominently in their diet. These birds of prey display not just speed, but also superb maneuverability in flight, when pursuing their quarry.

Birds of prey

Some avian predators feed mainly on other birds, such as the sparrowhawk (*Accipiter nisus*)—which is so-called because of its preference for hunting house sparrows (*Passer domesticus*). Another avian hunter, the peregrine falcon (*Falco peregrinus*), is among the most agile of all hunting birds. Strength is a feature of some species that prey on mammals, such as the golden eagle (*Aquila chrysaetos*), which can lift young lambs in its powerful talons, but often feeds on carrion. Yet other birds of prey target different groups of vertebrates,

Above: Vision is the main sense that allows most birds of prey, such as golden eagles (Aquila chrysaetos), to target their victims. These eagles have keen sight.

including fish and reptiles, while a great many species hunt insects and other invertebrates.

Hunting techniques

Many predatory birds hunt during the day, but not all, with most owls preferring to seek their prey at night. Mice and other creatures that are caught by owls are killed and eaten immediately. In contrast, Old World shrikes (Laniidae) have a grisly reputation because they kill more prey than they can eat immediately. They store the surplus as a so-called larder. They impale invertebrates such as grasshoppers, and even sometimes small vertebrates, onto sharp vegetation, and return to feed on them later. Caching, as this behavior is known, is especially common during the breeding period, and presumably developed as a way of ensuring that the shrikes have sufficient food to rear their young.

Some birds have evolved particular ways of overcoming prey in certain localities. In parts of Egypt, for example, eagles have learned to prey

Above: Like other cormorants, the white-necked cormorant (Phalacrocorax carbo) *brings fish that it catches underwater up to the surface before swallowing them.*

on tortoises by seizing the unfortunate reptiles in their talons, and then dropping them onto rocky ground from the air to split open their shells.

Not all birds of prey are aerial predators. Species such as secretary birds (*Sagittarius serpentarius*), which range widely across Africa in grassland areas, prefer to seek their victims on the ground. Secretary birds have developed long, strong legs and yet have surprisingly small feet. Snakes feature prominently in the diet of these birds, which raise their wings when confronting one of the reptiles. This has the effect of breaking up the bird's outline, making it harder for the snake to strike. Meanwhile the bird uses its feet to stun the reptile by jumping up and down on it, before killing it with a stab of its sharp bill.

Aquatic predators

The osprey (*Pandion haliaetus*) is an unusual bird of prey that literally scoops up large fish swimming close to the water's surface while in flight. Other birds actually enter the water in search of their prey. They may not have sharp talons, but many have powerful bills that enable them to grab slippery fish without difficulty.

Pelicans are equipped with a large, capacious pouch beneath the lower part of their bill, which they use like a net to trawl the water for fish.

Cormorants (Phalacrocoracidae) dive down after fish, and can remain submerged for some time. Kingfishers (Alcedinidae) have sharp eyesight. Having detected the presence of a fish from the air, they dive into the water, seizing their quarry in their pointed bill and then re-emerging immediately. They then kill the fish by battering it against their perch. The speed at which the kingfisher dives provides the necessary momentum to break through the surface, and it closes its wings once submerged to reduce resistance.

Aquatic predators always try to swallow their prey, such as fish, head-first. That way, gills and scales do not get stuck in their throat. On land, predatory birds that hunt victims such as rodents employ a similar technique so they do not choke on fur and tails.

Scavengers

Vultures are the best-known of all scavengers. They can home in on carcasses from a great distance away, and so have become regarded as harbingers of death. Lammergeiers (*Gypaetus barbatus*), have developed a technique that allows them to feed on bones that their relatives cannot break open. They smash the bones into pieces by dropping them from a great height. It is a skill that they learn to perfect by choosing the right terrain on which to drop the bones.

The small Egyptian vulture (*Neophron percnopterus*) survives by using its small size, which is no match

Above: American white pelicans (Pelecanus erythrorhynchos) *have expandable pouches that allow them to trawl for fish, and other edible items, in a variety of aquatic habitats.*

at the site of a kill, to advantage: it can become airborne soon after dawn—before the thermal air currents needed by its larger relatives have been created—and seek out overnight casualities. In some parts of Africa, these vultures smash tough ostrich eggs by repeatedly throwing stones at them.

Birds other than vultures also scavenge on occasion rather than hunting. Road kills of birds and other animals offer rich pickings for a host of such species, ranging from corvids such as crows and magpies to road-runners (*Geococcyx californianus*).

Below: Griffon vultures (Gyps fulvus) *and similar scavengers are able to spot a carcass on the ground using their keen eyesight, possibly combined with a sense of smell.*

DISPLAY AND PAIRING

Birds' breeding habits vary greatly. Some birds pair up only fleetingly, while others do so for the whole breeding season, and some species pair for life. For many young cock birds, the priority is to gain a territory as the first step in attracting a partner. Birds use both plumage and their songs to attract a mate.

A number of factors trigger the onset of the breeding period. In temperate areas, as the days start to lengthen in spring, the increase in daylight is detected by the pineal gland in the bird's brain, which starts a complex series of hormonal changes in the body. Most birds form a bond with a single partner during the breeding season, which is often preceded by an elaborate display by the cock bird.

Bird song

Many cock birds announce their presence by their song, which both attracts would-be mates and establishes a claim to a territory. Once pairing has occurred, the male may cease singing, but in some cases he starts to perform a duet with the hen, with each bird singing in turn.

Singing obviously serves to keep members of the pair in touch with each other. In species such as Central and

South American wood quails (*Odontophorus*), the pair coordinate their songs so precisely that although the cock bird may sing the first few notes, and then the hen, it sounds as if the song is being sung by just one bird. Other birds may sing in unison. In African gonoleks (*Laniarius*), it may even be possible to tell the length of time that the pair have been together by the degree of harmony in their particular songs.

Studies have revealed that young male birds start warbling quite quietly, and then sing more loudly as they mature. Finally, when their song pattern becomes fixed, it remains constant throughout the bird's life.

It is obviously possible to identify different species by differences in their song patterns. However, there are sometimes marked variations between the songs of individuals of the same species that live in different places. Local dialects have been identified in various parts of a species' distribution, as in the case of gray parrots (*Psittacus erithacus*) from different parts of Africa. In addition, as far as some songbirds are concerned, recent studies

Above: A male ruff (Philomachus pugnax) *at a lek, where males compete with each other in displays to attract female partners. Ruffs do not form lasting pair bonds, so the hens nest on their own after mating has occurred.*

Below: An American bittern (Botaurus lentiginosus), *well disguised in a reed bed. In spite of being solitary by nature, these waders have a remarkable territorial call, which booms out across the marshes, and has led to species becoming known locally as "Thunder-pumpers." The boom is created by use of the gullet to amplify sound, rather like a voice box.*

Below: A cock ruffed grouse (Bonasa umbellus) *displaying. The male is using his wings to create a loud drumming sound, uttering a series of quieter calls at the same time, in a bid to attract females. Drumming occurs at dawn and dusk, usually with pauses of about five minutes between displays.*

Above: Black-necked swans (Cygnus melanocoryphus) *of South America normally mate for life. Pairs typically breed on their own, but once the nesting period is over, large numbers unite to form great flocks of as many as 200 individuals—a spectacular sight on large stretches of water.*

have shown that over the course of several generations, the pattern of song can alter markedly.

Birds produce their sounds—even those species capable of mimicking human speech—without the benefit of a larynx and vocal cords like humans. The song is created in a voice organ called the syrinx, which is located in the bird's throat, at the bottom of the windpipe, or trachea.

The structure of the syrinx is very variable, being at its most highly developed in the case of songbirds, which possess as many as nine pairs of separate muscles to control the vocal output. As in the human larynx, it is the movement of air through the syrinx that enables the membranes here to vibrate, creating sound. An organ called the interclavicular air sac also plays an important role in sound production, and birds cannot sing without it. The distance over which bird calls can travel is remarkable— up to 3 miles (5km) in the case of some species, such as bellbirds (*Procnias*) and the American bittern (*Botaurus lentiginosus*), which has a particularly deep, penetrating song.

Breeding behavior

Many birds rely on their breeding finery to attract their mates. Some groups assemble in communal display areas known as leks, where hens witness the males' displays and select a mate. A number of species, ranging from cocks of the rock (*Rupicola*) to birds of paradise (Paradisaeidae), establish leks.

In other species, such as the satin bowerbird (*Ptilonorhynchus violaceus*), the male constructs elaborate bowers of grass, twigs and similar vegetation, which he then decorates with items of a particular color, such as blue, varying from flowers to pieces of glass. Male bowerbirds are often polygamous,

meaning that they mate with more than one female. African weaver birds, such as the orange bishop (*Euplectes orix*), demonstrate the same behavior. The males molt to display brightly colored plumage at the onset of the breeding season, and construct nests that are inspected by the females. Hens are often drawn to the older cocks, whose nest-building abilities are likely to be more sophisticated.

Pair bonding

Many male and female birds form no lasting relationship, although the pair bond may be strong during the nesting period. It is usually only in potentially long-lived species, such as the larger parrots and macaws, or waterfowl such as swans, that a life-long pair bond is formed.

Pair bonding in long-lived species has certain advantages. The young of such birds are slow to mature, and are often unlikely to nest for five years or more. By remaining for a time in a family group, therefore, adults can improve the long-term survival prospects of their offspring.

Below: Two greater male sage grouse (Centrocercus urophasianus) *circle each other at a lek. These prominent displays help watching hens to choose a partner. There are usually just one or two dominant males with whom the hens mate: younger males—also present—are likely to be ignored. Lekking takes place from early dawn to late morning.*

NESTING AND EGG-LAYING

All birds reproduce by laying eggs, which are covered with a hard, calcareous shell. The number of eggs laid at a time—known as the clutch size—varies significantly between species, as does egg coloration. Nesting habits also vary, with some birds constructing very elaborate nests.

The coloration and markings of a bird's eggs are directly linked to the nesting site. Birds that usually breed in hollow trees produce white eggs, because these are normally hidden from predators and so do not need to be camouflaged. The pale coloration may also help the adult birds to locate the eggs as they return to the nest, thus lessening the chances of damaging them. Birds that build open, cup-shaped nests tend to lay colored and often mottled eggs that are camouflaged and so less obvious to potential nest thieves.

Nesting holes

Many birds use tree holes for nesting. Woodpeckers (Picidae) are particularly well equipped to create nesting chambers, using their powerful bills to enlarge holes in dead trees. The diameter of the entry hole thus created

Below: African ostriches lay the largest eggs in the world, which can weigh up to 3.3lb (1.5kg). In comparison, a chicken's egg, shown in front of the ostrich egg, looks tiny. The egg nearest to the viewer is a hummingbird egg. These tiny birds lay the smallest eggs in the avian world, weighing only about 0.01oz (0.35g).

Above: A northern flicker (Colaptes auratus)—a member of the woodpecker family—returns to its nest hole. Tree holes offer relatively safe nesting retreats, although predators such as snakes may sometimes be able to reach them.

is just wide enough to allow the birds to enter easily, which helps to prevent the nest being robbed. Old World hornbills (Bucorvidae) go one stage further—the cock bird walls the hen up inside the nest. He plasters the hole over with mud, leaving just a small gap through which he can feed the female. The barrier helps to protect the nest from attacks by snakes and lizards. The female remains entombed inside until her young are well grown. At this stage she breaks out and then helps her mate to rear the chicks, having walled them back up again.

Nest-building

Some birds return to the same nest site each year, but many birds simply abandon their old nest and build another. This may seem a waste of effort, but it actually helps to protect the birds from parasites such as blood-sucking mites, which can otherwise multiply in the confines of the nest. Most birds construct their nests from vegetation, depending on which

The reproductive systems

The cock bird has two testes located within his body. Spermatozoa pass down the vas deferens, into the cloaca and then out of the body. Insemination occurs when the vent areas of the male and female bird are in direct contact during mating. Cock birds do not have a penis for penetration, although certain groups, such as waterfowl, may have a primitive organ that is used to assist in the transference of semen in a similar way.

Normally only the left ovary and oviduct of the hen bird are functional. Eggs pass down through the reproductive tract from the ovary. Spermatozoa swim up the hen's reproductive tract, and fertilize the ova at an early stage in the process. Generally, only one mating is required to fertilize a clutch of eggs. Spermatozoa may sometimes remain viable in the hen's body for up to three weeks following mating.

1 Testes	7 Magnum
2 Kidneys	8 Isthmus
3 Vas deferens	9 Egg with shell
4 Cloaca	contained in
	the hen's
5 Ova	reproductive tract
6 Infundibulum	10 Cloaca

Male   **Female**

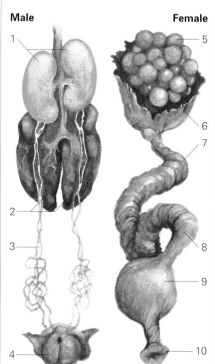

materials are locally available. In coastal areas, some seabirds use pieces of seaweed to build theirs. Artificial materials such as plastic wrappers or polystyrene may be used by some birds.

Nest styles

Different types of birds build nests of various shapes and sizes, which are characteristic of their species. Groups such as finches build nests in the form of an open cup, often concealed in vegetation. Most pigeons and doves construct a loose platform of twigs. Swallows are among the birds that use mud to construct their nests. They scoop muddy water up from the surface of a pond or puddle, mold it into shape on a suitable wall, and then allow it to dry and harden like cement.

The simplest nests are composed of little more than a pad of material, resting in the fork of a tree or on a building. The effort entailed in nest construction may reflect how often the birds are likely to nest. The platforms of pigeons and doves can disintegrate quite easily, resulting in the loss of eggs or chicks. However, if disaster does befall the nest, the pair will often breed again within a few weeks. At the other end of the scale, albatrosses expend considerable effort on nesting, because if failure occurs, the pair may not breed again for two years or so.

Cup-shaped nests are more elaborate than platform nests, being usually made by weaving grasses and twigs together. The inside is often lined with soft feathers. The raised sides of the cup nest lessen the likelihood of losing eggs and chicks, and also offer greater security to the adults during incubation. The hollow in the nest's center is created by the birds compressing the material here before egg-laying begins.

Suspended nests enclosed by a domed roof offer even greater security. They are less accessible to predators because of their design and also their position, often hanging from slender branches. Some African waxbills (*Estrilda*) build a particularly elaborate nest, comprising two chambers. There is an obvious upper opening, which is

Above: The piping plover (Charadrius melodus) *from North America breeds in the open and so must also rely on camouflage to hide its presence when sitting on the nest.*

always empty, suggesting to would-be predators that the nest is unoccupied. The birds occupy the chamber beneath, which has a separate opening.

Nest protection

Some birds rely on the safety of numbers to deter would-be predators, building vast communal nests that are occupied by successive generations and added to regularly. Monk parakeets (*Myiopsitta monarchus*) from South America breed in this way. Their nests may weigh over 4cwt (200kg) or more.

Other birds have evolved more sophisticated methods not only of protecting their nests, but also of minimizing the time that they spend

incubating their eggs. Various parrots, such as the red-faced lovebird (*Agapornis pullaria*) from Africa, lay their eggs in termite mounds. The insects tolerate this intrusion, while the heat of the mound keeps the eggs warm. Mallee fowl (*Leipoa ocellata*) from Australia create a natural incubator for their eggs by burying them in a mound where the natural warmth and heat from decaying vegetation means that the chicks eventually hatch on their own and dig themselves out.

Other birds, such as the cowbirds (*Molothrus*) of North America, simply lay and abandon their eggs in the nests of other species. The foster parents-to-be do not seem able to detect the difference between their own eggs and that of the intruder, so they do not reject the cowbird egg. They incubate it along with their own brood, and feed the foster chick when it hatches out.

Birds that nest on the ground, such as the long-billed curlew (*Numenius americanus*), are especially vulnerable to predators and rely heavily on their fairly drab plumage as camouflage. Skylarks (*Alauda arvensis*) have another means of protecting their nest site—they hold one wing down and pretend to be injured to draw a predator away.

Below: Most eggs have a generally rounded shape, but seabirds such as guillemots (Uria aalge), *breeding on exposed rocky outcrops by the ocean, lay eggs that are more pointed. This shape helps to prevent the eggs from rolling over the cliff.*

HATCHING AND REARING CHICKS

Birds are vulnerable to predators when breeding, especially when they have young in the nest. The chicks must be fed frequently, necessitating regular trips to and from the nest, which makes it conspicuous. The calls of the young birds represent a further danger, so the breeding period is often short.

Most birds incubate their eggs to keep them sufficiently warm for the chicks to develop inside. Larger eggs are less prone to chilling during incubation than small eggs, because of their bigger volume. In the early stages of the incubation period, when the nest may be left uncovered while the adult birds are foraging for food, eggs can withstand a lower temperature. Temperature differences also account for the fact that, at similar altitudes, incubation periods tend to be slightly longer in temperate areas than in tropical regions.

The eggshell may appear to be a solid barrier but in fact contains many pores, which are vital to the chick's well-being. These tiny holes allow water vapor and carbon dioxide to escape from the egg, and oxygen to enter it to reach the embryo.

Incubation

The incubation period often does not start until more than one egg has been laid, and sometimes not until the entire clutch has been completed. The interval between the laying of one egg and the next varies—finches lay every

Below: A fertile chicken's egg, showing the development of the embryo through to hatching. 1. The fertilized egg cell divides to form a ball of cells that gradually develops into an embryo. 2. The embryo develops, nourished by the yolk sac. 3. The air space at the rounded end of the egg enlarges as water evaporates. 4. The chick is almost fully developed and ready to hatch. 5. The chick cuts its way out, and its feathers dry off.

day, whereas gannets may lay only one egg every six days. If incubation does not start until egg-laying has finished, the chicks will all be of a similar size when they hatch, which increases their overall chances of survival.

The cock and hen may share incubation duties, as in the case of most pigeons and doves, or just one member of the pair may incubate. This is usually the hen, but there are exceptions. With ostriches (*Struthio*

Above: Breeding in one of the coldest places on Earth means that emperor penguins (Aptenodytes forsteri) *can lay only a single egg, which they incubate on top of their feet, where special blood vessels help to warm it. After hatching, the chick is carried here too.*

camelus) and most other large flightless birds, it is the male who incubates the eggs and cares for the resulting chicks. Anis (*Crotophaga*) breed communally, and all members of the group share the task of incubation.

1

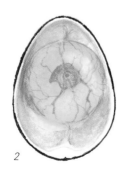

2

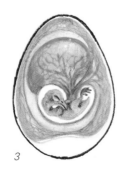

3

4

5

Hatching

Incubation periods vary among species, ranging from as few as 11 days in the case of some sparrows (*Spizella*), to over 80 days in some albatrosses (Diomedeidae). Before hatching, the chick uses the egg tooth on the tip of its upper bill to cut through the inner membrane into the air space at the blunt end of the shell, which forms as water evaporates from the egg. The chick starts to breathe atmospheric air for the first time. About 48 hours later, it breaks through the shell to emerge from the egg.

Chicks hatch out at various stages of development, and are accordingly able to leave the nest sooner or later.

Species that remain in the nest for some time after hatching, including parrots (Psittacidae) and finches (Fringillidae), hatch in a blind and helpless state and are entirely dependent on their parents at first. Birds in this group are known as nidicolous. If not closely brooded, they are likely to become fatally chilled. In contrast, species that leave the nest soon after hatching, known as nidifugous, emerge from the egg and are able to move around on their own at this stage. They can also see, and feed themselves, almost immediately. The offspring of many game birds such as pheasants, as well as waterfowl and waders, are nidifugous, which gives them a better chance of survival, as they can run to escape from predators. Young waterfowl cannot take safely to the water at first, however, because they lack the oil from the preen gland above the base of the tail to water-proof their feathers.

Rearing and fledging

Many adult birds offer food to their offspring, even some nidifugous species. This can be a particularly demanding period, especially for small birds that have relatively large broods. Blue-gray gnatcatchers (*Polioptila caerulea*), for example, must supply their offspring with huge quantities of insects, returning with food, and to clean the nest, several times each hour.

Young birds usually leave the nest from about 12 to 30 days after hatching. However, some species develop much more slowly. Albatross chicks are particularly slow developers, spending up to eight and a half months in the nest.

When they first leave the nest, many young birds are unable to fly, simply because their flight feathers are not fully functional. If these feathers are not fully unfurled from the protective sheaths in which they emerged, they cannot function effectively. The strength of the wing muscles also needs to be built up, so it is not uncommon for young birds to rest on the sides of the nest, flapping their wings occasionally, before finally taking to the air for the first time. Chicks that

Above: The tufted titmouse (Baeolophus bicolor) is typical of many birds that leave the nest before they are able to fly effectively. The young remain hidden in vegetation and are fed by their parents in these critical early days after leaving the nest.

are unable to fly immediately on fledging remain reliant on the adults, especially the cock, for food until they become fully independent.

For some young seabirds, fledging is a particularly hazardous process. From their cliff-ledge nests, they may simply flop down on to the water, where they are at risk from drowning until they master swimming skills. If they get swept out to sea, they may be caught by predators such as killer whales.

Below: The broad and often colorful gape of chicks allows parent birds such as this northern mockingbird (Mimus polyglottos) to feed their offspring quickly and efficiently. Weak chicks that are unable to raise their heads and gape at the approach of a parent will quickly die from starvation.

SURVIVAL

The numbers of a particular species of bird can vary significantly over time, affected by factors such as the availability of food, climate, disease and hunting. When the reproductive rate of a species falls below its annual mortality rate, it is in decline, but this does not mean it will inevitably become extinct.

For many birds, life is short and hazardous. Quite apart from the risk of predation, birds can face a whole range of other dangers, from starvation and disease through to human interference or persecution. The reproductive rate is higher and age of maturity is lower in species that have particularly hazardous lifestyles, such as black-capped chickadees (*Poecile atricapilla*), who often breed twice or more a year in quick succession.

Rising and falling numbers
Some birds have a reproductive cycle that allows them to increase their numbers rapidly under favorable conditions. The Galapagos Island penguin (*Spheniscus mendiculus*) is such a species. Fluctuating sea temperatures in the Pacific—part of the El Niño phenomenon—can drive sardines, its principal food source, away from the Galapagos. Very few chicks are reared during the lean years, as the native population faces starvation. During intervening periods,

Below: A flock of American blackbirds (Agelaius phoeniceus). *These New World birds have adapted very well to changes in their landscape brought about by agriculture. Although regarded as pests in some areas, they do consume large numbers of harmful invertebrates.*

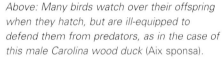

however, the penguin population recovers, as its food source returns. Ultimately, numbers are likely to fall, threatening the species with extinction.

Regular fall-offs in populations can occur on a cyclical basis, as shown by the case of snowy owls (*Nyctea scandiaca*) in North America. As the numbers of lemmings—the main component of the owls' diet—rise, so too does the snowy owl population. This is the result of more chicks per nest being reared successfully, rather than dying of starvation. When the numbers of lemmings fall again, due to a shortage of their food, owls are forced to spread out over a much wider area

Above: Many birds watch over their offspring when they hatch, but are ill-equipped to defend them from predators, as in the case of this male Carolina wood duck (Aix sponsa).

than normal in search of food, and their breeding success plummets accordingly. Later they gradually increase again over successive years, as the lemming population recovers.

Group living
Birds that live in flocks find mates more easily than other birds, and group life also offers several other advantages, including the safety of numbers. An aerial predator such as a hawk will find it harder to recognize and target individuals in a flying mass of birds, although stragglers are still likely to be picked off.

Coloration can also increase the safety of birds in flocks. In Florida, U.S.A., there used to be feral budgerigar flocks made up of multi-colored individuals. The different colors reflected the diversity of color varieties that were developed through domestication. Today, however, green is by far the predominant color in such flocks, as it is in genuine wild flocks, simply because predators found it much easier to pick off individuals of other colors. Greater numbers of the

Cryptic coloration

Camouflage, also known as cryptic coloration, enables a bird to hide in its natural surroundings. It offers distinct survival benefits in concealing the bird from would-be predators. Cryptic coloration has the effect of breaking up the bird's outline, allowing it to blend in with the background in its habitat. Posture and, in particular, keeping still can also help, as movement often attracts the attention of would-be predators.

Below: The common or long-tailed potoo (Nyctibius griseus) is a nocturnal species ranging from Mexico down to Argentina. It relies upon its camouflage to conceal its presence when resting during the day.

always the case. The expansion of agriculture in countries such as Argentina has resulted in the greater availability of both food and water for birds. This in turn has enabled populations, especially parrots like the Patagonian conure (*Cyanoliseus patagonus*), to grow by alarming degrees in recent years. Shooting and poisoning have been used as methods of population control, but it should be remembered that, overall, these birds have increased in numbers directly as a consequence of changes to the land pioneered by humans.

Other birds have benefited more directly from human intervention, as is the case with the common starling (*Sturnus vulgaris*). These birds have spread across North America, following their introduction from Europe in the late 1800s.

Similarly, the common pheasant (*Phasianus colchicus*) is now found across much of central North America, thanks to human interest in these game birds, which are bred in large numbers for sport shooting. Many more survive than would otherwise be the case, thanks to the attention of gamekeepers who not only provide food, but also help to curb possible predators in areas where the birds are released.

Slow breeders

Birds that reproduce slowly, such as albatrosses (Diomedeidae) and sandhill cranes (*Grus canadensis*), are likely to be highly vulnerable to any changes in

Above: Snowy owls (Nyctea scandiaca) are often seen near coasts outside the breeding season. They are opportunistic hunters, even catching fish on occasion.

their surroundings, whether caused by human interference, climate change, disease, or other factors. Great concern has recently been focused on albatross numbers, which are declining wordwide. Many of these birds have been caught and drowned in fishing nets in recent years. Albatrosses are normally very long-lived and breed very slowly. Any sudden decline in their population is therefore likely to have devastating consequences that cannot easily be reversed.

Below: Sandhill crane (Grus canadensis) with chick. Long-lived, slow-breeding birds such as cranes are the least adaptable when faced with rapid environmental changes of any kind.

green budgies survived to breed and pass on their genes to their descendants, and so green became the dominant color in the feral flocks.

Group living also means that when the flock is feeding and at its most vulnerable, there are extra eyes to watch out for predators and other threats. Within parrot flocks, birds take it in turns to act as sentinels, and screech loudly at any hint of danger.

Effects of humans

It is generally assumed that human interference in the landscape is likely to have harmful effects on avian populations. However, this is not

MIGRATION

Some birds live in a particular place all year round, but many are only temporary visitors. Typically, species fly north into temperate latitudes in spring, and return south at the end of summer. They have a wide distribution, but are seen only in specific parts of their range at certain times of the year.

Many species of birds regularly take long seasonal journeys. The birds that regularly undertake such seasonal movements on specific routes are known as migrants, and the journeys themselves are known as migrations. Many birds migrating from North to South America prefer to fly across Central America rather than the Caribbean. Birds migrate to seek shelter from the elements, to find safe areas to rear their young and, in particular, to seek places where food is plentiful. Birds such as waxwings (Bombycillidae) irrupt to a new location to find food when supplies become scarce in their habitat, but such journeys are less frequent and are irregular. The instinct to migrate dates back millions of years, to a period

Right: This diagram illustrates the main migratory routes in the Americas, where birds fly either down the Central American isthmus, or across the Caribbean via the local islands. In following these traditional routes over or close to land, the birds avoid long and potentially hazardous sea crossings.

Below: The routes taken by birds migrating back and forth to Africa from parts of Europe and western Asia are shown here. Again, crossings are not always made by the most direct route, if this would entail a long and possibly dangerous sea journey.

when the seasons were often much more extreme, which meant that it was difficult to obtain food in a locality throughout the year. This forced birds to move in search of food. Even today, the majority of migratory species live within the world's temperate zones, particularly in the northern hemisphere, where seasonal changes remain pronounced.

Migratory routes

The routes that the birds follow on their journeys are often well defined. Land birds try to avoid flying over large stretches of water, preferring instead to follow coastal routes and crossing the sea at the shortest point. For instance, many birds migrating from Europe to Africa prefer to fly over the Straits of Gibraltar. Frequently

---

Banding birds

Much of what we know about migration and the lifespan of birds comes from banding studies carried out by ornithologists. Lightweight aluminum bands placed on the birds' legs allow experts to track their movements when the ringed birds are recovered again. Unfortunately, only a very small proportion of ringed birds are ever recovered, so the data gathered is incomplete, but now other methods of tracking, such as radar, are also used to follow the routes taken by flocks of birds, which supplements the information from banding studies.

Below: Banding and collection of "biometric" data from shorebirds in New Jersey. By taking careful measurements of various parts of the body, and weighing the bird as well, scientists are able to build up a physical portrait of various bird populations.

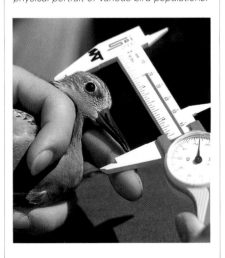

---

birds fly at much greater altitudes when migrating. Cranes (Gruidae) have been recorded flying at 16,400ft (5,000m) when crossing the mountainous areas in France, and geese (*Anser*) have been observed crossing the Himalayas at altitudes of more than 29,500ft (9,000m). Even if the migratory routes are known, it is often difficult to spot migrating birds because they fly so high.

Speed and distance

Migrating birds also fly at greater speeds than usual, which helps to make their journey time as short as possible. The difference can be significant—migrating swallows (*Hirundo rustica*) travel at speeds between 1.8–8.7mph (3–14km/h) faster than usual, helped by the greater altitude, where the air is thinner and resistance is less.

Some birds travel huge distances on migration. Arctic terns (*Sterna paradisea*), for example, cover distances of more than 9,300 miles (15,000km) in total, as they shuttle between the Arctic and Antarctic. They fly an average distance of 100 miles (160km) every day. Size does not preclude birds from migrating long distances, either. The tiny ruby-throated hummingbird (*Archilochus colubris*) flies over the Gulf of Mexico from the eastern USA every year, a distance of more than 500 miles (800km).

Preparing for migration

The migratory habits of birds have long been the subject of scientific curiosity. As late as the 1800s, it was thought that swallows hibernated in the bottom of ponds because they were seen skimming over the pond surface in groups before disappearing until the following spring. Now we know that they were probably feeding on insects to build up energy supplies for their long journey ahead.

Even today, the precise mechanisms involved in migratory behavior are not fully understood. We do know that birds feed up before setting out on migration, and that various hormonal changes enable them to store more fat

Above: Many birds, like this scarlet tanager (Piranga olivacea) migrate after molting. Damaged plumage can make the task of flying harder and more hazardous.

in their bodies to sustain them on their journey. Feeding opportunities are likely to be more limited than usual when birds are migrating, while their energy requirements are, of course, higher. In addition, birds usually molt just before migrating, so that their plumage is in the best condition to withstand the inevitable buffeting that lies ahead.

Navigation

Birds use both learned and visual cues to orientate themselves when migrating. Young birds of many species, such as swans, learn the route by flying in the company of their elders. However, some young birds set out on their own and reach their destinations successfully without the benefit of experienced companions, navigating by instinct alone. Birds such as swifts (Apopidae) fly mainly during daytime, whereas others, including ducks (Anatidae), migrate at night. Many birds fly direct to their destination, but some may detour and break their journey to obtain food and water before setting out again.

Experiments have shown that birds orientate themselves using the position of the sun and stars, as well as by following familiar landmarks. They also use the Earth's magnetic field to find their position, and thus do not get lost in cloudy or foggy weather, when the sky is obscured. The way in which these various factors come together, however, is not yet fully understood.

BEHAVIOR

Bird behavior, or avian ethology as it is known, is a very broad field. Some patterns of behavior are common to all birds, whereas other actions are very specific, just to a single species or even to an individual population. Interpreting behavior is easier in some cases than in others.

All bird behavior essentially relates to various aspects of survival, such as avoiding predators, obtaining food, finding a mate and breeding successfully. Some behavior patterns are instinctive, while others develop in certain populations of birds as a response to certain conditions. Thus, the way in which birds behave is partly influenced by their environment as well as being largely instinctual.

Age also plays a part in determining behavior, since young birds often behave in a very different way from

Above: An albatross (Diomedeidae) preens the downy plumage of its chick. This helps to cement the bond between them, as well as ensuring that the plumage around the bill does not become matted with food.

adults. Some forms of bird behavior are relatively easy to interpret, while others are a great deal more difficult to explain.

Garden birds

One of the first studies documenting birds' ability to adapt their behavior in response to changes in their environment involved blue tits (*Parus caeruleus*) in Britain. The study showed that certain individuals learned to use their bills to tap through the shiny metallic foil covers on milk bottles to reach the milk. Other blue tits followed their example, and in certain areas householders with milk deliveries had to protect their bottle tops from the birds.

The way in which birds have learned to use various types of garden feeders also demonstrates their ability to modify their existing behavior in response to new conditions when it benefits them. A number of new feeders on the market, designed to thwart squirrels from stealing the food,

exploit birds' ability to adapt in this way. The birds have to squeeze through a small gap to reach the food, just as they might enter the nest. Once one bird has been bold enough to enter in this fashion, others observe and soon follow suit.

Preening

Although preening serves a variety of functions, the most important aspect is keeping the feathers in good condition. It helps to dislodge parasites and removes loose feathers, particularly during molting. It also ensures that the plumage is kept waterproof by spreading oil from the preen gland at the base of the tail.

Preening can be a social activity too. It may be carried out by pairs of males and females during the breeding season, or among a family group.

Aggression

Birds can be surprisingly aggressive toward each other, even to the point of sometimes inflicting fatal injuries. Usually, however, only a few feathers are shed before the weaker individual backs away, without sustaining serious injury. Conflicts of this type can break out over feeding sites or territorial disputes. The risk of aggressive outbreaks is greatest at the start of the breeding season, as this is when the territorial instincts of cock birds are most aroused. Size is no indicator of the potential level of aggression, since some of the smallest birds, such as hummingbirds (Trochilidae) can be ferociously aggressive.

Below: A dispute breaks out between a pair of great-tailed grackles (Quiscalus mexicanus). *Such encounters rarely result in serious injury, as the weaker individual usually flies away to escape its rival.*

This behavior is seen in a variety of birds, ranging from parrots to finches. Some parrots perform mutual preening throughout the year, which reinforces the pair bond. In some of the Asiatic psittaculid parakeets, however, such as the Alexandrine (*Psittacula eupatria*), the dominant hen allows her mate to preen her only when she is in breeding condition, in which case preening may be seen as a prelude to mating.

Bathing

Preening is not the only way in which birds keep their plumage in good condition. Birds often bathe to remove dirt and debris from their plumage. Small birds wet their feathers by lying on a damp leaf during a shower of rain, in an activity known as leaf-bathing. Other birds immerse themselves in a pool of water, splashing around and ruffling their feathers.

Some birds, especially those found in drier areas of the world, prefer to dust-bathe, lying down in a dusty hollow known as a scrape and using fine earth thrown up by their wings to absorb excess oil from their plumage. Then, by shaking themselves thoroughly, followed by a period of preening, the excess oil is removed.

Sunbathing

Sunbathing may be important in allowing birds to synthesize Vitamin D3 from the ultraviolet rays in sunlight, which is vital for a healthy skeleton. This process can be achieved only by light falling on the bird's skin, which explains why birds ruffle their plumage at this time. Some birds habitually stretch out while sunbathing, while others, such as many pigeons, prefer to rest with one wing

Right: The natural waterproofing present on the plumage ensures that birds do not become saturated when swimming or caught in a shower of rain. This would destroy the warm layer of air surrounding the body created by the down feathering, and leave them vulnerable to hypothermia. Nevertheless birds do need to dry their plumage, which is what this American anhinga (Anhinga anhinga) is doing, with its wings outstretched.

raised, leaning over at a strange angle on the perch. Vasa parrots (*Coracopsis*), found on the island of Madagascar, frequently behave in this fashion, although sunbathing is generally not common in this group of birds.

Maintaining health

Some people believe that when birds are ill, they eat particular plants that have medicinal properties, but this theory is very difficult to prove. One form of behavior that does confer health benefits has been documented, however: it involves the use of ants. Instead of eating these insects, some birds occasionally rub them in among their feathers. This causes the ants to release formic acid, which acts as a potent insecticide, killing off lurking parasites such as mites and lice. Blue jays (*Cyanocitta cristata*) and also starlings (Sturnidae) and Eurasian blackbirds (*Turdus merula*) are among the species that have been observed using insects in this way. Members of the crow family have also been seen perching on smoking chimney pots or above bonfires, ruffling their feathers and allowing the smoke to penetrate their plumage. The smoke is thought to kill off parasites in a process that confers the same benefits as anting.

Above: Birds such as the cattle egret (Bubulcus ibis) form unusual associations with large mammals. They will mingle among herds as they feed, keeping a sharp watch for potential prey such as invertebrates, or other creatures, that may be flushed from the grass by the mammals as they move.

Below: A Gila woodpecker (Melanerpes uropygialis) feeding on cactus fruit. These desert-dwelling woodpeckers will also bore into larger cacti to create their nest site.

BIRDWATCHING

Thanks to their widespread distribution, birds can be seen in virtually any locality, even in the center of cities. You don't need any special equipment to watch birds, but a pair of binoculars will help you to gain a better insight into avian behavior, by allowing you to study birds at close range.

Birdwatching can be carried out almost anywhere around the world. Many people enjoy simply watching the birds that visit their garden. A greater variety of species can be seen if the birdwatcher ventures further afield, to local parks, woods or wetlands for example. Birdwatching vacations and sponsored birdwatching competitions offer opportunities to see an even greater variety of birds in different localities. Seasonal changes in bird populations mean that even if you visit the same area through the year, you will see new species at different times.

Drawing birds for reference

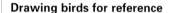

1. Sketching birds is relatively straight-forward if you follow this procedure. Start by drawing an egg shape for the body, with a smaller egg above, which will become the head, and another to form the rump. A center line through the head circle will form the basis for the bill. Now add circles and lines to indicate the position of the wings and tail. Add lines for the legs and then sketch in the feet and claws.

3. Colored pencils will allow you to add more detail after you have rubbed out any unwanted pencil markings.

2. Use an indelible fine-line felt-tip pen to ink in the shape of the bird that you have drawn previously in pencil, avoiding the unwanted construction lines.

4. If you take a number of prepared head shapes with you into the field, you can fill in the detail quickly and easily, enabling you to identify birds later.

Above: At many major reserves where birds congregate, special permanent birdwatching hides have been set up to give visitors a good view without disturbing the birds themselves.

Getting a good view

Binoculars can be purchased from camera stores and similar outlets, but it is important to test them before deciding which model to buy, particularly as they vary quite significantly in price. When purchasing binoculars, you will need to consider not only the power of magnification, but also how closely the binoculars can be focused, particularly if you going to use them at home, where the bird table is likely to be relatively close.

Binoculars vary according to their power of magnification and the length of the objective lens in millimeters, with the lens modifying the image. The lens' length and magnification are given in the specifications: binoculars described as 8x45 multiply the image by eight compared with how it would appear to the naked eye and have an objective lens of 45mm, which is important in determining the focus.

Two important considerations stem from the power of magnification. First, the depth of field is important, since it affects the area of the image that is in focus. The greater the magnification, the shallower the depth of field. A deep depth of field can be helpful, since it ensures that a larger proportion of the birds on view are in focus, which avoids the need to refocus constantly. If the depth of field is shallow, only the birds in the center will be in focus. Second, the degree of magnification also affects the field of vision—the area that you can see through the binoculars. A wide field of vision will help you to locate birds more easily.

Buying binoculars

A number of other factors may be considered when buying binoculars.
• Weight is important. Consider buying a lightweight pair if you intend using binoculars for long periods. They should also feel balanced in the hands.
• For people with large hands, small binoculars may be hard to adjust and not very comfortable to hold. Pay attention to the focusing mechanism—it should be easy to operate.
• Try the eyecups of the binoculars to see how comfortable they feel. If you wear glasses, it is important that the cups give you a full field of vision. Binoculars with adjustable eyecups are better for people who wear glasses.
• Is the design of good quality? It could be worthwhile paying extra for waterproofing. The better-quality

Above: A backyard bird table will attract many species to feed, like this starling (Sturnus vulgaris). If it is carefully sited, you should be able to see the birds from inside your home.

Right: Hanging feeders are increasingly popular in American backyards as a means of encouraging birds to visit. The positioning of this orange makes it easily accessible to this hungry Baltimore oriole (Icterus galbula), and other fruit-eating species, providing them with a vertical grip as well as a source of food.

models have their chambers filled with nitrogen gas to prevent any condensation developing.
• The design should be sturdy, with a solid protective casing.

Fieldscopes

Apart from binoculars, dedicated bird-watchers often use birding telescopes, called fieldscopes. These are ideal for use in hides as they can be mounted in various ways, using either a bench clamp fitting or a tripod. Fieldscopes are equipped with lenses similar to those in binoculars, but are more suited to long-term use, when you are watching a nest for example, as you do not have to keep holding the scope while waiting for a bird to return. Instead, attach the scope to a branch or bench and train it on the nest, then simply be patient until you see the bird return.

Making notes

When observing birds either in the garden or further afield, it is always useful to have a notebook handy to write down details and make sketches.

Below: A view of a hide. External camouflage, easy access and good viewing positions are essential features in the design of such units. Even so, it may take birds some time to accept the presence of a hide.

When sketching, proceed from a few quick pencil lines to a more finished portrait as time allows. Water-soluble pencils are helpful for coloring sketches, as the colors can be spread using water and a small paintbrush. If you spot a bird you cannot identify, jot down the details quickly in your notebook. Note the bird's colors and markings. Notice the length of the neck and legs, and the shape of its bill. Assess the bird's size in relation to familiar species, and try to decide which family you think it belongs to. Your notes can then be compared with a field guide or other sources of information to identify the bird.

FIELDCRAFT

*If you are seriously interested in birdwatching, you will need to develop fieldcraft skills. There is a
significant difference between watching birds casually in a garden and tracking down particular species
in remote areas, where preparation is important. Don't neglect your own safety in the wild.*

*Left: Hand-held binoculars or a viewing scope
attached to a tripod can help you to study
both common and rare species. Taking notes
is useful, especially if you intend to write up
details of your observations.*

Photography
In the past, birdwatchers relied on
35mm SLR cameras and telephoto
lenses to record their sightings. Today,
however, birders are increasingly using
digital cameras. These work very well
when combined via a connector to a
viewing scope that magnifies the
image, like a telephoto lens. Digital
cameras have the further advantage
that they do not require film, but store
images in their memory. Unwanted
pictures can simply be deleted, while
the best images can be transferred to a
computer and printed out. Although
you will not run out of film, digital
cameras do use a surprising amount of
power, so remember to take spare

Research and careful preparation are
vital to the success of any field trip.
You should also select clothing and
equipment suited to the particular
place where you intend to study birds.

Clothing and equipment
Suitable clothing is vital to keep you
warm and dry when birdwatching.
Waterproof footwear will be needed
when visiting wetlands, or after rain.
Dull-colored clothing will allow you to
blend in with the landscape so you can
approach the birds more closely.
A camping mat can be useful if you
intend spending time on the ground.

In addition to packing your
binoculars, camera equipment and
perhaps a viewing scope, you may also
want to take a notebook or sketchpad.
A field guide will help to identify birds,
while a waterproof knapsack will
protect all your belongings.

Preparation
It always helps to do your homework
before setting out. Investigating the
habits of the birds you hope to see will
help you to decide on the best place to
go, and the time of day when they are

most likely to be seen. It may be useful
to draw up a checklist highlighting key
features of the species concerned in
advance. You can then refer to these in
the field. Studying a local map prior to
your visit will help you to orient
yourself in new surroundings. Good
preparation is especially important in
areas where you are likely to be
unfamiliar with the birds concerned.

*Below: Plumage details, such as the
handsome markings of this blue jay
(Cyanocitta cristata), may be captured using a
conventional camera with a telephoto lens, or
using a digital camera or camcorder linked to a
viewing scope.*

batteries with you on field trips. Digital camcorders can also be linked with viewing scopes, and are more flexible than cameras. Not only does a camcorder enable you to record the bird's song—which can be significant, especially if there is any doubt about identification—but you can also obtain a sequence of still images, especially if you can see the bird from different angles. Flight patterns can be recorded in this way, which again can help with identification. Even in relatively dark surroundings, some camcorders will function well.

Using hides and cover

On recognized reserves, there are likely to be hides in the best localities for birdwatching. Hides allow you to observe birds at relatively close quarters, and also offer excellent opportunities to photograph or film birds in their natural habitat. Even so, patience is likely to be needed for successful birding, as there will be no guarantees that you will see the species you hope to spot.

In areas where no hide is available, take cover behind shrubs, tree trunks or raised banks, or even in a parked car. Birds are highly attuned to the

Below: There are now many organized trips taking keen birders to exotic localities, such as this tour of La Selva Biological Station, the center for rainforest research, in Costa Rica.

slightest hint of danger, such as humans approaching. In areas where no cover is available, stand, kneel or lie in a comfortable position and try to move as little as possible. When approaching birds, make sure your position is downwind, so the sounds of your approach don't frighten them away.

Seeking rarities

Birdwatching magazines can be useful in identifying sites where rarities have been spotted. For up-to-the-minute news, you will need to seek out either a regularly updated website or an information phone line giving details of the latest sightings. Birders with access to email can also receive

Above: In some areas, there may not be any natural cover or hides available. To get close to birds, you will need to dress inconspicuously so that you blend into the background, and try to keep as still as you possibly can. Birdwatching requires plenty of patience.

bulletins listing where particular rarities have cropped up. These are most likely to be recorded after bad weather such as fierce storms which can blow migrant birds off-course.

Bear in mind that many people will be drawn to a place where an unusual species has been sighted, and it is important not to create a disturbance or to trespass on private land. Similarly, it is a criminal offence in some areas to disturb breeding birds. Always act in a responsible manner when birdwatching.

Getting the best results

• Plan well beforehand, including checking tide times if relevant. Tidal areas can be particularly hazardous where there is quicksand.
• Remember that bird populations may vary according to the time of year.
• Never neglect your own safety. Let someone else know where you are going, and when you intend to return.
• Check the weather forecast first, and take a cell phone in case you get into difficulties.
• Take a local map and also a compass to guide you if you get lost. Allow enough time to locate and then observe the birds.

ZONES AND HABITATS

Birds have been exceedingly successful in colonizing the planet. Their warm-blooded nature and ability to fly have helped them to reach and then adapt to life in some of the world's most inaccessible places. They are found naturally on all continents, even successfully inhabiting Antarctica.

Zoologists divide the world into broad geographical zones, within which there are many different habitats. This approach reflects the movements of the Earth's landmasses through geological time, and so helps to show relationships between species occurring in various parts of the world today.

The Americas

In the distant past, North America was separated from its southern neighbor, and they had different origins. North America was originally attached to what is now Europe and later drifted westwards, while South America was once joined to a huge southern landmass that geologists call Gondwana, which included what is now the Indian subcontinent, Australia, Africa and Antarctica. South America split off at an earlier stage in

geological history than did North America—more than 100 million years ago—at a time when dinosaurs were in the ascendancy and the skies were occupied by flying reptiles called pterosaurs, rather than birds.

When birds began to evolve on this southern continent, they did so in isolation from the rest of the world. For this reason, the bird life that occurs today in this southern zone is known as neotropical, to distinguish it from that found in North America, which is known as nearctic. Later the avian populations of the Nearctic and Neotropical zones mingled somewhat by way of the Central American land bridge that was created when these two vast landmasses joined. However, unique forms still exist that are found only in South America, reflecting their isolated development in prehistory.

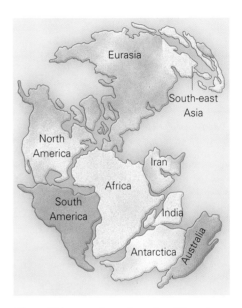

Above: This map shows how the different continents are believed to have formed and divided, giving rise to the familiar continents that we know today (see map below). These continental movements have, in turn, had a direct impact on the distribution of birds today.

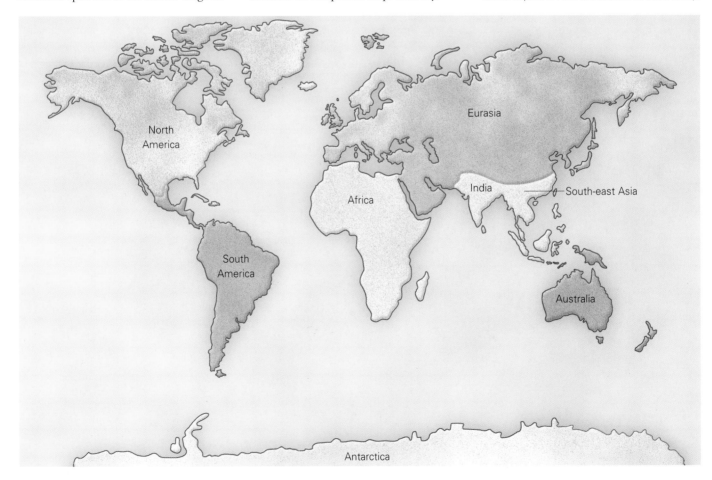

Above: Some birds can be seen far outside their natural range, thanks to human intervention. Escapes from aviaries by, and deliberate releases of, orange bishops (Euplectes orix), normally found in Africa, have led to the recent establishment of this species in Los Angeles and Phoenix, Arizona.

The Palaearctic

Europe has been separated from North America by the Atlantic Ocean for more than 50 million years, but the bird species of these now separate areas still show some evidence of their common past. In prehistory, Europe formed, and still forms, part of a much broader area known as the Palaearctic realm, which extends right across the northern continent from Iceland eastward to Japan. Fossilized remains suggest that this region was the cradle of avian evolution, where the first members of the group probably originated more than 80 million years ago. Most zoologists believe that the oldest-known bird, *Archaeopteryx,* was not in fact the first of the avian line, but as yet its immediate ancestors have not been discovered.

The distribution of avian species in the northern hemisphere has been affected in the more recent geological past by the spread and subsequent retreat of the ice sheets from the far north. Today, Europe and Asia experience a climate similar to that of the corresponding area of North America, ranging from arctic to subtropical according to latitude. The two regions even have some birds in common, especially in the far north, where certain species have a circum-polar distribution—they are found right around the polar region.

Africa, southern Asia and Australasia

As part of the great southern continent of Gondwana, Africa used to be attached to South America, but subsequently remained in contact with what is now the Indian subcontinent during the critical early phase in avian evolution, approximately 60 million years ago. This distant history is reflected even today by the large number of avian species found south of what has become the Sahara Desert. This zone is now described as the Ethiopian realm, although it covers virtually all of Africa.

The Indian subcontinent became a separate landmass when Gondwana broke up. It ultimately drifted north, colliding and eventually joining with what is now the Asian landmass, and creating the Himalayan mountains in the process. As in Africa, the broadly tropical climate and the landscape have altered little since then, which has meant that a number of the species that evolved here are found nowhere else in the world.

East and south of India lie the islands that comprise the Australasian realm, which includes Australia, New Guinea and New Zealand. These islands once formed part of the vast landmass of Gondwana, but later broke away and have been isolated from the rest of the world for millions of years. A diversity of bird species found nowhere else in the world can be seen here as a result.

Present distribution

Birds' current distribution throughout the world is affected by a number of different factors, as well as the history of their evolution. The ability to fly has allowed birds to become very widely distributed, as has their warm-blooded nature, which has meant that they are far less vulnerable to climatic factors than cold-blooded creatures. Lifestyle, and particularly the range of foods that are available, also play a part. As a result of all these factors, birdwatchers know that they are more likely to encounter certain groups of birds in specific types of habitat. The major, and richly diverse, avian habitats of the American world are listed on the pages that follow.

Below: Common, or European, starlings (Sturnus vulgaris) *are now well established outside their natural range. This picture was taken in the U.S.A. where, during the 1800s, the species was introduced. It has since spread widely across North America, and can also be found in Australia, and other localities.*

THE OCEANS

The world's oceans provide a very rich source of food for all birds able to exploit it. Fish and invertebrates such as squid and krill form the basis of the diet of seabirds, some of which range extensively across the world's oceans and are frequently sighted long distances from land.

The huge expanse of the oceans, and the difficulty of observing seabirds, means that relatively little is known about many species. This lack of knowledge was confirmed by the case of the Bermuda petrel (*Pterodroma cahow*). This species was believed to have become extinct during the 1600s, but, remarkably, a surviving population was rediscovered in 1951 after more than three hundred years. Seabirds survive out at sea with the help of special salt-excreting glands in

the nasal area (just above their bills) that allow them to drink seawater without getting dehydrated.

Breeding habits

Many seabirds are social by nature, forming huge breeding colonies on rocky outcrops by the sea. Indeed, one of the main factors restricting seabird populations can be the lack of nesting sites. By congregating in large colonies the birds can maximize their reproductive success while reducing the effects of predators on their numbers. Nest-raiders such as greater black-backed gulls (*Larus marinus*) may be unable to inflict damage on a breeding colony if the birds are so densely packed that the raiders cannot land.

Feeding

The feeding habits of seabirds have a significant impact on their lifestyle. Albatrosses (Diomedeidae), for example, spend most of their lives flying above the oceans. Their large wingspan allows them to glide almost effortlessly for long periods, swooping down to take food from the surface or even catching flying fish above the waves, rather than entering the water. Other species, such as gannets (Sulidae), dive beneath the surface to feed.

Above: Some seabirds spend their entire lives on the water, and will not venture any great distance from this habitat. Others, such as these knots (Calidris canutus), are only in the ocean for part of the year. They retreat inland during the breeding season, to nest in the far north on frozen tundra.

Below: Not all seabirds feed on fish. This white-vented storm petrel (Oceanites gracilis) is feeding on planktonic debris, while paddling with its feet on the surface of the water.

Right: The ocean can be a hostile environment, with rough weather sometimes making feeding conditions difficult. High winds can batter birds and blow them off course, while oil spillages have presented a new threat in recent times. Ultimately, all seabirds are forced onto land to reproduce. Many species seek out remote oceanic islands to do so. There they can breed without being harassed by people or encountering introduced predators such as domestic cats.

Birdwatching tips

• Seabirds such as albatrosses are attracted to passing ships because of the food that is thrown overboard. This means they are relatively easy to locate in certain areas—for example near shipping lanes.
• Ornithologists can often take trips on local boats to view seabird colonies. These and other ocean crossings may present a good opportunity to watch birds feeding out at sea.
• If you are prone to seasickness, don't forget to take medication beforehand if you think you may feel ill on a trip.
• Binoculars can easily be lost overboard from a small boat on choppy oceans. Always sling them (and any camera equipment) around your neck, rather than simply holding them in your hands.

Typical sightings in seas and oceans, depending to some extent on location:
• Auks
• Gannets
• Albatrosses
• Petrels

Below: For most ornithologists, organized charter boat trips present the only way to reach seabird colonies.

1 Great skua
2 Atlantic puffin
3 Razorbill
4 Common murre
5 Black-legged kittiwake
6 Northern gannets
7 Great black-backed gulls
8 Northern fulmar
9 Sooty shearwater

SEASHORE AND ESTUARY

Tidal rhythms have a significant impact on the habits of birds found on seashores and estuaries. These birds usually group together to feed on mudflats and sandbars that are uncovered at low tide. As the incoming tide encroaches, the birds are forced to retreat to the shoreline.

Gulls typify the image of the seashore more than any other group of birds, being a familiar sight on coasts the world over. These adaptable birds also venture well inland, especially to locations where food is available, such

Above: Sanderlings (Calidris alba) *demonstrate the features of a typical wader. The daily lives of such birds are directly influenced by the movements of the tide.*

Below: *It is very difficult to get close to seabirds such as these terns, as they tend to be wary and may take flight. It is therefore better to pick a well-concealed vantage point and wait for the birds to approach.*

as public parks with ponds and even the less salubrious surroundings of refuse dumps.

Lifestyle and feeding

Wading birds that frequent seashores typically have relatively long legs compared with perching birds, which enable them to walk through shallow water. Their narrow bills allow them to probe for invertebrates concealed in the mud. Some waders have evolved more specialized feeding habits, which are reflected in the shape of their bills. The American oystercatcher (*Haematopus palliatus*), for example, has a chisel-like tip to its bill that allows it to split open mollusk shells.

Shorebirds feed on a range of creatures, and can therefore be sighted further inland, even if only seeking sanctuary from storms. Some shorebirds are migratory, spending summer as far north as the Arctic Circle before heading south for winter again.

Breeding habits

Many birds that live close to the shoreline have to breed in the open. The eggs and chicks of such species,

which include curlews (*Numenius*), have markings that conceal them well among the sand or pebbles. This cryptic coloration also plays a part in adulthood, with typical shades of gray, brown and white plumage merging into the background of the shoreline.

Within the tropics, a number of shorebirds have adapted to living in coastal mangrove forests, the roots of which are submerged by the incoming tide. They include some of the most spectacular members of the group, such as the scarlet ibis (*Eudocimus ruber*). These birds use the mangroves for roosting and breeding because they can nest off the ground there.

Right: *The day-to-day distribution of seashore and estuarine birds is likely to be influenced by the weather. If conditions are stormy, birds often retreat to estuaries and coastal lagoons; in icy winter weather, a variety of unexpected species may be seen at estuaries, since these stretches of water do not freeze over, unlike surrounding areas of fresh water such as lakes and rivers.*

1 Roseate spoonbills
2 Scarlet ibis
3 Brown pelicans
4 Long-billed curlew
5 American oystercatchers
6 Knots
7 Herring gulls
8 Marbled godwit
9 Snowy egret
10 Fish crow

FRESHWATER LAKES, PONDS AND RIVERS

The speed of the water flow in freshwater habitats has a direct impact on the vegetation that grows there, which in turn influences the types of birds that may be seen. Some birds are drawn to lakes, ponds and rivers mainly for food, whereas others seek sanctuary from would-be predators there.

A wide variety of birds can be encountered by lakes, ponds and rivers, but not all are easy to observe. In areas of slow-flowing or still, shallow water where reed beds are well established, rails of various types (Rallidae) are often present, but these birds are shy by nature. Their mottled plumage provides camouflage, while their slim, tall body shape coupled with long, narrow toes allows them to move quietly through the vegetation.

Finding food
Many birds of prey hunt in freshwater habitats, swooping low over the water to seize fish by day and even at night. Ospreys (*Pandion haliaetus*) have very powerful, hooked talons, allowing them to hold onto slippery fish that they lift out of the water during flight. Other hunters rely on different tactics to catch food. Herons (Ardeidae) wait in the shallows and seize fish that swim in range of their sharp, powerful bills. Some fish-eating birds such as kingfishers (Alcedinidae) dive to seize their prey, which they may feed to their young in river bank nests.

Nesting
Some birds are drawn to lakes and rivers not so much by food but by nesting opportunities. Swallows (*Hirundo rustica*) collect damp mud from the

Above: A sharp bill, narrow head and powerful neck mean that birds such as the red-necked grebe (Podiceps grisegena) *are well equipped to seize aquatic prey.*

water's edge to make their nests, and may also catch midges flying above the water. Most birds that actually nest by ponds and rivers seek seclusion when breeding. They hide their nest away, or make it hard to reach by choosing a spot surrounded by water, while taking care to avoid sites that may flood. Trumpeter swans (*Cygnus buccinator*) construct large nests, which restricts their choice of sites. Both sexes, but especially the cob (male), defend the nest ferociously. These largish birds are capable of inflicting painful, damaging

blows with their wings on would-be wild predators, dogs or even people who venture too close.

Below: The keen eyesight and long legs of birds such as the great blue heron (Ardea herodias) help them to hunt effectively in freshwater habitats.

Below: A wattled jacana (Jacana jacana), *photographed here in Trinidad, has long toes which support its weight when walking across lily pads, and prevent it from sinking down.*

Birdwatching tips
• Patience is essential when watching freshwater birds, as many species are shy and easily frightened away.
• Certain localities, such as large lakes and gravel pits, are particularly good for spotting waterfowl in winter. Check local details in field guides or on websites.
• Quietly paddling a canoe up a river can be a good way to spot birds, but plan carefully and be alert to possible dangers, such as strong currents, weirs or waterfalls on the route.
• Take great care near rivers when there is a risk of flooding, such as after heavy rain.

Typical sightings by lakes, ponds and rivers, depending on location:
• Ducks, geese and swans
• Rails
• Herons
• Birds of prey

Right: Reedbeds associated with freshwater habitats provide cover for many species of birds. The dense vegetation in such areas means that birdwatching can be difficult. The narrow body shape and agility of many freshwater birds allow them to move easily through dense vegetation, avoiding detection. Fortunately, birds swimming into open water will be much easier to spot.

1 Whistling swans
2 Belted kingfisher
3 Yellow-headed blackbird
4 Osprey
5 Common loon
6 Lesser scaup
7 Canvasback
8 Wood duck family
9 Green heron
10 King rail
11 Great blue heron

TEMPERATE WOODLAND

The temperate woodlands of the Northern Hemisphere have altered significantly over time owing to climate change, receding in cold periods and expanding in warmer eras. Coniferous forests extend north to the treeless area known as the tundra, where it is too cold for even hardy trees to grow.

Bird life in coniferous forests is less varied than in deciduous, broad-leaved woodlands, largely because there are fewer feeding opportunities. Nonetheless some species manage to thrive in this cooler habitat.

Coniferous woodlands

Clark's nutcracker (*Nucifraga columbiana*) of the North American forests is one such success. Their curving bills allow these specialized members of the crow family to extract the seeds from pine cones effectively.

The food supply in this habitat is not guaranteed, however. There are barren years when the trees do not produce as many cones as usual, forcing the birds to abandon their regular haunts and fly elsewhere. These unpredictable movements, known as irruptions, occur when birds suddenly appear in large numbers outside their normal range, searching for alternative sources of food. They later disappear

Above: Some birds, like this wild turkey, (Meleagris gallopavo), nest on the ground, concealing their presence from other creatures as much as possible. The chicks are able to move immediately after hatching.

Above: A pileated woodpecker (Dryocopus pileatus) male returns to the nest site. Trees provide relatively safe nesting havens, especially for birds such as woodpeckers that can create their own nesting holes.

just as suddenly as they arrived, and may not return again for years. In northerly areas the landscape is covered in snow for much of the winter. Some species, including various corvids and woodpeckers, prepare for the cold weather by burying stores of nuts or hiding them in trees.

Owls are frequently found in coniferous forests, preying on the rodents that can be quite plentiful there. However, owls may also be forced to hunt elsewhere if the numbers of their prey plummet, as occasionally happens when there is a shortage of pine cones.

Deciduous woodlands

A greater variety of feeding opportunities exists for birds in deciduous forests. Such woodland is more open, which means that there is a significant understorey of vegetation and insects are more plentiful. Migratory birds take advantage of the feeding opportunities in these forests in summer. Ground birds of various types, including wild turkeys (*Meleagris gallopavo*), are also found here. During the breeding season they congregate in forest clearings to display and mate. These birds eat a

variety of foods, ranging from seeds to berries and invertebrates, depending on the time of year.

Below: Some predatory birds have adapted to life in temperate forests, especially owls such as this large-eared owl (Asio otis). These hunters depend largely on rodents for food.

Birdwatching tips

• Spring is a good time to spot birds in deciduous woodlands, before the trees are covered in leaves.
• Woodlands and particularly coniferous forests can be disorientating, so take a map and compass if you're going any distance in case you lose your bearings.
• In summer, woodland glades attract invertebrates, which in turn attract insectivorous birds in search of prey.
• Stand quietly in woodlands and listen— the song of woodland birds helps to reveal their presence.

Typical sightings in temperate woodlands, depending to some extent on location:
• Woodpeckers
• Finches
• Owls
• Warblers

Right: In many ways, temperate woodland is an ideal avian habitat during the warm months of the year, providing a wide range of food, excellent cover and a variety of nesting sites. During the winter months, however, life here can become much harsher. Once the leaves have fallen, the birds will be much more conspicuous, and food is likely to be harder to find. Survival will become even more difficult if snow blankets the ground.

1 Black-capped chickadee
2 Goshawk
3 Pileated woodpecker
4 Winter wren
5 Hermit thrush
6 Yellow warbler
7 Long-eared owl
8 Pine siskins
9 White-breasted nuthatch

TROPICAL RAINFOREST

Over long periods, tropical rainforests have provided relatively stable environments compared with temperate forests, and are home to some spectacular species. Unfortunately, many tracts of forest are not easily accessible. Choose locations carefully to maximize your chance of seeing a wide range of birds.

Many of the birds inhabiting rainforest areas are brightly colored, but their vibrant plumage is very effectively concealed in this dark, shadowy environment. Only flashes of color may be seen as the plumage is lit by shafts of sunlight penetrating through the dense canopy of the forest.

Rainforest diversity

The stable environment of the rainforest has undoubtedly contributed to the diversity of bird life found there. Fruit is especially plentiful, and specialist fruit-eating birds, known as frugivores, are therefore numerous. Their presence is essential to the long-term well-being of the rainforest, as they help to distribute the seeds of the fruits on which they feed. The seeds are excreted in their droppings, often some distance away from where the fruit was originally eaten. This method of seed dispersal helps to ensure the continued regeneration of the forest.

Birds of prey can also be observed in tropical rainforests, having adapted well to forest life, and there are even a

Below: A yellow-naped Amazon (Amazona ochrocephala) *feeding. The unchanging climatic conditions in rainforests mean that food is readily available here through the year.*

number of species that specialize in hunting other birds. These predators are relatively few in number, however, compared with the overall numbers of birds found in this habitat.

Many rainforest species have localized distributions. Although some toucans, for example, may have extensive ranges, the distribution of some of Hawaii's native birds may be confined to just a single island. Vast tracts of the world's rainforests are still so remote and inaccessible that even today, particularly on the South American continent, new species of birds are still regularly being discovered by explorers each year.

Threatened habitat

It is well known that the world's rainforests are being felled alarmingly quickly. The fast rate of destruction means that it is possible that some species may become extinct before they have even been identified. Museum collections around the world contain various hummingbirds (Trochilidae) and tanagers (Thraupidae), for example, that are known only from single specimens. The birds' distributions are unrecorded and nothing more has been documented about them.

Above: Toucans are among the most distinctive of all birds found in tropical rainforests. Their large but lightweight bills assist them in reaching fruits that would otherwise be inaccessible.

Birdwatching tips

• Rainforests are potentially dangerous places, so go with an experienced guide or group, and don't be tempted to wander off into the forest on your own.
• You are often more likely to hear rather than see birds in this leafy environment.
• Pausing quietly for a time should allow you to spot bird life more easily.
• Photography is often difficult in the forest because of the low light.
• The high humidity, almost daily rainfall and biting insects in rainforests can create additional problems.

Typical sightings in tropical rainforests, depending to some extent on location:
• Parrots
• Barbets
• Cotingas
• Trogons

Right: The dense upper canopy of the rainforest provides both a screen and a vantage point for birds, depending on their lifestyle. Hunters may perch among the tallest trees or fly over the canopy, seeking signs of possible prey beneath, while nearer to the ground, nectar-eating birds seek flowers to feed from. Fruit is also abundant in these lush forests, so frugivorous species are commonly encountered here too.

1 Sulphur-breasted toucan
2 Orange-winged parrot
3 Scarlet macaws
4 Resplendent quetzal
5 White-chinned hummingbird
6 Guianian cocks-of-the-rock
7 Green-tailed jacamar
8 Paradise tanager
9 White-plumed antbird
10 Chestnut-crowned ant pitta

TUNDRA AND POLAR REGIONS

Birds have successfully colonized many harsh environments, including the treeless tundra and freezing Antarctic. A surprisingly wide range of birds may be sighted on the tundra, especially in summer, when many migratory birds arrive to breed.

The treeless lands of the far north are inhospitable in winter, so many birds visit only for the summer. Icy Antarctica is even harsher, yet birds such as penguins are year-round residents on coastlines.

Antarctic survivors

As the huge landmass of Antarctica drifted gradually southward millions of years ago, so the seabirds there adapted their lifestyle to survive the harshest conditions on Earth. The freezing cold and biting winds combine to create a numbing wind-chill factor that few creatures could survive, but penguins have adapted to thrive in this habitat. The lack of nesting material and the threat of fatal chilling if the eggs or young are exposed to the elements for even a few seconds have affected their breeding habits. Emperor penguins (*Aptenodytes forsteri*) lay only a single egg, which is kept wedged between the top of their flippered feet

Above: Unlike many birds from the far north, the white plumage of these snow geese (Anser caerulescans) remains the same color throughout the year. There is, however, a much rarer pale blue form of the plumage.

and their abdomen. Emperors have an increased number of blood vessels here, to convey heat to the developing embryo through the eggshell.

Penguins have in fact reversed the general evolutionary path of birds to survive in this harsh environment. In the course of millions of years, most birds evolved increasingly lightweight bodies to facilitate flight, but the body weight of penguins increased because of a build-up of the subcutaneous fat that helps to insulate them against the bitter cold. The evolution of their

Below: Antarctic seabirds such as the cape petrel (Daption capense) benefit from the rich food supply in the southern oceans. These birds fly north to escape the worst winter weather, and only return to the shores of Antarctica during the brief summer to nest.

wings into flippers and their streamlined shape combine to make them highly effective marine predators.

The northern tundra

In the far north, the treeless tundra landscape is transformed during the brief summer months when the snow melts. The topsoil thaws too, and the ground becomes boggy because the melt water cannot drain away through the permanently frozen layer beneath. Instead, water forms shallow pools at the surface, where mosquitoes and other insects breed in large numbers. These invertebrates and other food attract a variety of birds as temporary visitors. The migrants nest and quickly rear their young before the weather turns cold and they head south again.

Right: Many birds found in areas where snow often blankets the ground and there is little natural cover have mainly white plumage. This is true of both predators such as snowy owls (Nyctea scandiaca) and also prey. Other adaptations that assist survival in cold habitats include extra feathering over the body extending to the feet, and greater reserves of body fat.

Birdwatching tips
• Wear pale or dull-colored clothing to conceal your presence in these cold, treeless areas where there is little natural cover. Of course, all clothing must be warm as well.
• Take mosquito repellent when visiting the tundra during the summer.
• Allow for the bright light when photographing in snowy landscapes. Glare reflecting off the snow may distort your camera's light readings, so you may need to compensate.
• An increasing number of ornithological trips to the Antarctic allow you to visit this part of the world accompanied by experienced guides.

Typical sightings in tundra or polar landscapes, depending on your location in the Northern or Southern Hemisphere:
• Waterfowl
• Snowy owls
• Waders
• Penguins

1 Gyr falcon
2 Canada geese
3 Ravens
4 Snow geese
5 Snowy owls
6 Black-bellied plover
7 Lesser yellowlegs
8 Snow buntings

GRASSLAND, STEPPE AND MOORLAND

Grasslands and moorlands offer relatively little cover to birds, and some are harsh places where both water and food may be scarce. A number of birds found in these areas are ground-dwellers, and they are often well camouflaged, which makes them hard to spot unless flushed from their hiding places.

Above: A male greater prairie chicken (Tympanuchus cupido) shows off the barred plumage that is a feature of many birds found in moors and grasslands.

Moors and grasslands are among the best habitats in which to spot predatory birds as they fly overhead seeking live quarry or carcasses to scavenge. Prey species are also present in numbers, but they are more difficult to spot because of their camouflage.

Spotting predatory birds

Large predators and scavengers such as condors (Cathartidae) fly high over grasslands, utilizing the warm air currents known as thermals, which allow them to remain airborne with minimal effort. Smaller hunters such as hawks swoop down much lower over the open countryside as they search for the small mammals or birds that form the basis of their diet.

Grassland birds

Perhaps not surprisingly, many of the birds living in this type of habitat are primarily terrestrial, essentially because —with the exceptions of boulders, crags or low-lying shrubs—there is little room for them to perch. The plumage on their backs is frequently barred and mottled. This serves to break up their outline from above, making it harder for predators passing overhead to spot them. If disturbed at ground level, some grassland birds will take off almost vertically, often with a loud whirring of the wings, and then subsequently glide for a distance at a low level, before dropping back down

Left: The crested caracara (Caracara plancus), native to the U.S.A. and South America, may survive by scavenging rather than hunting.

to the safety and cover of the vegetation. If pursued, they will take off again immediately, only staying on the ground once they feel secure.

Moorland camouflage

On moorlands and steppes the weather can become cold and snowy in winter. Some of the birds found in this terrain undergo a seasonal molt at the onset of winter, from which they emerge transformed by lighter-colored plumage to help conceal their presence.

Birdwatching tips

• Seek a good vantage point to increase your chances of spotting and following birds of prey.
• You will need a pair of powerful binoculars in grassland environments, as you will be combing relatively large and distant expanses of sky and land in search of birds.
• Use whatever natural cover is available to conceal your presence, such as tall vegetation and outcropping rocks.
• Horse riding can be a good way to cover long distances in grasslands and yet have a reasonable chance of spotting bird life, because birds are often less fearful of people on horseback.

Typical sightings in grassland habitats, depending to some extent on location:
• Eagles
• Vultures
• Grouse
• Hawks

Right: Avoiding predators is difficult in open countryside—especially hunters flying overhead. For prey species, the best strategy is to blend into the background and avoid being seen. While a relatively large number of mainly terrestrial birds are found in grasslands, therefore, these birds are often almost impossible to spot unless they take fright and fly up as you walk across the landscape. On the other hand, grasslands offer one of the best environments for observing birds of prey, since these birds are forced to spend relatively long periods on the wing searching for food.

1 Rough-legged hawk
2 Lark sparrows
3 Sage grouse
4 Burrowing owl
5 Prairie falcon
6 Western meadowlark
7 Lark bunting

URBAN LIFE

*Some birds display a remarkable ability to adapt to modern life, occurring right in the center of cities.
They use buildings for nesting and, in the case of birds of prey, as vantage points for hunting, just as they
would use trees or rocky crags in the wild. City parks, in particular, have become major refuges for birds.*

Cities, as densely populated areas, tend to be slightly warmer than the countryside, and this warm microclimate offers a number of advantages for birds. Drinking water is less likely to freeze in cold weather, and in spring, as plants bud and grow more quickly because of the warmth, insects are more readily available as food.

Residents and visitors

Some birds live permanently in cities, taking advantage of parks, whereas

*Above: Out of all birds, the feral pigeon
(Columba livia) has adapted best to urban life,
to the extent that it is now a common sight in
cities around the world.*

*Below: Some birds of prey, such as this turkey
vulture (Cathartes aura), have adapted to feed
in cities. They will often feed on the carcasses
of birds and other creatures killed by passing
traffic, and are a common sight near refuse
dumps, seeking anything edible there.*

others are more casual visitors, flying in to roost at night from outlying areas, or pausing there on migration. Deserted buildings offer a snug and relatively safe retreat for birds that roost in flocks, whereas birds of prey seek the inaccessible ledges of high-rise buildings. The abundance of feral pigeons (*Columba livia*) in built-up areas attracts peregrine falcons (*Falco peregrinus*), proving that they are just as adaptable as their prey. The falcons may keep pigeon populations in check, but if not, their numbers can be also curbed by feeding them with corn, which acts as a contraceptive.

A life above the bustle of city streets generally offers predatory species a fairly safe existence, compared with more rural areas where they risk being shot illegally. There are still dangers lurking on the city streets, however. High-rise office blocks with large expanses of glass can lure birds to a fatal collision.

Migrating birds still pass through cities on occasion, notably huge flocks of common starlings (*Sturnus vulgaris*). These congregate not just in city parks, but also roost on buildings and tree-lined streets when breaking their journey, creating a noisy chatter and plenty of mess.

*Above: Many gulls have left their seaside
haunts and moved inland, where they scavenge
on leftovers and city dumps, often ripping apart
plastic refuse sacks in search of food.*

Birdwatching tips
• City parks offer the best chances of spotting the largest number of species in urban environments, particularly if there is a sizeable pond or lake.
• Early morning is a good time to spot birds at close quarters in cities, before many people are on the streets.
• Don't forget about the dangers of traffic in your enthusiasm to spot particular birds.
• Join the local ornithological society to gain insight into the more unusual species found in local towns and cities.

Typical sightings in urban environments, depending to some extent on location:
• Falcons
• Owls
• Pigeons and doves
• Gulls

*Right: The spread of cities inevitably
influences the local avian populations, by
altering the neighboring habitat. When new
development encroaches on surrounding land,
for example, it becomes increasingly hard for
birds that have fairly specialist feeding
requirements, such as white storks, to obtain
enough food for themselves and their young.
Only opportunists such as pigeons are likely to
thrive in crowded city centers, but a wider
variety of birds use the oases of city parks.*

1 Starlings
2 House sparrows
3 Peregrine falcon
4 Feral pigeons
5 Mallard
6 Common crow
7 Moorhen
8 Black-headed gull

BACKYARDS

An amazing variety of birds have been recorded as backyard visitors. Cardinals, chickadees, sparrows and finches regularly visit bird tables, while jays, doves, woodpeckers and hummingbirds feed on the ground or from shrubs. Feeding stations help to attract birds, but they also visit as part of their natural behavior.

Tidy, immaculately manicured back-yards generally support less bird life than well-established ones with plenty of mature shrubs that can be used for roosting and nesting. If there are stands of trees nearby, or lining the street outside, the range of birds visiting the backyard will increase, and larger species will become more common. Artificial nesting sites, such as nest boxes of various types and sizes, can also help to increase the variety and numbers of birds that visit backyards regularly.

Birds face a major backyard hazard in the guise of the domestic cat. Huge numbers of individuals fall victim to these pets annually. The majority of the casualties are young fledglings, which lack the awareness and caution of adult birds. In areas where the cat population is especially high, there

Above: Bird tables and feeders help to attract birds into gardens by providing them with additional food sources. These are especially valuable during cold winter weather.

may be local declines in bird numbers. However, studies suggest that bird populations do not seem to be adversely affected by cats overall.

Helpers and pests

Birds are often regarded as gardeners' friends because they help to control the number of invertebrate pests. For example, titmice (Paridae) eat aphids on rose bushes, and thrushes (*Turdus*) hunt snails. At certain times of year, however, some birds can themselves become pests. Pigeons (*Columba*) often dig up newly planted seeds and eat them before they can germinate, unless the seeds are protected in some way. Later in the year, some species eat ripening berries.

Residents and migrants

Some birds are resident in backyard settings throughout the year. Others are temporary visitors, migrating to warmer climates for the winter period. Hummingbirds (Trochilidae), for example, are resident in northern parts of North America for only part of the year, and head south for the winter. Meanwhile, winter migrants from further north may descend on these

backyard habitats in place of the species that have already left. Studies provide clear evidence that actual shifts in the behavior and distribution of birds are currently occurring because of the availability of the kind of habitat and the provision of food there. The Eurasian blackbird (*Turdus merula*) has now become a common sight in backyards, while, in North America, the American robin (*Turdus migratorius*) has moved from its traditional woodland haunts into this type of environment too.

Above: A wide choice of bird food is currently available, along with various types of feeder to dispense it. These American goldfinches (Carduelis tristis) have been photographed eating sunflower seeds.

Right: In many respects, backyards offer an ideal habitat for birds. Food is readily available in these surroundings, as well as trees and shrubs, which provide good opportunities for roosting and nesting. Unfortunately, backyards can often be dangerous places for birds to visit, thanks to the popularity of cats as pets. Nor are cats the only danger in this type of habitat. Predatory birds, notably magpies (Pica hudsonia), will raid the nests of smaller birds, taking both eggs and chicks.

Birdwatching tips

• You can encourage invertebrate-eating birds to visit your backyard by creating a wild area or by establishing a compost heap where invertebrates can multiply.

• Positioning a bird table near a window will allow you to watch birds from inside the house, but take care to site it well away from cover where cats could lurk and ambush the birds.

• Keep a pair of binoculars handy indoors so you can get a better view of the bird table and any unexpected visitors to it, plus a notepad to record descriptions of any unusual birds you see.

• Try to avoid using insecticides in your backyard, as these reduce the food that will be available for birds.

• Ordinary slug pellets will poison slug-eaters such as thrushes. Use pellets that are described as safe for birds instead.

Typical sightings in gardens, depending to some extent on location:

• Finches
• Tanagers
• Woodpeckers
• Hummingbirds

1 Purple martins
2 Downy woodpecker
3 Eastern bluebirds
4 Cardinal
5 Blue jay
6 Purple finches
7 Common grackles
8 Ruby-throated hummingbird
9 Eastern phoebe
10 Tufted titmouse
11 Black-capped chickadee

ENDANGERED SPECIES AND CONSERVATION

It has been estimated that three-quarters of the world's birds may come under threat in the 21st century. Habitat destruction poses the most serious danger, so conservationists are striving to preserve bird habitats worldwide. Direct intervention of various kinds is also used to ensure the survival of particular species.

Around the world, threats to birds are varied and complex, but most are linked to human interference in the ecosystem, and will thus continue to grow as human populations increase.

Habitat destruction

Habitat destruction includes the deforestation of the world's tropical rainforests, which host a wide variety of birds, and also the conversion of many grassland areas into crop fields or livestock pasture. The first casualties of habitat destruction are often species with specialized feeding or nesting requirements, which cannot easily adapt to change.

In recent years, there have been a number of instances of opportunistic species adapting and thriving in altered habitats. One example is the common mynah (*Acridotheres tristis*), whose natural distribution is centered on India but has been introduced to other locations worldwide, often to control locust numbers. Such success stories are the exception rather than the rule,

Below: Lear's macaw (Anodorhynchus leari)—*native to Bahia, Brazil—is one of the most endangered of all South American parrots, with probably fewer than 150 left in the wild.*

Above: The northern spotted owl (Strix occidentalis caurina) *is currently threatened by the rapid felling of the ancient forests on the west coast of California.*

however. Generally, the diversity of bird life in an area declines drastically when the land is modified or cleared.

Hunting and pollution

Unregulated hunting of adult birds, eggs or young threatens a variety of species worldwide. The birds may be killed for their meat or feathers, or captured live and sold through the pet trade. In many countries, laws are now in place to protect rare species, but hunting and trading still go on illegally.

Overfishing is a related hazard facing seabirds, especially now that trawling methods have become so efficient. Global shortages of fish stocks are forcing fishermen to target fish that had previously been of little commercial value, but that are an important part of seabirds' diets.

In agricultural areas, pesticides and herbicides sprayed on farmers' fields decimate bird populations by eliminating their plant or animal food supplies. The deliberate or accidental release of industrial chemicals into the

air, water or soil is another hazard, while in the oceans, seabirds are killed by dumped toxins and oil spills. Disease is another major threat that may increase.

Climate change

In the near future, global warming caused by increased emissions of carbon dioxide and other gases is likely to impact on many bird habitats, and will almost certainly adversely affect birds' food supplies. If plants or other foods become unavailable in an area, birds must adapt their feeding habits or face extinction. As temperatures rise, the melting of the polar ice caps will threaten seabird populations by destroying their traditional nesting areas. Rising sea levels will also threaten low-lying wetlands favored by wading birds.

Threats to island birds

Some of the world's most distinctive birds have evolved in relative isolation on islands. Unfortunately, these species are also extremely vulnerable to changes in their environment, partly because their populations are small. One of the greatest threats comes from

Above: This guillemot (Uria aalge) *killed in Scottish waters is just one of the countless avian victims claimed by oil spillages each year. Large spills of oil can have devastating effects on whole populations.*

introduced predators, particularly domestic cats. Cats have been responsible for wiping out a host of island species, including the flightless Stephen Island wren (*Xenicus lyalli*) of New Zealand waters, which became extinct in 1894, thanks to the lighthouse-keeper's cat.

Cats are not the only introduced predators that can cause serious harm to avian populations. Grazing animals such as goats, introduced to islands by passing ships to provide future crews with fresh meat, have frequently destroyed the native vegetation, so reducing the birds' food supply.

Today, control of harmful introduced species is helping to save surviving populations of endangered birds on islands such as the Galapagos off Ecuador, home to the flightless cormorant (*Phalacrocorax harrisi*) and other rare birds.

Conservation and captive-breeding

Preserving habitat is the best and most cost-effective way to ensure the survival of all the birds that frequent a particular ecosystem. A worldwide network of national parks and reserves now helps to protect at least part of many birds' habitats. In addition,

conservationists may take a variety of direct measures to safeguard the future of particular species, such as launching a captive-breeding program. This approach has proven effective in increasing numbers of various critically endangered species, from the Californian condor (*Gymnogyps californianus*) of the U.S.A., to the echo parakeet (*Psittacula echo*) of Mauritius. In some cases, the technique of artificial insemination has been used to fertilize the eggs.

Artificially or naturally fertilized eggs can be transferred to incubators to be hatched, effectively doubling the number of chicks that can be reared. This is because removing the eggs often stimulates the hen to lay again more quickly than usual. Hand-rearing chicks on formulated diets helps to ensure the survival of the young once hatched. When hand-reared chicks are later released into the wild, it is vital that they bond with their own species and retain their natural fear of people, so glove puppets shaped like the parent birds are often used to feed the chicks.

Reintroduction programs

Breeding endangered species is relatively easy compared with the difficulties of reintroducing a species to an area of its former habitat. The cost of such reintroduction programs is

*Above: Glove puppets resembling the parent bird's head are often used when hand-rearing chicks, such as this peregrine falcon (*Falco peregrinus*), to encourage the birds to bond with their own kind when eventually released.*

often very high. Staff are needed not only to look after the aviary stock and rear the chicks, but also to carry out habitat studies. These assess the dangers that the birds will face after release and pinpoint release sites. The newly released birds must then be monitored, which may include fitting them with radio transmitters.

Ecotourism

Working with local people and winning their support is often essential to the long-term success of conservation programs. This approach has been used successfully on some of the Caribbean islands, such as St Vincent, home to various indigenous Amazon parrots (*Amazona*). Increasing clearance of the islands' forests, a growing human population and hunting all threatened these birds.

Effective publicity about these rare parrots, including portrayals of them on currency and postage stamps, helped to raise local people's awareness of the birds as part of their islands' heritage. A publicity campaign brought the parrots' plight to international attention and attracted visitors to the region, which brought in much-needed foreign currency. Thus, so-called "ecotourism" both helped the local economy and enlisted the islanders' support to conserve the parrots.

Left: The rapid destruction of the world's rainforests, seen here in Costa Rica, is the single most important threat facing tropical birds.

IDENTIFYING BIRDS

Recognizing birds is not always easy, particularly if you have only a relatively brief sighting. This part of the book has therefore been designed to simplify the task of identification as much as possible, by allowing you to link your sightings with the environment in which you spotted the bird. The section is divided into the particular habitats where birds are most likely to be spotted. It should be pointed out that this system is not infallible, as some birds are highly adaptable and range widely through different environments, but it is a useful starting point. Distribution maps accompanying all the illustrated entries provide a visual guide as to exactly where bird species are to be found within these regions, while the text provides information on the time of year and locations where the birds are most likely to be seen, in the case of migratory species.

The associated descriptions will help to clarify whether you have seen a cock bird or a hen, since there are often plumage differences between the sexes. Other information in these fact boxes about habitat, feeding and breeding habits should provide further help when it comes to identifying a particular bird. A bird's general shape, and the characteristic way in which it moves and behaves, all add up to what birdwatchers call its "jizz," which can help to identify birds even from a tiny speck in the sky or a dark shape scuttling behind a hedge.

Not every species in America is covered, but the representative sample featured in the following pages means that you should at least be able to identify the type of bird you spotted. Browsing through these pages also affords an opportunity to learn more about the varying lifestyles of America's birds, ranging from parrots living in the lush Amazon rainforests to the bitterly cold breeding grounds of puffins on the Alaskan peninsula, and the various pigeons and predatory birds that inhabit our city centers.

Note: Where an (E) appears after the scientific name of a bird, this indicates that it is an endangered species.

Left: Flamingos (Phoenicopteridae), one of the avian families present in America, often inhabit quite harsh environnments.

BIRDS OF AMERICA

There is a significant divide between the avifauna of the South American continent, and those families represented in North America, with the Central American isthmus serving as a crossover zone. This is partly a reflection of the feeding habits of the birds, with many fruit-eating species of the Amazonian region, for example, being restricted to this rainforest area, where they are guaranteed a constant supply of food throughout the year. Some of the most unusual birds in the world, including toucans with their bizarre and often colorful bills, are found in this region and nowhere else. Hummingbirds, which include the smallest bird in the world, do range across both continents, and through the Caribbean, although they reach their greatest diversity on the southern continent. The localized distribution of some birds in parts of South America, combined with the often inaccessible terrain, means that new species are still found there quite regularly.

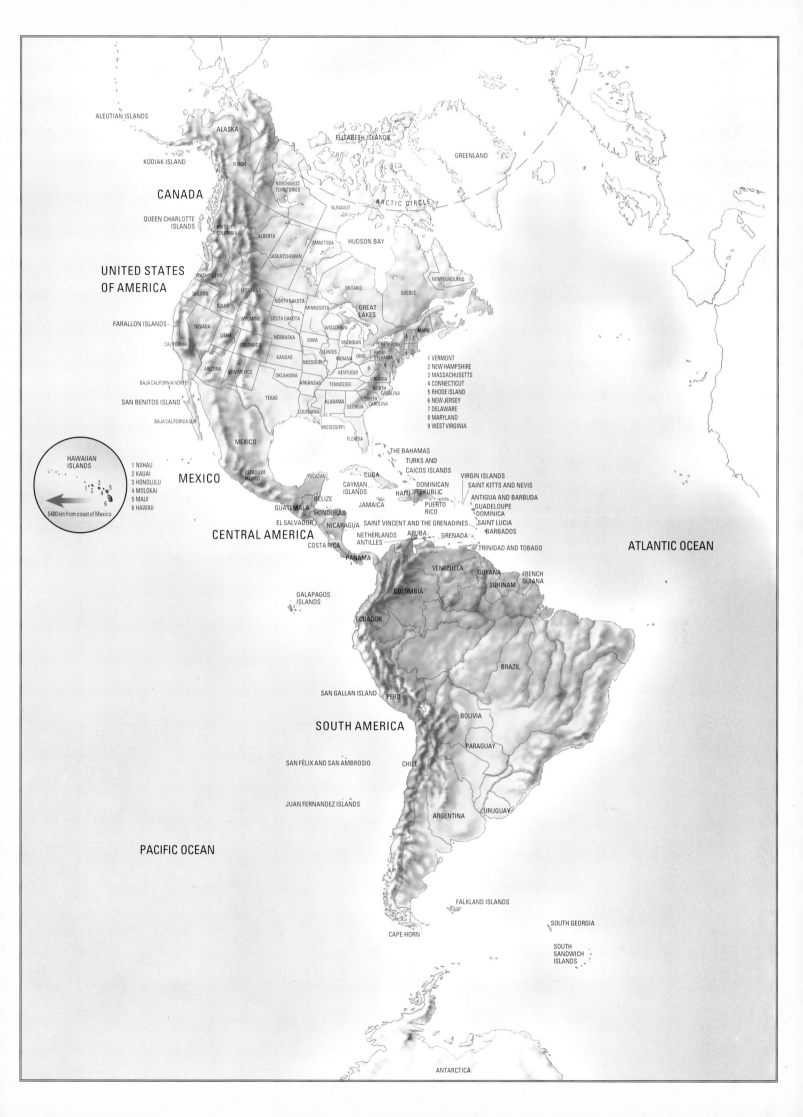

OCEAN WANDERERS

These birds often have a wide distribution, roaming far out from the shore over the oceans. They will only return to land in order to nest, frequently choosing remote islands for this purpose, so they are unlikely to be seen by the casual observer. However, they may be attracted to passing ships, particularly trawlers, in search of offerings of food.

Laysan albatross

Diomedea immutabilis

The Laysan is the most common albatross of the northern Pacific region. According to reports of sightings, especially from the larger islands, these birds now appear to be venturing closer to the shoreline of the Hawaiian islands. Unlike many albatrosses, the Laysan rarely follows ships, and comes to land only during the breeding season. It is thought that pairs remain together for life, and albatrosses rank among the longest-lived of all birds, having a life expectancy often exceeding half a century. These birds face few natural enemies, but, sadly, a number are dying prematurely after seizing baited hooks intended for fish left on long lines by fishing boats. Albatrosses usually feed by scooping up prey from the surface of the ocean while in flight.

Identification: Relatively small. Predominantly white with a sooty-brown back, upperwings, and tail, and dark feathering around the eyes. In flight, the largish, pinkish feet extend beyond the tail. Yellow curved bill has a black tip. Sexes are alike.

Distribution: Extends from the northern Pacific Ocean to the western coast of North America. Especially common on Midway and Laysan Islands, Hawaii.
Size: 36in (91cm).
Habitat: Open ocean.
Nest: Area of ground.
Eggs: 1, white, may be blotched.
Food: Fish and other aquatic creatures.

Short-tailed albatross

Diomedea albatrus (E)

Distribution: Occurs off the west coast of North America, up to the Gulf of Alaska. Has been sighted very rarely as far south as Hawaii.
Size: 37in (94cm).
Habitat: Open ocean.
Nest: Earth mound incorporating plant matter.
Eggs: 1, white.
Food: Mainly fish and squid.

Short-tailed albatrosses breed mainly on Torishima Island, which is part of the Izu group lying off the southeast of Japan. They return every second year, with the nesting season starting in October. However, Torishima has an active volcano at its core, which has led to a dramatic decline in their numbers, as repeated eruptions have decimated the breeding population. In addition to this, they were also once hunted for their plumage. These long-lived ocean wanderers were thought to have become extinct during the 1940s, but some of them had survived, and now about 70 chicks are reared annually on Torishima, where they are protected. Another breeding population is established on Minami-kojima, in the nearby South Ryukyu Islands, where the albatrosses use cliffs for nesting. Out at sea, birds may scavenge scraps thrown overboard from trawlers, and hunt squid at night.

Identification: Mainly white, with black patches extending from tips of wings and on tip of tail. Yellowish-orange on the head. Pinkish bill with pale blue tip. Sexes alike. Young have dark-brown plumage.

Red-billed tropic bird

Phaethon aethereus

These sleek, elegant birds swoop down from their cliff-top roosts and out over the oceans, catching their food by diving into the sea. The red-billed type is the largest of the tropic birds. Its elegant, long, streaming white tail distinguishes it from the red-tailed tropic bird (*P. rubricauda*), which ranges further across the Indo-Pacific Ocean to the south and also has paler, whitish wings. The bill of the Indian Ocean population is less brightly colored, serving to distinguish them from others of the species occurring elsewhere in the world. Islands, rather than mainland areas, are favored breeding sites, as their position means that the birds will be in less danger from their predators.

Above: Red-billed tropic birds nest in crevices in the ground.

Identification: Predominantly white with a black streak running through the eyes. Black is clearly visible on the primary flight feathers at the ends of the wings. Black streaking runs over the back and rump down to the base of the tail. Tail streamers are longer in the cock bird than the hen. Bill reddish orange with black edging.

Distribution: The Atlantic population extends from Central America through the south Caribbean, down the coast of South America and across the Atlantic Ocean, from Brazil to West Africa. Separate Pacific populations occur near Baja California and the Galapagos Islands.
Size: 41in (104cm) including streamers to 22in (56cm).
Habitat: Tropical and subtropical seas.
Nest: Rocky crevice or hollow on the ground.
Eggs: 1, pinkish with darker markings.
Food: Fish and squid. Agile enough to catch flying fish.

Wandering albatross (*Diomedea exulans*): 53in (135cm)
Circumpolar, and present right around the southern part of South America. White, with black extending partially across the wings from the tips, with cock birds becoming whiter with age. Often a slight orangish area on the ear coverts. Bill pinkish with pale horn-colored tip. Hens may have a light grayish band around the chest, and black tips on the tail feathers.

Black-footed albatross (*Diomedea nigripes*): 36in (91cm)
Found in the northern Pacific Ocean, extending from western North America to the Asiatic coast. Lives on the open ocean. Predominantly brownish gray with a white face and undertail coverts, although occasionally paler. Feet are black. Sexes are alike.

Waved albatross (*Diomedea irrorata*): 37in (93cm)
Occurs off the northwest coast of South America, west to the Galapagos Islands. Easily recognized by the combination of a whitish head and neck with a yellow suffusion, plus brown plumage elsewhere on the body. May be observed feeding at night, when squid are nearer the surface. Sexes are alike.

Northern fulmar

Fulmarus glacialis

Northern fulmars are versatile in their feeding habits. They often track the path of trawlers, and may congregate in large groups in the wake of boats, seeking food. These seabirds scoop up fish during the day and find squid at night, when these invertebrates rise up from the depths. If necessary, they will dive into the sea to catch food. They are also adept scavengers, feeding on the remains of whales and other marine mammals washed onto beaches. They nest communally, usually on sheer cliff faces, where they can colonize inaccessible ledges. In some parts of their range they may build their nests on buildings inland, but they generally favor islands and other remote sites rather than the mainland. Northern fulmars are thought to have a life expectancy of about 34 years. Fulmar chicks may not breed for more than a decade after fledging.

Distribution: Occurs right around the Northern Hemisphere, being present both on the Atlantic and Pacific coasts of North America, extending right up to the far north.
Size: 20in (50cm).
Habitat: Open ocean.
Nest: Bare cliff ledge.
Eggs: 1, white.
Food: Fish, squid and sometimes carrion.

Identification: Varies in color throughout its range, with light and dark morphs. The light form has a whitish head and underparts with gray above; dark morphs are grayish brown overall. Sexes are alike, but males are larger.

PETRELS

Many of the seabirds found in American waters have a wide distribution, which can be pan-global, often extending around the southern oceans and sometimes even further afield. Petrels are well adapted to spending virtually their entire lives over these waters, even to the extent of being able to scoop up their food directly from the surface of the ocean and sleeping on the wing as they glide.

Hawaiian petrel

Dark-rumped petrel *Pterodroma phaeopygia* (E)

The alternative name, "dark-rumped petrel," is not a clear guide to its identification, since various petrels display this feature. The Hawaiian petrel appears to be quite rare compared to other species and is thought to be declining in numbers. It spends its time at sea, coming onto land to breed. The largest colony is found around the Haleakala Crater on Maui. These petrels nest in underground burrows, remaining there during the day and emerging to search for food at night. Outside the breeding period, Hawaiian petrels are most likely to be sighted to the southeast of the Hawaiian islands.

Identification: Black upperparts, with white plumage just above the bill and extending right across the underparts. The undersides of the wings are also mainly white, with a black area evident on each of the leading edges when seen from below. There is usually a white, V-shaped marking present at the base of the uppertail coverts, above the tail. Sexes are alike.

Distribution: Pacific Ocean, Hawaiian and Galapagos Islands.
Size: 17in (43cm).
Habitat: Open ocean.
Nest: Sited in underground burrows.
Eggs: 1, white.
Food: Fish and other aquatic creatures.

Mottled petrel

Pterodroma inexpectata

Distribution: Very wide-ranging, occurring in the Pacific Ocean from the Gulf of Alaska southward down the west coast of North America, and has been recorded off the southern tip of South America.
Size: 14in (35cm).
Habitat: Lives at sea, only comes on land to nest.
Nest: Rocky crevices or underground, in colonies on remote islands and outcrops.
Eggs: 1, white.
Food: Fish, squid, and crustaceans.

These petrels spend most of their lives flying across the oceans. They range over a very wide area along the Antarctic coastline, with their distribution extending as far south as the pack ice. In the north, they occur throughout the central Pacific area but are rarely sighted close to land. Mottled petrels migrate south across the Equator before the nesting period, which begins in October. Only at this stage do they come to land, nesting colonially on small rocky outcrops and remote islands. The incubation period is lengthy, lasting approximately 50 days. After hatching, nestlings may spend up to three and a half months in the nest. By the time the petrels are ready to head north again, the dark days of the southern winter are descending. Mottled petrels have disappeared from some parts of their former breeding range, notably New Zealand and nearby islands, where the introduction of land predators such as cats has greatly reduced their success rate.

Identification: Upperparts are dark. A black stripe on the underside of each wing joins to form a characteristic M-shape when viewed from below. The sides of the head are grayish, with a black stripe through the eyes. The underparts are white, aside from a distinctive gray patch running across the center of the body. Sexes are similar in appearance.

Kermadec petrel (*Pterodroma neglecta*): 15in (38cm)
Ranges right across the southern Pacific, from the western coast of South America to Australia's east coast, and extending north up to Central America. Both light and dark morphs are recognized. Very pale gray suffusion on the head is a distinguishing feature of the light morph, while consistently blackish coloration over the entire body is a feature of the dark morph, although there are variants between these two extremes as well. Sexes are alike.

Soft-plumaged petrel (*Pterodroma mollis*): 14¹⁄₂in (37cm)
Distribution extends widely through the southern oceans from close to New Zealand around the world to southeastern South America. Generally only exists in a light phase, although the breadth of the dark throat collar varies in width and definition. Basic coloration otherwise similar to other related petrels, with dark upperparts and mainly white underparts.

Great-winged petrel (gray-faced petrel, *Pterodroma macroptera*): 16in (40cm)
Distribution extends from east of New Zealand through the southern oceans, coming close to the southern coast of South America. Distinguishable from other petrels in this region by its consistently dark brown coloration. Sexes are similar, but hens are smaller. The nearest breeding grounds to South America are on islands off the southwest coast of Africa. Nesting occurs during the southern winter.

Herald petrel

Pterodroma arminjoniana

The coloration of these petrels is quite variable, since intermediate forms exist between the light and dark color morphs. Darker birds tend to be more common in eastern parts of both the Atlantic and Pacific ranges. The variation in color can make these petrels hard to identify, particularly in areas where similar species are found. Herald petrels may be seen in the company of wedge-tailed shearwaters, which occur in similar color morphs. They seek out inaccessible breeding sites. They do not migrate over large distances, though young birds may travel further after fledging.

Distribution: One population occurs in the central Pacific, extending westward as far as northeastern Australia, while another is found in the Atlantic, off the eastern coast of South America. A third is isolated around Mauritius in the Indian Ocean.
Size: 15in (39cm).
Habitat: Open ocean.
Nest: Cliffs and underground burrows.
Eggs: 1, white.
Food: Squid; and probably other fish.

Identification: The Atlantic race (*P. a. arminjoniana*) is grayish-brown on its back and wings, with a similar band across the throat and around the eyes. The remaining underparts are white, with dark spotting on the flanks. The dark morph has darker underparts. Sexes are alike.

Stejneger's petrel

Pterodroma longirostris

As with many petrels, relatively little is known about the habits of this oceanic wanderer. There is little to constrain its range through the Pacific Ocean, so it is not surprising that there have been a number of reported sightings of Stejneger's petrels far away from where it is most commonly observed. Stejneger himself first recorded the petrel in Japan in 1893. The breeding period starts in November. Pairs return from further north to Alejandro Selkirk Island, part of the Juan Fernandez group off the west coast of South America. They nest inland in areas of tree fern forest, in underground burrows, usually alongside the Juan Fernandez petrel. The young possess darker plumage than the adults. They leave the nest by the following March, and then disperse over the Pacific, often not returning for several years.

Identification: Dark grayish-black lines create an M-shaped pattern over the wings when viewed from behind, with the center point of the letter being located on the lower back. The head is blackish, as is the tip of the tail, and the remaining upperparts are whitish. Pale white under-wing area, with a very faint bar running across the underside. Sexes are alike.

Distribution: Typically encountered from Japan down to the western-central coast of South America. Occasionally sighted outside this range in localities including coastal parts of California.
Size: 12in (31cm).
Habitat: Open ocean.
Nest: Burrows.
Eggs: 1, white.
Food: Probably fish and other marine creatures.

DEEP SEA HUNTERS

Keen eyesight, possibly assisted by a sense of smell, aids these seabirds in finding sources of food in the oceans. Marine invertebrates feature prominently in their diet, and they will often congregate in areas where krill are to be found, along with other predatory creatures such as whales. They tend to seek out inconspicuous places to nest, such as underground burrows or the crevices in a rocky cliff face.

Black-capped petrel

Pterodroma hasitata

Occurring further north than many petrels, this species ranges out into the Atlantic and has even crossed to the U.K. on very rare occasions. Its main breeding grounds are on Haiti, where it nests high up in the mountainous areas, seeking the safety of cliffs. Plants help to conceal the presence of its burrows. Nevertheless, black-capped petrels are still hunted there, and their numbers have fallen in recent years. It is even feared that the completely black melanistic race known as *P. h. caribbea*, which used to frequent the island of Jamaica, is now extinct. It is thought that mongooses brought to the islands in the 1870s to control the rat population started raiding the nests of these petrels, causing a rapid decline in their numbers. An unusual feature of the young of the surviving race is that they have yellow rather than gray down, reflecting the fact that their plumage overall is not as dark as that of many other petrels.

Identification: This species has white plumage on the back of the neck and black on the head. The wings are dark, the rump and uppertail coverts white. A narrow black streak extends down the sides of the neck. The body is white, with black stripes near the leading edge of the wings, and black wing tips. Sexes alike.

Distribution: North Carolina and both coasts of Florida southward via the Caribbean islands of Cuba and Hispaniola as far as the island of Guadeloupe, and reaching the coast of northeastern Brazil, but not Central America.
Size: 16in (40cm).
Habitat: Open ocean.
Nest: Rocky areas and underground burrows.
Eggs: 1, white.
Food: Fish, squid and perhaps jellyfish.

Audubon's shearwater

Puffinus lherminieri

Distribution: From north of Florida through the Caribbean region to the coast of northern South America. Another population is present in the southern Pacific Ocean, off the northwest coast of South America.
Size: 13in (33cm).
Habitat: Out over the sea.
Nest: Rocky hollows. Sometimes underground.
Eggs: 1, white.
Food: Fish, krill, and squid.

Audubon's shearwater has a discontinuous distribution through the world's oceans. There is a distinct, separate Pacific population off the coasts of Asia and Australia, and another in the Indian Ocean. Breeding periods vary accordingly in different parts of its range. Small, remote islands, many of which are uninhabited by people, are favored for breeding. These shearwaters usually stay close to the shore when nesting, breeding colonially yet preferring an inconspicuous site, which may sometimes be underground rather than on a bare cliff face. The young, who may not fledge until they are nearly 11 weeks old, disperse to the sea. They are slow to mature, and unlikely to breed until they have reached approximately eight years old. Individuals from the Caribbean population have occasionally been recorded as far north as northeastern Canada.

Identification: Brownish back and wings, with brown coloration extending to the sides of the head. The throat area and underparts are white, with brown edging visible on the extended underside of the wings. This species has a dark bill, pinkish legs and brown undertail coverts. Sexes are alike, and younger birds often closely resemble the adults.

Black storm petrel (*Oceanodroma melania*): 9in (23cm)
Extends along the California coastline and offshore islands. This is the most common and largest of the black-colored petrels, with a pale wing bar and a relatively slow flight pattern. Calls at night from underground burrows. Sexes are alike.

Black-bellied storm petrel (*Fregetta tropica*): 8in (20cm)
Occurs virtually throughout the oceans of the southern hemisphere up to the equator, including right around South America south of the equator, breeding on remote islands close to Antarctica. From beneath, a well-defined central black stripe bisects the white breast feathering, down to the black lower belly and undertail coverts. There are also whitish areas on the underside of the wings. Sexes are alike.

Least storm petrel (*Halocyptena microsoma*): 6in (15cm)
Relatively narrow range in the Pacific, sighted not far from the western coast of Baja California, breeding on small islands and rocky outcrops in the Golfo de California. This is the smallest storm petrel, dark in overall coloration, with paler edging apparent across the wing coverts. Forked tail feathers help with recognition. Sexes are alike.

Gray-backed storm petrel (*Garrodia nereis*): 8in (20cm)
There are three isolated sub-Antarctic populations. Regularly nests on the Falkland Islands, extending across the southern Atlantic. The head and leading edges of the wings are dark, remainder of under-parts and wings are white. Legs extend beyond tail feathers when in flight. Rump and uppertail coverts are gray; a black bar edges tail feathers. Sexes alike.

Wedge-rumped storm petrel
Galapagos storm petrel *Oceanodroma tethys*

These storm petrels often roam extensively through their range. However, on the Galapagos Islands there is a permanent population throughout the year, not just during the breeding period, which usually commences in May. There, however, they are vulnerable to short-eared owls (*Asio flammeus*), which regularly prey on them. Their other main breeding area is on the Piscadores and San Gallan Islands, off the coast of Peru. Part of the reason for their wandering is that they are able to track the Humboldt Current, which helps to provide them with a ready source of food. (Note that this can be disrupted during years when weather patterns and sea currents are affected by the El Niño phenomenon.) Wedge-rumped storm petrels catch their food in a variety of ways, including while swimming on the ocean surface and by diving underwater.

Identification: Distinguishable by the extensive area of white plumage on the rump and uppertail coverts, which separates this species from other storm petrels. The upper surfaces of the wings are dark, with light areas across the wing coverts, and a white central area on the underside of each wing. The head is dark. Sexes are alike.

Distribution: Extends through the eastern Pacific region, from California southward to Peru, including the Galapagos Islands.
Size: 8in (20cm).
Habitat: Out over the ocean.
Nest: Crevices in rocks or under plants.
Eggs: 1, white.
Food: Fish, krill, and squid.

Fork-tailed storm petrel
Gray storm petrel *Oceanodroma furcata*

The bluish coloration of the fork-tailed petrel sets it apart from all other related species. These birds are most likely to be seen over open sea, swooping down to break the surface of the water occasionally with their legs. They feed both on the wing and on the ocean surface. Like other storm petrels, they come ashore to breed, often on islands, seeking the security of underground burrows at this time. Breeding colonies can be savaged by introduced mammals, notably cats and rats. The nostrils of fork-tailed petrels are located in a tube above the bill, and serve to excrete excess salt from the body, ingested as a result of the bird's environment and diet.

Identification: Distinctive bluish-gray plumage is lighter on the throat and the undertail coverts. The tail is forked and the wings are a duskier shade of blue. Both the bill and the legs are black. The plumage around the eyes is mainly blackish. Sexes are alike.

Distribution: The west coast of North America and south to California. Also found on the Aleutians and nearby islands.
Size: 9in (23cm).
Habitat: Open ocean.
Nest: Underground burrow.
Eggs: 1, white.
Food: Fish, invertebrates and plankton.

SOME LONG-DISTANCE TRAVELERS

It is remarkable just how far some seabirds will fly to and from their nesting grounds each year.
They may effectively traverse the globe on an annual basis, as in the case of those that nest in the far
north and return to the Antarctic region by the start of the northern winter. These extensive journeys are
made all the more remarkable for entailing little or no rest on land.

Wilson's storm petrel

Oceanites oceanicus

Identification: Dark brownish, with a prominent white rump and square tail. Paler buff barring on wing coverts. Short wings and long yellow legs conspicuous in flight. Sexes alike.

Breeding Wilson's storm petrels may excavate their own nesting burrows, which typically extend about 15in (38cm) below ground, although on cliff faces and other rocky areas these seabirds seek out sanctuary in a suitable crevice. The nesting period typically begins in November. However, unpredictable snowstorms can sometimes obscure the entrances to nesting burrows, forcing the birds to abandon them. Incubation lasts about six weeks, with the chick fledging about 7¹/₂ weeks later. Both adult birds assist in its care. These storm petrels feed in a number of ways, sometimes swooping down to take krill from the water surface, and at others flying very close to the surface, just staying airborne. It is believed that Wilson's storm petrels rely partly on a keen sense of smell to find food, especially carrion, which may form part of their diet. They may also follow ships, particularly fishing vessels, in search of scraps.

Distribution: Has one of the most extensive ranges of any seabird, being found along the entire eastern seaboard of North America and the northern Caribbean, around South America, down to Antarctica, and across both Atlantic and Pacific oceans.
Size: 7¹/₂in (19cm).
Habitat: Open ocean.
Nest: Rocky crevice or underground burrow.
Eggs: 1, white.
Food: Krill and fish.

Long-tailed jaeger

Stercorarius longicaudus

The long tail feathers of this jaeger account for as much as 9in (23cm) of its overall length, and it is actually still the smallest member of this group of seabirds. Long-tailed jaegers breed in the Arctic region of North America, spending the winter at sea. Only on rare occasions are they observed on freshwater lakes. Jaegers can be considered the pirates of the skies, menacing gulls and terns and harrying them to drop fish or other quarry, which they quickly swoop down on and seize before the prey disappears into the water. The long-tailed jaeger is especially agile in flight, as is reflected by its long, pointed wings, while its hooked bill is a formidable weapon. On occasion, long-tailed jaegers have been known to resort to attacking other nesting seabirds, taking both their eggs and the chicks.

Identification: Characteristic long, narrow tail feathers. Underparts are whitish, with a grayer tone on the flanks and around the vent. Head is blackish and the wings are dark. Sexes are alike.

Distribution: Occurs throughout the far north of North America and Greenland during the summer breeding period. Then flies south to overwinter around the coasts of South America and western South Africa, extending down into sub-Antarctic areas.
Size: 23in (58cm).
Habitat: Mainly open ocean.
Nest: Depression on the ground.
Eggs: 1–2, olive with dark spots.
Food: Fish and other small aquatic and land creatures.

Parasitic jaeger

Arctic skua *Stercorarius parasiticus*

The diet of these jaegers alters dramatically though the year. They are known as parasitic jaegers due to their habit of stealing fish from other seabirds, preferring this method of feeding more than any related species. Yet they are also effective hunters, catching lemmings in their northern breeding grounds, and also feeding on insects and even berries during the brief Arctic summer. Their nests, in turn, are commonly raided by Arctic foxes (*Alopex lagopus*). Once the surviving chicks have migrated southward, beginning their journey in August, they may remain in the southern hemisphere for their first year rather than return back north. Unlike many seabirds, parasitic jaegers often migrate over land, possibly because they will stay close to coasts on arrival, rather than ranging widely over the ocean.

Identification: Sleek, gull-like appearance with long, narrow tail extensions averaging nearly 3¹/₂in (9cm) in the summer. Dark crown, with brownish-gray wings and tail, with white underparts at this stage too. The dark color morph displays no white plumage, while youngsters have a barred appearance. Sexes are alike. Young birds have blue legs.

Distribution: Overwinters south of the equator, including Atlantic and Pacific coasts of South America from Peru to Brazil. Migrates to breed in the north, including the U.S.A. and Greenland.
Size: 17in (44cm).
Habitat: Open ocean.
Nest: Scrape on the ground.
Eggs: 1–2, olive with dark spots.
Food: Fish and rodents.

Southern giant petrel (*Macronectes giganteus*): 39in (99cm)
Circumpolar in the Antarctic and up both sides of South America, to Chile in the west and Argentina in the east. Brownish overall, although darker on the lower underparts toward the vent. Paler grayish-brown head and neck. Bill is yellowish. White morph displays odd speckled brownish feathering on otherwise white plumage. Hens are smaller.

Fairy prion (*Pachyptila turtur*): 11in (28cm)
Found in three separate areas in the southern oceans, one extending eastward from the extreme southeast of South America. Gray crown, wings and back, with white underparts and a dark tail tip. Blackish patterning across the wings. Sexes are alike.

Blue petrel (*Halobaena caerulea*): 12¹/₂in (32cm)
Another circumpolar species of the southern oceans. Ranges from the Atlantic to the Pacific coast of South America, with young birds seen off the Peruvian coast. Bluish-gray wings with a black M-shaped marking over the rump to the tail. Tail has a distinctive black subterminal band, with broad white tips to the feathers. The top of the head, including the eyes is black, with white plumage below, extending to the underparts. Sexes are alike.

Black petrel (*Procellaria parkinsoni*): 18in (46cm)
Ranges from the west coast of Central America down to northwestern South America, typically far offshore, and across the Pacific to New Zealand. Relatively large, with black plumage. Bill yellowish-orange, darker at tip. Sexes alike.

Pomarine jaeger

Pomarine skua *Stercorarius pomarinus*

Pomarine jaegers are exceedingly effective predators of lemmings, and are even able to dig these small rodents out of their underground burrows using their strong bills. There is a direct link between the number of lemmings and the breeding success of these jaegers: when lemmings are plentiful, it is not uncommon for young pomarine jaegers to breed before they have acquired full adult plumage. However, during the periods following a collapse in the lemming population, food becomes scarce, forcing these jaegers to turn their attentions to other prey, which can include anything from carrion to the eggs of other birds. They will also kill and eat smaller seabirds. Pairs lay in the far north, directly on the ground, without constructing a nest of any kind. After leaving the tundra region in September, pomarine jaegers will feed mainly on fish, which they prefer to steal from other seabirds, rather than catch themselves.

Distribution: Breeds in the Arctic along the northern coastline of North America, and migrates south in the winter to both the Pacific and Atlantic coasts of Central America, occurring widely throughout the Caribbean. Also present on Hawaii. A separate population is found on the southeastern coast of South America.
Size: 20in (50cm).
Habitat: Open ocean.
Nest: Scrape on the ground.
Eggs: 2, olive with dark spots.
Food: Fish and lemmings.

Identification: Mainly black head; back of neck is pale yellowish. Back, wings and vent area dark gray. White underparts, with gray barring on chest and flanks. Bill pinkish with dark tip. Juvenile has white wing bars.

PREDATORS AND PIRATES

Seabirds are adaptable by nature, as shown by the way they will occasionally scavenge, following trawlers for unwanted parts of a catch that fishermen may throw back overboard. Some birds are even more resourceful, and aggressive, in obtaining their food, notably pirates such as skuas, which will harry other seabirds in order to steal their catch.

South polar skua

Catharacta maccormicki

South polar skuas are long-distance migrants, flying from their breeding grounds in the Antarctic up to the edge of the Arctic. The time of year obviously affects the likelihood of observing them. During the northern summer they can be seen on the Grand Bank of Newfoundland in relatively large numbers. They leave the north in August, after molting for the journey, and begin arriving at their breeding grounds in October. South polar skuas are highly territorial when breeding, with nest locality affecting breeding success. If both eggs hatch, the younger, weaker individual may be killed by its sibling. Many skuas seen in the northern hemisphere are young birds, not ready to breed until over six years old. In the Antarctic, the two color morphs are often observed in different locations: the dark morph more commonly on the Antarctic peninsula; the light morph in the Ross Sea.

Identification: Two distinctive color morphs recognized. Dark morphs are dark brown overall, with wings slightly darker than the body. In pale morphs the head and underparts are significantly paler than the brown wings. Males are darker overall and smaller in size.

Distribution: Occurs in the eastern Pacific, off the coast of North America in an area extending from Baja California to Alaska, and also on the Atlantic seaboard, extending right up to Greenland. Breeds in the Antarctic, in the Ross Sea area and on the Antarctic peninsula.
Size: 22in (55cm).
Habitat: Open ocean.
Nest: Scrape on the ground.
Eggs: 1–2, olive with dark spots.
Food: Mainly fish.

Great skua

Northern skua *Catharacta skua*

Distribution: Occurs in the vicinity of Newfoundland, Canada, and also through the outer Caribbean region down to the area off northern Brazil.
Size: 23in (58cm).
Habitat: Open ocean.
Nest: Scrape lined with grass.
Eggs: 1–2, olive green with dark spots.
Food: Mainly fish

These skuas are transatlantic migrants, breeding in the far north of Europe, with some individuals overwintering along parts of the eastern American seaboard. Most of these birds are thought to be of Icelandic origin, rather than from further east in Europe. Great skuas prefer to nest in fairly remote locations on level ground, often in proximity to other seabird colonies. They are very resourceful in obtaining food, since not only will they catch fish themselves, but they will also torment other birds, such as puffins (*Fratercula arctica*), into dropping their catches. They will feed on carrion too, as well as edible items thrown overboard from boats. Sand eels are often very significant in their diet during the breeding period. Great skuas migrate southward at the end of the summer, returning north to their traditional nesting grounds again in March. Occasionally, individuals may be found inland as the result of severe storms, young birds especially.

Identification: Large and predominantly brown, with a powerful black bill. The sides and top of the head are entirely dark in color, but there is lighter streaking down the neck onto the chest, broadening out over the wings. Short tail and blackish webbed feet. Sexes are alike.

Pink-footed shearwater

Puffinus creatopus

Pink-footed shearwaters overwinter off the shores of eastern North America, where they are sometimes sighted as far north as the Gulf of Alaska. They head south to their breeding grounds, on the Juan Fernandez islands, located off the coast of central Chile, arriving there by November. Their nesting sites are often located far away from the shore, as these birds will instinctively seek out areas where vegetation provides good cover for their burrows. Single eggs are laid underground. The young will have left their nests by the following April, when the shearwaters head north again, leaving the southern winter behind. They may sometimes disperse far outside their natural range, however, having been recorded on the other side of the Pacific, off the coasts of New Zealand and eastern Australia. When feeding, pink-footed shearwaters grab their prey at the surface of the water, but they are also adept at diving beneath the waves.

Identification: Predominantly grayish-brown, with paler underparts displaying a variable amount of mottled brown coloration, especially on the sides of the body. Paler plumage also under the wings. Flesh-pink bill with a dark tip, and similarly colored feet. Sexes and young birds are alike.

Distribution: Eastern Pacific, particularly off the coast of the Americas, although absent from the far north and extreme south. Also on Hawaii.
Size: 19in (48cm).
Habitat: Open ocean.
Nest: Underground burrows.
Eggs: 1, white.
Food: Fish and squid.

Manx shearwater (*Puffinus puffinus*): 14in (35cm)
Widely distributed through the North Atlantic, seen in the vicinity of Canada and breeding on Newfoundland. Overwinters down the eastern coast of South America. Sooty black upperparts, white beneath including the undertail coverts. Sexes are alike.

Black-vented shearwater (*Puffinus opisthomelas*): 15in (38cm)
Very limited distribution off the coast of Baja California, breeding on islands in this area. Upperparts are dark, as are the undersurfaces of the primaries. The whitish underparts are suffused with brown, with dark plumage around the vent. Sexes are alike.

Great shearwater (*Puffinus gravis*): 20in (51cm)
Present throughout the Atlantic Ocean, breeding on the Falkland Islands during the southern summer. Relatively large in size, with dark upperparts and a white band on the uppertail coverts. Underparts below the eyes are also whitish, with variable darker mottling on the belly, and dark edges to undersides of wings. Sexes are alike.

Brown skua (*Catharacta antarctica*): 25in (64cm)
Widely distributed through southern latitudes. Winters off the southeastern coast of South America, breeding in the Falkland Islands and southern Argentina. Large size, stocky appearance. Predominantly brown in color, with paler streaking extending down from the neck around the wings, which tend to be of a darker shade, although there can be considerable variation between individuals. Sexes are alike.

Sooty shearwater

Puffinus griseus

The largest populations of sooty shearwaters are found in the northern Pacific, rather than the Atlantic. Their location varies according to the season, however, with their American breeding grounds located at the very tip of South America, including the Falkland Islands. They nest in large colonies, with the breeding season commencing in October. Subsequently they will head north, remaining relatively close to the western coast of the continent while crossing the equator, although some will overwinter in southern waters. Sooty shearwaters are often observed feeding in the company of unrelated species, including penguins in the far south. They usually obtain their food underwater, rather than trawling for it at the surface while in flight. The difficulty of mastering this skill probably helps to explain why young birds will follow ships, especially trawlers, in the hope that edible items will be thrown overboard that they can scavenge.

Distribution: Occurs right around the entire coast of the Americas, except the Caribbean and the far north, ranging out across the Pacific and Atlantic oceans.
Size: 20in (50cm).
Habitat: Open ocean.
Nest: Underground burrows.
Eggs: 1, white.
Food: Fish and marine invertebrates.

Identification: Dark sooty black, reflecting its common name, with paler areas evident under the wings. Black bill and yellowish feet. Young birds resemble the adults. Sexes are alike.

AUKLETS

The six members of this group of seabirds occurring around the shores of America are much more at home on the sea surface than in the air. They often struggle to take off, paddling to raise their body up before they can use their wings to get clear of the water. Once in the air, a group will often fly behind each other in a straight line, rather than opting for a V-shaped formation.

Crested auklet

Aethia cristatella

Crested auklets spend much of the winter period at sea, before returning to their breeding islands in the spring after the snow has melted. Huge numbers, sometimes as many as 100,000 birds, may congregate at these colonies. Dominant individuals with the tallest crests are favored breeding partners, though members of an existing pair will return to breed together every year. Unusually, while males are responsible for brooding the young, it is the females who provide the majority of food for the chicks, frequently traveling distances of 31 miles (50km) or more from the nest site, carrying the food back in their throat pouches. Egg-laying occurs at roughly the same time in a colony, which means that most of the young will fledge together within a short period. This brings survival advantages by increasing the percentage of young that are likely to escape waiting predators. Once at sea, crested auklets remain in large groups.

Distribution: Extreme northern Pacific, extending between Alaska across to Asia, through the Gulf of Alaska, especially near Kodiak Island.
Size: 8in (20cm).
Habitat: Ocean and shore.
Nest: Rocky crevices and crags.
Eggs: 1, white.
Food: Mainly crustaceans, plus fish.

Identification: Dark gray underparts, blacker head, back and wings, with a white stripe behind the eyes. There is a forward-pointing, semicircular crest of feathers on the head. Breeding adults develop orange plates on the face. Sexes alike. Young have a tuft of feathers instead of a crest.

Parakeet auklet

Aethia psittacula

Distribution: Occurs in northern Pacific Ocean, extending between north-eastern Asia and the far northwest of North America, and southward down as far as California.
Size: 10in (25cm).
Habitat: Ocean and shore.
Nest: Underground holes.
Eggs: 1, white.
Food: Crustaceans and fish.

These auklets breed along the western coast of North America, as well as in the Aleutians and other islands. Large colonies may be formed in areas where nesting sites are available. Breeding underground offers a degree of security from larger predators, but the eggs and young chicks are still vulnerable to attack by voles. It takes approximately five weeks for the chicks to reach fledging size, at which stage they will emerge from the nest under cover of darkness and head directly to the sea. The young are unlikely to breed until they are three years old. Parakeet auklets have been known to dive as deep as 100ft (30m) in search of food, and they are capable of remaining underwater for at least a minute. They spend much of their winter at sea, typically heading south, away from the Gulf of Alaska, and are commonly seen in the vicinity of Washington and California.

Identification: Dark upperparts, with white underparts and an intervening mottled gray area. A thin white streak extends back from the eye on each side of the head. Bill reddish outside the breeding season, brighter in breeding adults. Sexes alike. Young birds are duller, with light blue rather than white eyes.

Cassin's auklet

Ptychoramphus aleuticus

These auklets do not venture across the Pacific, preferring to stay around the shore of northwestern North America. They remain close to their breeding grounds, even during the winter, although the nesting period varies significantly depending on the latitude. It can begin as early as March in southern California, but not until July in Alaska. Cassin's auklets may excavate their own nesting burrows, which can be 3ft (1m) in length, but elsewhere, in rocky areas, they seek out suitable retreats among the rocks. Nesting communally, however, often draws the attention of predatory species such as gulls, resulting in the loss of both eggs and chicks. Unique among members of the alcid family, the Farallon Islands population of Cassin's auklets regularly nests twice during the same season, with females laying both in April and July.

Identification: Rather stumpy, plump body shape, with a short, straight and rather broad bill with a pale spot at its base. Predominantly grayish, with small white, crescent-shaped markings above and below the eyes. The underparts are whitish. Sexes alike. Young birds have dark eyes and black bills.

Distribution: Through the Aleutian Islands to the coast of Alaska and south to Baja California, including offshore islands through this region.
Size: 9in (23cm).
Habitat: Ocean and shore.
Nest: Underground burrow or crevice.
Eggs: 1, white.
Food: Crustaceans and fish.

Least auklet (*Aethia pusilla*): 6¼in (16cm)
This auklet is found off western Alaska, wintering in the Aleutian Islands, and has sometimes been recorded as far south as California. White plumes extend back from each eye, with bristly feathers on the forehead and lores (between the bill and the eyes). There is a white area under the chin, and the underparts vary from lightly mottled to blackish, depending on each individual. With winter plumage, the upperparts are black with a white wing bar, and the underparts completely white. Sexes are alike.

Whiskered auklet (*Aethia pygmaea*): 8in (20cm)
The whiskered auklet ranges through the Aleutian Islands off the southwest coast of Alaska. Three relatively long, white plumes are present on each side of the face, and the auklet has a raised, forward-curling black crest of feathers in the center of the forehead. Undertail coverts are white, and the bill is bright red. Out of breeding condition, both plumes and crest are less evident, and the bill appears darker. Males and females are alike. Young birds lack the crest.

Rhinoceros auklet

Cerorhinca monocerata

Rhinoceros auklets congregate in areas where they can come ashore and excavate their nests in relative safety. They breed communally, with nesting densities of approximately seven birds per square yard (square meter) having been recorded on Forrester Island, Alaska. Rhinoceros auklets dig long underground tunnels, using their bills and feet to excavate these burrows during the night. It will typically take a pair about 14 nights to construct an average tunnel about 7ft (213cm) long. The hen lays a single egg in a chamber at the end.

Distribution: Western coast of North America, extending to the Aleutian Islands across the Bering Sea.
Size: 15in (38cm).
Habitat: Coastal areas.
Nest: Underground chamber, may be lined with vegetation.
Eggs: 1, white spotted.
Food: Fish, such as anchovies, sand launce, and herrings.

Identification: Dark brown upperparts. Underparts from the chin down to the chest and flanks are whitish, with a brownish-gray tone especially evident on the breast. White streaks evident on the face, creating a mustached effect, plus white crests extending from the eyes back to the nape of the neck that are less distinctive outside the breeding season. Orangish bill with characteristic horn-like swelling at the base of the upper bill, which largely disappears during the winter. Sexes alike.

PUFFINS AND AUKS

Although seabirds generally have a reputation for being quite dull in terms of coloration, members of this group often undergo a striking transformation in appearance at the onset of the breeding period. In flight or at a distance, puffins can generally be distinguished from other alcids since they tend to fly relatively high above the water, rather than skimming low over the waves.

Puffin

Fratercula arctica

These auks have unmistakable bills, said to resemble those of parrots. Young puffins have much narrower and less brightly colored bills than the adults. Puffins come ashore to nest in colonies on cliffs and in coastal areas where they can breed largely hidden from predators. Sand eels figure prominently in their diet at this time, and adult birds often fly quite long distances to obtain food.

When underwater, puffins use their wings like flippers, which enables them to swim faster. Adult birds fly back to their young with eels arranged in a row, hanging down each side of their bills. They can carry as many as ten fish at a time in this way.

Identification: Distinctive whitish sides to the face, with black extending back over the crown. Black neck, back and wings; underparts white, with a gray area on the flanks. Broad, flattened bill has a red area running down its length and across the tip, and a grayish base with a yellow area intervening. During the winter, the bill is less brightly colored, and the sides of the face turn grayish. Sexes are alike.

Above: The appearance of the puffin's bill varies depending on the bird's age and the time of year.

Right: Puffins excavate nesting tunnels underground or use existing holes.

Distribution: Extends from the far north of eastern Canada south, occasionally as far down as Long Island.
Size: 13in (32cm).
Habitat: Ocean and coastal areas.
Nest: Underground burrows.
Eggs: 1, white.
Food: Fish.

Tufted puffin

Fratercula cirrhata

After nesting at high densities, both on the coast of North America and on islands including the Aleutians, tufted puffins disperse widely through their extensive range. These puffins prefer to nest in burrows, which they dig in grassy areas. The single egg is laid at the end of the burrow on the bare soil, or sometimes on a bed of feathers. Puffins react badly to human disturbance when nesting, a likely reason why the small southerly breeding population in California has declined over the past century. Further north, in the breeding grounds on the Alaskan peninsula, predators such as Arctic foxes take their toll, while gulls are a hazard on the Aleutians. Young puffins leave the nest after dark and head out to sea.

Identification: Breeding plumage is mostly blackish, with prominent white areas on the face and long, straw-colored tufts of feathers that extend over the back. The large bill is red, with a prominent horn-colored area at its upper base. Entire body is grayish-black in winter, the bill being red with a brownish base (those of young birds are completely brown).

Distribution: Ranges right up into the polar region and throughout the northern Pacific, occurring as far south as the Farallon Islands off central California.
Size: 16in (41cm).
Habitat: Ocean and shore.
Nest: Burrows, sometimes rocky crevices.
Eggs: 1, white, often spotted.
Food: Fish and squid form the bulk of the diet.

Marbled murrelet (*Brachyramphus marmoratus*): 10in (25cm)
Extends from southeast Alaska across the Pacific to the coast of Asia via the Aleutian Islands, and south down North America's west coast to California. Dark brown coloration, especially on the sides of the head and over the back, with whitish mottling on the breast and underparts, but no white area there. In winter, black extends around the eyes, with a white collar evident on the back of the neck. Sexes are alike.

Kittlitz's murrelet (*Brachyramphus brevirostris*): 9in (23cm)
From the western coast of Alaska to Asia via the Bering Sea. Present also through the Aleutian Islands and in North America, on rare occasions as far south as California. Grayish-brown on the throat, breast and flanks, with only the center of the belly being white. Brown flight feathers and a brown area on the wing coverts. In winter, a black stripe extends over the top of the head. Wings and back predominantly grayish. Sides of the face and underparts are white, with slight mottling on the breast. Sexes are alike.

Craveri's murrelet (*Synthliboramphus craveri*): 8in (20cm)
Occurs on the western side of North America, in the Golfo de California and Baja California north as far as the San Benito Islands. This species has black upperparts, with white crescents directly above and below the eyes, and white underparts, with a blackish collar curving slightly onto the breast. Underwing area is gray. Narrow black bill. Sexes are alike.

Horned puffin

Fratercula corniculata

Horned puffins are most frequently observed in northern parts of North America. However, they do venture south outside their traditional wintering grounds, and can occasionally be seen on the shorelines of Oregon and California. Records reveal they may even reach the western Hawaiian islands. The determining factor that affects their range, especially at this time of year, is the availability of fish. Within a colony, egg-laying is a synchronized process usually occurring over the course of a week, which means that the chicks will subsequently hatch together. There may be a few later young, usually resulting from pairs who lost their initial egg soon after it was laid. (This in turn has the effect of triggering the hen to lay again.) Horned puffins will not stray far from their breeding grounds when obtaining food for their young, who are reared mainly on sand eels caught under-water by the adults.

Identification: White underparts and black on the upper body, with a huge bill and gray coloration on the sides of the face, distinguish this species. During the breeding period, the sides of the face become white and the bill, with its horn-colored base, is much brighter. Sexes alike. Young birds have dark and much narrower bills.

Distribution: Ranges right up into the polar region and throughout the northern Pacific, occurring as far south as the Queen Charlotte Islands, British Columbia.
Size: 16in (41cm).
Habitat: Ocean and shore
Nest: Rocky crevices and burrows.
Eggs: 1, white with dark spots.
Food: Mainly fish and squid.

Dovekie

Little auk *Alle alle*

The smallest of the auks, the dovekie has a relatively restricted distribution. Despite this, it is considered to be possibly the most numerous seabird in the world. It forms huge nesting colonies in the Arctic region during the brief summer, before heading south at the approach of winter as the ocean surface starts to freeze over. Little auks are often more likely to be spotted at this time of year, frequently flying very low over the waves or even through them on occasion. Sometimes, however, fierce storms make feeding virtually impossible, and in a weakened state, dovekies are driven into coastal areas. This phenomenon is often described as a "wreck."

Identification: In summer plumage, the head and upper part of the chest are black. The back, wings and upper surface of the tail feathers are also black, aside from white streaks apparent over the wings. During the winter, the black on the face is broken up by white, leaving a small band of dark plumage across the throat. Small, black bill. Sexes are alike.

Distribution: Northern Atlantic, extending from Greenland down the eastern seaboard of North America as far as North Carolina, and sometimes Florida.
Size: 8in (20cm).
Habitat: Ocean and coastal areas.
Nest: Cliffs or crevices.
Eggs: 1, pale blue.
Food: Microscopic plankton.

SOCIAL SEABIRDS

Although seabirds generally feed on fish, their bills can differ significantly in shape, as revealed by a comparison between the pointed bill of the guillemots, the relatively stumpy bill of the murrelets and the uniquely broad shape of the razorbill's beak. These differences can be very helpful when trying to identify birds such as these from their silhouettes.

Ancient murrelet

Gray-headed murrelet *Synthliboramphus antiquus*

The unusual name of these members of the auk family comes from the white streaks in the plumage of breeding adults, which suggest an old appearance. Though occurring right across the Pacific to the eastern coast of Asia, the ancient murrelet can sometimes be found on inland waters in North America, and may even extend as far south as northern Baja California. It is possible to distinguish between these and other murrelets thanks to their flight pattern, since they keep their head in a more upright position rather than extending it horizontally. Ancient murrelets prefer to nest in burrows that they excavate themselves. Weaning takes place rapidly, with the adult pair simply abandoning their young, forcing them to emerge. The family group then fly off, usually at night, and will travel a long distance, typically up to 30 miles (50km), within a day of leaving the nesting grounds.

Identification: White underparts and sides of the neck, with gray on the back and wings. Black bib and head, which is variably streaked with white. Black barring on the sides of the body too, usually concealed by the wings. Sexes are alike, and the throat region of young birds is mainly white.

Distribution: Represented through the Aleutian chain and southern Alaska southward along the North American coast to northern California.
Size: 11in (27cm).
Habitat: Ocean and shore.
Nest: Burrows and crevices.
Eggs: 2, brownish-green with darker spots.
Food: Crustaceans and fish.

Razorbill

Alca torda

The distinctive broad, flattened shape of the bill, resembling a cut-throat razor, explains the common name of these auks. They are often observed swimming with their tails held vertically, rather than flat, enabling them to be distinguished from seabirds of similar size and coloration. Razorbills are adaptable in their feeding habits, with diet varying according to locality. Pairs display a strong bond, and return to their traditional breeding sites, which may sometimes be no more than steep, inaccessible rocky stacks located off the coast. They show no tendency to construct a nest of any kind, with hens sometimes laying their single egg on a narrow ledge directly above the ocean. The pearlike shape of the razorbill's egg helps to prevent it rolling over the edge if accidentally dislodged. Even so, losses of eggs are fairly high, with predators such as gulls swooping down on unguarded sites.

Identification: Black upperparts, with white edging along the back of the wings, and a vertical white stripe across the bill. Black coloration more strongly defined in breeding birds, with a white horizontal stripe reaching from the eyes to the bill. Sexes are alike. Young birds have smaller bills with no white markings.

Distribution: Extends right across the North Atlantic, occurring on the eastern side of North America, from the far north of Canada south to Long Island, New York.
Size: 15in (39cm).
Habitat: Ocean and shore.
Nest: Cliff face crevices.
Eggs: 1, whitish with brown spots.
Food: Fish and crustaceans.

Pigeon guillemot

Cepphus columba

These guillemots are most conspicuous during the early summer when they come ashore to breed, with pairs returning to the same site throughout their lives. Southerly populations are likely to be seen around six weeks before egg-laying commences in April, returning about a month later further north. The adults are determined hunters, submerging to catch fish and other prey for up to 2^1/$_2$ minutes. They comb the seabed for fish, invertebrates, crabs, other crustaceans, and mollusks. Chicks are normally fed on fish such as sand eels. The young are independent once they leave the nest at just over five weeks old, although this period may be longer if food is scarce. They are unlikely to breed until at least three years old.

Identification: Relatively long neck and pointed bill. Adult breeding birds are black with a white area on the wings, and have a mottled back, whitish neck and white underparts in the winter. The area around the eyes remains dark, as does the bill. Sexes are alike. Young birds display more pronounced grayer mottling on the neck than the adults.

Distribution: Northern Pacific region, on both the east coast of Asia and the western coast of North America, reaching as far south as southern California.
Size: 14^1/$_2$in (37cm).
Habitat: Ocean and shore.
Nest: Rock crevices, burrows.
Eggs: 2, whitish with dark spots.
Food: Fish and marine invertebrates.

Thick-billed murre (*Uria lomvia*): 17in (43cm) Murres are members of the auk family. This species occurs right around the northern part of North America. It is occasionally recorded as far south as California, and is a regular sight around the Aleutian Islands. Has also been recorded as far south as Florida in the east, but normally only to the mid-Atlantic. As its name suggests, this murre has a broad, relatively short bill, which possesses an arched tip and a white line along the lower mandible. Black head, back and wings, with a white area across the underwing coverts. Sexes are alike.

Black guillemot (*Cepphus grylle*): 13in (33cm) Black guillemots occur on the northern shore of Alaska and more widely in the northeast, southward along the Atlantic coast as far as Maine. These seabirds are jet black in color, with a vivid white wing patch and red feet in summer. They are predominantly white in the winter, with mottling evident on the head and over the back, but with the back of the wings remaining blackish. Young black guillemots display more mottling on the head.

Xantus' murrelet (*Synthliboramphus hypoleucus*): 10in (25cm) This species is present off the coast of western North America, breeding on islands off southern California and Baja California. The southern Californian race (*S. h. scrippsi*) is very similar to Craveri's murrelet but lacks the black collar across the breast, with white rather than gray plumage under the wings. The subspecies occurring in Baja Californian waters (*S. h. hypoleucus*) has more extensive white markings on the sides of the face.

Common murre

Guillemot *Uria aalge*

The upright resting stance of the common murre and its ability to hop, combined with its black and white coloration and fish-eating habits, have led to these birds being described as the penguins of the north. However, unlike penguins they can fly. This enables them to reach their rocky and inhospitable nesting sites, where large numbers pack onto ledges. The sheer density of numbers there offers protection against raiding gulls since there is little space for the predators to land, and they will be met with a fearsome barrier of sharp, pointed bills if they swoop down. As many as twenty breeding pairs can crowd every 11 square feet (1 square meter). Fall-offs in fish stocks can have an adverse effect on numbers, as will oil pollution.

Identification: Black head, neck and upperparts, aside from a white area at the edge of the wing coverts. Slight mottling on the flanks, otherwise underparts completely white. Outside the breeding season the entire throat and sides of the neck are white. Sexes are alike. Dark plumage extends up the sides of the neck in young birds.

Distribution: Northern waters right across the Atlantic and Pacific oceans, from Alaska to California in the west down to the Gulf of Maine on the east coast.
Size: 17in (43cm).
Habitat: Ocean and shore.
Nest: Cliff ledges and crevices.
Eggs: 1, bluish-green, dark spots.
Food: Fish and marine invertebrates.

PELICANS AND BOOBIES

These large birds, which belong to the same family, both hunt fish, but whereas pelicans are well-equipped to trawl for fish by virtue of their pouches, boobies are more opportunistic, relying sometimes on their size to harry and dispossess other birds of their catches. Both groups possess webbed feet, which are ideally suited to swimming in watery habitats.

American white pelican

Rough-billed pelican *Pelecanus erythrorhynchos*

These pelicans are found mainly on stretches of fresh water, sometimes hunting in groups for fish and other creatures such as crayfish. They are also seen in saltwater habitats but do not venture far from coasts. Occasionally, they may fly long distances to obtain food if the waters that they inhabit have a low fish population. On migration, American white pelicans fly over land rather than the ocean, although populations in the southern part of their range will remain in the same region throughout the year. These birds breed communally, usually on quite inaccessible islands. Their chicks associate together in groups, known as pods, before they are fully fledged.

Identification: Predominantly white plumage with contrasting black primary flight feathers. The large yellow bill develops a distinctive raised area on the ridge toward the tip from late winter through the breeding season. Sexes are alike, but the female is smaller.

Distribution: Western and central areas of North America, extending as far south as Guatemala and Costa Rica during the winter.
Size: 70in (178cm).
Habitat: Both freshwater and saltwater areas, not ranging far out to sea.
Nest: On the ground.
Eggs: 2–3, whitish with darker markings.
Food: Fish and other aquatic creatures.

Left: The pelican's pouch is used to trawl for food.

Brown pelican

Pelecanus occidentalis

Distribution: Ranges down the Pacific coast of America, from California to Chile, and on the Galapagos Islands. Another population is centered on the Caribbean.
Size: 60in (152cm).
Habitat: Ocean and shore, but not venturing inland.
Nest: On the ground or in trees.
Eggs: 2–3, white.
Food: Mainly fish.

Brown pelicans trawl for fish at the surface, but also dive to depths of 30ft (10m), where small fish are numerous, returning to the surface to swallow their catch. They also fly in formation close to the surface and spot fish below with their good eyesight. Brown pelicans frequent ports in search of fish leftovers, but retreat to islands and other remote locations to breed. They usually nest on the ground, but build more substantial platform nests in mangrove swamps, with chicks taking longer to fledge there.

Identification: Golden-yellow area on head, grayish-brown body and white neck, with the white becoming browner in the breeding season. The top of the head becomes speckled when adults are rearing young. Sexes are alike. Young birds have brown heads and are duller overall.

Blue-faced booby

Masked booby *Sula dactylatra*

The blue-faced species is the largest of the boobies, and preys upon correspondingly larger fish, swallowing those of up to 16in (41cm) without difficulty. Although these birds often dive quite deeply in search of fish, they may also catch flying fish at the surface. They sometimes lose their catch to frigatebirds that harry them as they fly back to land. Blue-faced boobies live in colonies, and prefer to nest on cliff faces. On remote islands in the absence of major predators, however, pairs may breed on the ground. While the hen is likely to lay two eggs, only one chick is normally reared, and the weaker chick loses out to its stronger sibling in the competition for food. Blue-faced boobies are long-lived, and young birds may not breed until their third year. These birds frequent tropical oceans on both sides of America. Sadly, their numbers are declining in some areas due to increased development disturbing their habitat. A large colony can still be found around the Galapagos Islands, off the western coast of South America.

Identification: Predominantly white but with black on the wings and a distinctive black tail. Has dark feathering on the face around the eyes, with a bluish tinge extending onto the yellowish bill. In hens, the bill is significantly duller.

Distribution: Range is pan-global around the equator. This species occurs both on the Atlantic and Pacific coasts of America, and also in the Caribbean.
Size: 36in (91cm).
Habitat: Tropical oceans.
Nest: Constructed from accumulated droppings.
Eggs: 2, pale blue.
Food: Fish form the main element of diet.

Peruvian booby (*Sula variegata*): 30in (76cm)
Ranges along the western coast of South America, in the vicinity of the Humboldt Current. Breeds from northern Peru south to central Chile, sometimes being observed as far north as southwest Ecuador. White head and neck, with blackish bill and black area around the eyes. Brown wings with white edging over the feathers, and similar mottling behind the legs and on the rump. Dark feet. Sexes are alike.

Red-footed booby (*Sula sula*): 31in (77cm)
Occurs both in the Caribbean and southwest Atlantic, off the coast of Brazil. Also in the Pacific, with a distribution including the whole coast of Central America. Occurs in a variety of color morphs. Black-tailed white morph with black flight feathers is found on the Galapagos Islands. Brown morph also recognized. May also have a distinctive white tail in some cases. Sexes are alike.

Blue-footed booby (*Sula nebouxii*): 33in (84cm)
Eastern Pacific, extending from the Golfo de California south to Peru, and to the Galapagos Islands. Black area around the eyes and similar bill. Brown and white markings from top of head to base of neck. Throat and underparts whitish. Wings brown; plumage on back is edged with white. Distinctive blue feet. Sexes are alike.

Brown booby

Sula leucogaster

The noise of these boobies in a colony is deafening, but out over the sea they hunt quietly, often not far from the coast. They are very agile both above and below the water surface, able to catch flying fish as they break above the waves, as well as pursuing their prey underwater, using their wings like paddles. Brown boobies are rarely seen on the surface of the ocean, however. Females especially will also rob other seabirds of their catches as they head back to shore. Pairs usually nest on the ground, favoring offshore islands, nesting almost throughout the year in some parts of their range, although usually only one chick survives through to fledging. The young spend several months with their parents after fledging, before leaving the colony. This gives them a chance to learn basic fishing techniques that will be essential to survival.

Distribution: Virtually circumtropical. Populations present off the coast of Central America and in the Caribbean, as well as eastern-central South America.
Size: 32in (81cm).
Habitat: Ocean and shore.
Nest: Loose pile of twigs.
Eggs: 2, pale chalky blue.
Food: Flying fish and squid.

Identification: Adults generally have dark brownish head, upperparts and wings, with pale yellowish bill and feet. The remainder of the body is white, including much of the underwing area. Sexes alike. Young birds are entirely brown at first, and have duller coloration around the face.

CORMORANTS

Cormorants are generally dark, which can make it hard to distinguish between different species from a distance. These seabirds are often sighted on harbor poles and buoys, with their wings outstretched. This is essential behavior, allowing their plumage to dry off, since it is not as water-repellent as that of other seabirds. When in flight, cormorants flap their wings frequently, and they will dive down to catch fish.

Neotropic cormorant

Phalacrocorax brasilianus

Distribution: Southern U.S.A., east to Cuba and the Bahamas, also Central and South America to Cape Horn.
Size: 29in (73cm).
Habitat: Coastal areas and inland.
Nest: On ground, or in bushes.
Eggs: 1–7, whitish-blue.
Food: Fish, other aquatic creatures.

A widely distributed species likely to be found in a variety of aquatic habitats. These cormorants will even move into temporarily flooded areas, and are a relatively common sight in the Andean lakes. In coastal districts they seek out sheltered bays and coves, rather than venturing far out in open sea. Social by nature, neotropic cormorants will fish in groups, collaborating together. When breeding they form large aggregations, often in the company of other birds such as herons, and their nest site is directly influenced by their habitat. If trees or bushes are available they will nest off the ground, where they will be safer from predators, but on remote islands they can breed at ground level with little fear of persecution. Pairs often hatch more chicks than they can successfully rear, with the older, dominant individuals winning in the competition for food with their younger siblings.

Identification: Blackish plumage, more mottled over the wings. Dull yellow throat-patch edged with white, which becomes pinker in the breeding season. Long, hooked bill and characteristic long tail. Sexes alike. Young birds are much browner.

Double-crested cormorant

Phalacrocorax auritus

These cormorants are found mainly in coastal waters, sometimes using unorthodox sites such as wrecked ships as perches. They also venture to inland areas, where they are found on suitable stretches of water. They can form large flocks, often hunting together for fish, which form the main ingredient of their diet. In the past, double-crested cormorant numbers have plummeted in some parts of their range due to DDT entering the food chain. This pesticide has had a harmful effect on eggshell thickness, and, as a result, has significantly reduced the number of chicks that hatch. The ban on DDT has seen their numbers rise again. These cormorants have also benefited from the increasing number of freshwater reservoirs in various parts of their range, providing them with additional areas of habitat.

Identification: Adults are entirely black. Immatures show a whitish hue to their underparts. A double crest of feathers is evident on the back of the head during the breeding period, with a variable amount of white coloration. Has bare yellowish-orange skin around the face, with a powerful hooked bill. Females are smaller in size. Several different races are recognized through their range, differing in the extent of the white feathering forming the crest as well as in the depth of coloration.

Distribution: Much of the U.S.A., south to parts of Central America in the winter. Also in parts of the Caribbean, from Florida to Cuba.
Size: 36in (91cm).
Habitat: Areas of fresh water and sea water.
Nest: Built of sticks and often seaweed.
Eggs: 3–4, pale blue.
Food: Fish and other aquatic creatures.

Blue-eyed cormorant (Imperial shag, *Phalacrocorax atriceps*): 30in (76cm)
Southern South America, from Chile to Argentina and Uruguay, and the Falkland Islands. Loose black crest with black plumage extending from above the upper bill over the head, back and wings to the tail. White on the sides of the head down over the underparts, with white patches on the wings. Blue skin encircling the eyes. Sexes alike.

Great cormorant (*Phalacrocorax carbo*): 40in (102cm)
Great cormorants breed from Newfoundland and around the Gulf of St. Lawrence southward as far as Maine. May move further south for the winter, sometimes as far as Florida. Different races occur elsewhere in the world. Nominate North American race is blackish overall, with purplish hue on the wings and white patches in the throat region and near the top of the legs when in breeding condition. Bluish skin around the eyes, and horn-colored bill with a darker tip. Sexes alike.

Red-faced cormorant (*Phalacrocorax urile*): 35in (89cm)
This species occurs on southern coasts of Alaska extending via the Aleutian Islands to Asia. Blackish overall, with white plumage at the top of the legs. Slight crest on the top of the head and another behind. Red areas of bare skin encircle the eyes. Relatively pale bill. Crests and white areas are breeding characteristics. Hens are smaller in size.

Pelagic cormorant

Phalacrocorax pelagicus

Occasionally sighted as far south as Hawaii, the pelagic cormorant is smaller than related species from the American Pacific region. Their size enables them to colonize small rocky shelves on the faces of cliffs, which can be adopted for breeding purposes without conflicting with their larger relatives. Flying into a site such as this is one thing, but, with insufficient room to turn around, the birds may have to take off again by throwing themselves backward off the ledge. Pelagic cormorants usually nest in small groups, and in some locations individual pairs may even breed on their own. The nest is constructed of seaweed or similar material, held together by their droppings. It is unusual for more than four chicks to be reared successfully through to fledging, even in locations where fish are plentiful. Pairs will return in future years, renovating the nest site as necessary. On occasions, these cormorants may also be sighted inshore.

Distribution: Northern Pacific region, from Asia to North America southward from Alaska, including the Aleutian Islands, as far as north-western Mexico.
Size: 30in (76cm).
Habitat: Sea and seashore.
Nest: Cliff ledges and caves.
Eggs: 2-7, whitish-blue.
Food: Mainly fish.

Identification: Glossy greenish-black. During the breeding period gains white areas on the flanks, and tufts of longer feathers on the nape and crown, with the skin around the eyes also becoming redder. Sexes alike. Young birds are brown in color.

Brandt's cormorant

Phalacrocorax pencilliatus

The social behavior of these cormorants is fascinating to observe, as they sometimes join together in their hundreds to head out over the sea in search of fish. When a shoal is discovered the cormorants dive down, collectively harrying the fish and working together to maximize their catch. These birds also breed colonially, and, although males return to the same nest site each year, they may choose a new partner. The nest is sited on the ground on a larger area than the cliff nests of pelagic cormorants. Breeding success is influenced greatly by the availability of a plentiful supply of food, and in years when the El Niño effect alters the pattern of ocean currents off the coast, and thus the distribution of anchovies and other fish, success may plummet accordingly. This generally has no lasting effect on the cormorant population, however, because they are long-lived birds with a potential life expectancy of more than a decade.

Distribution: Restricted to the western coast of North America, from southern British Columbia down to Baja California in Mexico.
Size: 35in (89cm).
Habitat: Ocean and shore.
Nest: Gently sloping cliffs.
Eggs: 3–6, whitish-blue.
Food: Mainly fish.

Identification: Relatively large. Buff feathers across throat, pouch bright blue at outset of breeding. Plumage generally blackish, aside from a few white feathers on the head at this time. Sexes alike. Young birds brown.

PENGUINS AND SEA DUCKS

Bright plumage is not a feature generally associated with seabirds, in which more subdued hues of black, brown and white predominate. There are exceptions, however, most noticeably in the case of ducks that have spread to the marine environment from the freshwater haunts more usually occupied by waterfowl. These birds are also more predatory by nature.

Galapagos penguin

Spheniscus mendiculus

These penguins have colonized the volcanic outcrops of the Galapagos Islands, seeking out fish such as sardines, which feature prominently in their diet in coastal waters.

Galapagos penguins usually fish together in pairs but sometimes hunt in larger groups too. When there is a change in the pattern of the ocean currents owing to El Niño, and fish then become scarce, penguin numbers may plummet. This decline occurred most dramatically in the early 1980s, when just a few hundred Galapagos penguins survived. Their numbers have since undergone a good recovery, aided by the fact that they can breed throughout the year.

Above: Penguins may not be able to fly, but their wings make powerful flippers underwater.

Distribution: Confined to the Galapagos Islands.
Size: 21in (53cm).
Habitat: Coastal regions.
Nest: In caves or crevices.
Eggs: 2, whitish.
Food: Fish.

Identification: A relatively small penguin, especially when compared with related species. A very thin white stripe extends from the eye around the throat, and the sides of the face are dark. White area under the lower bill and over much of the underparts, aside from an uneven, mainly black circle of feathers. Bill is pinkish at the base. Sexes are alike, and patterning is less clearly defined in young birds.

Rockhopper penguin

Eudyptes crysocome

Distribution: Occurs on the southeastern side of South America. Other populations found off Australia's south coast and between Africa and Australia.
Size: 24¹/₂in (62cm).
Habitat: Ocean and close to the shoreline.
Nest: Made of grass and other available materials.
Eggs: 2, bluish white.
Food: Mainly krill. Some fish.

These penguins are so called because of the way they hop across land instead of walking. They live communally in rookeries, using their sharp bills to ward off gulls and other predatory birds that may land in their midst. Despite its relatively small size, the rockhopper is the most aggressive of all penguins. It is also one of the most adaptable, and is found even in temperate areas. These penguins feed underwater, using their wings like flippers to steer themselves. If danger threatens, they swim toward the shore and leap out of the water onto the land with considerable force.

Identification: White underparts. Black head, flippers and tail although the ear coverts appear slightly paler. The bill is red, as are the irises. A line of golden plumage forms a crest toward the rear on each side of the head. Hens are smaller and have less stout bills.

Above: These ungainly hopping penguins are elegant swimmers.

Humbolt penguin (*Spheniscus humboldti*): 28in (70cm)
Occurs in the vicinity of the Humbolt Current along the shores of Chile and Peru. Distinctive pink fleshy edges at the base of the bill. Otherwise black and white, with a prominent white area on the throat. Sexes alike.

Magellanic penguin (*Spheniscus magellanicus*): 30in (76cm)
This species occurs around the southern part of South America, from central Chile via Cape Horn north to central Argentina. Also present on the Falkland Islands. Similar to the Humbolt penguin, but can be distinguished by the much wider white stripe extending around the side of the head, and the pink coloration not extending below the level of the upper bill. This species is also slightly larger. Sexes alike.

White-headed flightless steamer duck (*Tachyeres leucocephalus*): 29in (74cm)
White-headed flightless steamer ducks are restricted to the coastal region of Chubut in Argentina, South America. The drake has a grayish head with white patches on the sides of the face and down the neck when in breeding condition. White is also evident on the wings, and the remainder of the plumage is grayish with black edging to the feathers. A narrow black band extends around the bill, which is yellowish. Ducks have a darker head, and reddish-brown, rather than whitish, plumage. The bill is also darker. Young birds have brown rather than gray markings on the head.

King eider

Somateria spectabilis

Like most birds from the far north, the king eider has a circumpolar distribution that reaches right around the top of the globe. Seasonal movements of these sea ducks tend to be more widespread than in other eiders, and they are remarkably common, with the North American population estimated at as many as two million individuals. Huge groups of up to 100,000 birds will congregate together during the molting period, although the groups split up during the breeding season when pairs nest individually across the Arctic tundra. King eiders are powerful swimmers and generally dive to obtain their food.

Identification: Orange area edged with black above the reddish bill in breeding condition. Light-gray plumage extends down the neck. Chest is pale pinkish white, with black wings and underparts. Ducks are mainly a speckled shade of brown, and the pale underside of their wings is visible in flight. In eclipse plumage, drakes are a darker shade of brown, with an orangish-yellow bill and white plumage on the back.

Distribution: Largely within the Arctic Circle.
Size: 25in (63cm).
Habitat: Tundra and ocean.
Nest: Hollow lined with down feathers.
Eggs: 4–7, olive buff.
Food: Predominantly crustaceans and marine invertebrates.

Oldsquaw

Long-tailed duck *Clangula hyemalis*

These sea ducks often congregate in large numbers, although in winter females and young birds tend to migrate further south in flocks than do adult drakes. They spend most of their time on the water, and obtain food by diving under the waves. They come ashore onto the tundra to nest, and ducks lay their eggs on the ground. The drakes soon return to the ocean, where they start to molt. When migrating, they generally fly quite low in lines, rather than in any other organized formation.

Identification: Black head, neck and chest, with white around the eyes and white underparts. Head becomes white across the top outside the breeding season, with patches of black evident on the sides. Gray rather than brown predominates on the wings. Long tail plumes present throughout the year. The smaller ducks undergo a similar transformation, and the sides of the face become white rather than blackish.

Distribution: Northern coasts, with circumpolar range. Winters further south.
Size: 19in (47cm).
Habitat: Coastal waters and bays.
Nest: Hidden in vegetation or under a rock.
Eggs: 5–7, olive buff.
Food: Mainly crustaceans and marine invertebrates.

GULLS

Gulls are linked in many people's minds with the seaside, but some species have proved very adept at adjusting to living closely alongside humans, and generally profiting from this association. A number of different gulls have now spread to various inland locations as a result. Shades of white and gray generally predominate in the plumage of these birds, making them quite easy to recognize.

Heermann's gull

Larus heermanni

Distribution: Occurs along much of the Pacific coastline of North America, being recorded from Vancouver Island down as far south as Panama.
Size: 21in (53cm).
Habitat: Ocean and shore.
Nest: Scrape on the ground.
Eggs: 2–3, buff-colored.
Food: Fish and various invertebrates form the bulk of the diet.

Like most of its kind, Heermann's gull is very adaptable, ever ready to obtain food opportunistically. These gulls may harry pelicans, persuading them to disgorge their catches, or dart in among feeding sea lions to grab food. They often follow fishing boats too, swooping on waste thrown overboard, and will scavenge on the shoreline for edible items. When Heermann's gulls obtain their own food they usually do so inland, seizing lizards and invertebrates, although they are able to catch fish in the ocean also. While most migrants head south for the winter, these gulls will often move further north. Some prefer to head to warmer climates further south of their breeding grounds, which are centered on Isla Raza and other neighboring islands in the Golfo de California, as well as the San Benito Islands, lying off western Baja California.

Identification: Dark gray back and wings, with the body being lighter in color and the tail edged with white. Head whitish, becoming streaked in winter. Bill bright red with a dark tip. Sexes alike. Young birds are dark brownish-black, lightening over successive molts and gaining a buff tail tip in their second year.

Black-headed gull

Larus ridibundus

These gulls are a common sight not only in coastal areas but also in town parks with lakes. They move inland during the winter and are often seen following tractors plowing at this time of year, seeking worms and grubs in the soil. Black-headed gulls nest close to water in what can be quite large colonies. Like many gulls, they are noisy birds, even calling at night. On warm, summer evenings, they can sometimes be seen hawking flying ants and similar insects in flight, demonstrating their airborne agility.

Identification: These gulls have their distinctive black heads only during the summer, with a white collar beneath and white under-parts. Wings are gray, and the flight feathers mainly black. In the winter, the head is mainly white, aside from black ear coverts, and a black smudge above each eye. In the winter, the bill is red at the base and dark at the tip.

Distribution: Occurs on the tip of Greenland and along the coast of Newfoundland south to New England. May also sometimes be seen from western Alaska southward.
Size: 15in (39cm).
Habitat: Coastal areas.
Nest: Scrape lined with plant matter.
Eggs: 2–3, pale blue to brown with darker markings.
Food: Typically mollusks, crustaceans, and other small aquatic creatures.

Above: The black feathering on the head is a transient characteristic, appearing only in the summer (above right).

Lesser black-backed gull (*Larus fuscus*): 22in (56cm)
The lesser black-backed gull ranges along the eastern coast of North America. Sometimes also encountered in Alaska and down the Pacific region. This species is similar to the great black-backed gull but smaller, and lacks the prominent white seen on the flight feathers when the wings are closed. The legs are yellow rather than dull pink. There is a much smaller area of white on the outstretched upper surface of the wings in flight. Sexes are alike.

Little gull (*Larus minutus*): 11in (28cm)
This species is now breeding in Ontario and Wisconsin, though its main area of distribution extends from central Europe to Siberia. Breeding population overwinters on the Great Lakes and the coastal area from New Brunswick south to New Jersey. Pale gray back and wings, with a black head, the black extending right down to the neck. Red legs and feet. In winter, has a dark spot toward the rear of the head, which is otherwise whitish apart from a mottled area on the crown. Sexes are alike.

Bonaparte's gull (*Larus philadelphia*): 13¹/₂in (34cm)
Bonaparte's gull breeds in Alaska and Canada. It winters on the Pacific coast of North America from Washington to Mexico, and on the Atlantic coast from New England south along the Gulf coast. This species has a black head with a white collar on the neck. Pale gray wings and white underparts are typical. The black bill is retained in winter, but black on the head is reduced to a spot behind each eye. Legs and feet are red. Sexes are alike.

Herring gull

Larus argentatus

These large gulls are often seen on fishing jetties and around harbors, searching for scraps. They have also moved inland and can be seen in areas such as garbage dumps, where they scavenge for food, often in quite large groups. Herring gulls are noisy by nature, especially when breeding. They now frequently nest on rooftops in coastal towns and cities, a trend that began as recently as the 1940s in the U.K. Herring gull pairs can become very aggressive at breeding time, swooping menacingly on people who venture close to the nest site or even near the chicks once they fledge.

Identification: White head and underparts, with gray on the back and wings. Prominent large, white spots on the black flight feathers. Distinctive pink feet. Reddish spot toward the tip of the lower bill. Some dark streaking on the head and neck in winter. Sexes alike. The young birds are mainly brown, with prominent barring on their wings and dark bills.

Distribution: Occurs extensively, including inland areas away from the shore in much of eastern North America. Pacific range tends to be more restricted to coastal areas.
Size: 24in (60cm)
Habitat: Coastal and inland areas.
Nest: Small pile of vegetation.
Eggs: 2–3, pale blue to brown with darker markings.
Food: Fish and carrion.

Left: The herring gull's pink legs are a distinctive feature.

Great black-backed gull

Larus marinus

These large gulls can be extremely disruptive when close to nesting seabird colonies. Not only will they harry returning birds for their catches of fish, but they also take eggs and chicks on occasion too. In winter, great black-backed gulls move inland to scavenge on garbage tips, although they are generally wary of people and are unlikely to be seen in urban areas. These gulls have now become relatively common on the eastern Great Lakes, and may be moving progressively westward in this part of North America, where there are large stretches of accessible water. When breeding, pairs can be quite solitary, especially near human habitation, but they are more likely to nest in colonies on uninhabited islands.

Identification: Has a white head and underparts with black on the back and wings. A large gull with a white-spotted black tail and a large area of white apparent at the wing tips in flight. The bill is yellow with a red tip to the lower bill. Has pale pinkish legs. Sexes alike.

Distribution: Extends down the northern Atlantic coastline, expanding its range progressively to Florida but still uncommon along the Gulf coast. This species occurs inland too.
Size: 29in (74cm)
Habitat: Coastal areas.
Nest: Pile of vegetation.
Eggs: 2–3, brownish with dark markings.
Food: Fish and carrion.

ISLAND GULLS

The adaptable nature of gulls is further revealed by the way in which they occur not just around the coastline, from the north right down to the south of America, but out to many of the world's more remote islands too, including Hawaii, the Galapagos Islands and the Falklands. Young gulls are usually easy to spot by their darker plumage.

California gull

Larus californicus

California gulls are particularly adaptable, as is reflected in the wide range of habitats they frequent. They will eat an equally diverse range of food, including grain and various types of invertebrates, and will scavenge at garbage dumps for anything edible. These gulls will also take eggs and hunt ducklings and other young birds, and may even cannibalize the carcasses of their own dead. They seem to have an insight into where food may be readily available, often appearing to plague strawberry farms for fruit when the crop is ripening. Famously, flocks of California gulls rescued the early Mormon settlers around the Great Salt Lake from imminent starvation by devouring a plague of locusts that was threatening to destroy their crops, an event marked by a statue in Salt Lake City. California gulls breed in colonies on islands in large inland lakes.

Identification: White underparts and head, with the back of the head being mottled in the winter. Wings gray, with the flight feathers appearing black and white with the wing closed. The bill is yellow with a red tip. Legs and feet are also yellow. Sexes alike. Young birds have brown mottling, a dark bill and pink legs.

Distribution: Central north-western North America, in the prairie regions, overwintering on the coast from Oregon south via California to Baja California.
Size: 23in (58cm).
Habitat: Coastal areas and inland.
Nest: Twigs and other vegetation.
Eggs: 2–3, buff-olive with blotches.
Food: Omnivorous.

Ring-billed gull

Larus delawarensis

Identification: Named for the black ring circling the yellow bill close to its tip. Typical gull patterning, with white head showing mottling in winter. Wings grayish, white markings on black wing tips. Legs yellow. Sexes alike. Young show light mottling.

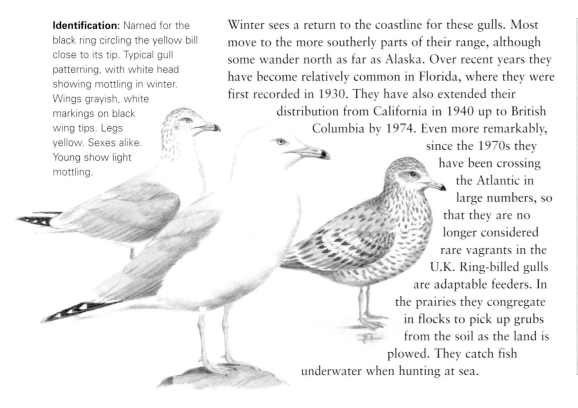

Winter sees a return to the coastline for these gulls. Most move to the more southerly parts of their range, although some wander north as far as Alaska. Over recent years they have become relatively common in Florida, where they were first recorded in 1930. They have also extended their distribution from California in 1940 up to British Columbia by 1974. Even more remarkably, since the 1970s they have been crossing the Atlantic in large numbers, so that they are no longer considered rare vagrants in the U.K. Ring-billed gulls are adaptable feeders. In the prairies they congregate in flocks to pick up grubs from the soil as the land is plowed. They catch fish underwater when hunting at sea.

Distribution: Range extends north to the prairie region of Canada, and east to the Great Lakes. Also extends down the Atlantic seaboard, past Florida and around the Caribbean to Central America.
Size: 21in (53cm).
Habitat: Coastal areas and inland.
Nest: Made of vegetation.
Eggs: 3, buff-colored and blotched.
Food: Omnivorous.

Glaucous-winged gull

Larus glaucescens

Glaucous-winged gulls breed in large colonies on islands and remote areas of coastline, returning during the spring and early summer to nest. Pairs are strongly territorial, driving away would-be rivals. However, violent squabbling between adjacent pairs can result in nearly half the chicks being killed, especially while they are young. When feeding, glaucous-winged gulls will hunt and scavenge for any edible animal matter, even learning to crack shellfish by dropping them onto rocks. In areas close to human habitation they have become scavengers, flying surprisingly long distances of over 40 miles (64km) to seek food on garbage dumps. As their range gradually expands, in some areas glaucous-winged gulls are increasingly hybridizing with related species, such as western gulls (*L. occidentalis*) in Washington state.

Identification: Pale gray wings and flight feathers with white edging, help to distinguish this gull. Head and underparts are white, the bill is yellow with a red spot, and the feet are pink. Sexes are alike. Young birds are predominantly fawn-brown with a dark bill.

Distribution: Extends right across the Pacific, from the coast of eastern Asia via the Aleutian Islands down the western coast of North America to Baja California.
Size: 27in (69cm).
Habitat: Ocean and shore.
Nest: Made of vegetation.
Eggs: 2–3, pale olive-brown with speckles.
Food: Omnivorous.

Dolphin gull (*Larus scoresbii*; previously *Leucophaeus scoresbii*): 18in (46cm)
Southern Chile around the Cape of Good Hope to southern Argentina and the Falklands. Light dolphin-gray head and underparts. Dark gray on head when not breeding. Wings slate-gray with white tips, flight feathers black with white markings. Red bill, legs, and feet. Sexes alike.

Olrog's gull (*Larus atlanticus*): 22in (56cm)
Ranges from Puerto Deseado in Argentina north to southeastern Uruguay; breeds solely in Argentina. White head and underparts, black wings. Black tail band, white band at bottom of tail feathers. Bill has yellowish base, blackish and red tip. Legs and feet yellow. Sexes alike.

Mew gull (*Larus canus*): 18in (46cm)
Widely distributed across Europe and Asia, as well as in western North America, ranging from Alaska southward to British Columbia, and seen inland to northern Saskatchewan. White head and underparts, gray back and wings. White tips to the flight feathers. Relatively small, greenish-yellow bill. Sexes alike.

Gray-headed gull (*Larus cirrocephalus*): 17in (43cm)
Found on both coasts of South America, ranging along the coastlines of Peru and Ecuador on the west. On the Atlantic coast from Argentina to central Brazil, ranging inland to Santa Fe. Characterized by gray head, with dark edge over back of head. Wings grayish, flight feathers black. Neck and underparts are white. Reddish bill, legs and feet. Sexes alike.

Belcher's gull

Band-tailed gull *Larus belcheri*

Belcher's gulls track the Humboldt Current, although much of their food is gathered along the shoreline rather than out over the sea. They will readily take eggs and young from colonies of other seabirds too. They generally associate in small groups, typically comprising less than 100 pairs. The largest colony is to be found on San Gallan Island, off central Peru, where thousands of these gulls may be present. Their eggs are laid on the ground, sometimes directly onto the sand above the high-water mark, or concealed among rocks on the shoreline. In the past, Belcher's gulls were subjected to heavy persecution at their breeding sites, since their droppings, known as guano, were sold in huge quantities as a fertilizer. Today their numbers can be adversely affected by the El Niño effect, which typically occurs every five years, altering the sea currents and thus the availability of fish in this region.

Identification: Dark wings and a broad black band across the base of the tail are evident in flight. This gull has a dark head in winter. Bill tip is red, with a black bar behind. Eyes have a yellow orbital ring. Sexes alike. Young birds have mottled brown wings and a dark head, with a black-tipped, dull yellow bill.

Distribution: Coastal area of South America, from northern Ecuador southward as far as central Chile, typically breeding between northern Peru and northern Chile.
Size: 20 1/2in (52cm).
Habitat: Ocean and shore.
Nest: Hollow on the ground.
Eggs: 1–3, dark olive-brown with speckles.
Food: Fish, shellfish and carrion.

LARGER SEABIRDS

Larger seabirds tend to be quite opportunistic in their feeding habits. Although they are able to catch fish very effectively, as shown by the gannet, some of these birds are often seen scavenging on the coastline or soaring around seabird colonies, seeking other opportunities to obtain food. This is a reflection of their aerial agility and strength. They tend to be long-lived as well.

Kelp gull

Larus dominicanus

These gulls have a wide global distribution, also occurring in the southern hemisphere along the shores of southern Africa, Australia and New Zealand. Birds belonging to the South American population may venture inland, sometimes being found on lakes in the Andean region. Their extensive range is matched by their opportunistic feeding habits. In addition to taking fish and crustaceans, they may attack other creatures ranging from geese and lambs to whales. Those gulls found in the Antarctic region, below Tierra del Fuego, remain there all year, frequenting open water away from the pack ice. The breeding period is typically between October and December. Pairs construct a relatively bulky nest from seaweed and similar material gathered on the shore, often concealed by rocks or trees which offer some security. The young fledge at seven weeks old.

Identification: A large, black-winged species with a white area at the rear of the flight feathers (most evident in flight). A red spot is present near the tip of the lower mandible. Sexes are alike. Dark area mottled brown in maturing young birds.

Distribution: Ranges from northern Peru down via Tierra del Fuego and up the Atlantic coast of South America to southern Brazil. Also present on the Falkland Islands.
Size: 26in (65cm).
Habitat: Ocean and shore.
Nest: Pile of vegetation.
Eggs: 3, olive-brown and speckled.
Food: Animal matter.

Black-legged kittiwake

Rissa tridactyla

Identification: Head usually whitish with a black marking on the back. Back and wings grayish. Flight feathers black, white spots on tips. Bill yellow, legs black. Sexes alike. Young birds have a black bill, plus a black band across the neck, wings, and on tail tip.

The largest breeding colonies of black-legged kittiwakes in the Arctic comprise literally hundreds of thousands of birds. They seek out high, steep-sided cliffs, with so many birds packing onto these ledges that both adults may encounter difficulty in landing at the same time. These sites are defended from takeover most of the year, not just during the nesting period. The nest is made using scraps of vegetation, especially seaweed, combined with feathers and bound together with mud. The narrow, shelf-like nature of the site may make it difficult for aerial predators to attack the kittiwakes, but in some parts of their range, such as Newfoundland, it also reduces breeding success. Away from the nest, these birds remain largely on the wing, swooping down to gather food from the ocean surface.

Distribution: Circumpolar, extending from the far north of Alaska southward as far as Mexico. Occurs down to the northeastern U.S.A. in the north Atlantic. Also on Greenland. The commonest gull in the Arctic region.
Size: 16in (40cm).
Habitat: Ocean and shore.
Nest: Cliff ledge.
Eggs: 2, buff-olive and blotched.
Food: Fish and marine invertebrates.

Iceland gull (*Larus glaucoides*): 25in (64cm) Iceland gulls occur in the north Atlantic, being present in Iceland, Greenland and northeast Canada. They overwinter south from Labrador down to Virginia and inland to the Great Lakes. This species has a relatively pale gray area on the back and wings, with the head and underparts being white. The bill is yellowish, with a red spot on the lower mandible. The legs and feet are pink. Sexes are alike.

Red-legged kittiwake (*Rissa brevirostris*): 15in (38cm) Red-legged kittiwakes are found in the northern Pacific, occurring off the southwest coast of Alaska and through the Aleutian Islands. Their head and underparts are white. The wings are relatively dark gray, with white edging on the longer feathers. The flight feathers are black with white markings. These birds have a white tail and yellowish bill. Their reddish legs and feet help to distinguish them from other species.

Northern Gannet

Sula bassana

This species is the largest of all gannets and can weigh up to 8lb (3.6kg). It is the only member of this group found around the North Atlantic. These gannets are powerful in the air. Their keen eyesight allows them to detect shoals of fish such as herring and mackerel in the ocean below. When feeding, gannets dive down into a shoal, often from a considerable height, seizing fish from under the water. Their streamlined shape also enables them to swim. Breeding occurs in the spring when the birds form large colonies in which there is often a lot of squabbling. The young mature slowly, and are unlikely to breed until they are at least four years of age.

Distribution: Occurs on both sides of the Atlantic, in North America ranging down most of the eastern coastline via the Gulf coast to Central America.
Size: 35–39in (88–100cm).
Habitat: Ocean.
Nest: Usually on cliffs, built from seaweed and other marine debris held together by droppings.
Eggs: 1, whitish.
Food: Fish.

Identification: Mainly white, aside from pale creamy yellow plumage on the head extending down the neck, and black flight feathers. Tail feathers are white, and the feet are dark gray. Sexes are alike. Young birds are dark brown in color.

Man o'war bird

Magnificent frigatebird *Fregata magnificens*

Distribution: Throughout the eastern Pacific Ocean, Gulf of Mexico and tropical parts of the Atlantic Ocean.
Size: 40in (101cm).
Habitat: Oceanic coastlines.
Nest: Platform of sticks.
Eggs: 1, white.
Food: Fish and invertebrates, including jellyfish. Also preys on baby turtles and seabird chicks.

These birds can glide for long periods, relying on their huge 7½ft (229cm) wingspan to help keep them airborne on the air currents. The male's throat pouch, prominent at close quarters, is far less visible when in the air. Pairs nest on the coast in areas where there are other smaller, fish-eating seabirds that can be harried for their catches, so that the frigatebirds do not have to obtain their own food. If necessary, however, they often catch flying fish, as well as other creatures found near the surface, including baby turtles. It is believed that although cock birds may breed annually if the opportunity is there, most hens nest only every second year.

Identification: Jet black, with a bare, bright red throat patch that can be inflated for display purposes. Hens are similar, but can be easily distinguished by white feathering on the breast. In immature birds, the plumage on the head is also white.

TERNS

Terns as a group can usually be distinguished quite easily, even from gulls, by their relatively elongated shape. Their long, pointed wings are an indication of their aerial ability, and some terns regularly fly longer distances than other migrants. Not surprisingly, their flight appears to be almost effortless. When breeding, terns generally nest in colonies.

Black skimmer

Rynchops niger

Distribution: Southern North America, from California in the west and North Carolina on the Atlantic coast south through Central and South America as far as Chile and northern parts of Brazil.
Size: 18in (46cm).
Habitat: Coastal areas and rivers.
Nest: Depression in the sand.
Eggs: 2–6, bluish with dark spots.
Food: Mainly fish.

As their name suggests, these narrow-bodied birds with long wings have a distinctive way of feeding, skimming over the surface of the water with their mouth open and lower bill beneath the water level. Contact with a fish will result in the skimmer snapping its bill shut, with its head briefly disappearing under its body before it moves forward and takes off. The catch is consumed either in flight or once it has landed. This fairly specialized method of fishing is most suited to the shallows, so when hunting inshore in rivers these birds favor areas near sandbars, becoming most active in tidal rivers at low water. Black skimmers breed colonially, with up to 1,000 pairs nesting on beaches in remote localities. The North American population overwinters in Central America. Those breeding in South America also head south, while pairs nesting along rivers in eastern Brazil move to coasts.

Identification: Recognizable by uniquely longer lower bill, red with a black tip. Top of head and wings black, white collar evident in winter. Face and underparts white. Females smaller. Young have brown mottled backs.

Sandwich tern

Cabot's tern *Sterna sandvicensis*

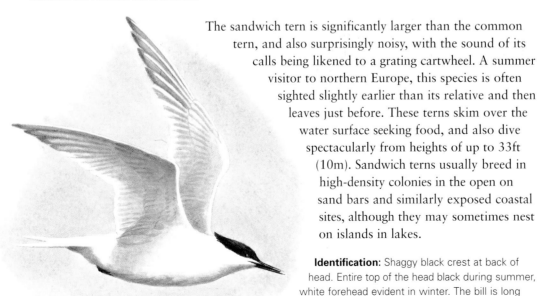

The sandwich tern is significantly larger than the common tern, and also surprisingly noisy, with the sound of its calls being likened to a grating cartwheel. A summer visitor to northern Europe, this species is often sighted slightly earlier than its relative and then leaves just before. These terns skim over the water surface seeking food, and also dive spectacularly from heights of up to 33ft (10m). Sandwich terns usually breed in high-density colonies in the open on sand bars and similarly exposed coastal sites, although they may sometimes nest on islands in lakes.

Identification: Shaggy black crest at back of head. Entire top of the head black during summer, white forehead evident in winter. The bill is long and black with a yellow tip. Rest of the head and underparts white, wings gray. Sexes are alike.

Distribution: Eastern North America, from Virginia southward through the Caribbean and down the Pacific coast of South America to Peru and Uruguay in the east.
Size: 17in (43cm).
Habitat: Coastal areas.
Nest: Scrape on the ground.
Eggs: 1–2, brownish white with darker markings.
Food: Fish, especially sand eels.

Gull-billed tern (*Sterna nilotica*): 17in (42cm)
The gull-billed tern is present in California, wintering as far south as Ecuador. Also from New Jersey, in the U.S.A., down as far as Argentina, on the Atlantic coast. Black cap on the head extends down to the nape of the neck. Frosty gray wings, back and tail feathers, which have white edges. Remainder of the plumage is white. In winter, the black cap is replaced by blackish ear coverts. Relatively short, black bill. Sexes are alike.

Common tern (*Sterna hirundo*): 14in (36cm)
This tern is widely distributed over much of northeastern North America, including the Great Lakes, and in parts of Central America, extending down the Pacific coast of South America. Also found down the eastern Atlantic coast of South America, to the Falkland Islands. Black on the top of the head extends down the back of the neck. Rest of the face and underparts whitish-gray. Back and wings grayish with long flight feathers. Narrow white streamers on the tail. Bill red, with a dark tip that turns black in the winter, as the plumage in front of the eyes becomes white. Legs and feet are red. Sexes are alike.

Roseate tern (*Sterna dougallii*): 14in (36cm)
The roseate tern is present in America along the Atlantic coast, from Nova Scotia to New York, and through much of the Caribbean region. Also occurs along the northern and northeastern coast of South America. There is a slight pinkish suffusion on the whitish underparts. Relatively long tail streamers and quite short wings. Bill primarily blackish with a red base in summer, when the entire top of the head turns black as well. The forehead turns white in winter. Sexes are alike.

Arctic tern

Sterna paradisaea

It can be very difficult to distinguish this species from the common tern, but the Arctic tern's bill is shorter and does not have a black tip in the summer. The tail, too, is longer, and the tail streamers are very evident in flight. Arctic terns undertake the most extensive migrations of any birds, flying almost from one end of the world to the other. Breeding in the vicinity of the Arctic Circle, these birds then head south, often beyond Africa to Antarctica, before repeating the journey the following year. However, it appears that at least some young birds stay for their first full year in the Antarctic Ocean. Arctic terns will nest communally, often frequenting islands for breeding purposes. They react aggressively to a potential predator in their midst, with a number of individuals turning on and mobbing any intruder. Arctic terns may steal food from other birds, such as puffins, in some parts of their range.

Identification: Black area covering the entire top of the head, with white chest and underparts. Wings gray. Bill dark red, becoming black in the winter when the forehead is white. Sexes are alike.

Distribution: Right across the Arctic region of North America, occurring as far south as British Columbia in the west and New York in the east. Overwinters at the tip of South America and in the Antarctic.
Size: 15in (38cm).
Habitat: Ocean and fresh water.
Nest: Hollow on the ground, lined with vegetation.
Eggs: 2, brownish, bluish or greenish with dark markings.
Food: Fish and invertebrates.

Bridled tern

Sterna anaethetus

This tern has a pantropical distribution, but rarely ventures further than 30 miles (50km) from the shore. It feeds mainly on small fish that school near the surface, swooping down to seize them in its bill. Breeding birds typically return each year to the same beach, and attempt to conceal the nest site among rocks or vegetation. Bridled terns often associate with related species, such as sooty terns, at this time. Incubation lasts about a month. The young stay in the nest for seven weeks and then remain with the colony for a month or so after fledging. They are unlikely to nest themselves until four years old. Bridled terns live for about 18 years.

Distribution: Two distinct American populations, one off the western coast of Central America; the other in the southern Caribbean.
Size: 15in (38cm).
Habitat: Ocean and shore.
Nest: Scrape on the ground.
Eggs: 1, brownish with darker markings.
Food: Fish, squid, and crustaceans.

Identification: Long narrow wings are brownish-black with a white collar. A black patch toward the back of the head narrows to a stripe connecting eyes and bill. White patch above the eye. White underparts and underwing coverts with black flight feathers. Deeply forked tail. Young have white edging to dark plumage on back and wings, black area on head is mottled.

SANDPIPERS

This group of waders tend to have a fairly compact body shape, and are not especially brightly colored.
They have thin, narrow bills that are used for probing, although they also provide a very efficient means
of grabbing the invertebrates that feature in their diets. The way in which they feed and move
on the ground can aid identification.

Spotted sandpiper

Actitis macularia

Distribution: Northern Alaska through most of Canada and the U.S.A. Moves south in the winter, heading down into South America.
Size: 8in (20cm).
Habitat: Shores and waterways.
Nest: Scrape in the ground.
Eggs: 4, greenish buff with brown spots.
Food: Invertebrates and fish.

In spotted sandpipers, some aspects of the traditional breeding roles of male and female are reversed. It is the female that returns first to the breeding grounds in the far north and establishes the breeding territory, driving off would-be rivals. During the breeding season she is likely to mate with a number of males, producing several clutches of eggs in succession. These are incubated and hatched by the male on his own, although occasionally the bond is strong enough for the female to stay and assist him. Spotted sandpipers start to leave the breeding grounds in June, heading south. Although some birds may only travel as far as British Columbia, the majority fly much closer to the equator, overwintering in the Caribbean and as far south as northern parts of Chile and Argentina. They are also not uncommon on the Galapagos Islands at this time.

Identification: Dark upperparts with darker brown speckling, white stripe above each eye and a long red bill with a dark tip. Underparts are white with dark spotting, with streaking on the sides of the face. Outside the breeding period the underparts are white, with speckling also absent from the wings, and the bill is yellowish-brown. Sexes are alike. Young birds resemble adults not in breeding plumage.

Dunlin

Red-breasted sandpiper *Calidris alpina*

Identification: The Alaskan (*C. a. pacifica*) and Canadian (*C. a. hudsonia*) races are the largest. Coloration is quite variable. Generally grayish head and wings in winter, with streaking on the breast. Underparts white. In summer, underparts display black streaking, with brownish and black on wings. Center of abdomen black, flanks white. Sexes alike.

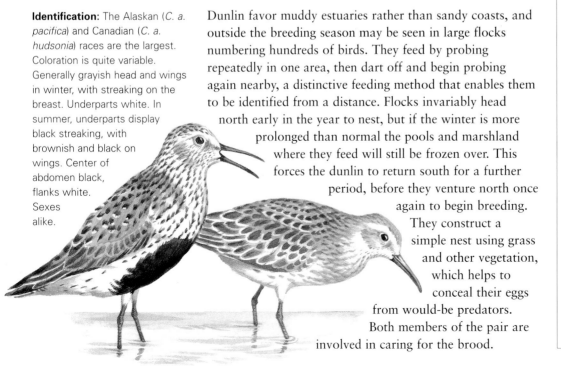

Dunlin favor muddy estuaries rather than sandy coasts, and outside the breeding season may be seen in large flocks numbering hundreds of birds. They feed by probing repeatedly in one area, then dart off and begin probing again nearby, a distinctive feeding method that enables them to be identified from a distance. Flocks invariably head north early in the year to nest, but if the winter is more prolonged than normal the pools and marshland where they feed will still be frozen over. This forces the dunlin to return south for a further period, before they venture north once again to begin breeding. They construct a simple nest using grass and other vegetation, which helps to conceal their eggs from would-be predators. Both members of the pair are involved in caring for the brood.

Distribution: Circumpolar, breeding along the coast of Alaska and through northern Canada around to the western shore of Hudson Bay. Winters south down the Pacific coast of North America, and along much of the Atlantic coast too.
Size: 8in (20cm).
Habitat: Frequents tundra and beaches.
Nest: Cup on the ground.
Eggs: 4, greenish brown with dark spotting.
Food: Invertebrates are the main constituent of diet.

Baird's sandpiper

Calidris bairdii

The female Baird's sandpiper lays her eggs on a scape in dry ground on the tundra, with both members of the pair incubating the clutch. Once the breeding season ends in July, these sandpipers begin to head south, with the females setting out first, followed by their partners and finally the young birds, who are unlikely to be seen in Argentina before the end of August. Here the sandpipers can be encountered in a wide range of habitats, with some found in the vicinity of lakes in the high Andes. They start to head north again during March, passing back over Central America and the prairies of North America, where they are likely to be observed during late April and early May. Baird's sandpiper is less social by nature than some of its kind and does not form large groups when feeding. These birds often prefer to seek their food along the shoreline, rather than actually wading.

Identification: Mottled appearance over the back and wings, with more of a striped pattern on the sides of the face and upper chest during the breeding period. Underparts are white, and the narrow bill is blackish. Upperparts more uniform in color, with light edging to the brownish plumage. Sides of the face whitish with a brownish breast band. Legs and feet are dark. Sexes are alike. Young birds have an evident scaly patterning on their wings and streaky buff feathering on the chest.

Distribution: Summer breeding range is circumpolar. Overwintering grounds are mainly in the southern half of South America, including the Falkland Islands.
Size: 7^1/$_2$in (19cm).
Habitat: Breeds on tundra.
Nest: Scrape in the ground.
Eggs: 4, olive with dark markings.
Food: Invertebrates.

Sanderling (*Calidris alba*): 8in (20cm)
Breeds in the far north of Canada and Greenland, overwintering along the Atlantic coast of the U.S.A. down through the Caribbean. Also present from southern Alaska right down the Pacific coast. Reddish coloration and black speckling on the breast. The underparts are white, while the back and wings are gray with black and buff markings. In winter plumage, reddish markings are less evident, but a broad wing bar with black edging is seen in flight. Sexes are alike.

Red-necked stint (*Calidris ruficollis*): 6in (15cm)
Migrates regularly from eastern Asia across the Bering Sea to western Alaska and its offshore islands. Variable depth of reddish coloration on the head and upper chest, with the underparts being white. In paler individuals throat area may be whitish. Wings are chestnut and black, with white edging to the plumage. Bill and legs are blackish. Sexes are alike.

Purple sandpiper (*Calidris maritima*): 9in (23cm)
This species breeds on the southern coast of Greenland, plus Queen Elizabeth and neighboring islands off Canada's northern coast. Streaked patterning is evident on the head, with a dark crescent-shaped marking seen behind the eyes. The back is mottled, with the wings being mainly brownish. Underparts becoming whiter, with striations down the flanks. The bill and legs are yellowish in color, and the bill has a dark tip. Dark, grayish-brown head in winter plumage. Sexes are alike.

Stilt sandpiper

Calidris himantopus

The long legs of stilt sandpipers help distinguish them from similar species. Wading through water, they will submerge their heads as they search for food such as aquatic snails. They are observed feeding with dowitchers. Males lay claim to breeding territories on the tundra, flying conspicuously and calling loudly to attract females. The pair both incubate the eggs, the cock bird typically sitting through the day and his partner at night. In due course, they leave their young for the southerly wintering grounds. From mid-July the females head south, followed by their partners. Fledglings spend a further month before departing. Most fly straight down across North America, but some take a more easterly route down the Atlantic coast.

Identification: Breeding adults have a chestnut patch on each side of the head, conspicuous behind the eyes. White underparts are heavily barred, top of the head is darker. Black and white markings on back and wings. In winter, much grayer overall, with underparts much whiter. Long, narrow bill is still blackish. Sexes alike. Young lack chestnut patches.

Distribution: Northern Alaska and Canada eastwards as far as Hudson's Bay. Moves south to southern California, Florida, and parts of South America for the winter.
Size: 8^1/$_2$in (22cm).
Habitat: Tundra and coastal areas.
Nest: Hidden in grass.
Eggs: 4, buff with brown markings.
Food: Mainly invertebrates.

WADERS

Like their smaller counterparts, these birds may travel long distances to and from their breeding grounds, which are typically in the Arctic region. The nature of the climate here means the nesting period is necessarily short, and cover in this treeless part of the world is limited. In this environment, barred plumage of any type is helpful in providing camouflage.

Wilson's phalarope

Phalaropus tricolor

This is the largest species of phalarope. It moves inland when overwintering in South America, and is found around lakes and ponds rather than at sea like its relatives. A distinctive feature of Wilson's phalarope is the way its legs change color during the year, being dull yellow in non-breeding birds before darkening to black at the start of the nesting period. Hens are more colorful, and will compete with each other to attract mates. Having laid her eggs, the hen leaves her partner to hatch them and rear their chicks alone. Wilson's phalarope has a very slender bill, which enables it to hunt invertebrates very effectively. Unlike other phalaropes this species does not have webbed feet, and so swims less frequently, but it does possess an unusual habit of stirring up the water by spinning around, and then looking for invertebrate food items that have been disturbed.

Identification: Breeding females have a broad reddish area down the side of the neck, with similar spots of coloration on the gray wings. Orange feathering on the throat. Underparts white with yellowish edging. Cock birds are duller in color, with brownish wings. In winter plumage, both sexes have gray upperparts and white underparts. Young birds have brownish, mottled wings and white underparts.

Distribution: Generally breeds in an area from southern Yukon and Minnesota south to California and Kansas. Occasionally in the Great Lakes region, and also Massachusetts. Migrates south to the tropics for the winter, but some individuals may remain in California and Texas.
Size: 9$\frac{1}{2}$in (24cm).
Habitat: Coastal bays and lakes.
Nest: Scrape on the ground.
Eggs: 4, buff with brown spotting.
Food: Invertebrates.

Red phalarope

Gray phalarope *Phalaropus fulicaria*

Identification: Breeding hens have reddish underparts, black on top of head, and white cheek patches. Cocks are less vividly colored. In winter, head is mainly white with black near the eyes; back is gray with a black strip reaching to the tail. Young have orangish chest band.

This phalarope is tied much more closely to the ocean, but may be seen on inland water after severe storms. Unlike all other waders, it migrates over the oceans rather than over land. In its North American range it occurs predominantly along the Pacific coast, with peak numbers being seen here in fall. They are often sighted in the company of whales, feeding on the skin parasites of these marine mammals. Red phalaropes also congregate in areas where plankton is present, providing them with rich feeding. They feed close to the water surface, sometimes dipping down with their strong bills to obtain food. In their breeding grounds in the far north the female leaves after egg-laying, sometimes seeking another partner. Male red phalaropes hatch and rear the young alone.

Distribution: Breeding range includes north Alaska and Canada up to the Queen Elizabeth Islands. Migrates to South America for winter, when often sighted at sea.
Size: 8$\frac{1}{2}$in (22cm).
Habitat: Tundra, coast and ocean.
Nest: Scrape on the ground.
Eggs: 2–4, buff-olive with dark spots.
Food: Invertebrates and fish.

Long-billed curlew

Numenius americanus

The distinctive song of these birds helps to explain their name, and announces their return to the northern breeding grounds each spring. Over the past century, however, their numbers have declined significantly. They nest in grassland areas, but are most likely to be seen feeding in groups on mudflats when the tide is low. They use their long bill to probe in the mud for worms and similar edible items. They are shy by nature, and will not generally tolerate a close approach. Long-billed curlews move south from May onward, traveling relatively short distances in flocks to their wintering grounds, which include parts of Central America. They are opportunistic feeders, particularly when migrating. Their diet may include marine invertebrates caught on beaches and grasshoppers on the prairies, as well as berries and even seeds on occasion.

Identification: Brownish overall, with barring running across the feathers of the back and wings. Underparts slightly paler, less cinnamon in coloration, with striations becoming less apparent on the abdomen. Long, slightly down-curving bill, with gray legs and feet. Sexes are alike. Young birds are similar but have shorter, straighter bills.

Distribution: Breeding range extends from southern Canada down to northern California, running through parts of Utah, New Mexico, and Texas. Overwinters in southern U.S.A. southward.
Size: 23in (58cm).
Habitat: Salt marshes and prairies.
Nest: Grass-lined scrape.
Eggs: 4, olive with darker spotting.
Food: Mainly invertebrates, occasionally berries, seeds.

Bristle-thighed curlew (*Numenius tahitiensis*): 18in (46cm)
The bristle-thighed curlew breeds only in Alaska, overwintering in parts of Asia, including Pacific islands. Very similar to the whimbrel, with mottled plumage and a dark streak behind the eyes, but distinguishable by the buff coloration of the rump and tail. There are stiff feathers on the flanks. Black, down-curving bill and gray legs. Sexes are alike.

Red-necked phalarope (*Phalaropus lobatus*): 8in (20cm)
Red-necked phalaropes breed throughout Alaska and northern Canada. Spend the winter largely at sea in the southern hemisphere. Females have a chestnut area on the neck which extends to the upper chest. Grayer area on the sides of the chest spread over the wings, which have yellow barring. White underparts. Male paler, with white throat. Grayish-black upperparts, with white underparts in the winter.

Magellanic plover (*Pluvianellus socialis*): 8in (20cm)
This species occurs on the southeastern side of South America, in coastal parts of Argentina. Pale gray upperparts, with a darker eye stripe, white throat and a broad gray band across the chest. Remainder of the underparts are white. A darker gray central stripe is evident on the tail. Bill blackish, legs pinkish. Sexes are alike. Young birds have mottled gray upperparts and white streaking on the breast.

Whimbrel

Numenius phaeopus

The relatively large size of the whimbrel makes it conspicuous among smaller waders. Although it may probe for food, it often snatches crabs scampering across the sand. In their tundra nesting grounds, whimbrels have a more varied diet, eating berries and insects too. Both adults help to incubate and raise the young. They begin their journey south in July, when they are often seen flying over land, seeking out inland grassy areas, including golf courses, in search of food. Two months later, some are sighted at Tierra del Fuego, at the southern tip of South America. However, many whimbrels spend winter on North American coasts. They return to their breeding grounds by April and May.

Distribution: Breeds from western Alaska along the northern coast of Canada to southern part of Hudson Bay. Winters on southern coasts of California, and on the east coast as far north as Virginia.
Size: 17 1/2in (45cm).
Habitat: Tundra and shore.
Nest: Grass-lined scrape.
Eggs: 4, olive with dark blotches.
Food: Invertebrates, berries.

Identification:
Brown crown with lighter central stripe. Fainter brown line through eyes. Brown streaks on silvery background on rest of body, back and wings darker brown. Long, down-curving bill. Sexes alike. Young have shorter, straighter bill.

OTHER NORTHERN WADERS

In the inhospitable region of the far north there is a restricted choice of food, but the presence of mosquito larvae, breeding in the shallow pools that develop here as the water is trapped by the deep-frozen permafrost beneath, guarantees a valuable source of protein for nesting birds, which they can use as a rearing food for their young.

Willet

Catoptrophorus semipalmatus

The loud calls of the willet help to betray its presence, particularly as when alarmed it calls more frequently. Its unusual name is derived from its contact call, which sounds like "pee ... wee ... willet." Occurring in small flocks, willets keep in touch with each other by calling, especially if disturbed on their feeding grounds. They are found in a range of habitats, from mud flats to salt marshes, sometimes venturing into water to grab prey. Small crabs often feature prominently in their diet. Willets breed over a relatively wide area. The Caribbean population does not stray far, but those breeding further north head toward warmer climates in July. The young birds later follow their parents.

Identification: Breeding adults have a vibrant mottled appearance, with a white central area to the abdomen, and grayish wings with black flight feathers. Birds from the east have more evident barring than those from the west, as well as being slightly smaller too. The bill is long and straight. In winter plumage, gray overall becoming lighter on the underparts. Sexes are alike, with brownish tone to the back and wings.

Distribution: Breeding range extends from central Canada to northeastern parts of California and Nevada. A second breeding population extends south from Nova Scotia down along the Gulf coast.
Size: 15in (38cm).
Habitat: Muddy shores and coastal marshes.
Nest: Grassy scrape.
Eggs: 3–4, buff with darker spots.
Food: Invertebrates and seeds.

Greater yellowlegs

Tringa melanoleuca

The muskeg area of Canada, characterized by its marshy ponds and relatively few trees, is the greater yellowlegs' breeding habitat. They move further south for the winter, where they are found on muddy coasts and sometimes further inland, in areas of both brackish and fresh water. These sandpipers will wade into deep water, up to the top of their legs, and have developed diverse feeding techniques. They chase after small fish, bending to seize them with their long bill, and pick up invertebrates on the shoreline. These waders undertake a relatively long migration, with some birds leaving as early as July, stragglers as late as November. They return from South America in March, reaching the breeding grounds again in April. Some young birds may remain behind, not heading north until ready to breed the following year.

Identification: Legs can vary in color from yellow through to orange. Black lines on the neck are more distinctive in breeding plumage, with brown areas apparent on the wings. Center of the abdomen is white. The contrast in coloration is less distinctive in birds in winter plumage, with the brown and black areas in the wings becoming gray. Sexes are alike. In young birds, more brownish coloring is seen over the wings.

Distribution: Breeds in southwest Alaska, and across Canada to Newfoundland. Overwinters in coastal and southern U.S.A., from Washington southward and Virginia in the east, and through South America.
Size: 14in (36cm).
Habitat: Wet meadows and marshes.
Nest: Scrape on the ground.
Eggs: 4, dark spotted buff or grayish.
Food: Small fish and invertebrates.

Wandering tattler

Heteroscelus incanus

As its name suggests, the wandering tattler travels over a very wide area and can be found in a diverse range of habitats, depending on the time of year. Pairs breed alongside flowing streams in Alaska, nesting on the ground on gravel, sometimes constructing a nest for their eggs. They remain there between late May and August, before heading south to their wintering grounds, which include Hawaii. It is not common to see wandering tattlers feeding in large groups, but they will roost communally, and are not unduly shy. They sometimes seek to avoid danger by freezing rather than taking flight, although they are very agile on the wing and able to fly with little obvious effort. Away from their breeding grounds, these waders are often found in rocky areas, rather than the mudflats favored by the related Siberian or gray-tailed tattler (*H. brevipes*).

Distribution: Breeds in south-central Alaska and northern British Columbia. Overwinters on Pacific islands and along the Pacific coast from central California south as far as Ecuador.
Size: 11in (28cm).
Habitat: Coastal areas and mountain streams.
Nest: Made of twigs and leaves.
Eggs: 4, greenish and spotted.
Food: Invertebrates.

Identification: Dark gray upperparts, with the head and breast being heavily streaked and barred with gray markings. Pointed black bill, with yellow legs and feet. Outside the breeding season the markings on the underparts are replaced by consistent gray coloration on the breast and along the flanks, with a white central area on the underparts. Sexes are alike. Young birds similar but distinguishable by white spots on their upperparts.

Lesser yellowlegs (*Tringa flavipes*): 10¹/₂in (27cm)
Breeds from Alaska southward across Canada to southern shores of Hudson Bay. Winters further south from Florida along Gulf coast and also on Pacific coasts into Central America. Similar to greater yellowlegs, but smaller. Bill is shorter, darker, and without upward curve. Barring on flanks when breeding is also less evident.

Black turnstone (*Arenaria melanocephala*): 9in (24cm)
Breeds around the Alaskan coast, moving further south to Baja California in winter. Mainly black upperparts with some white markings, including conspicuous spot above bill. Underparts white. In winter head, back, and breast are brown.

Hudsonian godwit (*Limosa haemastica*): 15in (38cm)
Far north of North America, wintering in the southeastern part of South America. Grayish head and neck, with chestnut featuring on the underparts. Speckled white plumage on the wings, with distinctive black underwing feathering. Long bill, reddish at the base. Hen is larger, with whiter underparts.

Buff-breasted sandpiper (*Tryngites subruficollis*): 8in (20cm)
Northern coast of Alaska eastward to the Queen Elizabeth Islands when breeding, migrates to South America for winter. Buff coloration on sides of face and underparts, becoming white. Large eyes, narrow black bill, yellow legs. Blackish-brown feathering edged with white on the back. Sexes are alike.

Ruddy turnstone

Arenaria interpres

Pairs of ruddy turnstones return to their Arctic breeding grounds during May, using their distinctive facial patterning and fanning their black and white tails for display. They will subsequently travel widely to their overwintering grounds, which lie in coastal areas and even on Pacific islands such as Hawaii. As their name suggests, ruddy turnstones have a distinctive way of seeking food. They utilize their strong neck and bill to flip over small rocks, shells, and seaweed on the beach, which may be hiding small crabs and other invertebrates. In sandy areas these sandpipers will dig too. They also scavenge on the remains of invertebrates caught by oystercatchers for example, and will even eat carrion. Ruddy turnstones are relatively tame birds and often seek to run away from danger, only taking flight as a last resort.

Distribution: Northwestern Alaska and Canadian Arctic, including Queen Elizabeth Islands. Found all along the coastline from Oregon to Connecticut in the U.S.A., and all around South America.
Size: 9¹/₂in (24cm).
Habitat: Coastal tundra.
Nest: Scrape on the ground.
Eggs: 4, grayish-green with darker markings.
Food: Invertebrates.

Identification: Distinctive ruddy coloration on wings in breeding plumage, broken by black. Black markings around the eye down onto the chest, with remaining underparts white. Bill black, legs reddish. Hens not as brightly colored. In winter, brown and blackish streaks appear on head and back, with black wing patch and bib unaltered. Young birds have browner heads.

PLOVERS AND DOWITCHERS

Many shorebirds occur over a wide area, but on occasion they may additionally be sighted in areas well outside their natural range. The young birds especially can become disorientated and end up in the wrong location, sometimes after being blown off course by gales and storms, which may force them to travel further inland than normal.

Ringed plover

Charadrius hiaticula

Distribution: Far northeast of North America, in Canada and also present on Greenland.
Size: 7¹/₂in (19cm).
Habitat: Coastal areas and tundra.
Nest: Bare scrape on the ground.
Eggs: 4, stone-buff with black markings.
Food: Freshwater and marine invertebrates.

Ringed plovers are relatively small in size. These waders have strong migratory instincts. They breed mainly in the far north, migrating to Canada via Iceland and Greenland from more southerly areas in Europe. This is quite different from the more standard migratory patterns among shorebirds, which generally move in a north-south direction through America. Ringed plovers typically breed on beaches and on the tundra. They can be seen in reasonably large flocks outside the nesting season, when they often seek food in tidal areas. If a nesting bird is disturbed it will try to lure the would-be predator away from the vicinity of its nest site by feigning a wing injury. The mottled appearance of the eggs and the absence of an elaborate nest provide camouflage.

Identification: Black mask extends over the forehead and across the eyes. There is a white patch above the bill and just behind the eyes. A broad black band extends across the chest, forming a bib. The underparts are otherwise white. Wings are grayish-brown, and the bill is orange with a black tip. In winter plumage the black areas are reduced, apart from the bill which becomes entirely blackish. White areas extend from the forehead above the eyes. Cheek patches are grayish-brown with a grayish-brown band on the upper breast. Hens have less black on their head.

Wilson's plover

Thick-billed plover *Charadrius wilsonia*

Wilson's plovers, also known as thick-billed plovers, are widely distributed in North America. They frequent sandy coasts and mud flats, where they use their relatively large bill to feed on crabs and other invertebrates. They tend to avoid hunting directly on the shoreline, preferring the upper areas of the beach instead. Wilson's plovers nest on sandy beaches, sometimes close to coastal lagoons, but they do not usually venture far inland. In winter the northern population heads south as far as Brazil, leaving just a remnant overwintering population in southern Florida. On the Pacific coast, many of the Wilson's plovers that spend the summer there retreat as far south as central Peru for the duration of the winter. The young birds molt rapidly, and are indiscernible from the adults within months of fledging. It is not uncommon to see Wilson's plovers in the company of similar species.

Distribution: Breeding range from southern New Jersey south to Texas and Florida. Winters mainly in Florida, along the Gulf coast and in northern South America.
Size: 8in (20cm).
Habitat: Sandy beaches and mud flats.
Nest: Scrape in sand.
Eggs: 3–4, buff with dark markings.
Food: Invertebrates.

Identification: In breeding plumage males have a black area on the center of the crown and a broad black chest bar, with brown areas on the head and extending down over the wings. The underparts are white. Hens lack the male's black areas, which are replaced by brown feathering; this also applies to cock birds outside the breeding period. Young birds have scaly areas on the head, chest, back, and wings.

Short-billed dowitcher

Limnodromus griseus

Breeds in northern areas, typically the marshy and sparsely wooded muskegs of Canada. The short-billed dowitcher is one of the first shorebirds that nest in this region to head back south again, with females leaving in late June. The young will follow slightly behind the adults, seeking out their coastal wintering grounds. These dowitchers can be encountered on both Atlantic and Pacific coasts, as well as through the Caribbean region, though some travel down to South America. The three distinctive races all follow separate routes as they leave the Arctic. Short-billed dowitchers form large flocks in their wintering grounds. They feed by probing with their bills for edible items underwater, often submerging their heads while doing so. On the return journey, southerly populations start to pass through the U.S.A. from March onward.

Identification: Crown of breeding birds dark, with pale orange area on underparts broken by blackish speckling. Wings are black and gray with pale edging, although races differ. Sexes are similar. Silvery-gray winter plumage, becoming paler on the underparts. Young birds resemble breeding adults, but underparts are much whiter.

Distribution: Breeding range from southern Alaska across central Canada to Hudson Bay and northern Quebec. Overwinters on coasts south from California in the west and Virginia in the east as far as tip of South America.
Size: 11in (28cm).
Habitat: Tundra and tidal marshes.
Nest: Scrape on the ground.
Eggs: 4–5, white.
Food: Invertebrates.

Black-bellied plover (*Pluvialis squatarola*): 12in (30cm)
Breeds from northern Alaska eastward to the vicinity of Hudson's Bay. Migrates south for the winter to the Pacific coast of North America and via Florida through the Caribbean. Prominent black area on the face and belly, with white patches on the sides of the body. Mottled black and white plumage over the wings and white undertail coverts. Hens are similar, but black on the underparts has white barring. During the winter upperparts are silvery-gray, with similar streaking on the white underparts.

Pacific golden plover (*Pluvialis fulva*): 10in (25cm)
Breeds in western Alaska, overwintering mainly in Asia, but some birds remain in North America, being sighted as far south as California. Black areas on sides of face extend over chest and underparts, which are bordered by white feathering and barring. Coarse mottled pattern of brown, black and white plumage on the wings. In winter plumage underparts are mottled with black and white feathering too. Sexes alike.

Long-billed dowitcher (*Limnodromus scolopaceus*): 12in (30cm)
Breeds on the north Alaskan coast and offshore islands, migrating south to the Pacific coast and across the southern U.S.A. into Central America. Only the hen has a longer bill than the short-billed dowitcher. In breeding plumage all of the underparts are orangish, with a white stripe above the eyes. In winter, these birds become silvery-gray with whiter underparts.

American oystercatcher

Haematopus palliatus

This wader's large size and noisy nature make it quite conspicuous. The powerful bill is an adaptable tool, used to force mussel shells apart, hammer limpets off groynes, prey on crabs and even catch worms in the sand. Individuals will defend favored feeding sites such as mussel beds from others of their kind. They are not likely to be observed in large groups, and tend to be quite sedentary. It takes young birds two years to gain their full adult coloration.

Identification: Black head, white underparts, brown back and wings. White wing bar. Large reddish-orange bill, reddish eye ring, legs and feet pink. Sexes alike. Young birds have brown head with speckled wings.

Distribution: Breeding range from Baja California in the west to Massachusetts in the east. Winters along the Gulf coast from North Carolina, and into South America.
Size: 18¹/₂in (47cm).
Habitat: Tidal mud flats.
Nest: Scrape on the ground.
Eggs: 2–4, light buff with blackish-brown markings.
Food: Various invertebrates.

LARGER WADERS

Colorful in some cases and highly adapted to their environment, larger waders use their bills as sensory devices, probing for aquatic prey concealed in mud or under loose stones underwater. Their long legs facilitate feeding in beyond the shallows, while their height allows them to spot potential prey, such as a shoal of fish, from some distance away.

Scarlet ibis

Eudocimus ruber

The beautiful appearance of these ibis is derived in part from their diet, which helps to provide the pigment that gives them their characteristic coloration. They live in groups and comb the mud flats for crabs and other food with their stout but pointed bills. The scarlet ibis prefers to nest on islands, building a loose nest of sticks off the ground, often in mangrove swamps above the waterline. This can bring dangers, however, from crocodiles that lie in wait, hoping to seize chicks that have just left the nest and fall into the water.

Identification: Brilliant scarlet plumage, besides blackish ends to four longest primary flight feathers. Bill black in breeding birds, reddish rest of year. Sexes alike. Young birds are duller, with brown and white areas.

Distribution: Concentrated in northern South America, from parts of Colombia and Ecuador through Venezuela (including Guyana [formerly British Guiana] to French Guiana) along the coast of Brazil to the Amazon Delta. Has reappeared around São Paulo at Santos Bay, Brazil.
Size: 27in (69cm).
Habitat: Mangroves, mud flats and estuaries.
Nest: Sticks.
Eggs: 2, pale blue or greenish with brown blotches.
Food: Crustaceans, small fish and amphibians.

White ibis

Eudocimus albus

These ibis use their long bill to probe underwater, seeking out the crabs that figure prominently in their diet, although they will also prey on other creatures, including fish and amphibians. White ibis are usually seen in groups, roosting and breeding in colonies which may number many thousands of birds, and which are frequently centred in mangrove areas. The eggs take three weeks to hatch, with the new chicks initially having a covering of black down. The young will leave the nest five weeks after hatching. Although populations are largely sedentary, these ibis may fly some distance to find food. When flying in groups they adopt a typical V-shaped formation. Numbers have declined in some areas, but there are still colonies of up to 40,000 ibis in parts of southeastern U.S.A.

Identification: Snow-white plumage and red legs. Reddish bill with a darker tip and bare reddish facial skin, which becomes darker as birds come into breeding condition. Blackish tips to the primary feathers are revealed in flight. Sexes alike. Young birds have brown streaking on the head and neck, brownish wings and white underparts. Bill and legs paler than in adults.

Distribution: From North Carolina in the east, west to Baja California, and down through the Caribbean and Central America to Colombia and northwest Venezuela. Extends to western Ecuador and northwestern Peru.
Size: 25in (64cm).
Habitat: Mangrove and wetland areas.
Nest: Platform of sticks.
Eggs: 2–3, bluish-green with dark blotches.
Food: Crustaceans, small vertebrates.

Little egret (*Egretta garzetta*): 26in (65cm)
One of the Old World species that occasionally crops up on the east coast of North America during the summer, recorded from Newfoundland down to the mid-Atlantic states. White plumage with a blue-gray area at the base of the bill. Long white nuptial plumes at breeding time. Legs are blackish, but with highly distinctive yellowish toes. Sexes are alike.

Glossy ibis (*Plegadis falcinellus*): 26in (65cm)
Eastern coast of the U.S.A., down through Florida and along the Gulf coast. Has been recorded as far west as Colorado. Dark brown overall, but some white streaking on head. Wings and rump green, legs and bill dark. Green and brownish plumage on head replaced by streaking in winter. Sexes are alike.

Cattle egret (*Bubulcus ibis*): 22in (56cm)
Established in America after arriving from Africa. Moved north to Florida by the 1950s, reaching California by the 1960s. Pale buff coloration on head and throat extends onto breast, also on back and rump. Remaining plumage white. May have traces of white plumage around yellow bill.

Western reef-heron (*Egretta gularis*): 25$\frac{1}{2}$in (65cm)
Occurs on Puerto Rico, Barbados and St. Lucia. Dark phase birds are gray with darker band on wings and browner underparts. White at base of bill, down to throat. Legs dark, with yellowish-green feet. White phase birds are pure white with two long plumes on hindneck. Sexes are alike. Young birds are brown and white.

Tricolored heron

Egretta tricolor

Although most commonly found in coastal areas, tricolored herons may occasionally be seen inland as well, with breeding records from both Kansas and North Dakota. They frequent both mud flats and mangrove swamps, the latter providing them with trees where they can construct their nests in relative safety. They prefer to nest there rather than on the ground. Although rather solitary when seeking food, these herons will breed in relatively large colonies, sometimes alongside related species, with as many as 1,500 nests being recorded in the same area. Tricolored herons display some seasonal movements, with the U.S.A. populations usually heading south to northern parts of South America to overwinter, swelling the local population. In recent years the species has also ranged further north up the U.S. Atlantic coast.

Distribution: From southern and eastern parts of the U.S.A. through the Caribbean and along the northern coast of South America. Also present on the western coast, through Ecuador down to northern Peru.
Size: 26in (66cm).
Habitat: Salt marshes and mangrove swamps.
Nest: Platform of sticks.
Eggs: 3–4, greenish-blue.
Food: Fish and other aquatic creatures.

Identification: Bluish head, back and wings, with white underparts to the body and a brownish area over the back. Sexes alike. Young birds have a chestnut hind neck, with the chestnut extending onto the wing coverts.

Reddish egret

Egretta rufescens

Only young reddish egrets are likely to venture inland, and even they are a rare sight. These egrets are most commonly sighted around the shoreline. They are solitary hunters, catching food in a variety of ways. This includes scratching in the water with a foot to stir up creatures lurking on the bottom, and opening the wings to create a shadow on the water, which may draw fish within reach. They may even chase larger quarry through the shallows. Reddish egrets prefer to nest on islands or in mangroves, which provide some protection from predators. The color morphs can be distinguished on hatching, since the white birds have corresponding white down. This form is only likely to be seen in the Bahamas, however. The overall range of reddish egrets has declined during the past century, initially as the result of hunting, as plumage was used to decorate hats.

Identification: Shaggy reddish-chestnut plumage on head and neck extends to upper chest, with grayish-black plumage over rest of body, and cobalt-blue legs. Pure white form has same bill and leg colors. Plumage less shaggy and bill dark when not breeding. Sexes alike. Young birds grayish, with cinnamon on head.

Distribution: Extreme south of the U.S.A., around the Gulf coast on the eastern side, and eastern Mexico as well as parts of the Caribbean. Also occurs in South America in the most northerly parts of Colombia and Venezuela.
Size: 32in (81cm).
Habitat: Shallow salt pans.
Nest: Made of sticks.
Eggs: 2–7, greenish-blue.
Food: Mainly fish.

WATERFOWL AND RAILS

While members of both these groups are typically more widespread in freshwater zones, there are certain species which have adapted to living in proximity to tidal areas. In the case of rails, the regular fall-off in water level in this type of environment provides increased feeding opportunities. Like waterfowl, they can feed both in water and on land.

Mottled duck

Anas fulvigula

Distribution: From just north of Florida on Atlantic coast around the Gulf of Mexico down to south Mexico. Now introduced to South Carolina.
Size: 22in (56cm).
Habitat: Coastal waters.
Nest: Made of grass.
Eggs: 4–18, grayish-green.
Food: Aquatic vegetation and invertebrates.

Closely related to the well-known mallard (*Anas platyrhynchos*), these dabbling ducks are usually encountered in relatively shallow waters, where they dip their heads down under the surface to obtain water plants and invertebrates. During the summer they are more likely to be found on stretches of fresh water, but will usually be seen in salt marshes through the winter period. Flocks start to pair off early in the year, beginning in January. They breed on the ground, choosing a secluded site under vegetation for their nest and lining it with feathers. The incubation period takes approximately four weeks, with the young ducklings having dark brown upperparts at first, and much lighter underparts. They will be sexually mature at one year old. Mottled ducks can be distinguished from mallards by their darker overall plumage, with females having no white area in their tails.

Identification: Drake has a yellow bill with a dark tip. Predominantly brownish plumage, with paler, unstreaked sides to the face and on the throat. Mottled underparts, with more evident scalloping to the feathers on the flanks, and over the back and wings. Blue wing speculum. Yellowish-orange legs and feet. Sexes similar, although females can be instantly recognized by the greener coloration of their bills.

Brant goose

Branta bernicla

Brant geese start breeding in June. A site close to the tundra shoreline is often favored, with pairs lining the scrape with plant matter and down. It takes about nine weeks from egg-laying until the young geese are ready to leave the nest, subsequently heading south with their parents to milder climates for the winter. The goslings may then not breed until they

are three years old. While on the tundra, brant geese will graze mainly on lichens, moss and other terrestrial vegetation. Over the winter period they will feed mainly on aquatic plants, including seaweed, which is plucked from under the water as the goose up-ends its body. On land, these geese graze by nibbling the shoots directly from plants.

Distribution: Circumpolar, ranging from the far north of the U.S.A. and Canada eastward to Greenland. Winters further south along both the Pacific and the Atlantic coasts of North America, as well as in Europe and Asia.
Size: 26in (66cm).
Habitat: Bays and estuaries.
Nest: Scrape on the ground.
Eggs: 1–10, whitish.
Food: Plant matter.

Identification: Black head and neck, with trace of white on lower neck. Wings gray-black. White flanks with barring. Abdomen white in American brant (*B. b. hrota*) from the east, but often dark in its western relative, the black brant (*B. b. nigricans*). Sexes are alike. Young may lack white neck patches.

Clapper rail

Rallus longirostris

The population of clapper rails has declined in some areas, notably on the west coast, as a result of the introduction of red foxes (*Vulpes vulpes*), which hunt these birds to the extent that the brightly colored subspecies *R. l. levipes* is now regarded as endangered. There are approximately 21 different subspecies of this rail recognized through their New World distribution, differing not just in coloration but also in size. Clapper rails were given their name because of the sound of their distinctive calls. They use their long bills to probe for food, hunting by sight in most cases, although they can catch fish by diving underwater. The best time to spot these secretive birds is when the tide is low, but they rarely emerge from cover for long and will dart back at the slightest hint of danger. Pairs are very territorial when nesting.

Identification: Grayish sides to the face, with a speckled brown back. The throat is white with variable brown and white barring on the flanks and white undertail coverts. The chest area can be cinnamon, although duller in some cases, depending on the species concerned. Long, dark-colored straight bill. Hens are significantly smaller in size.

Distribution: Occurs mainly in coastal areas, extending through Mexico and parts of the Caribbean region southward to northern Peru and southern Brazil in South America.
Size: 16in (41cm).
Habitat: Salt marshes.
Nest: Cup-shaped.
Eggs: 3–14, creamy-white with dark blotches.
Food: Small invertebrates and seeds.

West Indian whistling duck (mangrove duck, *Dendrocygna arborea*): 22in (56cm)
Occurs widely through the Caribbean, from the Bahamas south via Cuba, the Cayman Islands and Jamaica east to Puerto Rico, Antigua, and Barbuda. Also on the Virgin Islands. Dark crown, neck and wings. Yellowish-brown markings on the sides of the face; and white upper throat is mottled with black lower down. Prominent black and white markings on the flanks. Brown on chest, becoming mottled and paler on lower underparts. Sexes alike. Young birds duller.

Flying steamer duck (*Tachyeres patachonicus*): 28in (71cm)
Southern South America, on both sides of Cape Horn, from Chile to northern Argentina, and also on the Falklands. Plain gray head, with black edging to the gray feathering on the body. White wing speculum. Gray back and white underparts. Drakes have yellowish-orange bills with a black tip, whereas hens have a darker bluish shade on the bill. Yellow legs.

Barrow's goldeneye (*Bucephala islandica*): 21in (53cm)
Western North America, from the Aleutian Islands and southern Alaska down the Pacific coast to California. Also occurs on northeastern Canada and Greenland. Metallic green head, black over the back with white underparts, and a prominent white area on each side of the black bill, with golden eyes. Hens, in contrast, have brown head and grayish underparts, with a dull yellow tip to the bill. Drakes out of color resemble hens, aside from their dark bill and black and white wing markings.

Little wood rail

Aramides mangle

Since it was first described back in 1825, very little has been documented about the habits of this species, which is the smallest of the wood rails. In some parts of its range, however, it does appear to be quite numerous. The best time to see little wood rails is at low tide, when the falling water level draws the birds out from the relative sanctuary of the mangroves to search for food on the mud banks. It is thought that little wood rails feed chiefly on invertebrates. They also venture further inland on occasions, being recorded from forests near the mangroves. Little wood rails are shy by nature, and if disturbed will fly up and perch in branches, where they will be relatively safe from danger. It is likely that they will nest off the ground too, but no information is recorded about their breeding habits, nor their eggs. Even the appearance of the young birds remains unrecorded, though it is probable they are simply not as brightly colored as the adults.

Distribution: Restricted to South America, where it can be found in the eastern coastal areas of Brazil.
Size: 11in (32cm).
Habitat: Coastal swamps and mangroves.
Nest: Unknown.
Eggs: Unknown.
Food: Probably invertebrates.

Identification: Bluish-gray plumage on the head, extending down the back, with the chin and throat being whitish. Olive-green coloration extends down to the upper back, while the lower back and rump is sepia. Tail and surrounding region are black, with the underparts being tawny-red. Lower flanks and abdomen are olive. The sharp, pointed bill is yellowish-green. Legs and feet are red. Sexes alike.

LOCALIZED SPECIES

Coastal areas, including mangroves, are home not just to various types of water birds but also to members of groups such as sparrows, whose relatives are typically found further inland. These species have adapted well to this type of habitat, and yet in a number of respects their lifestyles are not entirely dissimilar to those of their more widely distributed relatives.

Mangrove cuckoo

Coccyzus minor

Hard to spot in the mangroves and forested areas where they occur, these cuckoos effectively conceal their presence by perching near the center of a tree, rather than on the outer branches. Their slim shape enables them to slip through vegetation without creating a disturbance or drawing attention to themselves. Mangrove cuckoos fly straight and fast, slipping out of sight rapidly. They are more likely to reveal their location by their song, which can be heard during the nesting period. Unlike many cuckoos, the mangrove rears its own chicks. The nest is built in trees or bushes, where it is well concealed, sometimes at a relatively low height. As with other related species, the young will grow quickly, and are reared mainly on invertebrates.

Identification: The Florida race (*C. m. maynardi*) has a grayish-white throat with yellow underparts. In other cases, however, this part of the body is entirely yellowish-buff. The head is grayish, with a black band behind each eye and browner wings and tail. Underside is black and white. It has a powerful, down-curving bill. Sexes alike. Young birds have paler faces, and the contrast on the tail is less marked.

Distribution: Occurs in southern Florida and throughout the Caribbean. Also occurs on mainland parts of Central America, from Mexico extending south along the west coast of South America.
Size: 12in (30cm).
Habitat: Mangrove swamps.
Nest: Bowl of twigs.
Eggs: 2, white.
Food: Invertebrates, some berries.

Fish crow

Corvus ossifragus

It can be difficult to distinguish this species from the American crow, especially from a distance, although fish crows are a little smaller, with longer tails. The situation is made more complex by the fact that these two corvids sometimes feed together. However, the calls of the two species offer a means of distinction, with fish crows uttering short, low-pitched "car" notes and higher-pitched, two-tone "ca-hah" calls, whereas adult American crows utter a more strident "caw." Fish crows hunt along the seashore, and will even wade into the water in search of food. They are sufficiently agile to catch small fish by plucking them from the water with their claws while hovering overhead. Fish crows may form small colonies when breeding in the spring, but each pair occupies its own tree, with the nest of twigs being built in a convenient fork. The young fledge with blue eyes, although these soon darken to the brown of adult birds.

Identification: Jet black, but can be distinguished from the similar American crow (*C. brachyrhynchos*) by its slightly smaller size, and perhaps most noticeably by its longer tail. The head and bill are also smaller, while in flight it has a more jerky flight pattern. Sexes alike. Young have a more dusky head and underparts.

Distribution: Occurs in eastern parts of the U.S.A., from New England down to Florida and along the Gulf coast to the vicinity of Galveston, Texas. May be sighted further inland during the summer, in the Mississippi valleys as far as southern Illinois.
Size: 15½in (39cm).
Habitat: Salty marshes and rivers.
Nest: Bowl of twigs.
Eggs: 4–5, bluish green with dark blotches.
Food: Omnivorous.

Black-whiskered vireo

Vireo altiloquus

Distribution: Centered on the Caribbean, sometimes recorded on the Caribbean coast. Also ranges north to Florida.
Size: 6¼in (16cm).
Habitat: Mangrove swamps.
Nest: Cup of grass.
Eggs: 2–3, white with brown spots.
Food: Invertebrates and berries.

These small insect-eaters are relatively inconspicuous, especially when obscured in vegetation, but they have a surprisingly loud song, which betrays their presence, reported to sound like the words "Whip Tom Kelly." In the Caribbean, these vireos have developed various local song dialects. Their characteristic stripe is not that apparent unless the bird is seen at close quarters. Typically occurring in mangroves, as in the vicinity of Miami on the mainland, black-whiskered vireos construct a small nest in a tree fork. While in some parts of their range, as in the Lesser Antilles, they are present throughout the year, populations from elsewhere migrate southward to northern South America in September, after the end of the breeding season, and return early the following year.

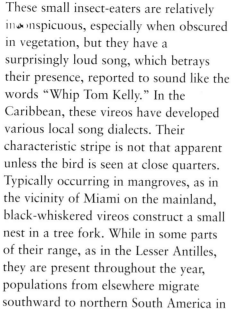

Identification: A characteristic black stripe extends down each side of the face from the base of the bill. The crown is gray, and there is also a broad gray stripe running through the eyes, which have bright orange-red pupils, with a whitish stripe above. The wings and back are olive-green, and the underparts are a whitish shade, with yellow suffusion on the flanks. Sexes are alike.

Saltmarsh sharp-tailed sparrow (*Ammodramus caudacutus*): 5in (13cm)
Found on the eastern coasts of the U.S.A. Dark crown, with orange area on the sides of the face, encircling the gray patches behind each eye. Underparts streaked on the chest and flanks, center of abdomen white. Some chestnut coloration on the wings, with three rows of distinctive white markings down the back. The bill is relatively long and flat.

Boat-tailed grackle (*Quiscalus major*): cock 16½in (42cm); hen 14½in (37cm)
Ranges down the Atlantic coast through Florida to coastal areas of Louisiana and Texas. Mature cock birds have iridescent bluish-black coloration, with a long, keel-shaped tail. Eye color varies from brown to yellow. Hens significantly smaller and tawny brown, with wings and tail darker.

Tricolored blackbird (*Agelaius tricolor*): 9in (23cm)
Occurs on southwestern coast of the U.S.A. extending inland, nesting in marshes. Breeding cock is predominantly black, with a bold red wing patch and white stripe behind. Hens sooty-brown overall, with speckled lines running over the breast and a light stripe above the eye. Grayish-buff edging on the upperparts seen in both sexes following the late summer molt.

Gray kingbird (*Tyrannus dominicensis*) 9in (23cm)
Found in the Florida Keys, occasionally north up the Atlantic seaboard, and along the Gulf coast to Texas. Often seen in mangroves. Darker gray head and back, with broad black streak through the eyes. Red patch on crown is hard to spot. Underparts whitish with a yellowish suffusion extending to undertail coverts. Forked tail, strong black bill. Sexes are alike.

Seaside sparrow

Ammodramus maritimus

Distribution: From New England down to Florida on the eastern side of the U.S.A., and along the Gulf coast as far as Texas.
Size: 6in (15cm).
Habitat: Tidal marshes.
Nest: Woven grass.
Eggs: 4–5, white with brown blotches.
Food: Invertebrates and seeds.

These unusual finches live in the grasslands of tidal salt marshes, having adapted to this habitat, with local races also having arisen. (These included the sadly extinct Cape sable sparrow [*A. m. mirabilis*], which had particularly strong green coloration, and the dusky seaside sparrow [*A. m. nigrescens*], one of the latest additions to the annals of extinct North American birds, the last known example dying in June 1987. The contrast in the plumage of *A. m. nigrescens*, between its dark upperparts and darkly streaked white underparts, was particularly marked.) The habitat has influenced the diet of seaside sparrows, since they feed more on small creatures such as crabs and snails in the tidal area rather than on seeds. They are inconspicuous, often spending time near the ground foraging, but can also be seen singing in prominent sites.

Identification: Differs quite widely in coloration, depending on the individual race. The common nominate race (*A. m. maritimus*) has grayish-olive upperparts with brown marking on the wings, and a small yellowish area above each eye. Throat is whitish-gray, with a darker stripe extending from the corner of the bill. Underparts are grayish, with darker streaked patterning. Sexes alike. Young birds are browner.

LOONS AND GREBES

Most wetland birds that breed in the far north during the summer cannot stay there throughout the year because the winter conditions are too harsh. While some head to warmer climates further south, others may seek sanctuary along the coast, where the ocean is unlikely to freeze even in winter. This shift usually brings a dramatic change in both the bird's lifestyle and diet.

Red-throated loon

Red-throated diver *Gavia stellata*

Distribution: Throughout far north of North America and in parts of Greenland when breeding. Overwinters further south, from the Aleutians down to California in the west and on the Atlantic seaboard down to Florida.
Size: 25in (64cm).
Habitat: Pools, open country.
Nest: Pile of vegetation.
Eggs: 1–3, olive-brown with dark spots.
Food: Mainly fish.

Red-throated loons pair up for life and stay together throughout the year. In May they return to their northern nesting grounds, revisiting the same location each year. Their nest, usually located among vegetation and surrounded by water, is simply a loose pile of plant matter. This is added to during the incubation period, potentially developing into a large mound. Both parents share incubation duties, although the female normally sits for longer than the male. Young red-throated loons can take to the water almost immediately after hatching, but usually remain at the nest for the first few days. Even once the chicks have entered the water they may still occasionally be carried on their parents' backs. Survival rates can be low, but if they make it through the critical early months of life, these divers may live for up to 23 years.

Identification: Distinctive red throat patch present in adults of both sexes during the breeding period. The head is gray, and the back of the neck is streaked black and white. Upperparts are brown, underparts white. During winter it has a pale gray crown, with speckling extending down the back of the neck and white spotting on the back, while remaining underparts are white. Yellowish-gray bill. Young birds can be identified by their grayish-brown heads.

Horned grebe

Podiceps auritus

Horned grebes return to their freshwater breeding grounds in spring, after overwintering in bays and other sheltered locations along the coast. The nest consists of a mass of floating aquatic plants, although it is sometimes built on rocks. The young, which hatch covered in striped down, can take to the water almost immediately, but prefer to be carried on their parents' backs. Horned grebes obtain much of their food by diving rather than feeding at the surface. Their natural underwater agility enables them to catch fish with ease. Diet varies according to season and location. At sea during winter they eat mostly fish, while brine shrimps are important when passing the Great Salt Lakes on migration. Diet is more varied on the breeding grounds.

Distribution: Breeds in much of Alaska and southeast across Canada to the shores of the Great Lakes. Overwinters through the Aleutians and down the west coast of Canada to mainland U.S.A., and down the eastern seaboard to Florida and Texas on the Gulf coast.
Size: 13½in (34cm).
Habitat: Marshland, ponds and lakes.
Nest: Pile of vegetation.
Eggs: 1–7, bluish-white.
Food: Fish and invertebrates.

Identification: Distinctive golden horns created by raised feathers on each side toward rear of head. A red-brown area extends from bill to eyes, with others on the neck and flanks. Remainder of head black, as are wings. Much duller plumage in winter, when black on top of head extends down back of the neck to the wings. Throat and area below eyes remain white. Iris is reddish, bill black. Sexes alike.

Western grebe

Aechmophorus occidentalis

Identification: Black head, encompassing the eyes when breeding, with a narrow white stripe running to the bill. Black plumage extends down back of neck over back and wings, with some mottling on flanks. Iris reddish, bill black in center, with yellowish sides. Area around eyes mottled in winter. Sexes are alike.

Western grebes hunt fish by diving, becoming most active when the sun is high in the sky, illuminating the water and improving visibility. Their habitat alters significantly through the year, as they range between the coast and their freshwater breeding haunts in the north. Western grebes begin nesting during May, often forming large groups comprised of thousands of birds. It is not uncommon for hens to lay in nests other than their own, which can result in some nests containing ten or more eggs. Once the chicks have fledged, typically about ten weeks after hatching, the grebes head south to their wintering grounds, migrating over land during the hours of darkness. The habits of the Mexican population are rather different, as they have a more extended nesting season, with egg-laying continuing until October. Mexican birds are also more sedentary by nature, and significantly smaller in size than their northern cousins.

Distribution: Breeds in south-central and south-western parts of Canada, and in western and central parts of the U.S.A. Overwinters down the Pacific coast to Baja California, with a separate Mexican population. Also present on the Gulf coast in winter.
Size: 25in (64cm).
Habitat: Lakes and reservoirs, overwinters on coasts.
Nest: Pile of vegetation.
Eggs: 3–4, bluish-white with buff markings.
Food: Fish form the bulk of the diet.

Common loon (great northern loon, *Gavia immer*): 35in (86cm)
Breeds on Greenland and from Alaska through Canada. Winters further south on both Pacific and Atlantic coasts and inland, notably south-eastern U.S.A. Black head, with barring on throat and neck. The back is patterned black and white, with white spots. Underparts white. Less contrast in winter, when white extends from lower bill and throat down over underparts. In winter eyes are dark rather than red. Sexes alike.

Least grebe (*Tachybaptus dominicus*): 10in (25cm)
Southern Texas and Baja California to northern Argentina and southern Brazil, also Caribbean. Grayish head and neck, darker crown, browner on chest, with dark flanks. Chin and throat are white, and flanks pale, outside the breeding season. Iris is yellowish. Sexes are alike. Young resemble non-breeding adults, except for stripes on sides of the head.

White-tufted grebe (*Rollandia rolland*): 14in (36cm)
Found in central Peru and southeastern Brazil down to tip of South America; also Falklands. Has a unique black and white tuft of feathers on head, with black crown, neck, chest, and wings. Red-brown barring on flanks and red-brown underparts. Browner overall when not breeding, with a white throat and underparts. Sexes alike. Young birds similar to adults out of breeding color, but with black striping across the cheeks.

Sungrebe

Heliornis fulica

The sungrebe is the smallest member of the finfoot family. Shy by nature, its habits have proved hard to determine, partly because it prefers wooded areas with dense vegetation by waterways. Sungrebes usually feed on the water, but may also venture onto land. They feed on insects such as dragonflies and their larvae, also hunting crayfish and amphibians. When breeding, males choose a nest site overhanging the water, typically only 3ft (1m) from the surface. The incubation period is short, lasting just ten days. The male sungrebe then carries the helpless chicks in a special pocket created by a skin fold under each wing, and can even fly with them in there. This method of care is completely unique.

Identification: Black and white stripes on top of head, running through eyes. White throat and underparts, yellowish hue on upper breast. Back and wings are brownish. Legs and especially feet banded gray and yellow. White tail tip. Breeding hens have chestnut area on sides of the head and red upper bill, plus scarlet eyelids.

Distribution: Extends from southeastern Mexico through Central America down to Peru in the west, and across much of northern South America east of the Andes down as far as northern Argentina.
Size: 13in (33cm).
Habitat: Streams, rivers and lakes.
Nest: Platform of twigs.
Eggs: 2–3, buff with darker markings.
Food: Mainly aquatic invertebrates.

FLAMINGOS AND OTHER LARGER WATERBIRDS

A number of relatively large birds, including flamingos and cranes, have evolved to live in wetland areas, where their height can be an advantage in finding food and wading through the water. Unfortunately, some have become so specialized in their habits that changes in their environment, such as pollution of waterways or clearing of land, could have serious consequences.

American flamingo

Phoenicopterus ruber

The distinctive coloration of these birds comes from their diet of algae or small creatures that have eaten the microscopic plants. They feed in a unique fashion by walking along with their head submerged, their long neck allowing them to filter relatively large quantities of water by sweeping their unusually shaped bill from side to side. As a result of their highly specific feeding requirements, American flamingos are vulnerable to habitat loss or pollution of the shallow coastal lagoons that they inhabit. Young are reared on nests of mud raised above the water level, and are covered in a whitish-gray down at first. At a month old, they molt into a brownish down. Their bills are short and straight at this stage. American flamingos are known to live for more than 30 years in the wild.

Identification: Bright, almost reddish plumage on the neck, with a paler pink body. Bill also has a pink hue behind the black tip. Outstretched wings in flight show black areas. Sexes alike.

Distribution: The Caribbean Islands, Mexico, the north coast of South America and the Galapagos Islands. Other subspecies found in parts of southern Europe, Africa, and Madagascar, extending through the Red Sea into Asia.
Size: 57in (145cm) tall.
Habitat: Shallow saline lagoons.
Nest: Mud.
Eggs: 1, white.
Food: Small mollusks, crustaceans, and plant matter.

Chilean flamingo

Phoenicopterus chilensis

Distribution: Ranges from highlands of Peru to Tierra del Fuego at the tip of the continent.
Size: Up to 41in (105cm) tall. Hens shorter and smaller.
Habitat: Highland salt lakes.
Nest: Mud.
Eggs: 1, white.
Food: Algae and invertebrates.

This is the most widely distributed South American flamingo, with a range extending more than 2,500 miles (4,000km). In the altiplano region of the Andes, they are usually observed at altitudes of 11,500–15,000ft (3,500–4,500m), but in parts of Argentina, east of the Andes, they occur at lower levels. In suitable areas, Chilean flamingos will congregate in large numbers, and as many as 100,000 have been counted on Lake Poopo in Bolivia. Lake Titicaca, found on the Bolivian border with Peru, is home to even greater numbers. Their calls are similar to the honking notes of geese.

Identification: Pinkish with crimson coloration over the back. Black area on the tip of the bill, extending back beyond the bend, with the remainder being whitish. No yellow coloration is evident here. Characteristic reddish knee joints and feet. Sexes alike.

Sandhill crane

Grus canadensis

Young sandhill cranes take around $2^1/_2$ years to acquire full adult coloration. However, adults may smear themselves with iron-rich mud when preening, which gives their plumage a reddish-brown color, not dissimilar to that of immature birds. Sandhill cranes migrate long distances to the Caribbean from their tundra breeding grounds, but are often difficult to spot as they fly at a high altitude. Southern populations tend to be more sedentary, although they may move in search of food. During late summer and early fall they are more likely to be sighted in agricultural areas, feeding on spilt corn and taking invertebrates such as earthworms.

Identification: Mostly gray, with whitish color on sides of face and throat. Vibrant red area on crown and lores; bill, legs, and feet gray. Sexes alike. Young birds have a tawny neck and head, and brownish mottling on the body, but no red area.

Distribution: Breeds along the Arctic coast of North America, and at Great Lakes. Winters in southern U.S.A. and Mexico. Also found in Florida and the Caribbean.
Size: 48in (122cm).
Habitat: Wetland areas.
Nest: Mound of vegetation.
Eggs: 2, buff with brown markings.
Food: Omnivorous.

Puna flamingo (*Phoenicopterus jamesi*; previously *Phoenicoparrus jamesi*): 36in (92cm)
Confined to a small part of the Andes, the Puna has the smallest range of any flamingo. Pinkish suffusion to the head and body, with a whitish neck and a reddish-pink streak along the breast and back when breeding. Flight feathers are black. Bare red skin around the eyes; yellowish bill with a black tip. Pink legs and feet, with no hind toe on either foot. Young birds have fawn-colored feathering with black streaking across upperparts.

Southern screamer (*Chauna torquata*): 37in (95cm)
South America, extending southward from Bolivia and southern Brazil down to northern Argentina. Mostly gray, darker over back and wings, with a short crest at the back of the head. Bare red skin around the eyes; bill is grayish. Narrow white band around the neck, with a broader black band beneath. In flight, a white area can be seen on the wings. Sexes alike. Young birds are duller in color with shorter spurs on the feet.

Northern screamer (*Chauna chavaria*): 36in (91cm)
Northwest Colombia and neighboring northwestern Venezuela. Predominantly dark, slate-gray with whitish striations on the breast. Top of the head is paler gray, with a backward-pointing crest and a large white area extending from the top of the head down under the bill. Neck is almost entirely black. Sexes alike. Young birds duller in coloration overall.

Whooping crane

Grus americana (E)

Distribution: Restricted areas of Canada and U.S.A.
Size: 56in (142cm).
Habitat: Peat bog and marshland.
Nest: Flat mound.
Eggs: 2, buff with darker blotches.
Food: Omnivorous.

Standing up to $7^1/_2$ft (229cm) in height, this is the tallest bird found on the North American continent, as well as one of the most critically endangered. Its breeding grounds are in Wood Buffalo Park adjoining the Great Slave Lake in Canada. The population moves south in fall to the wintering grounds at the Arkansas Refuge in Texas. The cranes pause on the long flight to feed on lakes and other similar stretches of water. Their name comes from the distinctive whooping sound of their call. The graceful dancing display of males is considered one of the most spectacular sights in the natural world. Pairs form a lifelong bond. Nesting usually starts in May.

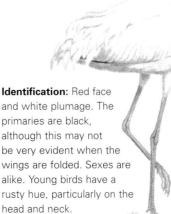

Identification: Red face and white plumage. The primaries are black, although this may not be very evident when the wings are folded. Sexes are alike. Young birds have a rusty hue, particularly on the head and neck.

LONG-LEGGED WADING BIRDS

These birds are all well equipped to forage in wetland areas, their long legs enabling them to wade easily through the shallows while also giving them a good field of vision to detect possible prey. A powerful bill and rapid reflexes make them formidable hunters of small aquatic creatures. They may also be encountered in open areas close to stretches of water.

Wood stork

Wood ibis *Mycteria americana*

Although usually it is most likely to be encountered in freshwater areas, the wood stork may be seen in mangrove swamps where food is abundant. These birds are opportunistic predators, and are equipped with a powerful bill to seize creatures ranging from fish to young turtles and alligators. These large birds breed colonially, often on nesting sites surrounded by water. Up to 50 pairs or more may be found in the same area where conditions are favorable. Pairs accomplish nest-building quite quickly, in about three days, and the hen lays the eggs on a nest lining of leaves. These storks are long-lived, and their young are therefore slow to mature, often not breeding until they are five years old.

Identification: Bare, dark and unfeathered head is offset against the white plumage. The black feathering is confined to the wings and tail. Long bill, powerful at its base. White plumage in young birds tends to appear slightly soiled.

Distribution: Southern parts of the U.S.A. south as far as northwest Argentina.
Size: 47in (119cm).
Habitat: Marshland and lakes.
Nest: Made of sticks.
Eggs: 2–5, creamy white.
Food: Fish, amphibians, and crustaceans.

White-faced ibis

Plegadis chihi

Studies have revealed the long distances that these ibises may travel, even in the southern part of their range where they do not undergo any apparent seasonal migrations. Not surprisingly, they may occasionally be encountered well outside their normal range, occurring as far south as Tierra del Fuego and even on Hawaii on rare occasions, though they fly over the ocean less than related species. White-faced ibises feed in large flocks, sometimes comprised of thousands of individuals. They eat a range of invertebrates, some of which may be gathered in water, while others such as earthworms are found by probing in mud. Unfortunately, in some areas pesticide residues have had an adverse affect on their numbers, since they interfere with the hatching of their eggs. The nest site is usually well concealed in vegetation. These ibises often nest together in large colonies, sometimes in the company of other birds, including gulls.

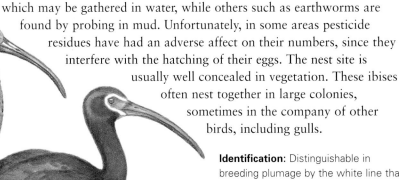

Identification: Distinguishable in breeding plumage by the white line that encircles the bare red skin on each side of the face. The remainder of the plumage is chestnut and green, with bronzy tones apparent over the wings. The legs and feet are reddish, while the horn-colored bill is long and down-curving. In winter, the appearance is much duller, with brown and black streaking extending over the head and neck, no greenish cap on the crown, and paler red skin. Sexes are alike. Young birds are much less brightly colored, being predominantly brownish on the head, with speckled feathering.

Distribution: Occurs in the northwest U.S.A. and central California, extending down the coasts of Mexico. Also found in southern-central parts of South America, from Paraguay, southern parts of Bolivia, and Brazil southward to northern parts of Chile and Argentina. Also occurs in Uruguay.
Size: 23in (58cm).
Habitat: Shallow areas of fresh water.
Nest: Cup-shaped, made of reeds.
Eggs: 3–5, pale green.
Food: Mainly invertebrates.

Great white egret

Egretta alba

Identification: Tall and snow-white, with plumes over the back and on the chest of breeding birds. Skin in front of eyes blue, bill yellowish with bluish hue on top. Legs and feet are black. Sexes alike. Birds lack both plumes and blue coloration in winter.

By the early 1900s, the great white egret had become a very rare species in the U.S.A. These birds were heavily hunted for their plumes, which were used to decorate women's hats. Numbers have now recovered and their range has expanded up the Atlantic coast. These birds move south to the Caribbean for winter, while further west, populations are found from California down through Central America. Great white egrets are adaptable, and are found on farmland and even in pasture some distance from water. Here they feed on rodents and other small mammals, insects, and reptiles such as snakes. Breeding occurs in colonies sometimes consisting of several hundred pairs. Nests may be sited either on the ground or high in trees, usually over water, which offers protection from predators.

Distribution: Breeds south of the Great Lakes in the eastern U.S.A., and along the Atlantic coast. Winters in southwest U.S.A., through much of Central America and the Caribbean down across most of South America, as far as central Argentina.
Size: 39in (99cm).
Habitat: Marshland, flooded areas.
Nest: Stick-type nest.
Eggs: 3–5, pale blue.
Food: Fish and small invertebrates.

Green ibis (*Mesembrinibis cayennensis*): 23in (58cm)
Eastern Costa Rica and Panama across much of South America east of the Andes. Very dark overall with greenish suffusion on wings and loose greenish plumage at back of head. Young lack the gloss on their plumage. Sexes alike.

Whispering ibis (*Phimosus infuscatus*): 21in (54cm)
Two separate populations: one across northern South America from eastern Ecuador eastward; the other south of the Amazon in Brazil, Bolivia, Paraguay, Argentina, and Uruguay. Blackish overall, with a bare area of reddish skin on the face. Bill is yellowish, legs reddish. Sexes alike.

Buff-necked ibis (*Theristicus caudatus*): 30in (76cm)
Colombia, Venezuela, and French Guiana south to northern Argentina and Uruguay. Buff neck, darker on the crown. Mainly gray wings, with a characteristic white area. Buff on the chest, with black underparts. Sexes are alike.

Agami heron (chestnut-bellied heron, *Agamia agami*): 28in (71cm)
Southeastern Mexico to Ecuador and Amazon region in Brazil. Very colorful: dark mauve head with white stripe down throat. Lower neck and back silvery-blue, with plumes of this color on crown. Metallic green wings, rufous underparts. Long, narrow, straight bill. Sexes are alike. Young birds browner, with a white stripe.

Limpkin

Aramus guarauna

This large bird, about the size of a goose, can be recognized by its long, pointed bill. It is not easily observed, being shy by nature and mostly active at night, when its wailing call echoes across the marshes. This disconcerting noise, which can sound like a person crying out, has led to the limpkin being called the crying bird. The impression of distress is reinforced by the fact that the birds have a limping gait which suggests they are in pain. Limpkins use their pointed bill to feed on aquatic apple snails, and are able to pull the mollusks from their shells without crushing them. They also prey on other invertebrates and amphibians. Pairs usually nest in secluded sites on the ground, but occasionally choose a low bush and use sticks to make a nest platform.

Identification: Tall, brownish with prominent white streaking on the head and neck, extending down over the upper wings. Strong, powerful, darkish horn-colored bill, with a blackish tip. Grayish-green legs and feet, with long toes. Sexes are alike. Young birds paler overall in coloration.

Distribution: Northern breeding range is centered on Florida, occasionally seen in neighboring parts of southern U.S.A. Also parts of Central America and South America east of the Andes.
Size: 26in (66cm).
Habitat: Wetlands, swamps.
Nest: Pile of vegetation.
Eggs: 5–8, buff with dark markings.
Food: Aquatic invertebrates and amphibians.

BITTERNS AND OTHER WATERBIRDS

Although some waterbirds, such as bitterns, feed in a similar fashion to waders, their larger size allows them to wander into deeper water, giving greater opportunities to feed and enabling them to take larger prey such as fish. Certain waterbirds, such as the anhinga, will actually disappear under the water in search of food, rather than hunting from above.

American bittern

Botaurus lentiginosus

These shy birds adopt a characteristic frozen pose when alarmed, with their head pointing vertically upward, in the hope of avoiding detection. This disguise is very effective in the reed beds that they frequent, especially as they move their head slightly to resemble a reed waving in the wind. Their presence is clearly audible during the nesting period, however, thanks to their booming calls, which can be heard over ¹/₂ mile (0.8km) away. American bitterns are solitary hunters, becoming active at dusk. These waders rely simply on standing quietly and seizing unsuspecting prey that comes within reach, though with their long neck and slim shape they can also chase prey through the water. Aside from fish, American bitterns will feed on a host of other creatures, including amphibians and reptiles, as well as invertebrates such as water snails and crayfish.

Identification: White streak extending above the eye. Throat is also white, with dark edging apparent, and striped throat markings too. The back and wings are mottled, and the flight feathers are dark. Underparts slightly paler around the vent. Bill is yellowish, as are the legs and feet. Sexes alike. Young birds lack the black markings on the throat.

Distribution: Breeds central Canada eastward along the southern shore of Hudson Bay to the Atlantic seaboard. Overwinters south of the breeding range and along the Pacific coast, notably throughout Central America and the Caribbean.
Size: 28in (71cm).
Habitat: Marshland and shallow water.
Nest: Platform made of marsh plants.
Eggs: 2–6, buff.
Food: Mainly fish.

Sun bittern

Eurypyga helias

The sun bittern has no close relatives and resembles a rail in some respects. It has a relatively long tail, and there is no webbing apparent between its toes. This bird has a fiery, brilliant coloration on the flight feathers and uses these to stunning effect during its mating display. Relatively little is known about the habits of these rather shy birds, which are most likely to be encountered on their own, or sometimes as pairs in damp areas of tropical forest. These bitterns use their bills to probe for food in wet areas, but rarely enter the water itself, and they do not fly far.

Identification: Black head with prominent white stripes above and below the eyes, and another white area on the throat. Neck and upperparts are brownish, broken with variable markings ranging from chestnut through gray to black. Orange areas on the wings are most apparent in flight. Dark markings also on the brownish breast, which becomes paler, almost whitish, on the underparts. Bill is straight and yellowish on the lower part. Legs are orangish-yellow. Sexes alike.

Distribution: From southern Mexico south to western Ecuador and east to northern parts of Brazil. Occasionally seen in Chile.
Size: 19in (48cm).
Habitat: Near streams in wooded areas.
Nest: Globular in shape, made of vegetation and mud.
Eggs: 2, buff with dark spots at the larger end.
Food: Invertebrates.

South American bittern (*Botaurus pinnatus*): 30in (76cm)
Eastern Mexico south across northern South America to Ecuador and the north of Argentina. Pale brown and black striations across neck, with further black markings over the back. Buff area behind the eyes, with a narrow white stripe here and white plumage under the throat. Brown and white underparts. Hens smaller, with brown rather than black tail feathers. Young birds reddish.

Least bittern (*Ixobrychus exilis*): 14in (36cm)
Breeds from southern Canada near the Great Lakes, southward across eastern U.S.A. Also Pacific coast down to Baja California, Caribbean and through Central America to northern and eastern parts of South America. Cock bird has a black stripe over head, less prominent in hen. Sides of face and neck yellowish-brown, back blackish with a white stripe on each side. White stripes on underparts too. Large buff areas on wings.

Stripe-backed bittern (*Ixobrychus involucris*): 13in (33cm)
Occurs in four separate areas of South America. Distinctive dark stripes on the head and down the wings and back. Sides of the head grayish, with a whitish throat. Rest of body light brown, with whitish stripes on underparts. Bill, legs, and feet yellowish. Sexes alike.

Anhinga

Snakebird *Anhinga anhinga*

The shape of the anhinga's body in the water has led to these darters being known as snakebirds. They swim with their body submerged, the long, narrow neck above the water giving the impression of a snake. Since their feathering is not waterproof, anhingas favor stretches of water with trees close by so they can roost and dry their plumage. They are most often seen perching with wings held out to dry, or flying high in circles over a favored tree. Anhingas feed mainly on fish, the rough edges on the sides of the bill making it easier to grasp their quarry. They catch fish by first stabbing them and tossing them into the air, then catching and swallowing them head-first. Amphibians and reptiles, even baby alligators, may also be taken.

Distribution: Breeds from North Carolina to Florida and west to Texas, up along the Mississippi to southern Missouri and Kentucky. Range contracts southward in winter, from South Carolina along the Gulf coast. Also Central America south to northern Argentina and the Caribbean.
Size: 35in (89cm).
Habitat: Ponds and swamps.
Nest: Sticks, with leaf lining.
Eggs: 3–5, chalky-blue.
Food: Mainly fish.

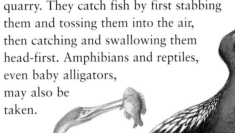

Identification: Cock bird has predominantly black plumage with a green iridescence. White and silvery-white spotted markings are evident on the wings. During the breeding period the bare facial skin becomes brighter in color, and long, fine plumes can be seen on the back of the neck. Hens have brownish heads.

Roseate spoonbill

Ajaia ajaja

The distinctively enlarged and flattened tips on the spoonbill's beak are very sensitive. They act like a pair of hands, allowing these birds both to detect and grab crabs and similar creatures underwater without difficulty. Roseate spoonbills sometimes immerse their entire head when feeding, although they are more likely to be observed sweeping the head from side to side, rather like the American flamingo and other tall waders. These birds are often seen in small flocks on marshes and similar wetlands near the coast. They nest off the ground, building loose piles of sticks.

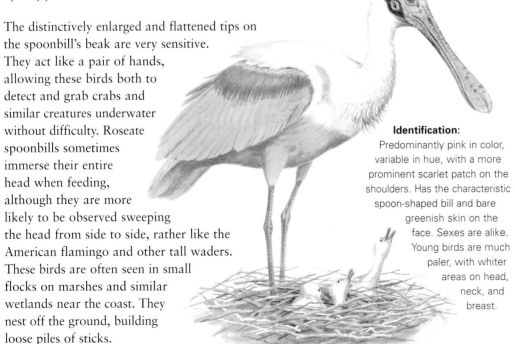

Identification: Predominantly pink in color, variable in hue, with a more prominent scarlet patch on the shoulders. Has the characteristic spoon-shaped bill and bare greenish skin on the face. Sexes are alike. Young birds are much paler, with whiter areas on head, neck, and breast.

Distribution: From southern U.S.A. into northern and eastern parts of South America as far south as Argentina. Also occurs in the Caribbean.
Size: 32in (81cm).
Habitat: Wetland areas, typically coastal areas including mangrove swamps.
Nest: Made of sticks.
Eggs: 3, white, brown spots.
Food: Small fish, amphibians, and other aquatic creatures.

HERONS

Colorful in some cases and highly adapted to their environments, herons are well equipped for their predatory lifestyle, with powerful, sharp bills and long necks enabling them to lunge at prey which would otherwise be out of reach. In spite of their size, however, herons are not always easy to observe, being shy by nature and blending in well with their surroundings.

Boat-billed heron

Cochlearius cochlearius

Unique among herons, the characteristic broad bill of this species is thought to have evolved to enable it to scoop up food whether in water or on land. Boat-billed herons rarely feed during the day, seeking their prey as dusk falls. They do not actively pursue their quarry, relying instead on stealth, and will sometimes catch small mammals as well as aquatic creatures. Their breeding season varies through their wide range, influenced by the rains that make it easier to obtain food for the nestlings. Pairs nest on their own or in small groups, occasionally associating with other herons. They may return to the same nest each year, adding new material to it, or even adopt an abandoned nest of another bird. Boat-billed herons prefer wooded areas of habitat close to water, and can be seen in mangroves as well as freshwater areas.

Identification: Black area runs across the top of the head and down the center of the back. Wings are grayish, with rufous underparts. Sides of the face and breast vary in color depending on race, from white through to reddish-gray, with a similar area of color just above the bill. Hens have smaller crest plumes. Young birds are duller, with rufous back and wings.

Distribution: Extends south from both the Caribbean and Pacific coasts of Mexico, through parts of Central America and via Panama to South America. Here the species ranges east to French Guiana and over a broad area in the center, as far south as northeast Argentina.
Size: 20in (50cm).
Habitat: Lakes and marshes.
Nest: Platform of sticks.
Eggs: 2–4, pale blue.
Food: Invertebrates and small vertebrates.

Whistling heron

Syrigma sibilatrix

Distribution: Two distinct populations in South America: one in eastern Colombia and Venezuela; the other further south, extending from Bolivia as far as southeast Brazil and northeast Argentina.
Size: 24in (61cm).
Habitat: Mainly wet grassland.
Nest: Platform of sticks.
Eggs: 3–4, pale blue with speckles.
Food: Invertebrates, also amphibians and reptiles.

Unlike most members of the heron family, the Ardeidae, the whistling heron is often encountered in areas of wet grassland rather than standing in water, although it may be observed in flooded fields and similar locations. The slender but stout bill enables it to capture both invertebrate and vertebrate prey, the latter including frogs and reptiles. In suitable areas where food can be found in abundance, these herons may congregate in groups of more than 100 birds, although they are more likely to be observed individually or in pairs. Their name is derived from their whistling calls, which have been likened to the sound of a flute.

Identification: Rigid black plumes at the rear of the head. The face is mainly black, with a white area under the chin and a large area of blue skin encircling the eyes. The neck and breast are a buff color, becoming paler on the underparts. The back is grayish with black edging to the brownish feathers on each wing. The legs are fairly dark. The reddish bill becomes dark at the tip. Sexes are alike. Young birds have streaking on the neck.

Bare-throated tiger heron

Tigrisoma mexicanum

Distribution: Range extends from coastal and western parts of Mexico down through Central America and as far south as northwestern Colombia in South America.
Size: 32in (81cm).
Habitat: Both streams and rivers.
Nest: Platform of sticks.
Eggs: 1–3, pale blue.
Food: Mainly fish.

Tiger herons are so-called because of their evident striped patterning, and this is the only species characterized by a lack of throat plumage. It is found further north than its two relatives, and also has a more limited area of distribution. Bare-throated tiger herons are often found not just in marshland and wooded swamps but also in coastal areas, where they hunt in mangroves. They are generally solitary when seeking food, and prefer to feed at dusk, often being content simply for unsuspecting prey to wander within reach of their sharp bills. In addition to fish, these herons also take amphibians and larger invertebrates, including crustaceans. The breeding period varies through their range, being delayed further north. The nest is usually constructed in a tree overhanging water, which affords the birds greater security from predators at this vulnerable time. The site may be up to 48ft (15m) off the ground.

Identification: Black area extending over the top of the head, gray sides to the neck, with horizontal black striations running around the neck down to the sides of the body. Wings marked with black and brown lines. White area on the chest extends to the flanks, underparts are pale rufous. Bare area around eyes, and also lower bill, yellowish-green. Bare skin on the throat yellowish, especially in breeding birds. Legs and feet grayish. Sexes alike. Young birds have brownish barring and spotting, with darker wings than adults.

Zig-zag heron (*Zebrilus undulatus*): 13in (33cm)
Precise distribution is unclear, but range probably extends from parts of eastern Colombia and Venezuela across to French Guiana and northern Brazil; also eastern Peru and northeast Bolivia. Dark, heavily mottled body in various shades of brown, with darker barring over the back and wings. Sexes are alike. Young birds have a more rufous coloration overall.

Black-crowned night heron (*Nycticorax nycticorax*): 26in (65cm)
Global range, including from southern Canada southward as far as northern Chile and Argentina in South America. Also present in the Caribbean. Breeds in central parts of North America, moving southward and to the coast during the winter. Predominantly black top to the head, with a thin white streak above the bill extending above the eyes. White areas on sides of the face, with the underparts grayish. The wings are black, with a white area on the back.

Rufescent tiger heron (*Tigrisoma lineatum*): 30in (76cm)
Southeast Mexico through Central America down to Ecuador and over much of northern South America, from Amazonia to the Brazilian coast and southward as far as northeast Argentina. Head and neck rufous, with gray back and wings. Black-edged white stripe extending down both sides of the chest from the base of the bill to the flanks. Underparts also reddish-brown. Sexes are alike. Young birds are a paler cinnamon-buff, with black barring on their bodies disappearing lastly from the neck region.

Little blue heron

Egretta caerulea

These herons are a common sight through much of their range. They prefer to feed on invertebrates rather than fish, hunting crayfish in the water, and crickets on drier ground. These birds sometimes follow behind plows to hunt worms brought to the surface. Breeding starts in April in the north, earlier in Florida and the Caribbean. Pairs often breed in mixed groups with larger herons. Young birds are occasionally seen well beyond their normal range, even as far as Greenland and Paraguay.

Distribution: Southern parts of the U.S.A.; breeds in various locations from southern California east to New England. Moves south in winter from New Jersey down to Florida, along the Gulf coast, and down through Central America to southern Peru and southern Brazil.
Size: 24in (61cm).
Habitat: Ponds, lakes, marshes.
Nest: Platform of sticks.
Eggs: 3–5, pale blue-green.
Food: Invertebrates.

Identification: Slate-blue, with dark purple feathers on head and neck. In breeding birds, these areas are reddish-purple, with plumes on the chest and a head crest. Legs and feet change from dull green to black. Sexes alike. Young birds white, with black tips to flight feathers.

CRAKES

The rail family, Rallidae, to which crakes belong, includes coots and gallinules as well as rails. These birds may be observed in the open, but if frightened will usually dart back into cover along the edges of the water. They can all be recognized by their relatively narrow body shape, which enables them to slip easily and quietly through reeds and similar vegetation.

Moorhen

Common moorhen *Gallinula chloropus*

Identification: Slate-gray head, back and underparts. Grayish-black wings. A prominent white line runs down the sides of the body. The area under the tail is white and has a black central stripe. Greenish-yellow legs have a small red area at the top. The bill is red apart from a yellow tip. Sexes are alike.

Although usually found in areas of fresh water, moorhens are occasionally seen in brackish areas, with infrequent sightings in eastern parts of the U.S.A., such as Connecticut. Their long toes enable them to walk over aquatic vegetation, and they also feed when swimming or browsing on land. Their diet varies according to the season, although seeds of various types make up the bulk of their food. Moorhens are less wary than most rails or crakes, swimming in open water. If danger threatens, they will either dive or swim underwater. They are adept divers, remaining submerged by grasping onto underwater vegetation with their bills. In public parks, moorhens can become quite tame, darting in to obtain food provided for ducks. During the breeding season, pairs of moorhens set up and defend territories and perform complex courtship rituals.

Distribution: South from the Great Lakes to much of the eastern U.S.A. Also Florida, the Gulf Coast and California, right through Central America. Common in much of South America except the northeast and far south.
Size: 12in (30cm).
Habitat: Ponds and other areas of water edged by dense vegetation.
Nest: Domed structure hidden in reeds.
Eggs: 4–7, buff to light green with dark markings.
Food: Omnivorous.

Gray-necked wood rail

Cayenne wood rail *Aramides cajanea*

These rails may expand their range during the wet season, moving into areas of tropical forest that have become flooded. Like many rails, they are shy, unobtrusive birds, preferring to escape danger by slipping away through undergrowth rather than by flying and revealing their presence. They are highly adaptable feeders, using their powerful bills to kill snakes and snails and to smash open palm nuts to feed on the edible kernel. They are even known to dig in cattle dung, to feed on insects there. Gray-necked wood rails form lifelong pairs. Their nest, constructed using a range of materials, is well-hidden, usually situated off the ground but remaining close to water. The chicks hatch after about three weeks, and leave the nest a day or two later. They grow rapidly, becoming indistinguishable from adults by the age of seven weeks old.

Identification: Appearance varies throughout its wide range. Characterized by the gray coloration of the neck, sometimes with a red cap on the crown. Wings are pale brown, with orange-chestnut underparts, and the rear of the body is dark blackish-brown. Legs and feet are red. Bill is yellow, being greener at the tip.

Distribution: Occurs over much of South America, extending south from southern Mexico via the Yucatan Peninsula to eastern Ecuador and Peru, and across Brazil to northern parts of Argentina and Uruguay.
Size: 17in (42cm).
Habitat: Forested areas with water.
Nest: Bowl of vegetation.
Eggs: 3–7, creamy-buff with brownish markings.
Food: Invertebrates, frogs, fruits, seeds and nuts.

Giant wood rail (*Aramides ypecaha*): 18in (45cm)
Eastern and southeastern Brazil, Bolivia, Paraguay, northeastern Argentina and Uruguay. Bluish-gray sides to the face extend over the breast, with a white area under the bill. Back of the head and neck chestnut, as are most of the underparts. Mantle, back and wings are greenish-brown. Rump and the corresponding undertail coverts are black. Area at the top of the legs is gray. Stout, pointed bill is yellowish-green, with legs and feet red, as is the iris. Hens similar, but smaller. Young birds duller overall, with brownish-black plumage.

Brown wood rail (*Aramides wolfi*): 14in (36cm)
Northwest Colombia south to western parts of Ecuador, and probably the far northwest of Peru. Ash-gray head and nape, with white throat. Upper back and underparts are rufous-chestnut, with the rest of the back and wings olive-brown. Rump and tail are black. A small yellowish patch is apparent on the center of the forehead, above the greenish-yellow bill. The legs are reddish. Sexes are alike.

Blackish rail (*Pardirallus nigricans*): 13in (32cm)
Widely separated distribution across South America, with several areas of population in the northwest, from southwestern Colombia down through Ecuador and Peru. Also in Bolivia, Paraguay, and over much of eastern Brazil, south to northeastern Argentina. Dark in color, with a bluish-slate head and underparts, except for a white area on the throat. Back and wings brownish, with the lower belly, undertail and uppertail coverts, and tail all black. Bill greenish-yellow. Legs and feet red, as is the iris. Sexes alike. Young birds have browner plumage.

American purple gallinule

Porphyrio martinica; previously Porphyrula martinica

These gallinules are very agile, athletic birds, able to walk across lily pads, climb trees, swim, and even dive underwater. They are also powerful in flight, with much of the North American population migrating across the Gulf of Mexico each year. Occasionally they are sighted far outside their usual range, in locations as far apart as Greenland and the Falkland Islands. Elsewhere, except at the far south of their range, these gallinules do not migrate. The breeding season begins in May in the U.S.A., but not until December in Argentina. Pairs may also breed regularly through the year, as in Costa Rica. Both parents help to incubate and rear the young. Chicks start to seek out food for themselves at three weeks old, but cannot fly for a further two weeks or more after this.

Identification: Bluish shield on the top of the head. Head also has a purplish area, becoming bluer on the underparts and much greener on the back and wings. White undertail coverts. Prominent bill is reddish, with a yellow tip. Legs and feet are also yellow. Sexes are alike. Young birds are predominantly brownish, with greenish suffusion on the wings and lighter underparts.

Distribution: Breeds in the eastern U.S.A., almost to the Great Lakes. Winters further south, along the Gulf coast and south through Central America as far as Argentina. Also in the Caribbean.
Size: 13in (33cm).
Habitat: Marshes and swamps.
Nest: Built on floating vegetation.
Eggs: 3–10, buff with red markings.
Food: Mainly plant matter.

Azure gallinule

Little gallinule *Porphyrio flavirostris*

The smallest member of its genus, the azure gallinule has a discontinuous distribution through South America. It tends to favor areas of deep water where there is much vegetation growing over the surface. In spite of its long legs, it can swim if necessary, as well as sometimes flying up and perching to escape danger. Azure gallinules also use their long legs to climb up and trample down seeding grasses, which allows them to extract the seeds. They are more likely to be seen in forested areas rather than savanna, and are known to undertake seasonal movements.

Identification: Azure plumage on the wings. The sides of the head down to the breast are a bluish gray, and the rest of the underparts are white. A band of brown extends from the center of the head down over the back and part of the wings. The bill and shield are a greenish-yellow color. Sexes are alike.

Distribution: From Colombia eastward to French Guiana and south through Peru to Bolivia, southern Brazil and into northern Argentina.
Size: 10in (25cm).
Habitat: Marshland with good cover.
Nest: Open cup of vegetation.
Eggs: 4–5, creamy with reddish-brown spots.
Food: Grass seeds and invertebrates.

OTHER RAILS AND RELATED SPECIES

Although shy by nature, members of this group are sometimes sighted in cultivated areas. Their large toes help to prevent them from sinking into marshy ground, and leave an unmistakable impression in mud at the water's edge. Some species of rail display a distinctive flattened, unfeathered area, known as the frontal shield, above the bill.

Giant coot

Fulica gigantea

Occurring in the puna zone of the Andes at altitudes as high as 21,320ft (6,500m), these coots are reputedly not able to fly when adult, although young birds will fly quite readily, often moving down to lakes at lower altitudes for a time. They then return to their traditional haunts for breeding, and have specific nesting requirements. Giant coots construct huge platforms of water weed, often 10ft (3m) or more in length, in the shallows for nesting. The hen lays her eggs in a relatively small, raised cup area, and the same nest site is used and maintained over a number of years. The rim of the nest helps to conceal the chicks once they hatch and also protects them from cold winds.

Identification: Predominantly dark slate gray, blacker on the head, neck, and undertail coverts. Bill is red, white and yellow, with the latter two colors on a flattened area called the shield, which extends over the top of the head. Sexes are alike.

Distribution: Central Peru to Bolivia, Chile and north-west Argentina.
Size: 23in (59cm).
Habitat: Shallow lakes and smaller areas of water.
Nest: Large platform built on dense patches of water weed.
Eggs: 3–7, creamy gray with reddish-brown spots.
Food: Aquatic vegetation.

American coot

Fulica americana

Although there are no striking plumage differences between the cock and hen, they can easily be distinguished by a marked difference in their calls. Unlike some related species, American coots have proved to be highly adaptable, to the extent that their numbers appear to have increased overall in recent years. They rapidly colonize new areas of suitable habitat, although populations can be adversely affected by very cold springtime weather, which makes food hard to find. American coots often migrate south in large numbers to avoid the worst of the winter.

Identification: Predominantly slate gray, more blackish on the head. White undertail coverts. Bill is whitish, with red near the tip, enlarging into a broad shield with red at the top. Sexes are alike, although hens are often significantly smaller. Young birds are predominantly brown, with duller bills.

Distribution: From Alaska southward across much of North America through Central America and the Caribbean into parts of Colombia in South America.
Size: 17in (43cm).
Habitat: Permanent areas of wetland.
Nest: Floating heap of dead aquatic vegetation.
Eggs: 3–12, buff with dense, fine blackish spotting.
Food: Diet consists of aquatic vegetation.

King rail

Rallus elegans

Distribution: From southern Canada through eastern U.S.A. to parts of Mexico. Also present on Cuba and the neighboring Isle of Youth.
Size: 19in (48cm).
Habitat: Freshwater and brackish marshes.
Nest: Cup-shaped.
Eggs: 10–12, creamy buff with purplish-brown spots.
Food: Both plant and animal matter.

Like many of the rails occurring in North America, king rails move south in winter to areas where the temperature is unlikely to drop significantly below freezing, as this would turn their feeding grounds to ice. Aquatic invertebrates feature prominently in their diet, but they are actually omnivorous, eating grass seeds and even fruit, such as blackberries, on occasion. They also prey on frogs and small water snakes. Sadly, in some parts of their range the numbers of king rail have fallen dramatically because of use of pesticides on agricultural land. Many are killed each year by passing traffic. They can also fall victim to a wide range of predators that may include alligators, raccoons, and great horned owls.

Identification: Rusty brown, with darker scalloped patterning over the back and wings. Gray on the ear coverts behind the eyes. Cinnamon underparts with vertical black and white barring on the flanks. Long bill, brown at the tip and orangish further back. Sexes are similar but hens are smaller in size.

Yellow rail (*Coturnicops noveboracensis*): 7in (17cm)
Marshland in central and southeastern parts of Canada to northeastern U.S.A., wintering further south in Louisiana and Texas. Brown on top of the head, with a buff stripe above the eyes, and a brown stripe running across the eye. Sexes are alike, but males may be slightly larger.

Eurasian coot (*Fulica atra*): 16½in (42cm)
Sometimes seen in Newfoundland and Labrador, as well as the Pribilof islands. Sooty, gray, plump body with a black head and neck. Distinguishable from the American coot by virtue of its darker overall coloration, lack of white undertail coverts and the completely white frontal shield.

Sora (Carolina rail, *Porzana carolina*): 10in (25cm)
Freshwater marshland from southeastern Alaska across much of the U.S.A., also in brackish marshes when migrating. Black area at base of bill extends to forehead, white spot behind eyes, with grayish sides to face, and barring on flanks. Upperparts show dark streaks. Sexes alike.

Galapagos rail (*Laterallus spilonotus*): 6in (15cm)
Endemic to the Galapagos Islands. Dark, mainly chocolate-brown coloration, with a blackish head. Dark gray neck and breast, belly dark chocolate with white spots. White barring on undertail coverts. White spotting on wings and back when breeding. Bill blackish, legs and feet dark. Iris is orange. Hens may have paler throat coloration. Young have no white spots on their underparts.

Red rail

Ruddy crake *Laterallus ruber*

Much still remains to be discovered about the red rail. It may only be present in Costa Rica for part of the year. It is shy by nature, blending in with the vegetation, but may be recognized by its calls, which are uttered with increasing frequency in the breeding season. The most obvious of these is a loud trilling call, which falls off in frequency. These rails hide for much of the time, but will emerge into the open by day in search of food. If frightened, they run to cover or fly off with their long legs hanging down. They probably feed mainly on invertebrates, with some seeds. Red rails appear to nest in reed beds, constructing a woven nest lined with thin stems of grass, and a narrow entrance at one side.

Distribution: Occurs in eastern Mexico, also down the west coast and possibly right across the southern part of Mexico too, ranging to parts of Honduras and Nicaragua in Central America, as far south as Costa Rica.
Size: 6in (15cm).
Habitat: Marshland and ditches.
Nest: Ball of grass and other plants.
Eggs: 3–6, cream with dark reddish markings.
Food: Unknown.

Identification: Cock has blackish area over top of the head, with bluish ear coverts. Throat whitish, underparts reddish. Back and wings brownish, darker on the flight feathers. Hen similar, but darker area to uppertail coverts is reddish. Legs and feet pinkish, iris orange, bill black. Young resemble adults but pale on belly.

WATERFOWL

This group of birds has diversified to occupy a wide range of habitats, and has adopted a correspondingly broad range of lifestyles, ranging from grazing in wetland areas through to hunting for fish. Breeding habits vary significantly too, with some members of the group choosing to breed on the ground, while others prefer the relative safety afforded by tree hollows.

Carolina wood duck

American wood duck *Aix sponsa*

Distribution: Occurs widely over much of North America and south to Mexico, being present in western, central and southeastern parts of the continent, as well as on western Cuba.
Size: 20in (51cm).
Habitat: Wooded stretches of fresh water.
Nest: In tree holes.
Eggs: 5–9, buff.
Food: Mainly vegetable matter, from acorns to aquatic plants.

Although these ducks have been seen as far north as Alaska, they move south to warmer climates for the winter months. In some areas their numbers have benefited from the provision of artificial nesting boxes, so that today they rank among the most common water-fowl in the United States. Carolina wood ducks are likely to be seen dabbling for food in open stretches of water, dipping their heads under the surface, but they also come ashore to nibble at vegetation. Although vagrants sometimes appear in the Caribbean, Carolina wood ducks observed in other parts of the world will be descendants of escapees from waterfowl collections.

Identification: Crest with glossy green and purple tones in breeding plumage. The lower neck and breast are chestnut with white speckling, while the abdomen is buff with barring on the flanks. Cock in eclipse plumage resembles the hen, but with a more brightly colored bill. The hen is duller in overall coloration, with dark brown underparts.

Muscovy duck

Cairina moschata

These dull-colored waterfowl are far removed in appearance from their more brightly colored domesticated counterparts. They prefer freshwater areas but sometimes move into saltwater lagoons during the dry season. Muscovies live in groups and are arboreal by nature, with powerful claws that help them to climb trees and roost easily on branches. They generally prefer to nest off the ground, but in areas where they are not commonly hunted, hens may lay eggs on the ground in spots that are well camouflaged by surrounding vegetation. The young develop the white wing patches at one year of age.

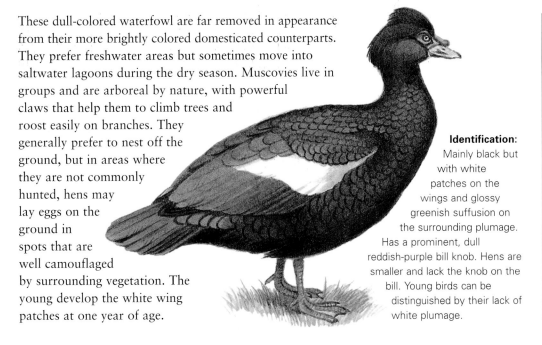

Identification: Mainly black but with white patches on the wings and glossy greenish suffusion on the surrounding plumage. Has a prominent, dull reddish-purple bill knob. Hens are smaller and lack the knob on the bill. Young birds can be distinguished by their lack of white plumage.

Distribution: From Mexico south to parts of Argentina and Uruguay.
Size: 33in (84cm).
Habitat: Forested lakes and marshes.
Nest: Usually in a tree hollow.
Eggs: 8–15, white with greenish suffusion.
Food: Omnivorous.

Hooded merganser

Lophodytes cucullatus

These ducks occur only in small groups of often less than a dozen individuals. They can be difficult to observe, either when resting by the water or even when swimming and darting under the surface in search of food. In the far north, hooded mergansers fly south when their freshwater habitat starts to freeze at the onset of winter, often moving to coastal estuaries. They breed off the ground and sometimes nest as high as 80ft (25m) up in suitable trees. These waterfowl can fly well, displaying great maneuverability at low levels.

Identification: Drakes have a white fan, edged with black, at the rear of the head. The face is black. The chest is white with black-and-white striping behind. The flanks are chestnut and the back is black. Ducks are mainly brown with a bushy crest. Cocks in eclipse plumage resemble hens but have yellowish rather than brown irises, and darker bills.

Distribution: Two distinct populations, one ranging south from Alaska on the western side of North America. The other extends widely over the east of the continent.
Size: 20in (50cm).
Habitat: Lakes and slow-flowing areas of water near woodland.
Nest: In tree hollows.
Eggs: 6–12, white.
Food: Mainly fish.

Northern pintail (*Anas acuta*): 24in (62cm)
Throughout North America and the Caribbean. Moves south in winter, when rarely seen north of the Great Lakes. Long, narrow black tail. Head blackish, with white stripes on breast. Gray flanks. Wings grayish with prominent stripes. Hens brown, with darker patterning and a long, pointed tail with white edge to wings in flight.

Ruddy duck (*Oxyura jamaicensis*): 17in (43cm)
Much of North America and down the west side of South America. Broad bill and upright tail feathers. Chestnut-brown coloration (brown in eclipse), with black and usually white on head. Some regional variations. Hens mainly brown.

White-winged scoter (*Melanitta fusca*): 24in (60cm)
Breeds in Alaska and west and central Canada. Overwinters along west coast of North America as far south as California and on the Atlantic coast from Newfoundland to the Carolinas, and even Florida and Texas. Drakes blackish, with white secondaries and a white area behind the eyes. Ducks brown with white patches on sides of head. Young similar to hens but paler brown.

Black scoter (common scoter, *Melanita nigra*): 21in (53cm)
Breeds in western Alaska, and also Labrador and Newfoundland. Overwinters on the Pacific from Alaska to California, and from Newfoundland down to the Carolinas in the east, sometimes south to the Gulf coast; also on the Great Lakes. Drake blackish with mainly yellow bill. Ducks dark brown with paler sides to head and neck. Young similar but with white bellies.

Common merganser

Goosander *Mergus merganser*

Like many waterfowl found in the far north, the common merganser occurs at similar latitudes in Europe and Asia. Diving rather than dabbling ducks, they are called sawbills because of the small sharp projections running down the sides of their bills, which help them to grab fish more easily. Seen in wooded areas close to water, pairs will nest in a hollow tree or even a nest box, lining it with down to insulate the eggs and prevent them rolling around. Outside the breeding period, common mergansers form large flocks numbering thousands of birds on lakes and similar stretches of fresh water. They may, however, prefer to fish in nearby rivers, returning to the lake at dusk. Common mergansers tend to remain in their nesting location until the water starts to freeze over, whereupon they head south.

They pair up mainly over winter, returning north to breed the following spring.

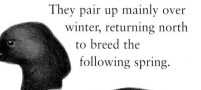

Distribution: Ranges right across North America, from Alaska to Newfoundland, moving southward to overwinter in southern parts of the U.S.A. and Mexico.
Size: 25in (64cm).
Habitat: Lakes and rivers.
Nest: Uses a tree hole.
Eggs: 6–17, ivory or pale buff.
Food: Predominantly fish.

Identification: Narrow body shape. Drake has dark green head and neck, with green on the primary flight feathers evident in flight. Underparts white, back is grayish. Ducks have chestnut-brown head and white area under throat. Bill and legs red. Drakes in eclipse plumage have white areas at front of wings.

DUCKS

Waterfowl are generally conspicuous birds on water, but their appearance and distribution can differ markedly through the year. Drakes often resemble hens outside the breeding season, when their plumage becomes much plainer. Some species are migratory, heading to warmer climates to escape freezing conditions, although others may fly to coastal areas, seeking out estuaries and sheltered bays.

American wigeon

Anas americana

These wigeon are sometimes seen well outside their normal range, with reports of sightings in locations as far apart as Hawaii, the Komandorskie islands off Siberia, and Europe. Almost every year a few vagrant American wigeon are recorded by birdwatchers in the British Isles. The ability of these ducks to cross the Atlantic Ocean is all the more surprising because they are essentially vegetarian in their feeding habits, browsing on plants in and out of the water. A number of American wigeon also migrate south each year to South America, and are observed here in larger numbers outside the breeding season.

Identification: In breeding condition, a prominent white stripe extends back over the top of the head, with a broad dark green area incorporating the eyes, and speckling beneath. The remainder of the plumage is brownish with a white belly and broader white area on the lower body close to the tail. Ducks have completely speckled heads and lack the drake's white forewing, which is retained in the eclipse plumage. The duck has paler chestnut coloration than the drake in eclipse plumage.

Distribution: Much of North America, including the far north. Often moves southward in winter.
Size: 22in (56cm).
Habitat: Freshwater marshland.
Nest: In a hollow often hidden in grass, lined with down feathers.
Eggs: 6–12, creamy white.
Food: Aquatic vegetation, small aquatic invertebrates.

Hawaiian duck

Koloa *Anas wyvilliana*

Considered a smaller relative of the mallard, Hawaiian ducks have declined over recent years. This is due to a combination of hunting pressures, drainage schemes and predation by introduced species such as cats and mongooses. However, it has proved possible to breed these waterfowl successfully in captivity, and this has provided the nucleus of stock for release schemes in areas where they formerly occurred. Already there are indications that they may be re-establishing themselves on Oahu. Hawaiian ducks are shy. Where they do occur in the company of mallards, the populations tend not to mix, although hybridization is a possibility, confirming their close relationship. Hawaiian ducks usually breed between March and June, choosing a well-hidden site for their nest. Although often feeding by dabbling in the water, these ducks may sometimes feed on land, especially in agricultural areas.

Identification: Some variation in appearance. Drakes have a dark greenish top to their heads, with a fine brown speckled area on the cheeks and neck. Chestnut markings with black scalloping on the chest, and brownish underparts. Darker over the back and wings. Drakes have an olive-green bill. Ducks similar, but of a lighter shade overall, with a dull orange or sometimes grayish bill.

Distribution: Restricted to the Hawaiian Islands, mainly on Kauai but reintroduced to both Oahu and Hawaii. Formerly also on Maui, Molokai, and Niihau.
Size: 19in (49cm).
Habitat: Freshwater areas.
Nest: Scrape on the ground.
Eggs: 7–16, grayish-green.
Food: Plant matter and invertebrates.

Green-winged teal (*Anas crecca*): 15in (38cm)
Occurs throughout most of North America, overwintering south of the Great Lakes. Brown head with broad green stripes running across the eyes, and yellow stripes above and below. Chest is pale yellow with black dots. Body and wings are grayish, the wings having white on their trailing edges, with a yellow area under the tail. Hens are mottled brown with a whitish area beneath the tail and a green area on the wings. The bill is dark. Drakes in eclipse plumage resemble hens.

Garganey (*Anas querquedula*): 16in (41cm)
One of a number of primarily Eurasian species sometimes sighted in North America, especially in the Pacific states. Prominent white stripe from the eyes down along the neck. Remainder of the face and breast area brown with black barring. Grayish area on the body, and grayish-black wings. Brown mottling seen over the hindquarters. Hens have mottled plumage with a distinctive buff-white area under the chin. Drakes in eclipse plumage resemble hens but with grayish areas on the wings.

Gadwall (*Anas strepera*): 20in (50cm)
Ranges extensively through North America, up as far as southern Canada. Winters further south, down to Mexico, and also on various Caribbean islands including Jamaica. Drake is finely speckled on the breast, browner on flanks, with a relatively dark crown and black bill. A black area runs through the eyes, with a white area on the wings. In eclipse plumage, the flanks and wings are speckled and the bill is yellowish. Ducks are mottled with rufous edging on the feathers, especially on the wings.

Blue-winged teal

Anas discors

Blue-winged teal return to their northern breeding grounds in May, nesting on their own rather than in colonies and choosing sites concealed in vegetation. The eggs take nearly four weeks to hatch, with the young being unable to fly for a further five weeks or so. They feed by dabbling, upending themselves rather than diving for food. They feed on aquatic snails, crustaceans, and virtually any plant matter. Blue-winged teal are long-distance travelers. Their regular migratory routes take them over land to South America rather than across the Gulf of Mexico. Strong and fast in flight, they are sometimes found well outside their usual range, including on Hawaii and the Galapagos Islands. Blue-winged teal also regularly cross the Atlantic to reach the U.K. and sites as far south as northwest parts of Africa.

Distribution: Breeds in south Alaska, Newfoundland, and central U.S.A. Winters along Pacific and Atlantic coasts. Also present in Caribbean and Central America, extending to northern part of South America, even as far as Chile.
Size: 16in (41cm).
Habitat: Marshes and shallow lakes.
Nest: Down-lined scrape.
Eggs: 6–15, grayish-green to buff.
Food: Plants, invertebrates.

Identification: Blue upperwing coverts with a green speculum. Drake has a white area around base of bill, and a grayish head with darker crown. Underparts red-brown with black speckles. White areas on sides, black rump. Male in eclipse similar to female. Duck brownish, with whitish area at base of bill. Young have spotted underparts.

Shoveler

Northern shoveler *Anas clypeata*

The broad bills of these waterfowl enable them to feed more easily in shallow water. They typically swim with their bill open, trailing it through the water to catch invertebrates, although they also forage both by upending and by catching insects on reeds. Shovelers choose wet ground, often some distance from open water, as a nesting site, where the female retreats from the attention of other drakes. Like the young of other waterfowl, young shovelers take to the water soon after hatching.

Identification: Dark metallic-green head and orange eye. White chest and chestnut-brown flanks and belly, and a black area around the tail. Both back and wings are black and white. The remainder of the body is predominantly white. Broad blue wing stripe, which enables drakes to be recognized even in eclipse plumage, when they resemble hens. Very broad black bill. Hens are predominantly brownish, but with darker blotching. The bill has yellowish edges. A paler area of plumage can be seen on the sides of the tail feathers.

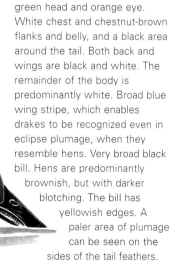

Distribution: Breeds in western North America, moving south to winter in warmer parts such as Texas and Central America. Smaller populations on east coast.
Size: 20in (52cm).
Habitat: Shallow coastal and freshwater areas.
Nest: Down-lined scrape.
Eggs: 8–12, green to buff white.
Food: Plants, invertebrates.

OTHER COMMON DUCKS

Ducks are a fairly diverse group of waterfowl, but can be distinguished by their relatively small size compared with swans and geese. They inhabit stretches of open water, though typically become more secretive when nesting. Drakes usually molt into more colorful plumage before the onset of the breeding season. For the rest of the year they have duller "eclipse" plumage more closely resembling the hens.

Mallard

Anas platyrhynchos

Distribution: Occurs throughout much of North America, though is more scarce in the far north of Canada. Also in Mexico.
Size: 24in (60cm).
Habitat: Open areas of water.
Nest: Scrape lined with down feathers.
Eggs: 7–16, buff to grayish green.
Food: Plant matter and some invertebrates.

These ducks are a common sight, even on stretches of water in towns and cities, such as rivers and canals. They may congregate in quite large flocks, especially outside the breeding season, but they are most evident in the spring, when groups of unpaired males chase potential mates. The nest is often constructed close to water and is frequently hidden under vegetation, especially in urban areas. These birds feed both on water, upending themselves or dabbling at the surface, and on land.

Identification: Metallic-green head with a white ring around the neck. Chest is brownish with gray underparts, and blackish area surrounds the vent. Bluish speculum in the wing, most evident in flight, bordered by black and white stripes. Hen is brownish-buff overall with darker patterning, and displays same wing markings as drake. Hen's bill is orange, whereas that of male in eclipse plumage is yellow, with a rufous tinge to the breast.

Redhead

Aythya americana

In April, redheads return to their northern breeding grounds in the prairie marshes, constructing a nest from dead vegetation concealed in among reedbeds. Although these waterfowl tend to nest singly, rather than in groups, it is not unusual for ducks to lay in the nests of other redheads. As a result, the number of eggs in a nest can vary significantly. Females may even deposit their eggs in the nests of other waterfowl. After breeding, large numbers of redheads often congregate over the winter period, when they can be seen in coastal districts as well as inland. They have even been recorded overwintering as far west as the Hawaiian islands in the Pacific Ocean. Redheads usually feed by diving, rather than dabbling at the surface, and although they feed mainly on plant matter they will also prey on crustaceans in coastal areas.

Identification: Drake has a chestnut-red head, with a black chest and smoky-gray back and sides. Black feathering also around the base of the tail. Bill is very pale blue with a dark tip. Ducks are brownish overall, darker on the crown, with a slaty bill and a narrow whitish area around the black tip. Out of color, the drakes resemble the ducks.

Distribution: Mainly in south-western Canada to western parts of the U.S.A., with a small population in central Alaska. Found near the Great Lakes, overwintering on the east coast through Florida and much of Central America south to Guatemala. Also in parts of the Caribbean.
Size: 19in (48cm).
Habitat: Ponds, lakes, and marshes.
Nest: Made of vegetation.
Eggs: 6–9, greenish-gray.
Food: Mainly plant matter.

Bufflehead

Bucephala albeola

The bufflehead's breeding grounds spread through the forested areas of northern North America, where they are likely to be seen close to water. These waterfowl will dive in search of invertebrate prey, feeding mainly on insects during the summer and switching to snails and crustaceans in winter. They also take plant matter. Breeding starts in April, with a pair often colonizing a hole made by a common flicker or other woodpecker. When not nesting, these ducks spend most of their time on the water. They are less social than many other diving ducks, rarely forming large aggregations even outside the nesting period. It appears that their range in the eastern part of North America, in the vicinity of the Great Lakes, is expanding, but these and other tree-nesting waterfowl are obviously adversely affected by deforestation.

Distribution: Ranges from Alaska eastward through Canada, reaching the Great Lakes and Hudson Bay. Overwinters further south, from the Aleutians down the southern coast of Alaska south to Mexico. Also ranging over much of southern U.S.A. as well as down the north-eastern seaboard to Florida.
Size: 13¹/₂in (34cm).
Habitat: Ponds and small lakes.
Nest: Hollow trees.
Eggs: 5–12, pale green.
Food: Invertebrates, some fish.

Identification: When in color, drakes have an unmistakable large, fluffy white area on the head, extending back behind the eyes. The front of the face and neck are glossy black. Back and wings are dark, contrasting with the white underparts. The duck's head is brownish-gray, with a smaller patch of white plumage below the eyes. Wings are darker, and flanks appear grayish rather than white. Males out of color indistinguishable from females.

Common pochard (*Aythya ferina*): 19in (49cm) Primarily Eurasian, but also the Aleutian and Pribilof islands, and from southern Alaska down to southern California. Similar in appearance to the redhead (see left), with a chestnut-brown head and neck, black chest, a broad gray band encircling the wings and body, and black feathering on the hindquarters. Hens have a brownish head and chest, grayer over rest of the body. Bill has distinctive black band extending down over the nostrils, not seen in redheads.

Canvasback (*Aythya valisineria*): 21in (53cm) Drake has a rufous head and black chest, with a silvery area on the back and wings, and black plumage on the rear. In eclipse plumage, chest area becomes blackish-brown, with silvery-brown coloration in place of the silver. Bill has a distinctive prominent silvery band across it. Ducks also display this feature, being recognizable by the pale stripe through the eye. Head and chest brownish overall. Young birds are a more even shade of brown.

Ring-necked duck (*Aythya collaris*): 18in (46cm) Drakes in breeding plumage have a blackish head, chest, back and wings, with silvery flanks and a distinctive white ring on the underside of the body at the base of the neck. Ducks are much browner, with a band of white plumage at the base of the bill and a similar eye-stripe. Their underparts are mainly brownish. Young birds are similar to hens, but with a less apparent white eye-stripe. They also lack the white bill stripe seen in adults, behind the black tip.

Torrent duck

Merganetta armata

Torrent ducks are associated with the Andes but may also be found at lower altitudes, even close to sea level in some areas. The appearance of these waterfowl varies throughout their extensive range, with six different races being recognized. However, some of these may be naturally occurring color morphs. Torrent ducks favor fast-flowing rivers, where they probe for food around boulders. They will also dive in search of prey, including small fish. Their nests are generally well-concealed, often on cliff ledges or in rocky crevices.

Distribution: Extends down the western side of South America, from Venezuela through most of the Andean region via Bolivia and Chile to Argentina.
Size: 18in (46cm).
Habitat: Fast-flowing rivers.
Nest: Dry plant matter.
Eggs: 3–4, pale green.
Food: Aquatic invertebrates.

Identification: Drake has a black stripe extending down the center of the head and neck, with another stripe through the eye. Body color varies significantly with race, with chests being black or speckled. Hens have chestnut throats and underparts. The rest of the head is grayish, with a similar band around the bill. Young birds are grayish, with streaking on the back and barring on the flanks.

SWANS AND GEESE

These large, unmistakable birds regularly fly long distances to and from their breeding grounds. They rank among the longest-lived of all waterfowl, with a potential life expectancy of more than two decades. Young birds are unlikely to breed until they are three or four years old. When observing them, remember that both geese and swans can be aggressive, especially when breeding.

Coscoroba swan

Coscoroba coscoroba

The status of this swan is a cause for debate among zoologists, with some suggesting that it represents a link between the true swans (of the genus *Cygnus*) and geese. Others regard this species as a relative of the whistling ducks. Coscoroba swans feed by dabbling in the shallows, although they will also seek food on land by grazing. Pairs tend to be solitary by nature. They build a typical swan-like nest consisting of a pile of vegetation, often concealed in a reed bed or on an island. The center of the mound is lined with soft downy feathers, serving as a receptacle for the eggs. The nesting period varies throughout their range. Once the young birds hatch they will swim after their parents, but, unlike other swans, these waterfowl do not appear to carry their cygnets on their backs. Subsequently these South American swans may be seen in flocks, numbering as many as a hundred individuals.

Distribution: Southern part of South America, extending north from Tierra del Fuego to central parts of Chile and northern Argentina. This species overwinters further north in Brazil.
Size: 45in (115cm).
Habitat: Lakes and lagoons.
Nest: Mound of vegetation.
Eggs: 4–7, pale green.
Food: Plant matter and invertebrates.

Identification: Predominantly whitish overall, but with distinctive black tips to the primary feathers that are even apparent when the wings are closed. Bill, legs and feet pinkish. A brown rather than reddish iris distinguishes the hen. Young birds have brownish feathering on the head.

Tundra swan

Whistling swan *Cygnus columbianus*

Tundra swans arrive on their breeding grounds during May. They choose an elevated nest site, and are very territorial at this stage. The majority of pairs breed in western Alaska, and adopt set flight paths to and from their northern range. In the vicinity of Niagara Falls, the swans can easily be swept over the falls to their death if they misjudge the current in the river, since their weight renders them unable to take off directly from the water's surface without paddling along first to gain momentum. The swans leave the tundra in October, roughly splitting into two groups and flying south to their wintering grounds on either side of the U.S.A. Here they may sometimes invade areas of farmland to feed on crops, especially winter cereals. Despite their alternative name of the whistling swan, these waterfowl honk, not whistle.

Distribution: Breeds across the extreme northern coast of North America, moving south to coastal locations in western and eastern parts of the U.S.A. for the winter.
Size: 52in (132cm).
Habitat: Tundra, ponds, and lakes.
Nest: Mound of vegetation.
Eggs: 2–6, pale green.
Food: Mainly vegetation.

Identification: Large, white with blackish legs and a mainly black bill. Small yellow area below each eye. This feature is larger in the Eurasian form, Berwick's swan, seen occasionally on the west coast. Males often larger. Young have gray-pink bills.

Ross's goose (*Anser rossii*): 26in (66cm)
Breeds in the far north of central Canada, near the Perry River, wintering in southwest U.S.A. and along the Mexican border. Occurs in both snow (white) and blue phases, like its relative, the snow goose, retaining the white plumage on the head in its blue phase. Sexes are alike, but males are often larger.

Pink-footed goose (*Anser brachyrhynchus*): 29¹/₂in (75cm)
Breeds in eastern Greenland, and occasionally in North America from Newfoundland to eastern Pennsylvania. Brown head with white streaking on the neck, and white markings on the wings and underparts. Bill is pinkish but dark at the base. Legs and feet are pinkish. Sexes are alike.

Barnacle goose (*Branta leucopsis*): 27¹/₂in (70cm)
Most westerly breeding location is northeast Greenland. Can be seen in the Maritime provinces, but birds encountered elsewhere are likely to be escapees from waterfowl collections. Black line extends from the bill to the eyes. Facial area mainly white, neck and upper breast are black. Whitish underparts with gray barring. Wings are gray, traversed by black and white lines. Sexes alike.

Mute swan (*Cygnus olor*): 63in (160cm)
A European species becoming established in various parts of North America, from southeast of Vancouver Island, British Columbia to the Midwest, the Great Lakes, and on northeastern coasts of the U.S.A. Mainly white, with a black area extending from the eyes to the base of the orange bill. A swollen knob protrudes over the upper bill near the base. Legs and feet blackish. Hens are smaller. Young birds are brownish.

Canada goose

Branta canadensis

A number of different races of Canada goose are recognized, which all differ from one another a little in terms of plumage and size. This species has proved to be highly adaptable. Its numbers have grown considerably in Europe, especially in farming areas, where these geese descend in flocks to feed on crops during the winter once other food has become more scarce. When migrating, flocks fly in a clear V-shaped formation. In common with many waterfowl, Canada geese are not able to fly when molting, but they take readily to the water at this time and can dive to escape danger if necessary. These handsome black-necked geese prefer to graze on land, returning to the relative safety of the water during the hours of darkness.

Identification: Distinctive black head and neck. A small area of white plumage runs in a broad stripe from behind the eyes to under the throat. A whitish area of feathering at the base of the neck merges into brown on the chest. The wings are dark brown, and there is white on the abdomen. The legs and feet are blackish. Sexes are alike.

Distribution: Breeds across North America from Alaska to Labrador, south to California and south of Great Lakes. The smallest race occurs in western Alaska, while geese from the Canadian prairies are almost four times as heavy. Overwinters near west and east coasts of the U.S.A., south to the Caribbean.
Size: 22–43in (55–110cm).
Habitat: Usually near water.
Nest: Vegetation on the ground.
Eggs: 4–7, whitish.
Food: Vegetarian.

Snow goose

Anser caerulescens

Although most common in the far north, migratory snow geese also visit the southerly coasts of the U.S.A., and can even be seen in northern Mexico. These geese are especially attracted to farmland, where grazing opportunities are plentiful, and this appears to be helping them to extend their range. As with all waterfowl, however, there is always the possibility that sightings of snow geese indicate an escape from domestic waterfowl collections, rather than actual wild individuals. The calls of snow geese have been likened to the barking of a dog.

Above: Blue geese are less common than white-phase geese.

Identification: Blue-phase birds (above) are dark and blackish, with white heads and white borders to some wing feathers. Young birds of this color phase have dark heads. White-phase birds (left) are mostly white, with dark primary wing feathers. Young have grayish markings on their heads. Sexes are alike.

Distribution: Breeds in the high Arctic, migrating to the Klamath marshes and south to California, while some remain at Puget Sound. Others overwinter on the east coast, and along the Gulf coast to Mexico.
Size: 33in (84cm).
Habitat: Tundra and coasts.
Nest: Depression lined with vegetation.
Eggs: 4–10, whitish.
Food: Vegetarian.

SHY WADERS

There are a number of long-legged yet small birds that inhabit freshwater locations. They are rather shy by nature, and tend to be found in the shallows, although some species are capable of not only swimming but also diving, and are able to escape would-be predators and obtain food in this way. Although their feet are not webbed like those of waterfowl, their toes are frequently elongated.

Northern jacana

Jacana spinosa

The long toes of this jacana help to distribute its weight over a wide area as it walks, enabling it to move over dense aquatic vegetation on the surface of pools and shallow lakes. This species feeds almost entirely on invertebrates, using its slender bill to probe in surface vegetation and among the roots of water plants. Small fish and water-lily seeds are sometimes eaten too. Breeding habits are unusual, since it is the female who maintains a larger territory, encompassing that of several males. The nest, constructed by the male, is often partially submerged, and the hen will mate with, and lay in the nests of, all males sharing her territory. In turn, each male is responsible for hatching the eggs, and rears the chicks until they are three months old.

Identification: Head and neck are black, merging into dark rufous body and wings. Flight feathers yellow, evident in flight. Frontal shield bright yellow, with bluish area above bill. Gray legs, and very long toes. Prominent spurs at the bend of the wings. Hens larger. Young birds have white underparts, with a white stripe running from each eye down the neck, and adjacent plumage is black. Back and wings brown.

Distribution: May breed as far north as southern Texas, but usually ranges from Mexico south through Central America to western parts of Panama. Also occurs in the Caribbean region, on Cuba, the Isle of Pines, Hispaniola, and Jamaica.
Size: 9^1/$_2$in (24cm).
Habitat: Marshes and ponds.
Nest: Made on floating vegetation.
Eggs: 4, pale buff with black markings.
Food: Invertebrates.

American avocet

Recurvirostra americana

These avocets head north to their breeding grounds in April, nesting around shallow lakes and similar expanses of water, sometimes in large numbers. Females sometimes lay in nests other than their own. Both sexes share the incubation and rearing, with the young fledging at around four weeks of age. American avocets leave their nesting grounds from August, often heading to coasts. They are less common on the eastern seaboard, but appear to be increasing there again after being hunted and almost exterminated in the 1800s. These birds have a distinctive method of feeding in water, sweeping their head from side to side in search of worms, crustaceans, and other prey. On land they catch grasshoppers in a more conventional way, grabbing them with their bill, and sometimes eat seeds too.

Identification: Slender and long-legged, with a narrow, grayish bill slightly upturned at its tip, especially in females, and longer in males. Black areas on the wings separated by a broad white band, with the underparts being white. The head and neck are of a rusty shade when breeding, becoming grayish-white in winter. Young birds have a slight cinnamon wash on their neck.

Distribution: Breeds from southeastern parts of British Columbia across to south-western Ontario, down to Baja California and central Texas. Also occurs in the eastern U.S.A. and central Mexico. Winters in the vicinity of Florida, Texas and the Caribbean, as well as California. Also ranges south to Guatemala.
Size: 18in (46cm).
Habitat: Marshes and ponds.
Nest: Grass-lined scrape.
Eggs: 4, olive-buff with darker spots.
Food: Invertebrates.

Black-necked stilt

Himantopus mexicanus

This species is sometimes regarded as a subspecies of the black-winged stilt (*H. himantopus*), which has a much wider distribution especially in southern latitudes. Other subspecies occur on the Hawaiian islands and southern parts of South America. The black-necked stilt can be distinguished from other mainland forms, which have a white top to the head, by its black top. These stilts breed in colonies and defend their nests aggressively, harrying would-be predators by dive-bombing and calling loudly. Later birds in northern parts migrate southward for winter, but nearer the equator they remain all year around. They seek invertebrates in water by probing and swinging their bill from side to side. Black-necked stilts also take fish, and on land are known to catch butterflies and other insects.

Identification: Slender, with a straight, narrow bill. Distinctive red legs and feet. Upperparts of the cock are predominantly black, with a white area at the base of the bill and above each eye. Black feathering extends out at the base of the neck. Hens are blackish-brown, while young birds have brown rather than black upperparts.

Distribution: Widely distributed through western and central parts of the U.S.A., and via Central America to parts of Ecuador and Peru in western South America, extending as far as northeastern Brazil. Also occurs in the Caribbean.
Size: 16in (41cm).
Habitat: Marshland.
Nest: Grass-lined scrape.
Eggs: 3–4, buff with darker markings.
Food: Mainly invertebrates.

Pied plover (*Vanellus cayanus*): 9in (22^1/$_2$cm)
Occurs in Northern South America, east of the Andes from the Caribbean south to Argentina. Broad black stripe on the sides of the face, extending down the neck and encircling the lower breast. Black cap on the head; remainder of throat, breast and head is white. Broad black stripes run across the wings, with the upperparts being grayish. Underparts are white. Legs and feet red. Sexes are alike. Young birds are brownish where adults have black markings.

Wattled jacana (*Jacana jacana*): 10in (25cm)
From western Panama through Colombia and Venezuela, across much of South America east of the Andes to northern Argentina and Uruguay. Separate population exists in Ecuador and Peru. Distinctive red frontal shield above and on the sides of the yellowish bill. Head and chest are a glossy bluish-black; wings are chestnut red with yellow evident in the flight feathers. Legs and long toes are gray. Regional variations exist, with the northern race blackish, with no chestnut markings on the back and wings. Hens larger, with bluish edging to the upper part of the comb. Young have a smaller frontal shield.

Andean avocet (*Recurvirostra andina*): 19in (48cm)
Found throughout western South America, from central Peru and western Bolivia to northern Chile; also northwest Argentina. Found high in the Andes. White head and body, blackish wings, and narrow, up-curved black bill. White feathering on breast is often stained. Orange-red iris. Grayish feet and legs. Sexes are alike.

Marbled godwit

Limosa fedoa

The call of these birds, most commonly uttered when they are nesting, explains why they are known as godwits. They eat a variety of foods, depending on habitat, feeding largely on insects when breeding. Marbled godwits nest in small colonies close to pools, and may start to lay as early as May. Both parents share the three-week incubation, with the young fledging after a further three weeks. Soon after the birds head south, mostly overwintering on coasts, especially in North America. Occasionally they may head much further south, with records of this species as far south as northern Chile. One of the best sites to see flocks returning north is at Cheyenne Bottoms in Kansas, where they traditionally break their journey. Marbled godwits can be long-lived, with a life expectancy in excess of 25 years.

Identification: Long, slightly upturned bill, orangish-pink at its base and dark at the tip. Tawny-brown overall, with relatively heavy black mottling on the upperparts and lighter barring beneath, especially during the winter months. Cinnamon plumage under the wings evident in flight. Sexes alike. Young birds resemble adults in winter plumage.

Distribution: Breeds in North America from Saskatchewan to Minnesota, also in southern Alaska and south of Hudson Bay. Moves south for winter to California, and from Virginia along Gulf coast to Panama and South America.
Size: 18in (46cm).
Habitat: Grassy areas, shallow waters.
Nest: Grass-lined scrape.
Eggs: 4, olive-buff with darker markings.
Food: Mainly invertebrates.

KINGFISHERS

There are only seven species of kingfisher in America. Although fish feature prominently in the diets of these birds, they may also hunt invertebrates in flight. Their dependence on stretches of open water means that they leave the freezing latitudes of the far north for the winter, and may sometimes move to coasts during unexpected cold spells elsewhere.

Ringed kingfisher

Ceryle torquata; previously *Megaceryle torquata*

Ringed kingfishers are rather solitary by nature, and hence not especially conspicuous. They are very patient when fishing, and can spend up to two hours on a favored branch waiting for a fish. The bird then dives down to seize the fish, returning to the perch to stun it before swallowing it head-first. Ringed kingfishers tend to be sedentary, but in southern areas they move north from Tierra del Fuego for winter. Pairs usually nest in river-banks. The tunnel leading to the nest chamber is up to 8.8ft (2.7m) long, while the chamber itself is small. The young remain there until five weeks old, and can fly from the time of fledging.

Identification: Male has pale gray head, with a white spot in front of the eye and a narrow white line beneath. A broad white collar encircles the neck. Back and wings are gray, with gray and white upper tail feathers. Underparts rufous, with white undertail coverts. Hens have a gray area on the breast with a narrow white band below, and rufous underparts. Young birds similar to females, but gray of the breast has a rufous suffusion.

Distribution: Ranges as far north as the Rio Grande and south Sinaloa down through Central America. Also present on Guadaloupe. Occurs through much of South America apart from the Andean region.
Size: 16in (40cm).
Habitat: Lakes and rivers.
Nest: In a burrow.
Eggs: 3–6, white.
Food: Mainly small fish.

Belted kingfisher

Ceryle alcyon; previously *Megaceryle alcyon*

The loud, rattling call of these kingfishers, uttered in flight, betrays their presence. Their preference for fish means they will move south in the winter, to areas of water that will not freeze over. They are generally found on tranquil stretches of water, where they can observe fish easily, but on occasions they have been spotted feeding up to 0.6miles (1km) offshore. They may also visit garden ponds. Various invertebrates from butterflies to crayfish feature in the diet of belted kingfishers. Their large size means they can also prey on water shrews and the young chicks of other birds. If faced with a shortage of food in winter, they will even resort to feeding on berries. The area beneath their regular roosting spot is littered with regurgitated pellets containing the indigestible remains of their prey. As in the case of owls, this evidence enables zoologists to pinpoint the feeding preferences of these and other kingfishers.

Identification: Cock birds are mainly gray on the head, back, and wings, except for a white collar, white underparts below a gray breast-band, and a white spot by each eye. Hens have a rufous breast-band with gray markings. and are rufous on the flanks too. Young have a second tawny breast-band.

Distribution: Ranges from the Aleutian Islands into southwest Alaska and down through southern Canada to the Gulf coast and Mexico. May be seen in other parts of Central America, the Caribbean and along the northeastern coasts of South America in winter.
Size: 14¹/₂in (37cm).
Habitat: Ponds, lakes, and rivers.
Nest: In a burrow.
Eggs: 5–8, white.
Food: Mainly fish.

Amazon kingfisher

Chloroceryle amazona

As their name suggests, Amazonian kingfishers are more common in South America than further north, preferring lowland areas of habitat. Their calls are quite harsh, but they do have a song that is occasionally uttered when perched, with the bird's wings held open and its bill raised vertically. A pair will excavate the nest tunnel in a vertical bank, extending back up to 5¼ft (1.6m) and broadening into a chamber about 10in (25cm) wide and 18in (45cm) long. The narrow dimensions of the nest mean that adult birds are forced to back out along the tunnel, rather than being able to emerge again head-first. Both members of the pair share the incubation, which lasts about 22 days, and subsequently care for the young, which leave the nest site when just over a month old.

Identification: Dark green head and back, with some prominent green streaks on the flanks. A white collar extends around the neck, beneath the black bill. A rufous area is present on the breast of cock birds, with the underparts being white in hens.

Distribution: From the Yucatan Peninsula in Central America southward to Ecuador and across central and eastern South America as far as central Argentina.
Size: 12in (30cm).
Habitat: Wooded areas near water.
Nest: In a burrow.
Eggs: 3–4, white.
Food: Fish and prawns.

Green kingfisher (*Chloroceryle americana*): 9in (22cm)
May be seen as far north as Arizona and New Mexico, and more frequently in Texas, down through Central America across much of northeastern South America to Argentina, as well as the northwestern coastal area, reaching northern Chile. Cock birds have a green head, back and wings, with two lines of white barring extending across the wings. The throat is white, with a collar extending from the throat around the neck. Rufous chest and white underparts, aside from prominent black spotting on the flanks and across the lower chest. Hens similar, but with a very pale rufous chest band and a speckled greenish band.

Green and rufous kingfisher (*Chloroceryle inda*): 9½in (24cm)
The green and rufous kingfisher ranges from southeastern Nicaragua, Costa Rica, and Panama southward through northern South America east of the Amazon, and south as far as Santa Catarina in Brazil. Also present down the western coast of South America through Ecuador and Peru. Head, back, and wings dark green, with pale white spots on the wings. Underparts are rufous. A small rufous stripe extends back to the eye on each side of the head from the base of the dark bill. Hens can be easily recognized by the green speckling on a white band across the upper breast.

American pygmy kingfisher

Chloroceryle aenea

Quiet by nature and blending in well with their forest background, these small kingfishers are often difficult to observe. They are not uncommon, however, and are most likely to be found near streams and other areas of water. American pygmy kingfishers hunt in a similar way to their larger relatives, perching on a convenient branch overlooking a calm stretch of water and waiting for small fish, tadpoles or other aquatic creatures to come to the surface. These kingfishers catch insects in flight too. They are solitary except when breeding. The nest may be excavated a short distance into a riverbank, or sometimes in an arboreal termite mound, where the termites help to protect the birds from predators.

Distribution: Extends southward from the Sierra Madre del Sur and Puebla in Mexico down through Central America and eastward across South America as far as Rio de Janiero.
Size: 5in (13cm).
Habitat: Forest pools and rivers.
Nest: In a burrow.
Eggs: 3–5, white.
Food: Fish and invertebrates.

Identification: Cock has a bright green head, back and wings, with a rufous collar. The chest and flanks are rufous, with the center of the underparts being white, as are the undertail coverts. A rufous area extends from the bill above the eye. Hens can be distinguished by their green breast band. Young birds have pale speckling on the wings and very pale rufous upperparts.

OTHER FRESHWATER PREDATORS

As with other species, there are a number of predatory birds which have adapted to lakes, rivers, and other freshwater habitats, while their relatives are more commonly encountered in other localities. Examples here include several fish-eating species, ranging from a freshwater tern to various birds of prey, with their lifestyles varying accordingly.

Large-billed tern

Phaetusa simplex

These unusual terns are typically found on freshwater lakes and rivers, where they breed on sand bars. They sometimes nest in large colonies of up to 100 pairs. Large-billed terns lay directly onto the sand but change their breeding sites annually, possibly to avoid predation. Nevertheless, nesting on the ground still has its dangers, with a variety of predators, including boa constrictors, seeking out their nests. Outside the breeding period they may be found in other habitats, often moving to coasts. Large-billed terns mostly feed by diving into the water, but may also swoop down and trawl at the surface using their large bill. Along with aquatic prey they also catch flying insects, and on farmland may seek out invertebrates exposed by the plow.

Identification: Black cap on the head, with black also on the primary flight feathers and adjacent areas. Back and leading edges of the wings are gray, the rest is white. Forehead paler when not breeding. Large bill and feet are yellow. Sexes are alike.

Distribution: Mainly eastern half of South America, with a small population in western Ecuador, down to Argentina and Uruguay. May range further north in spring, being recorded in Ohio, Illinois, and New Jersey in the U.S.A., and also from Bermuda as well as Cuba.
Size: 14^{1}/2in (37cm).
Habitat: Freshwater areas.
Nest: On sand bars.
Eggs: 2–3, brownish with darker markings.
Food: Fish and invertebrates.

Common black hawk

Buteogallus anthracinus

Common black hawks are summer visitors to North America, migrating south in the fall, although they appear to be sedentary further south. Occupying large territories means these birds of prey are not especially evident. A study in Mexico along the River Bavispe revealed that individual pairs typically occupy a territory of some 1.8miles (3km) long, although in other areas they may occur at higher densities. They are not very conspicuous, often perching quietly in trees, and briefly swooping down to seize their quarry. Fish figure prominently in their diet, although a wide range of other prey, from crabs to iguanas, may also be eaten. Breeding pairs in North America start laying in May, while nesting takes place earlier closer to the equator. The incubation period lasts nearly six weeks, with fledging occurring after a further six weeks.

Identification: Predominantly blackish, with a white tip to the tail and a broader white band across the tail. Some relatively inconspicuous white flecking on the thighs and also at the base of the primary flight feathers, evident in flight. Cere area incorporating the nostrils is yellow, as are the legs. Sexes are alike. Juveniles have streaked underparts, with a series of bands across the tail. Yellow on the face less prominent.

Distribution: Ranges from southern Utah, Arizona, New Mexico, and Texas down through western and eastern Central America to Colombia, Venezuela, and Guyana. Present on various Caribbean islands as well. Generally migrates south from the U.S.A. for winter.
Size: 21in (53cm).
Habitat: Wooded areas near rivers.
Nest: Made of sticks.
Eggs: 1–3, white and spotted.
Food: Amphibians, crabs, and fish.

Osprey

Pandion haliaetus

The natural range of the osprey extends to all inhabited continents, making it one of the most widely distributed of all birds. Ospreys have adapted to feeding on stretches of fresh water as well as on estuaries and even the open ocean, swooping to grab fish from just below the surface using their powerful talons. They are capable of carrying fish typically weighing up to 11oz (300g) without difficulty, although there are reports of birds being dragged underwater and subsequently drowning while grappling with extremely heavy prey. They live in coastal colonies and often return to the same nesting grounds year after year. Their call is a high, rapidly repeated and rather plaintive whistle.

Left: Osprey feed only on fish, pouncing on those just below the surface.

Identification: Brown stripes running across the eyes down over the back and wings. Eyes are yellow. Top of the head and underparts are white, with brown striations across the breast, which are most marked in hens. Tall, upright stance, powerful gray legs and talons. Hens significantly heavier than cocks.

Distribution: Ranges across North America, from British Columbia to eastern coasts north of the Great Lakes. Breeding grounds are also extensive, stretching from Florida to Labrador. Winters from South Carolina to north and eastern South America.
Size: 23in (58cm).
Habitat: Close to stretches of water.
Nest: Platform of sticks in a tree, high off the ground.
Eggs: 3, white with darker markings.
Food: Fish exclusively.

Rough-legged hawk (*Buteo lagopus*): 22in (56cm)
Breeds across the far north of North America, wintering in the northeast and across much of the U.S.A., except for the southeast. Heavily streaked brown and white plumage, with a brown area on the wings. Tail is banded in males, solid brown in females, edged with narrow black barring on lower side; feathers have white tips. Young birds have buff-colored thighs. A dark morph also exists.

Slate-colored hawk (*Leucopternis schistacea*): 17in (43cm)
Amazonia region, from southern Colombia and Venezuela eastward to French Guiana and northern Brazil. Also south via Ecuador and Peru to Bolivia. Slaty-gray overall, with a red area encircling the eyes and over the cere. Legs also red. Tail black with a white band across it, and a narrow white tip. Hens slightly larger. Young birds have narrow white barring on underparts and undersides of wings.

Barred owl (*Strix varia*): 21in (53cm)
Northwestern U.S.A. up to southern Alaska, across Canada and down across eastern U.S.A. Dark circle outlining the face, with a line running to the top of the yellow bill. Thick brown barring across the upper breast, with streaking over rest of underparts. Back and wings have brown and white patterning. Whitish feathers on the feet, with the exposed tips of the toes being yellowish. Sexes are alike.

Crane-hawk

Geranospiza caerulescens

Despite their extensive distribution relatively little is known about crane-hawks, so-called because of their long legs and upright posture. These birds of prey are found in a variety of habitats, usually near water. They are adaptable hunters, catching quarry in flight as well as dropping down to seize prey on the ground. Their legs are double-jointed, allowing one foot to be used rather like a hand while the hawk anchors itself with the other; this is useful for reaching into tree holes or vegetation to grab small creatures. The breeding period extends through much of the year, apparently influenced by location, occurring in Venezuela during the rainy season. The nest site is located high up and lined with fresh vegetation. Egg-laying is preceded by aerial courtship displays.

Identification: Varies with race. Grayish to black overall. Long, broad tail has two prominent white bands. Dark bill, with red skin encircling the eyes, and pinkish-red legs. Sexes alike, but females larger. Young display white streaking on head, and brownish suffusion, with barring and buff on underparts.

Distribution: An isolated population in northwestern Mexico, with the main range extending south through the rest of Central America and across much of northern South America to the north of Argentina and Uruguay.
Size: 20in (51cm).
Habitat: Often close to water.
Nest: Platform of sticks.
Eggs: 2, white and spotted.
Food: Larger invertebrates and vertebrates.

COTINGAS

The cotingas include some of the most colorful of all tropical birds, although their name comes from an Amazonian native American word meaning "washed white," which is used locally to describe the white bellbird. Their diet consists mainly of fruits and berries, and this group of birds is important in the dispersal of plants, as undigested seeds from their food are passed onto the ground.

Scarlet cock-of-the-rock

Andean cock-of-the-rock *Rupicola peruviana*

With their spectacular bright red plumage, males frequently congregate together at traditional display sites called leks, often deep in the forest. Here they seek to entice hens to mate with them. Their display calls have been likened to the squealing of pigs, although these cotingas are not noisy by nature. Their brilliant plumage blends into the dark background in the forest, making them hard to observe. The hen constructs her nest using damp mud.

Distribution: Colombia and Venezuela to parts of Ecuador, Peru, and Bolivia.
Size: 12¹/₂in (32cm).
Habitat: Humid, rocky areas of forest, often in ravines close to water.
Nest: Cup made of mud, located in a secluded rocky outcrop or cave.
Eggs: 2, buff with darker spotting.
Food: Mainly berries and other fruit.

Identification: Brilliant red dominates in the plumage, with crest feathers extending down over the bill, contrasting with black on the back and wings. Hens are significantly duller in color, and are generally reddish brown with a smaller crest.

Fiery-throated fruiteater

Pipreola chlorolepidota

This is the smallest of the Andean fruiteaters. It is found at a lower altitude than related species, typically less than 3,280ft (1,000m) above sea level, in the foothills of the Andes. These members of the cotinga clan are most likely to be observed singly or in pairs. They may breed throughout the year, building a moss nest lined with small roots, usually close to the ground and often disguised in a creeper. The fiery-throated fruiteater is unusual in that it does venture up into the canopy of the forest, although it is also commonly seen in the lower levels, often seeking food in the company of other birds.

Identification: The underparts are dark green, with a yellowish-orange throat area; remainder of the plumage is also green. Bill is reddish. Hens closely resemble female scarlet-breasted fruiteater (*P. frontalis*), being predominantly green, with yellow barring extending from the throat over the entire underparts.

Distribution: Eastern areas of Ecuador and Peru.
Size: 4in (11cm).
Habitat: Humid tropical forest.
Nest: Cup-shaped.
Eggs: Probably 2, creamy and spotted.
Food: Mainly berries and other fruit, also invertebrates.

Orange cock-of-the-rock (Guianan cock-of-the-rock, *Rupicola rupicola*): 12¹/₂in (32cm)
Found in French Guiana west to Colombia, also in northern Brazil. Unmistakable shade of brilliant orange. The hen is mainly olive brown with an orange suffusion on the rump.

Pompador cotinga (*Xipholena punicea*): 8in (20cm)
Extends from Colombia eastward to French Guiana and south to northwest Brazil. Wine-red plumage with white areas on the wings. Hens are gray, with white edging to some wing feathers. The eyes are whitish.

Plum-throated cotinga (*Cotinga maynana*): 7¹/₂in (19cm)
Ranges from southeastern Colombia to northern Bolivia and Amazonian Brazil. Turquoise with a small plum-colored throat patch. Hens are brown with pale edges to the feathers. They have cinnamon plumage on the lower abdomen.

Barred fruiteater (*Pipreola arcuata*): 8¹/₂in (22cm)
Found in the Andean region of western South America at altitudes of 10,500ft (3,200m) in cloud forest. Blackish head, with barring confined to the chest and underparts, which are green in hens.

Red-crested cotinga (*Ampelion rubrocristatus*): 9in (23cm)
Found in the Andean region of Colombia and western Venezuela south to northern Bolivia. Grayish-brown, with a blacker tone on the head, back, and wings. Reddish crest at the back of the head is often kept flat. Undertail coverts are streaked with white. White areas on the underside of the tail. Bill is white with a black tip. Iris is red. Sexes are alike.

Long-wattled umbrellabird

Cephalopterus penduliger

As the name suggests, the male of this species has a bizarre black-feathered wattle extending down from his chest that measures approximately 12in (30cm) long. It is inflated as part of his display, but shortened during flight and held close to the chest. The flight pattern of umbrellabirds is not dissimilar to that of woodpeckers, low and strong over the trees. Quiet by nature, solitary and rarely observed, males are most likely to be seen displaying on bare branches, when their booming calls are uttered. These calls are heard with increasing frequency during the nesting season, although it appears that the hen alone is responsible for rearing the offspring.

Identification:
Predominantly black in color. Very long wattle, which is greatly reduced in females. Both have relatively small crests. Brown eyes help to distinguish these cotingas from related umbrellabirds.

Distribution: Western Colombia and northwestern Ecuador.
Size: 20in (51cm) cock; 18in (46cm) hen.
Habitat: Lowland tropical forest.
Nest: Platform of twigs.
Eggs: 1, khaki-colored.
Food: Mainly palm fruits and insects.

Purple-breasted cotinga

Cotinga cotinga

One of the most striking features of these cotingas is their small yet broad bills, which allow them to pluck and swallow quite large fruits whole. They belong to the group often known as the blue cotingas, so-called because of the predominant color of the cock bird. Individuals are most likely to be seen perching on dead treetops, although they fly with a strange rattling noise, which is thought to be caused by the modified shape of their flight feathers. Little is known about their breeding habits, but it is believed that hens incubate and rear their chicks on their own.

Identification:
Silhouette is like that of a dove. Distinctive reddish-purple feathering from the throat down to the middle of the belly; the remainder of the body is violet blue, apart from the black wings and tail. Small yet broad bill. Hens are dark brown, with white edging to the feathers, creating a scaly appearance over the whole body.

Distribution: Eastern Colombia to the Guianas and Brazil.
Size: 7¹/₂in (19cm).
Habitat: Lowland tropical forest.
Nest: Small, flimsy, and cup-shaped.
Eggs: Probably 1–2, bluish with rusty-brown markings.
Food: Primarily fruit.

JACAMARS, MOTMOTS AND PUFFBIRDS

These birds are unique to America. Jacamars are mainly found in South rather than Central America, and are characterized by their relatively slim body shape, long narrow tail, and slender bill. Motmots are easily recognized by the enlarged rackets on their surprisingly flexible tail. Like puffbirds, they feed on invertebrates and even small vertebrates.

Paradise jacamar

Galbula dea

Distribution: Northern South America to parts of Brazil, Peru and Bolivia.
Size: 12in (30cm).
Habitat: Occurs in forest and more open country.
Nest: May excavate into the mounds of arboreal termites or a suitable bank.
Eggs: 2–4, glossy white.
Food: Invertebrates.

The jacamars form a group closely related to woodpeckers, and are members of the avian order *Piciformes* (which includes woodpeckers and trogons). Like trogons, they have a zygodactyl perching grip, with two toes directed forward over the perch and two behind. In common with related species, the paradise jacamar has a long, thin bill. It hunts insects on the wing, using its bill to grab prey in flight. These are not especially shy birds, and are most likely to be seen either in pairs or small parties in forest clearings or sometimes when swooping out across water. Their call note is a distinctive "pip" sound that is repeated frequently. These jacamars, unlike other species, often remain in the tree canopy, where they are difficult to observe thanks in part to their coloration. Paradise jacamars will often accompany groups of other birds, seizing any invertebrates that are disturbed as a result of the other birds' movements.

Identification: Distinctive dark body and a long tail that tapers along its length. White feathering under the throat and dark, glossy, green wings. Bill is long and black. Sexes are alike. The color of the crown may be either pale gray or dark brown, depending on the race.

Rufous-tailed jacamar

Galbula ruficauda

Distribution: Ranges from the southeastern part of Mexico along the Atlantic seaboard down through Honduras into South America, extending to Ecuador in the west and down as far as Argentina on the eastern side.
Size: 9in (22¹/₂cm).
Habitat: Evergreen forests.
Nest: In a burrow.
Eggs: 2–4, glossy white.
Food: Mainly flying insects.

Identification: Metallic green head, chest, and wings with glossy, iridescent upperparts and rufous-brown underparts. The bill is long and narrow, tapering to a point. Throat area in cock birds is white, and a pale cinnamon or buff color in hens.

Like other jacamars, this wide-ranging Central and South American species perches for relatively long periods during the day, remaining alert to feeding opportunities. When an insect ventures within range it will dart off in pursuit with a swooping flight pattern. Having seized its quarry, it will return to beat the invertebrate fiercely against its perch. Dragonflies and butterflies rank amongst its favorite prey. Rufous-tailed jacamars inhabit evergreen forests including second growth forests, where they frequent forest clearings. They have very loud calls, which have been likened to human screams, and it is usually these that betray their presence in the forest, especially since they favor perches that are relatively exposed. Pairs will nest in burrows, with the nest often located at a relatively low height in a bank. The tunnel can be up to 18in (45cm) in length. Both members of the pair share incubation duties. The cock bird sits mainly during the day, with the hen taking over at dusk. The young birds, which have duller plumage, remain in the nest until they fledge at about three weeks old.

Blue-crowned motmot

Momotus momota

Blue-crowned motmots frequent lower branches in the canopy, sometimes venturing into more open areas of countryside, especially in the vicinity of rivers. They have a very distinctive way of moving their tail feathers from side to side, rather like the pendulum of a clock, usually when excited, and will also perch with their tail held at an angle. These motmots hawk insects on the wing and hunt small vertebrates such as lizards, as well as eating fruit and berries on occasion. They also follow columns of army ants moving across the forest floor, swooping down not on the ants but on other small creatures attempting to escape from these aggressive insects. The call of the blue-crowned motmot is rather like that of an owl, often consisting of a double hooting, frequently uttered just before sunrise. A hole in a bank, often near water, is used for breeding, with the tunnel extending back some distance and broadening to form a nesting chamber at the end.

Identification: Quite variable, depending on the race. Black stripe, edged with blue, extends back a short distance down the side of the neck through the eyes. The crown may be blue (as in the northeast Mexican race *M. m. coeruliceps*) or can be black at the center with a blue surrounding area. Upperparts may be green or olive-green, sometimes with a chestnut collar. Underparts are olive-green. The tail is long, green at the base and blue toward the tip, with two evident rackets. Sexes are alike.

Distribution: Range includes much of Central and South America, extending from Mexico down to north-western Peru and eastward to Paraguay, northwest Argentina and southeastern Brazil. Also occurs on Trinidad and Tobago.
Size: 16in (41cm).
Habitat: Mainly forested areas.
Nest: In a burrow.
Eggs: 2–5, white.
Food: Invertebrates form the bulk of the diet.

White-eared jacamar (*Galbalcyrhynchus leucotis*): 8in (20cm)
Northern part of the Upper Amazonian region. Recognizable by its large, pinkish bill and white areas of plumage behind the eyes. Reddish-chestnut overall with dark wings. Sexes alike.

White-necked puffbird (*Notharchus macrorhynchus*): 10in (25cm)
The five recognized subspecies of these puffbirds have a fairly extensive range through South America, from sightings in Mexico and Guatemala south as far as northern parts of Argentina. White on the forehead, chest, and abdomen. Black elsewhere, in a band across the chest, around the eyes and on the wings. Barred on sides of body. Sexes are alike.

Spotted puffbird (*Bucco tamatia*): 7in (18cm)
Northern South America, including Colombia and Venezuela, south through Ecuador to Peru and east into Brazil. Cinnamon plumage across the throat, black-and-white barring beneath, with a black bar on the lower cheeks. Sexes are alike.

Rufous-capped motmot (*Baryphthengus ruficapillus*):16in (40cm)
Ranges from eastern Honduras down to parts of Brazil and northern Argentina. Head and underparts are rufous, apart from an area of black feathering extending back from the bill. There may also be a small black spot on the belly. Back and wings are green, as is the tail and the area around the vent. Isolated south-eastern population lacks rackets on the tail and has olive underparts.

White-whiskered puffbird

Malacoptila panamensis

It is easy to miss these dark-colored birds in the forest gloom. Puffbirds avoid the canopy, preferring to spend much of their time perching quietly at lower levels, flying only short distances. They hunt close to the ground, catching insects and small vertebrates in their stocky, hooked bills. Puffbirds are typically seen either on their own or in pairs. They nest in an underground tunnel, usually excavated on slightly sloping ground, which extends down to a depth of 2ft (60cm), and the eggs are laid in a chamber on a bed of leaves. Unusually, the male white-whiskered puffbird is largely responsible for incubating the eggs and brooding the chicks once they hatch, while the female is responsible for obtaining food. The entrance to the tunnel is carefully concealed with leaves and twigs, and the puffbirds fly directly up to the branches overhead as they leave the nest.

Identification: Cinnamon-brown streaking, with white spots over the back and wings. Paler brown underparts, with prominent white bushy lores and mustache. The iris is a deep reddish shade. Hens are paler and grayer overall, again with a white area surrounding the bill. Young birds are recognizable by the scaling on their upperparts, and they possess a smaller mustache.

Distribution: Ranges from southeastern Mexico down through Central America to Ecuador.
Size: 8in (20cm).
Habitat: Evergreen forest.
Nest: In burrows.
Eggs: 2–3, white.
Food: Mainly invertebrates.

QUETZALS, TROGONS AND MANAKINS

Quetzals have a special mythical significance in ancient Central and South American culture and feature prominently in Mayan legend and symbolism. Trogons as a group have a much wider distribution, with relatives in Africa. They have a similar body shape to quetzals, with a broad, square-ending tail. Manakins form another colorful group of fruiteating forest birds.

Crested quetzal

Pharomachrus antisianus

Distribution: Colombia and western Venezuela to Brazil in the east and southwards as far as Bolivia.
Size: 13in (33cm).
Habitat: Humid forest. Typically occurs in cloud forest in the Andean region up to an altitude of about 9,840ft (3,000m).
Nest: In tree holes or termite nests.
Eggs: 2, light blue.
Food: Berries, other fruit, and also invertebrates.

Quetzals have a distinctive, upright stance when perching, and they rest so quietly that they are easily overlooked. They are most likely to be seen close to the fruiting trees on which they feed. These quetzals have an undulating flight pattern, and their calls are a loud sequence of rolling notes. The plumage of crested quetzals, like that of related species, is brightly colored but fades quite rapidly after death, so museum specimens rarely display the vibrancy of living birds. Another unusual feature is their very thin skin.

Identification: Distinguished from other quetzals by the white undersides to the tail feathers; hens have barred feathering. The hen can also be distinguished from the cock by her brown rather than green head, and a reduced area of red on the underparts. Young birds resemble the female.

Golden-winged manakin

Masius chrysopterus

These small birds are most likely to be spotted flying through the understorey in forests, sometimes heading up into the canopy in search of fruit. Golden-winged manakins normally seek out berries, which they can pluck on the wing, as well as invertebrates, which figure more prominently in their diet during the breeding period when there are chicks in the nest. Little is known of the habits of golden-winged manakins, but they appear to be relatively solitary by nature. The males use their bright wing coloration for display purposes.

Identification: This species has a distinctive golden-yellow edging to the wings and a yellow crest on the forehead, with this color extending onto the throat and back over the head, where it becomes orangish. The remainder of the plumage is glossy black. The hen is greenish, but with prominent yellow feathering in the vicinity of the chin and belly.

Distribution: Occurs in the Andean region of South America, notably in Colombia, Venezuela, Ecuador and Peru.
Size: 4in (11cm).
Habitat: Cloud forest and woodland.
Nest: Suspended cup-shape, made of moss and rootlets.
Eggs: 2, cream with brown spots.
Food: Berries and some invertebrates.

White-tailed trogon

Trogon viridis

Like other trogons, the white-tailed may be sedentary for long periods, but is sufficiently agile to feed on fruit in flight, as well as to catch invertebrates on the wing. These trogons will also swoop on small vertebrate prey, such as lizards. The bill is short, but has a wide gape to facilitate swallowing. Their perching grip is unusual too, with two toes being directed in front of and behind the perch, rather than the more usual 3:1 perching configuration. In common with other trogons, they do not build a nest, with hens simply laying their eggs in a suitable chamber. They have even been known to use a termite nest, where the presence of termites deters would-be predators. Here the nesting chamber is a hollow, constructed at the end of a tunnel that usually leads in an upwardly diagonal direction.

Identification: Glossy violet feathering from the head to the chest. Yellow underparts and a dark green back, with a distinctive, mainly white underside to the tail. Blue eye rings. Bill is bluish-white. The hen is duller in appearance, slate in color with orangish-yellow underparts and a dusky upper bill.

Distribution: Costa Rica and Panama south to Colombia, Ecuador, Peru, and Brazil. Also on Trinidad.
Size: 11in (28cm).
Habitat: Humid forest.
Nest: Usually in a tree hole.
Eggs: 2, light blue.
Food: Berries, other fruit, and some invertebrates.

Pavonine quetzal (*Pharomachrus pavoninus*): 13in (33cm)
The only quetzal found east of the Andes, ranging south to northern Bolivia. Distinctive red bill and red lower underparts, otherwise the plumage is metallic emerald green. Hen is less colorful, with a black underside to the tail.

Black-throated trogon (*Trogon rufus*): 10in (25cm)
Ranges from southeastern Honduras down to Paraguay and northeastern Argentina. Distinctive green-and-yellow coloration, separated on the chest by a thin white band. The hen is distinguished from the cock by her brown and yellow feathering.

Striped manakin (*Machaeropterus regulus*): 3½in (9cm)
Colombia and Venezuela south to Peru, Bolivia, and Brazil, occurring in the Andes up to 4,900ft (1,500m). Brilliant red cap, with reddish streaking on the undersides. The hen is a dull shade of green overall, with paler, yellowish underparts and a white underside to the tail feathers. There are also darker streaks on the sides of the body, with a rufous hue on the flanks.

Violaceous trogon (*Trogon violaceus*): 9in (22cm)
Eastern Mexico, Central America down into Ecuador and Brazil. Entire head and throat of cock is purplish-blue, with a white border separating this area from the bright yellow underparts. The back is a dark metallic shade of green, while the underside of the tail is white with black horizontal banding. Bill is horn-colored and has a darker base. Hens have white feathering encircling each eye.

Elegant trogon

Trogon elegans

Elegant trogons frequent fruiting trees in the forest, being most commonly sighted individually or in pairs. Despite the bright coloration of the cock bird in particular, they blend in well with the background and are not easily observed. Elegant trogons are not especially active by nature. Their calls consist of chattering and hooting sounds. They may use their bill to excavate a nesting chamber, boring into rotten wood if no natural hole is available. Trogons may also dig into a wasps' nest or arboreal termite nest without disturbing the occupants, benefiting from the protection they offer.

Distribution: Occasionally observed in southern Arizona, more typically in Mexico and southward to northern parts of Costa Rica.
Size: 12in (30cm).
Habitat: Forested areas.
Nest: In hollows.
Eggs: 2–3, whitish.
Food: Fruit and invertebrates.

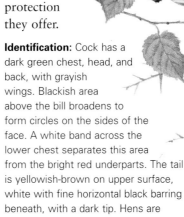

Identification: Cock has a dark green chest, head, and back, with grayish wings. Blackish area above the bill broadens to form circles on the sides of the face. A white band across the lower chest separates this area from the bright red underparts. The tail is yellowish-brown on upper surface, white with fine horizontal black barring beneath, with a dark tip. Hens are brownish, with a white area behind the eyes. There is a faint white band across the chest, with red on the lower underparts. Upper surface of the tail is reddish-brown, with pronounced barring beneath and a narrow dark tip.

BARBETS, BELLBIRDS AND FRUITCROWS

These birds are typical inhabitants of tropical forests. While fruitcrows and bellbirds are confined to America, barbets are well represented in parts of Asia and Africa. Like other fruiteating species, they all have an important role in helping to spread the seeds of the plants on which they feed. A number of these species are found at high altitudes in the Andes, and may have a limited area of distribution.

Toucan barbet

Semnornis ramphastinus

Distribution: Western parts of Colombia and Ecuador. Typically between 3,280 and 7,870ft (1,000 and 2,400m).
Size: 8in (20cm).
Habitat: Humid mountain forests.
Nest: Tree hollow.
Eggs: 2, white.
Food: Berries, other fruit, and invertebrates.

The coloration of these barbets is not dissimilar to that of mountain toucans, which is how they got their name. Their bills, in contrast, are both stocky and powerful, enabling them to bore into wood to create or enlarge a nest in a tree hollow. Their tails are flexible, and can be carried either down or raised into a more vertical position. The toucan barbet's range is relatively restricted, and they tend not to be common, with just odd birds or pairs being sighted rather than groups. Like many barbets, they can call loudly, with members of a pair taking part in a duet of loud honking notes with each other. Calling of this type is most common during the nesting season.

Identification: Prominent bluish-gray areas on the sides of the face and chest. Orangish-red underparts, becoming more yellowish toward the vent, with an olive-brown back and yellowish rump. Wings and tail are bluish-gray. Bill is tipped with black. Sexes are alike.

Five-colored barbet

Capito quinticolor

These barbets are not perhaps as colorful as their name might suggest. They have a localized distribution on the western (Pacific) side of the Andes, and they are not especially easy to observe, often occurring just as individuals hopping through the vegetation, or in pairs. They sometimes associate with other birds, possibly hoping to snatch invertebrates that may be disturbed as the flock moves from tree to tree. Five-colored barbets do not range up into the mountains, but are found in lowland areas, at altitudes of 330ft (100m) or below.

Identification: Distinctive yellow V-shape at the top of the mainly black wings. The chest is predominantly white. Underparts are yellowish-orange, with black spotting on the flanks and olive thighs. Hens have streaked upperparts and spotted underparts, and lack the crimson crown and nape seen in cocks.

Distribution: Restricted to western parts of Colombia, extending from Quibdó, Tadó, and Chocó southward along the Pacific coast as far down as western Nariño.
Size: 7in (18cm).
Habitat: Forested areas of the coastal lowlands.
Nest: Cavity in a tree.
Eggs: 3, white.
Food: Berries, other fruit, and invertebrates.

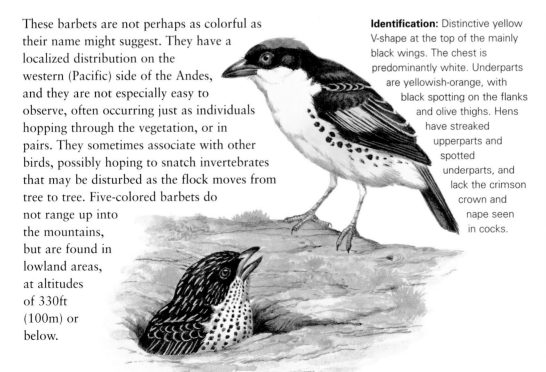

Prong-billed barbet (*Semnornis frantzii*):
7in (18cm)
Western Panama and Costa Rica. Olive-green
upperparts with buff coloration on the upper breast.
Crown is a dull, golden-brown shade, with a raised
crest of glossy black feathers at the back of the
head. Lower bill is divided, with the tip of the upper
bill lying in the notch created where the two halves
join. Hens lack black feathering.

Red-headed barbet (*Eubucco bourcierii*):
5¹⁄₂in (14cm)
Colombia, western Venezuela, Ecuador, and the far
north of Peru. Cock birds have a bright red head and
upper breast, merging into the orange of the upper
abdomen and becoming yellow on the lower
underparts. A narrow whitish collar encircles the
back of the neck, separating the red here from the
green wings. Hens easily distinguished by the black
plumage on the forehead, blue on the sides of the
face and yellow-to-green shading over the back. The
throat is gray, while all of the underparts are yellow.
Lower underparts are whitish, with green streaking.

Scarlet-crowned barbet (*Capito aurovirens*):
6¹⁄₂in (16cm)
Occurs in southern Colombia, Ecuador, western
Brazil, and the northern half of Peru. Cock bird has a
bright red crown and nape, with brown on the sides
of the face, extending over the back and wings.
There is a white area under the chin. The upper
breast is yellowish-red and the lower underparts
olive-brown. Legs and feet are gray. Lower bill
grayish with a black tip; upper bill is mostly black.
Eyes have a vivid orange iris. Hens have whitish
crown and nape, and a yellow breast.

Bare-throated bellbird

Procnias nudicollis

Bellbirds are named
because of the
sounds of the cock
bird's call, which
ranks as one of
the loudest and
most distinctive in
the avian world.
The hens, in
contrast, remain
quiet. When calling,
the cock bird chooses
a tall branch
in the tree
canopy, often
in quite a conspicuous
position, and subsequently
drops down to another
favored branch lower in the
canopy. It is here that mating
may take place. The cock often uses
these two perches to carry out a
jumping display, dropping down onto
the lower branch to land in a crouched
position with his tail feathers spread.
Studies on this species have revealed
that bare-throated bellbirds move
seasonally, descending to lower altitudes
outside the breeding season.

Distribution: Southern Brazil,
northeastern Argentina,
and Paraguay.
Size: 9¹⁄₂in (24cm).
Habitat: Montane forest.
Nest: Light and bowl-shaped,
often in a tree fork.
Eggs: 1, light tan with
brown mottling.
Food: Almost exclusively
frugivorous, feeding on
berries and other fruit.

Identification: Snowy-white
feathering, with blackish bill and
feet, plus a bare bluish-green
area under the throat, extending
just around the eyes. Contrasting
dark irises, bill, and legs. The
cock bird's calls are made by
the syrinx, located in the throat.
Hens are strikingly different,
with a dark head, green wings,
and yellow-streaked underparts,
which become yellower on the
lower abdomen. Young birds
develop their bare throats by the
time they are one year old.

Purple-throated fruitcrow

Querula purpurata

Like bellbirds, these are cotingas, not corvids as their
common name might suggest. Purple-throated
fruitcrows are not active birds by nature, which means
they can be easily overlooked in forested areas. They are
most conspicuous either when in flight or feeding,
especially when they dart out quickly to seize berries or
feed in the company of other frugivorous birds such as
trogons. These fruitcrows live in groups of three or four
individuals, and although only the female incubates, all
members of the group provide
food for the young bird.
When displaying,
males inflate their
purple gorget of
feathers, which then
resembles a shield.

Distribution: Costa Rica and
Panama south to Amazonian
region of Brazil and
northern Bolivia.
Size: 11in (28cm).
Habitat: Tropical forest.
Nest: Cup-shaped, relatively
high off the ground.
Eggs: 1, blackish.
Food: Berries, other fruits,
and invertebrates.

*Left: The fruitcrow's nest may be
at least 70ft (22m) off the ground.*

Identification: Predominantly black, with a distinctive area of purplish
plumage under the throat. Hens are entirely black in color, as are young
birds of both sexes. The tail is quite short, and wings are rounded.

TOUCANS, ARACARIS AND TOUCANETS

Members of the toucan clan are virtually unmistakable, although not all of them have large, brightly colored bills. Active and restless by nature, they often congregate in large numbers in fruiting trees, hopping from branch to branch. When roosting and breeding in tree holes where their bill could be an encumbrance, they pull their tail feathers up vertically and tuck their bill over their back.

Crimson-rumped toucanet

Aulacorhynchus haematopygus

The term "toucanet" is applied to smaller members of this family, with green predominating in the plumage of all six *Aulacorhynchus* species. These toucanets are active and quite noisy birds, hopping from branch to branch in search of food. Eating is a two-stage process. Fruit is plucked and then skillfully tossed up into the air and swallowed whole. Pits are regurgitated later. Larger items can be held against the perch with the foot, allowing chunks to be torn off and then eaten in a similar way. The zygodactyl arrangement of these birds' toes, with two toes directed forward and two behind the perch, helps them to hold their food securely.

Identification: Predominantly green, darker on the wings with distinctive red plumage over the rump. Dark, reddish-brown bill, with white at the base and prominent dull reddish skin encircling the eyes. Sexes are alike.

Distribution: Colombia, Venezuela, and Ecuador.
Size: 16in (41cm).
Habitat: Humid forest and secondary woodland.
Nest: Tree hollow.
Eggs: 3–4, white.
Food: Fruit, small vertebrates and invertebrates. May also steal eggs and chicks.

Toco toucan

Ramphastos toco

Distribution: Guyana, Surinam and Guiana, south to Brazil, Paraguay, Bolivia, and northern Argentina.
Size: 21in (53cm).
Habitat: Unusual in ranging from forest to savanna. On rare occasions, large flocks have moved into towns where ripening fruit is plentiful nearby.
Nest: Hollow in tree, sometimes previously occupied by woodpeckers.
Eggs: 2, white.
Food: Berries, other fruit, and invertebrates. Also raids nests of other birds.

Just why toucans have such large, brightly colored bills is something of a mystery. These lightweight, honeycombed structures contain a long, fringed tongue. Its function is unknown, but it probably helps the toucans to swallow food. It is thought that the bill may enable these birds to pluck fruits that would otherwise be out of their reach at the end of thin branches. The bright colors set against their subdued plumage may also be a useful defensive aid, and certainly, the serrated edges of the bill can inflict a painful wound. Toco toucans are less social by nature than other members of the family, although they may congregate in large groups in areas where food is plentiful. They have a call that has been likened to the sound of deep snoring.

Identification: Largest of the toucans. Glossy black plumage with prominent white bib on the throat and red around the vent. Bare area of bright blue skin around the eyes, with small area of surrounding yellow feathering. Large, broad bill displays shades of yellow and yellowish-orange coloration, black at the base, with a prominent black tip to the upper bill. Sexes are alike.

Lettered aracari

Pteroglossus inscriptus

These aracaris get their name from the traces on their upper bill, which look like lettering. Aracaris are social by nature, and are most likely to be observed in groups. It is thought that in some cases, the young of the previous year may remain with their parents and assist in the rearing of the following year's young. The chicks hatch with heel pads that help them to keep their balance, although their bills at this time are relatively small. These pads fall off once the young birds have left the nest. Aracaris and other toucans rely on an adequate number of tree holes for breeding purposes because, unlike woodpeckers, their bills are not strong enough to allow them to bore effectively into trees.

Identification: The lack of banding across the yellow feathering of the chest is distinctive. Upperparts are greenish. Traces similar to letters on the upper bill, whereas lower bill is mainly black. Sexes are alike.

Distribution: Eastern Colombia to central and southern Brazil, and into northern Bolivia.
Size: 14½in (37cm).
Habitat: Forested areas and more open woodland.
Nest: Tree holes.
Eggs: 2–3, white.
Food: Berries, other fruit, invertebrates, and small vertebrates.

Red-billed toucan (*Ramphastos tucanus*): 24in (61cm)
Occurs in Venezuela, Guyana and French Guiana into parts of Brazil and eastern Bolivia. Dark reddish sides to the bill, yellow on top, with a white chest and red band beneath. Has mainly black plumage elsewhere, although the vent area is red. Sexes are alike.

Sulphur-breasted toucan (Keel-billed toucan, *Ramphastos sulfuratus*): 19in (48cm)
Found in Central America, from southern Mexico to northern Colombia and Venezuela. Bill is pea-green with orange stripe on upper part. Brilliant yellow plumage on the chest, predominantly black elsewhere. Sexes are alike.

Golden-collared toucanet (*Selenidera reinwardtii*): 13in (33cm)
Found in southern parts of Colombia, extending to parts of Ecuador, Peru, and Brazil. Bill is a deep shade of red with a black tip. Plumage is mainly black and green, with a yellow collar and ear flashes. Hen has rufous coloration, not black.

Spot-billed toucanet (*Selenidera maculirostris*): 13in (33cm)
Confined to Brazil. Predominantly ivory bill with black markings. Mainly black head and chest, whereas the hen has reddish-brown plumage. Lower underparts are yellowish.

Many-banded aracari (*Pteroglossus pluricinctus*): 17in (43cm)
From Colombia and Venezuela south to northern Peru and Brazil. Black apart from ivory area down the sides of the upper bill. Two black bands run across the underparts, which are pale yellow with reddish markings. Upperparts are dark. Blue skin around the eyes. Rump is red. Sexes are alike.

Plate-billed mountain toucan

Andigena laminirostris

The four species of mountain toucan are all found at relatively high altitudes, and can be distinguished from the *Ramphastos* genus by their smaller bill. The plate-billed mountain toucan is so-called because of the presence of raised yellowish patches on each side of the beak. The function of these is unclear. Blue features prominently in the coloration of all mountain toucans, and the plumage is soft and quite loose. The wings of these toucans have the typical rounded shape associated with other members of the family, which means that they do not fly especially powerfully.

Identification: Characteristic yellow plate on each side of the upper bill, with black elsewhere and dull reddish base. Dark, sky-blue plumage on the underparts, with black cap on the head extending down the neck. Wings are olive brown. Sexes alike.

Distribution: Colombia and western parts of Ecuador.
Size: 20in (51cm).
Habitat: Humid and wet mountain forests.
Nest: Tree hollow.
Eggs: 2–3, white.
Food: Berries, other fruit, invertebrates, and small vertebrates.

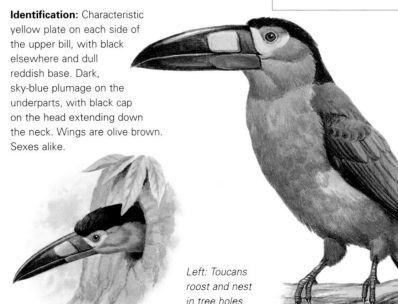

Left: Toucans roost and nest in tree holes.

CRACIDS, TINAMOUS AND GROUND BIRDS

There are a number of relatively large birds represented in America. The curassows, guans, and chachalacas together form the family Cracidae. They tend to be more arboreal than the tinamous, which form a separate group. Antpittas and trumpeters are primarily ground-dwelling birds from this region, and they live and feed mainly on the forest floor.

Great tinamou

Tinamus major

Approximately 40 different species of tinamou occur from Mexico to the tip of South America. Like others of its kind, the great tinamou is difficult to observe, in spite of its size. These birds rarely fly unless there is danger close by, and they move quite quietly through the forest, where their coloration helps them to merge into the background. Their call consists of whistling notes, sometimes heard after dark. The nest is always well concealed in thick, inaccessible vegetation. The cock bird is believed to be largely responsible for incubating the eggs. The eggs themselves can vary quite widely in color, even being violet in some cases. The chicks are able to move readily within a day of hatching. Their flight feathers grow rapidly, so that the young birds can fly when they are little bigger than a robin.

Identification: Large, plump appearance. Grayish-brown underparts, with a more olive hue across the back. White areas on throat, with chestnut feathering on the crown in many cases. Sexes are alike but hens may be larger. Young birds are darker in color than adults.

Distribution: From Mexico south to parts of Ecuador, Peru and Brazil, with approximately a dozen different subspecies being found throughout the area up to about 3,280ft (1,000m).
Size: 18in (46cm).
Habitat: Generally lowland areas in humid forests.
Nest: Leaf-lined scraping on the ground, often disguised in buttress roots.
Eggs: 6–7, glossy turquoise ranging to violet.
Food: Berries, seeds, and invertebrates.

Andean guan

Penelope montagnii

These large birds are primarily arboreal by nature, living in groups of three to six individuals outside the breeding season. They tend to be encountered at higher altitudes than other guans, certainly in Colombia where they have been observed up to 11,500ft (3,500m). They sometimes leave the cover of dense forest in search of fruit, venturing into isolated trees where such food is plentiful. They usually forage in the branches, however, rather than on the ground. Andean guans have a loud honking call, which is heard more frequently during the breeding period. These birds have been heavily hunted, like related species, are shy, and avoid areas near human settlements.

Identification: Brownish overall, with grayish markings on the plumage extending from the head down to the breast. A small area of bare red skin forms the dewlap, which is often hard to observe from a distance, and the throat is more feathered than in other guans. Legs are reddish. Sexes are alike.

Distribution: In the Andean region of Colombia, north-west Venezuela, Ecuador, Peru, and Bolivia. This species may extend as far south as northwestern parts of Argentina, although this is doubtful.
Size: 24in (61cm).
Habitat: Forested areas at relatively high altitudes.
Nest: Platform of leaves and twigs.
Eggs: 1–3, white.
Food: Berries, other fruit, and seeds.

Gray-winged trumpeter

Common trumpeter *Psophia crepitans*

Distribution: Northwestern South America eastward through to French Guiana.
Size: 24in (61cm).
Habitat: Rainforest.
Nest: Leaf-lined tree cavity.
Eggs: 6, white.
Food: Fruits, plant matter, and invertebrates.

Trumpeters are a common sight around native American settlements, and are easily tamed if obtained young. They make useful watchdogs, uttering loud grunts as warning calls. They are also valued for their snake-killing abilities, and these reptiles may feature as part of their natural diet. The plumage on the head and neck is short and has a velvety texture. Their overall appearance resembles that of miniature rheas, although trumpeters retain four toes on each foot. Their legs are powerful, allowing them not just to run but also swim effectively. Trumpeters spend most of their time on the ground, although they prefer to roost in trees when not active after dark.

Identification: Plumage predominantly black, with purplish feathering at the base of the neck. The plumage on the head is very short and has a plush texture. Gray coloration is apparent on the wings. Upright stance. Sexes are alike.

Great curassow

Crax rubra

Distribution: Mexico southward to Colombia and Ecuador.
Size: 36in (91cm).
Habitat: Lowland forest.
Nest: Platform off the ground.
Eggs: 2, rough-shelled, white.
Food: Plant matter.

The curassows tend to be more terrestrial than other cracids, although they invariably roost off the ground. Pairs also nest off the ground, sometimes at heights of up to 100ft (30m) in a suitable tree. Great curassows are most likely to be encountered individually or in pairs, rather than in larger groups. Cocks of this species have a deep, booming call and also utter high-pitched whistling notes. Their range has contracted in some areas, such as along the Pacific coast of Colombia, because of the combined effect of overhunting and deforestation. In areas where great curassows are not persecuted, these large birds are quite conspicuous.

Identification: Mainly black, with a white abdomen and undertail coverts. Striking yellow knob on the upper bill, which is absent in hens and immatures. Hens are mainly chestnut, but with black-and-white barring on the head and neck. Those from Central America may be darker and display more barring.

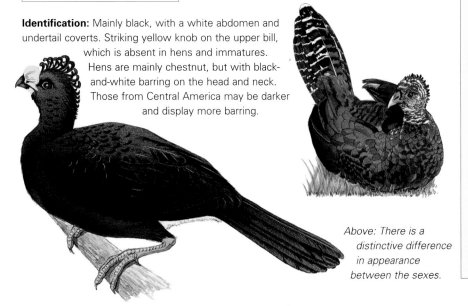

Above: There is a distinctive difference in appearance between the sexes.

Plain chachalaca (*Ortalis vetula*):
25in (64cm)
Southern Texas in the U.S.A. south to Mexico and Nicaragua, as well as the Honduran island of Utila. Predominantly brownish, with bare, blue skin on the face and a flesh-colored throat. Relatively noisy and quite adaptable by nature, in the face of primary deforestation. Sexes alike.

Band-tailed guan (*Penelope argyrotis*):
26in (66cm)
Found in parts of Venezuela and Colombia. Large red dewlap under the throat and frosty white plumage on the sides of the head. Has a distinctive pale tail band not seen in other guans, and also has a stocky appearance compared with related guans. Predominantly brown with white streaking on the breast and mantle. Sexes are alike.

Wattled curassow (*Crax globulosa*):
35in (89cm)
Southeastern Colombia south to northern Bolivia and the western upper Amazonian region of Brazil. Predominantly black with a curly crest. Two distinctive red wattles at the base of the lower mandible, with a similar knob on the top of the bill at its base. These swellings are sometimes yellowish. Sometimes a marbled plumage patterning is evident over the wings. Hens have no wattles or knob, and have a white rather than chestnut belly and undertail coverts.

Giant antpitta (*Grallaria gigantea*):
$10^1/_2$in (27cm)
Occurs in parts of Colombia and Ecuador, and lives on the forest floor. Reddish-brown with black barring on the underparts. Olive-brown upperparts and grayish suffusion on the head. Sexes are alike.

GAMEBIRDS

A variety of gamebirds are found in the woodlands of North America, extending southward. The most significant is undoubtedly the wild turkey, the original ancestor of all modern domestic strains worldwide. Grouse also occur in this region. All are shy and wary by nature, relying on cover to elude detection, and seeking their food at ground level. A number migrate.

American woodcock

Scolopax minor

The mottled appearance of the American woodcock provides exceptional camouflage when on the ground in forests, where these birds blend in with the leaf litter. They tend to rely on camouflage to escape danger, but if flushed will take off with a noisy flapping of their wings, flying not in a straight line but swerving from side to side. The courtship display of these woodcocks is spectacular, with males taking off and flying almost vertically before circling and plunging down again. The nest is sited in a secluded spot, and even the eggs blend in with the leaves, which are used to line the nest scrape. American woodcocks have relatively large eyes, which help them see well in the gloom of the forest. The position of the eyes high on the head also gives them excellent vision, so it is difficult for predators to creep up on them. The long bill is used to extract worms from muddy ground and catch insects.

Identification: Pale buff sides to the face, a barred crown, and gray above the bill and around the throat. A gray stripe extends down the edge of the wings, with a broader gray area across the wings. The rest of the back is mottled. Pale rufous-brown underparts, with the undersides of flight feathers gray, and a black band across a very short tail. Long, tapering bill. Sexes alike.

Distribution: Ranges from Newfoundland and southern Manitoba in Canada down through eastern parts of the U.S.A. as far as Texas, Florida and the Gulf coast. Overwinters in these southerly areas.
Size: 11in (28cm).
Habitat: Wet woodland.
Nest: On the ground.
Eggs: 4, buff with brown spots.
Food: Invertebrates including earthworms and insects of various kinds.

Wilson's snipe

Gallinago delicata

Not easy to observe, Wilson's snipe tends to feed either at sunrise or toward dusk, probing the ground with jerky movements of its stocky bill. It remains out of sight for most of the day. If surprised in the open these birds will sometimes freeze in the hope of avoiding detection, relying on their cryptic plumage to provide camouflage. More commonly they take off in a zigzag fashion, flying quite low and fast before plunging back down into suitable cover. Cocks perch and call loudly on their display grounds in the far north. When plummeting down as part of their display flight, the movement of air through their tail feathers creates a distinctive hooting sound, which has been likened to the call of the boreal owl. They migrate south in the fall, flying in flocks under cover of darkness. Subsequently they split up and forage separately, which helps to conceal their presence.

Identification: Pale buff stripe runs down the center of the crown, with pale stripes above and below the eyes. Dark mottled plumage on chest and wings. Blackish stripes on sides of the body, with white underparts. Wings have white stripes, tail is rufous. Long, pointed bill. Sexes alike.

Distribution: Breeds right across northern Alaska and Canada, southward to New Jersey in the east and California in the west. Wintering grounds extend up to British Columbia, to western and southeastern U.S.A., and all along the Gulf coast.
Size: 11in (28cm).
Habitat: Lightly wooded areas, and fields offering plenty of concealment.
Nest: Hidden in grass.
Eggs: 4, olive-brown with black spots.
Food: Mainly invertebrates.

Wild turkey

Meleagris gallopavo

These large members of the fowl family are difficult to spot in their natural woodland habitat because the barring on their plumage breaks up their outline very effectively to create good camouflage. Shafts of sunlight filtering through the trees highlight the natural iridescence in the plumage, with shades of green appearing on the feathering from some angles. The wild turkey is unmistakable, especially when the male erects his tail feathers into a fan-shape as part of his courtship display. The color of his bare skin intensifies during the breeding season, and he often utters a loud gobbling call. Males, called stags, frequently live in the company of several females. It is only these wild turkeys that have rusty brown tips to their tail feathers, those of domestic turkeys being white.

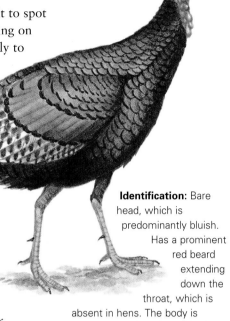

Identification: Bare head, which is predominantly bluish. Has a prominent red beard extending down the throat, which is absent in hens. The body is bronzy brown in color, with black barring on the wings and tail.

Distribution: Southern U.S.A. south into Mexico. It has a very patchy distribution that has given rise to numerous localized subspecies, especially in western parts of the range.
Size: 48in (120cm) cock; 36in (91cm) hen. Birds from the north are larger than those found further south.
Habitat: Wooded areas, including swampland.
Nest: Scrape on the ground.
Eggs: 8–15, buff with dark brown spots.
Food: Berries, seeds, and nuts, also invertebrates.

Spruce grouse (*Dendragapus canadensis*): 16in (41cm)
From Alaska south to northern parts of the neighboring U.S.A. Prominent red area above the eye. Forehead down to the throat and upper breast are black with a white border. White barring on the flanks. Grayish upperparts. Hens are much duller, lacking the red and black areas, and are significantly smaller in size.

Ruffed grouse (*Bonasa umbellus*): 18in (46cm)
Alaska and northwest Canada to central U.S.A. Distinguishable by the slight crest and ruff of black or reddish-brown feathering on the neck. There are two color phases; the reddish-brown rather than gray phase predominates in south-west British Columbia. Hens have a shorter ruff and an incomplete tail band.

Blue grouse (*Dendragapus obscurus*): 20in (50cm)
Western North America, from southeast Alaska down to San Francisco Bay. Also further inland in the Sierra Nevada and Rocky Mountains. Cock has sooty-gray plumage from the back of the neck to the yellow-orange comb on the head. Mottled brown markings with an inflatable neck sac apparent on the sides of the head, and surrounding plumage is white with brown edging. Brown plumage on the legs extends to the toes. Broad fan-shaped tail with whitish plumage around the vent. Hens much plainer, with mottled brown plumage edged with white. Flight feathers brown, spotted with white. Broad brown subterminal band across the tail feathers.

Ocellated turkey

Meleagris ocellata

Ocellated turkeys are shy, and despite their relatively large size are not easy to spot in the wild. However, the species has been domesticated in some parts, where birds are seen near settlements. They naturally live in groups, comprised of a single stag and several hens, and may emerge from wooded areas into clearings in search of food on the ground. If disturbed, they often run off rather than fly, as they are fairly clumsy in the air. When displaying, the stag inflates his wattle, which otherwise hangs down over his bill, and utters a call that has been likened to a motor being started. The nest is hidden in vegetation. The young grow rapidly but develop slowly, only gaining adult plumage at around three years old.

Distribution: Restricted to specific areas of Central America, such as the Yucatan Peninsula in Mexico, Belize and Guatemala.
Size: 40in (102cm) cock; 33in (84cm) hen.
Habitat: Largely deciduous woodland.
Nest: Scrape on the ground.
Eggs: 8–15, buff with brown markings.
Food: Seeds, berries, and invertebrates.

Identification: Male has greenish-blue neck, underparts, and back, merging with brown. Prominent copper wing patch. Whitish flight feathers. Broad tail with blue and coppery patches like ocelli. Pale blue skin on the head has warty areas. Female much smaller, with a pinkish bill. Young birds have grayish-brown feathers.

SPECIALIST FOREST-DWELLERS

Some of the smaller birds found in woodland environments tend to have the most specialized habits, as shown by the various birds featured here. Unfortunately, observing nocturnal species like the oilbird in the field, especially when they fly long distances, is difficult, but the widespread use of low-cost infra-red viewing equipment now gives a better insight into their behavior than ever before.

Oilbird

Steatornis caripensis

Distribution: Western Panama through Colombia to Ecuador and Peru, and east to French Guiana.
Size: 19in (48cm).
Habitat: Caves and cliffs.
Nest: Made from regurgitated seed.
Eggs: 2–4, white with brown blotches.
Food: Fruit.

The oilbird is the only fruit-eating bird in the world that feeds at night. It spends its days roosting in the black interiors of caves. Oilbirds have large eyes that glow red when a light is shone at them. Like bats, they rely on a navigation system known as echolocation to avoid collisions with objects when flying around in darkness. The system involves the bird uttering a constant series of high-pitched calls while in flight, and listening to the echoes that bounce back, to avoid flying into objects. Oilbirds fly up to 16 miles (25km) from their roosting caves in search of fruit each night. A keen sense of smell may help the birds to find ripe fruit, which they swallow whole and digest the next day.

Identification: Prominent hooked bill and very long wings. Rufous-brown upperparts with white spots edged with black running across the wings. Similar but smaller white-spotted patterning on the head and underparts, which are otherwise cinnamon-white. Long, tapering tail barred with black. Cock is grayer than the hen.

Great potoo

Nyctibius grandis

The potoo family, the Nyctibiidae, contains about seven species of nocturnal birds, all living in Central and South America, and in the West Indies. The group is named after the wailing cry of some species. All potoos feed mainly on insects. During the daytime, the large eyes of the great potoo are dark, but they take on an eerie orange glow at night when these birds become active. They hunt large flying insects on the wing, swooping down to catch them. During the day great potoos rest motionless on a tall branch in a hunched-up position. Their cryptic coloration provides good camouflage, helping to conceal their presence from enemies. They generally call only on moonlit nights, when their vocalizations comprise a series of guttural notes followed by louder, harsh, grating sounds. When breeding, the hen does not build a nest but simply lays her single egg in a suitable hollow in a tree where it cannot roll away.

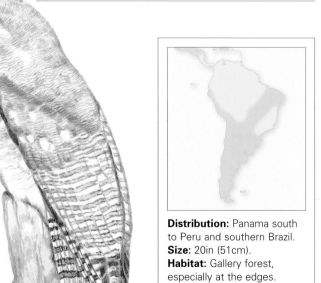

Distribution: Panama south to Peru and southern Brazil.
Size: 20in (51cm).
Habitat: Gallery forest, especially at the edges.
Nest: Knotholes or similar hollows in trees.
Eggs: 1, white with darker markings.
Food: Mainly insects.

Identification: Large birds with variable coloration. Typically grayish-white to brown upperparts, and white underparts that are finely barred. Black spots on the breast. Tail feathers are barred with black borders. Sexes are alike.

Lyre-tailed nightjar (*Uropsalis lyra*):
30in (76cm) cock; 10in (25cm) hen
In highland areas of Colombia and Venezuela to
Ecuador and Peru. Very distinctive ribbon-like
tail, up to three times as long as the body.
Brownish-black with rufous barring and spots.
Hens have shorter tails that lack the white tips.

Squirrel cuckoo (*Piaya cayana*): 17in (43cm)
Ranges from northwestern Mexico south to
Bolivia, Paraguay, Argentina, and Uruguay, with
18 different races being recognized. Chestnut-
brown head and wings, with grayish lower
underparts. Long tail with pale tips to the
feathers. Bare skin around the eyes is red in
birds found east of the Andes Mountains;
greenish yellow elsewhere. Sexes are alike.

Scaly-throated leaftosser (*Sclerurus
guatemalensis*): 7in (18cm)
Extends from southeastern parts of Mexico
down the Atlantic side of Central America to the
western coast of Colombia and western Ecuador
in South America. Predominantly dark brownish
overall, with relatively inconspicuous paler
markings on the throat. Long, straight, dark bill.
Dark legs and tail. Sexes are alike.

Long-billed gnatwren (*Ramphocaenus
melanurus*): 5in (12cm)
Extends from southeastern parts of Mexico
down through South America as far south as
northeastern Peru in the west, and southeastern Brazil. Long narrow bill, with white
throat offset against cinnamon plumage on the
face and underparts. The vent area is also
whitish. Upperparts grayish, with a relatively
long, narrow tail, marked black and white.

Ovenbird

Seiurus aurocapillus

These unusual warblers spend most of their
time on the ground searching for insect prey,
walking rather than hopping like most
birds. Ovenbirds prefer mature areas of
woodland, where there is relatively little
undergrowth. Their presence may be
revealed by their song, which sounds like
the word "teacher" repeated constantly.
Their precise song pattern varies with
region, with several dialects being identified.
The ovenbird gets its name from the
appearance of its nest, a domed structure
that has been likened to a Dutch oven. The
nest is located on the ground and made
from a pile of leaves and other vegetation.
The entrance hole is to the side, and the
interior is lined with grass. Some males have
more than one mate, while on occasions
several males have been
observed feeding a
brood of chicks.

Identification: Rufous stripe edged
with black extending back from the bill
and up the crown. Upperparts are olive-
brown, throat is white with a dark stripe
running down the sides from the lower corner
of the bill. Dark streaking on the underparts,
including the flanks. Narrow ring of white
feathers encircles each eye. Bill darker on
the upper surface, paler below, and the
legs and feet are pinkish. Sexes alike.

Distribution: Breeds in North
America from western and
central parts of Canada to the
east coast and south to South
Carolina and northern Gulf
states. Moves southward for
the winter, around the
Caribbean including much of
Central America down to
northern parts of South
America.
Size: 5¹⁄₂in (14cm).
Habitat: Mature woodland.
Nest: Dome of vegetation.
Eggs: 4–5, white with brown
spots.
Food: Invertebrates.

Tawny-throated leaftosser

Sclerurus mexicanus

Relatively little is known about the habits of this group of
forest birds, which were previously more commonly known
as leafscrapers. Their current name is a more accurate
reflection of their lifestyle, however, as they use their long
bill to grab and flip over leaves on the forest floor in search
of invertebrate prey lurking underneath. Leaftossers spend
most of their time at ground level, normally flying a short
distance if disturbed, calling loudly, before
settling onto a low branch, bobbing up and
down there at first. Tawny-throated
leaftossers are most likely to be found
in dense vegetation, where they
are usually observed on their
own. Pairs of these birds will
breed in banks, digging out their
nesting tunnel, which terminates in
a larger chamber at the end, where
the female lays her eggs.

Identification: Brown head and
wings. Relatively short brown tail
feathers with elongated tips.
Throat and chest are chestnut in
color, as is the rump. Sexes alike.

Distribution: Various
populations occur from
eastern parts of Mexico
down through Central
America and over a wide area
of South America, from
Colombia to French Guiana
and the eastern coast of
Brazil, south into Ecuador and
Peru, and down to Bolivia.
Size: 6¹⁄₂in (16cm).
Habitat: Humid forest.
Nest: A burrow.
Eggs: 2, white.
Food: Invertebrates.

MACAWS

The macaws include the largest and most spectacular members of the entire parrot family. All 17 species are characterized by their long tails and the prominent, largely unfeathered areas of skin on their faces. Their distribution ranges from Central America through to the southern parts of South America.

Blue and gold macaw

Blue and yellow macaw *Ara ararauna*

Distribution: Eastern Panama and Colombia south through Amazonia to southeastern Brazil, Bolivia, and Paraguay.
Size: 30–33in (75–83cm).
Habitat: Forested areas near water.
Nest: Tall hollow tree.
Eggs: 2, white.
Food: Nuts, fruits, and seeds.

Wooded areas are the normal habitat of these colorful macaws, which usually feed in the treetops. Their presence there is revealed by their loud, raucous calls, which are also uttered when the birds are in flight. Although normally observed in pairs or small family groups, blue and gold macaws do form larger flocks, consisting of up to 25 individuals on occasion. They are most likely to be observed during the morning and again at dusk, as they fly back and forth between their roosting and feeding sites. One of the main factors restricting the distribution of these macaws is the availability of suitable palms as nesting sites. They are quite adaptable in their feeding habits, eating a wide variety of plant matter and even sometimes seeking nectar from flowers.

Identification: Predominantly blue upperparts, with contrasting golden-yellow underparts. Greenish area on the forehead above the bill. Bare, unfeathered white skin on the sides of the face, with small tracts of black feathers there and a black band beneath the throat. Sexes alike. The rare Bolivian blue-throated macaw (*A. glaucogularis*) is similar in its overall coloration, but can be distinguished by its prominent blue cheek patches.

Red and green macaw

Green-winged macaw *Ara chloroptera*

As in related species, these large macaws display isolated feather tracts across the bare areas of skin on each side of their face. Rather like fingerprints, this feature is sufficiently distinctive to enable individuals to be identified at close quarters. Young birds display odd maroon rather than crimson feathers there, and also have dark eyes. Adult pairs remain together throughout the year, although they may not breed annually. They can live for more than 50 years. Red and green macaws usually feed in the canopy, and are sometimes seen there in the company of blue and gold macaws. These parrots are able to use their feet like hands to grasp their food. Pairs frequently engage in mutual preening when resting in trees during the hottest part of the day.

Identification: Rich crimson feathering predominates, with both bluish and distinctive green feathering evident on the lower part of the wings. Sexes are alike.

Distribution: Eastern Panama in Central America south across the Amazon Basin to Bolivia, Brazil, and northern Argentina. Now very rare in Panama and also at the southern tip of its range in Argentina, where there never appears to have been an established population.
Size: 29–37in (73–95cm).
Habitat: Forested areas.
Nest: Large hollow trees, sometimes on cliff faces.
Eggs: 2, white.
Food: Fruits, seeds and nuts.

Spix macaw (Little blue macaw, *Cyanopsitta spixii*, E): 22in (56cm)
The last known survivor of this species in the wild disappeared toward the end of 2000, so the future of the species now depends on captive breeding of approximately 60 individuals surviving in collections around the world. These small macaws have only ever been sighted iin northern Bahia, northeastern Brazil. Bluish plumage with a dark, grayish area of bare skin on the face. Sexes are alike.

Great green macaw (Buffon's macaw, *Ara ambigua*, E): 30–33in (77–85cm)
There are several widely separated populations throughout its wide range, which extends from eastern Honduras to western parts of Colombia. Mainly green plumage with a prominent area of red plumage above the bill. Whitish facial skin. Blue flight feathers, and a long reddish tail with a blue tip. Sexes are alike.

Illiger's macaw (Blue-winged macaw, *Ara maracana*, E): 15in (39cm)
Deforestation has led to the disappearance of these small macaws from Argentina. They occur in wooded parts of Brazil, south of the Amazon, and to the south in Paraguay. Mainly green, with white skin around the eyes and a red forehead and rump. Some red on the belly. Sexes alike.

Red-bellied macaw (*Ara manilata*): 18in (46cm)
Northern South America, including Trinidad, south to Bolivia, Peru, and northeast Brazil. Mainly green, with a bluer head and flight feathers. Bare yellowish area of skin surrounding the eyes. Reddish belly. Sexes are alike.

Red and gold macaw
Scarlet macaw *Ara macao*
(E: Central America)

There are two different populations, with birds of Central American origin being recognizable by the blue tips to the prominent yellow feathers on the wings. Red and gold macaws are sometimes encountered in certain areas with other related multicolored macaws, such as red and green macaws, although they do not appear to hybridize in the wild. Such mixed groups are most commonly observed congregating to feed on the soil of mineral-rich cliffs in parts of Peru. The mud that the parrots consume here is believed to neutralize plant toxins that they absorb as part of their diet. It appears that, certainly within some parts of their distribution, these macaws move seasonally in search of more plentiful feeding opportunities. They eat a considerable variety of foods, feeding in trees, rather than on or near the ground, which enables them to range widely across Central and South America.

Identification: The plumage of these large macaws is scarlet-red rather than crimson, which helps to distinguish them from the red and green macaw. Bright yellow plumage on the wings provides a further simple means of recognition. Sexes alike.

Distribution: Southern Mexico to Panama; widely distributed across the Amazonian region to Bolivia.
Size: 31–38in (80–96cm).
Habitat: Forested areas and savanna.
Nest: Hollow chamber in a tall tree.
Eggs: 2, white.
Food: Fruits, seeds, and nuts.

Hyacinthine macaw
Hyacinth macaw *Anodorhynchus hyacinthinus* (E)

These vividly colored macaws are the biggest parrots in the world. They fly with slow wingbeats and are usually seen in pairs or small family groups. Young hyacinthine macaws are unlikely to breed until they are seven years or even older, but these are potentially long-lived birds, with a life expectancy that can be measured in decades. They face relatively few predators, although in spite of their size and very powerful bills, they can fall victim to harpy eagles. In some areas hyacinthine macaws can be seen flying after dark, when the moon is shining. They are often noisy by nature, uttering a wide range of calls.

Identification: Predominantly a distinctive, deep shade of glossy blue, with prominent areas of bare yellow skin encircling the eyes and also present on the sides of the lower bill. Sexes are alike.

Distribution: North-eastern Brazil, extending south and westward to parts of Bolivia and Paraguay.
Size: 35–39in (90–100cm).
Habitat: Areas where Mauritia and other palms are growing.
Nest: Either a hollow tree or among rocks on inaccessible cliff faces.
Eggs: 2, white.
Food: Palm nuts, fruits, and even water snails.

CONURES

Conures are a group of parakeets whose distribution is confined to parts of Central and South America. Their unusual name comes from the old generic name Conurus. *They are quite social birds by nature and are often seen in noisy flocks, congregating in large numbers where food is plentiful, and even invading agricultural regions on occasion.*

Queen of Bavaria's conure

Golden conure *Guaruba guarouba* (E)

Ranking among the most colorful of all conures, this species is most commonly seen in small groups. It occurs in regions where the forest is not subject to seasonal flooding, and so is absent from areas immediately adjacent to the Amazon River. Females sometimes share the same nest hole, with chicks of widely different ages being reared inside. The nesting chamber can be surprising deep, extending down for at least 6¹/2ft (2m). Deforestation is having an adverse effect on the numbers of these beautiful parrots, since they are dependent on older, more mature trees for nesting sites. Small flocks will sometimes descend to feed in fields, taking crops such as ripening maize, but they more commonly eat a variety of rainforest fruits and flowers.

Identification: Heavy bill, bright yellow coloration with no orange hues. Sexes are alike. Young are a darker coloration, with green streaks on their upperparts.

Distribution: Centered on the Amazonia region of Brazil, south of the Amazon, and may range further afield.
Size: 14in (36cm).
Habitat: Rainforest extending to the edge of cultivated areas.
Nest: Cavity within a tree, up to 100ft (30m) above the ground.
Eggs: 2–4, white.
Food: Fruit and seeds, occasionally making raids on maize fields.

Sun conure

Aratinga solstitalis

The fiery coloration of these conures explains their common name. They are very social by nature, but in spite of their bright plumage, they can be hard to spot when roosting quietly on branches. When in flight, however, their sharp, harsh calls are often heard, drawing attention to the flock as it passes overhead. The coloration of sun conures often differs slightly between individuals, with some being of a brighter shade than others. The pattern of coloration is quite variable too, so it is often possible to distinguish between individuals in a flock. Large numbers of these conures may feed together on trees, and they have also been observed eating the fruits of cacti on the ground. It is possible that they move through their range according to the season, splitting up into smaller groups for much of the year.

Identification: The orange hues on the yellow plumage, black bill and smaller size distinguish this conure from Queen of Bavaria's conure. Sexes are alike. Young are much duller, being largely green.

Distribution: Occurs in northeastern parts of South America, being found mainly in parts of Guyana, Surinam and northern areas of Brazil. May also occur in French Guiana to the east.
Size: 12in (30cm).
Habitat: Palm groves, savanna, and dry forest.
Nest: In hollows in palms or other trees.
Eggs: 3–4, white.
Food: Berries, other fruits, seeds, and similar items. Sometimes cacti fruits.

Blue-crowned conure (*Aratinga acuticaudata*): 14in (36cm)
Occurs in separate populations in northeast, east, and central-southern parts of South America. Green with dull bluish coloration on the crown. Sexes are alike.

Nanday conure (Black-headed conure, *Nandayus nenday*): 12in (30cm)
The range of this conure extends from southeastern Bolivia via parts of Brazil and Paraguay to Argentina. The entire head, including the bill, is black in color, with a variable band of reddish feathers bordering the black. There is a pale blue wash in the vicinity of the throat, and red plumage at the top of the legs. The flight feathers are dark blue, with the underside of the tail being dark. The remainder of the body is green, slightly lighter on the rump and underparts. Sexes are alike. Blue wash less evident in young birds.

Dusky-headed conure (*Aratinga weddellii*): 11in (28cm)
The dusky-headed conure ranges from southeastern parts of Colombia southward to eastern Bolivia. Dark, scaly-gray coloration is seen on the head, with the bill being black. The pale-colored iris is surrounded by white peri-orbital skin. The flight feathers are dark.

Green conure (*Aratinga holochlora*): 12½in (32cm)
Extends from the far south of Texas in the U.S.A. south through Central America, occurring in eastern and southern Mexico south to northern Nicaragua. Predominantly green with a prominent white eye ring of bare skin and a pale bill. May be traces of yellow on the edge of the wings. The southern subspecies, known as the red-throated conure (*A. h. rubritorquis*), is easily distinguishable by its reddish throat.

Red-fronted conure

Wagler's conure *Aratinga wagleri*

Most conures of the genus *Aratinga* are predominantly green in color, with the brighter coloration on their heads serving to distinguish the individual species. Red-fronted conures are noisy by nature, and their call notes resemble the braying of a donkey. They often congregate in large flocks consisting of as many as 300 individuals. Cliffs are favored both as roosting and breeding sites, and are an important factor in determining the precise distribution of these conures within their range.

Flocks of red-fronted conures sometimes descend into agricultural areas, where they are capable of causing serious damage to cultivated crops.

Identification: Red plumage may extend over the top of the head to just behind the eyes, depending on the race. Scattered red feathering may also be present on the throat. Thighs are red. Sexes are alike. Young birds have greatly reduced area of red on the head.

Distribution: Discontinuous distribution down the western side of South America in the Andes Mountains, from Venezuela to Peru.
Size: 14in (36cm).
Habitat: Most often in forested areas with cliffs nearby.
Nest: Often located on cliff faces.
Eggs: 3–4, white.
Food: A variety of wild and cultivated seeds and fruits, including maize crops.

El Oro conure

Pyrrhura orcesi

The *Pyrrhura* conures are sometimes known as the scaly-breasted conures because of the characteristic barring across their chest. Most of the species have restricted areas of distribution, and the El Oro conure was not discovered until 1980. It is believed to have a very restricted range, which may be no more than 60 miles (100km) long and 6 miles (10km) wide. There has been relatively little deforestation in this area, and the population appears to be quite stable where the forest is undisturbed. These conures are most likely to be observed feeding in the forest canopy, or flying overhead calling. They are typically seen in groups numbering from four to 12 individuals.

Identification: Red on the crown and bend of the wing. Chest barring is relatively indistinct in this particular species. Pale bill. Sexes are alike. Young birds display less red.

Distribution: Apparently centered on El Oro province, Ecuador.
Size: 9in (22cm).
Habitat: Cloud forest between 2,000–4,300ft (600 and 1,300m).
Nest: Probably tree hollows.
Eggs: Not recorded.
Food: Fruits and seeds.

CONURES AND PARROTS

In America, parrots are generally restricted to Central and South America, where they range widely, although they used to occur regularly in North America too. The northern continent was home to the now extinct Carolina parakeet, a species thought to have vanished around 1920. It should be noted that not all members of this family lay their eggs in hollow trees.

Thick-billed parrot

Rhynchopsitta pachyrhyncha (E)

Distribution: Restricted largely to western and central parts of Mexico. Range formerly extended north into New Mexico and Arizona.
Size: 15in (38cm).
Habitat: Coniferous (pine) forests.
Nest: In a tree hole.
Eggs: 2–4, white.
Food: Pine seeds and other vegetable matter.

Thick-billed parrots formerly ranged northward from Mexico to New Mexico and Arizona, and particularly to the Chiricahua Mountains in the U.S.A. However, they have been severely affected by the clearance of pine forests, since pine cones provide a major source of food and the trees afford them nesting sites. Their breeding cycle is also closely tied to the ripening of the cones, which provide a plentiful supply of soft food for rearing the young. Their calls are very loud and raucous, and are audible at distances of up to 2 miles (3km). This can make it difficult to locate their precise whereabouts within a particular area. Attempts have recently been made to reintroduce these endangered parrots to Arizona, using individuals which had been illegally brought into the U.S.A. as well as captive-bred birds, but this has not proved entirely successful.

Identification: Large, stocky build. Mainly green, with a scarlet area on the forehead extending behind the eyes, which are encircled by white peri-orbital skin. Scarlet also on shoulders, leading edges of wings, and legs. Heavy black bill, with gray legs and feet. Sexes alike. Young birds are much greener, but with a red-brown band over the bill, and gray skin encircling the eyes.

Monk parakeet

Quaker parakeet *Myiopsitta monarchus*

Identification: Gray on forehead, crown, and down to underparts, which may show barring. Rest of underparts yellowish-green, with darker upperparts and bluish-purple flight feathers. Sexes alike. Young birds greener on the forehead.

The breeding habits of the monk parakeet are very different to other parrots. This has helped this species to spread beyond its native range. Rather than nesting in tree holes, these conures construct their own roosts out of sticks. Pairs often nest communally in these structures, which are added to over time, and may eventually become so large they collapse. Some nests accommodate twenty or more pairs, and weigh over 40lb (200kg). The entrance hole is directed downward, so that the birds fly in from below, making it harder for predators to gain access. A number of other species, including caracaras and storks, may take advantage of these substantial tree platforms to build their own nests on top.

Distribution: Extends from the central region of Bolivia, parts of Paraguay, and southern Brazil southward to central parts of Argentina. Also introduced to various locations including Puerto Rico in the Caribbean, and parts of the U.S.A.
Size: 12in (30cm).
Habitat: Dry, wooded areas.
Nest: Usually built of sticks.
Eggs: 4–6, white.
Food: Seeds, vegetable matter.

Patagonian conure

Cyanoliseus patagonus

Occasionally found in large flocks of up to a thousand birds, these conures can inflict serious damage in agricultural areas, especially when grain is ripening. In open country they are seen in groups perching on telephone lines, calling loudly, especially when alarmed. Patagonian conures nest communally in holes in either sandstone or limestone cliffs. Their breeding season varies through their range, with birds returning to nest sites in Argentina in September, as the peak laying period there is November and December. Most of these birds leave again by April, moving north for the southern winter. The distinctive Chilean race (*C. p. bloxami*) is bigger and has more extensive whitish areas on the sides of the breast, which often create a collar.

Identification: Mainly olive-brown on the head and upperparts, with blue flight feathers. White skin encircles the eye. Underparts are rich yellow, with a reddish central area. Bill is black, legs pinkish. Sexes alike. Newly fledged young have mainly white bills, with a blackish central stripe.

Distribution: Southeastern South America, centered on Argentina but also present in Uruguay. A small, distinctive, residual population also occurs in central Chile.
Size: 18in (45cm).
Habitat: Wooded areas and more open country.
Nest: In burrows.
Eggs: 2–4, white.
Food: Seeds and nuts.

Austral conure (*Enicognathus ferrugineus*)
13in (33cm)
Chile and Argentina down to Tierra del Fuego. Mainly green, with darker upperparts. A reddish area evident on the belly, with a smaller area above the bill. Body plumage is barred with dark edging. The tail is a dull reddish shade, with the bill dark on its upper surface. Sexes are alike. Young birds less brightly colored overall.

Maroon-fronted parrot (*Rhynchopsitta terrisi*):
18in (45cm)
Restricted to the Sierra Madre Oriental, north-eastern Mexico. Similar to the thick-billed parrot, with a mainly green body. Red feathering on the leading edges of the wings, shoulders, and at the top of the legs. Dark maroon patch on the forehead. Sexes are alike. Young birds have a brownish rather than black bill.

Golden-plumed conure (*Leptosittaca branickii*, E): 14in (35cm)
Andean region in forested areas. Recognizable by elongated, tufted band of yellow plumage under the eyes; rest of the plumage is green. Orangish suffusion on the breast. Sexes alike.

Yellow-eared parrot (*Ognorhynchus icterotis*, E) 16¹⁄₂in (42cm)
North Andean region of Ecuador and Colombia. Bright yellow plumage on the forehead extends to the lower bill and past the eyes. Yellowish suffusion on the underparts, while undersides of the tail feathers are rufous. Remainder of the body green. Dark, heavy bill, with narrow whitish area of skin encircling the eyes. Sexes alike.

Slender-billed conure

Enicognathus leptorhynchus

The elongated upper bill of these conures is used to dig for edible roots. It is also used to split open the tough-cased nuts of the monkey-puzzle tree. Slender-billed conures live in flocks with a well-defined structure. When the flock is feeding, one bird perches nearby and alerts its companions by calling loudly if danger threatens. Large numbers gather at their roosting grounds, calling as dusk falls. Slender-billed conures nest communally, with several pairs occupying hollows in the same tree. Occasionally they lay on cliff faces and are even known to build nests of sticks in bamboo or trees. This species was thought to have declined as a result of the deadly Newcastle disease, which can spread from flocks of chickens, but numbers now appear stable.

Distribution: Occurs on the western side of Chile extending from Mocha Island, off Bio Bio, northward to Santiago.
Size: 16¹⁄₂in (42cm).
Habitat: Wooded areas.
Nest: In a tree hole.
Eggs: 5–6, white.
Food: Seeds and roots.

Identification: A vivid red area extends back from the forehead through the eyes, and a red patch is present on the belly between the legs. Apart from the dull reddish tail feathers, remainder of the body is green with darker barring, which is often most noticeable on the head. Has a long, pointed upper mandible that extends well below the lower bill. Sexes alike. Young birds have less red coloration and a shorter upper mandible.

AMAZONS AND OTHER PARROTS

Amazon parrots are widely distributed in America from the extreme south of the U.S.A. to Mexico south through Central America and the Caribbean to South America. They are sometimes described as green parrots because this color predominates in the plumage of many species. Pionus parrots are smaller in size, while the bizarre hawk-head is the only member of its group.

Imperial Amazon

Dominican Amazon *Amazona imperialis* (E)

The largest of all 27 species of Amazons, these parrots are also unusually colored because most Amazons are predominantly green. It is sometimes seen in the company of the red-necked Amazon, and both are most likely to be seen in the vicinity of Dominica's highest mountain, Morne Diablotin. Hurricanes and agricultural development pose serious threats to the survival of these Amazons. Imperial Amazons have a wide range of call notes, which are often loud. Their alarm call has been likened to the sound of a trumpet. Pairs nest in hollow trees, but research suggests that they may breed only every two years or so, rather than annually, and then produce only a single chick.

Distribution: The Caribbean island of Dominica in the Lesser Antilles.
Size: 18in (45cm).
Habitat: Mountainous forest.
Nest: Tree cavities.
Eggs: 2, white.
Food: Fruits, nuts, seeds and palm shoots.

Identification: Green back. Purple neck and underparts. They can be confused with birds of prey, owing to their large size and flight pattern (wingbeats followed by gliding). Sexes alike. Young have green on the cheeks.

Black-billed Amazon

Amazona agilis

Distribution: Central and eastern parts of Jamaica.
Size: 10in (25cm).
Habitat: Wet limestone forests and agricultural areas.
Nest: Tree cavities at least 59ft (18m) off the ground.
Eggs: 2, white.
Food: Fruits, seeds and nuts.

Two distinctive species of Amazon parrot inhabit the Caribbean island of Jamaica and sometimes associate together in mixed flocks. As its name suggests, the black-billed type can be easily distinguished from the yellow-billed (*A. collaria*) by its beak coloration. Breeding occurs between March and May. These Amazons are shy birds by nature, and rarely tolerate a close approach. Their green plumage helps to conceal them in forests, making them very hard to spot, especially because they will remain silent if disturbed. Sadly, deforestation in various parts of the island is thought to be having an adverse effect on their numbers.

Identification: Mainly dark green with a bluish hue on the top of the head, black ear coverts and black edging to the feathers on the back of the head. Black bill. Sexes alike, although hens may have some green feathers on the edge of the wings. Young birds lack any trace of red feathering on the wing edges, and this area is entirely green.

Mealy Amazon (*Amazona farinosa*):
15in (38cm)
Range extends from Central America, home of the distinctive blue-crowned race (*A. f. guatemalae*) across much of northern South America to Brazil. A large, green Amazon with a particularly raucous call. Sexes are alike.

Red-necked Amazon (*Amazona arausiaca*, E): 16in (40cm)
Restricted to the Caribbean island of Dominica. Distinguished from the imperial Amazon by its predominantly green coloration and distinctive red area of plumage across the throat, often extending to the upper breast. Sexes are alike.

Tucuman Amazon (Alder parrot, *Amazona tucumana*): 12in (30cm)
Occurs in the eastern Andean region of Bolivia and Argentina. Predominantly green overall, with black scalloping on the plumage, especially on the back. Red forehead and a red area on the upperwing. White peri-orbital skin and horn-colored bill. Sexes alike. Young birds have a much reduced red area on the head, and none on the wing.

Dusky pionus (*Pionus fuscus*):
9¹/₂in (24cm)
Occurs in lowland forests from the Colombian–Venezuelan border east to northeastern Brazil. Unusual pinkish, purple and bluish-brown tones in its plumage. Sexes are alike.

Hawk-headed parrot

Red-fan parrot *Deroptyus accipitrinus*

Completely unique among parrots, the hawk-headed type displays a stunning ruff of blue-edged, claret-red feathers at the back of its neck, which it can raise like a fan as part of its display. These parrots may be seen in small groups outside the breeding season. They feed largely in the treetops rather than descending to the ground, and raise their young either in natural tree hollows or in old woodpecker nests. Hawk-heads are noisy parrots, possessing a wide array of call notes. They often call loudly and fan the ruff of feathers around their neck if alarmed.

Distribution: Northern South America, to the east of the Andes Mountains.
Size: 12in (31cm).
Habitat: Lowland rainforest.
Nest: Tree hollows, sometimes occupying old woodpecker nests.
Eggs: 2–3, white.
Food: Fruit, seeds, nuts and leaves.

Identification: These parrots fly quite slowly, with their tail feathers spread slightly apart. They may be confused with small hawks, thanks to the rounded tips of the wings and tail. Green back, wings and tail. Sexes are alike. Young have some green feathering on the crown.

Blue-headed pionus

Blue-hooded parrot *Pionus menstruus*

The most widely distributed of the seven members of the *Pionus* genus, and one of the commonest New World parrots, the blue-headed is often seen either singly or in pairs, rather than in flocks. They do congregate in larger numbers in certain mineral-rich areas, consuming the soil in the company of other parrots. The mineral-rich soil is thought to neutralize toxins absorbed from their food, which is usually gathered in the forest canopy, although they occasionally raid maize fields. Blue-headed pionus are sometimes observed flying quite high and fast in a loose formation, when they become more conspicuous than many parrots. They often call loudly when in flight.

Identification: Rich dark blue head with black ear coverts. Otherwise green plumage overall. Bill has reddish markings on the sides. Sexes alike. Young birds have mainly green heads.

Distribution: Two separate populations: from southern Costa Rica to northern South America; also present over a wide area of central South America east of the Andes.
Size: 11in (28cm).
Habitat: Lowland tropical forest, into agricultural areas.
Nest: Tree cavities, or nest sites created by other birds.
Eggs: 2–4, white.
Food: Seeds, fruit, and nuts, and sometimes maize.

SMALLER PARROTS AND PARAKEETS

The parrots of South America display a great range in size, from large macaws down to the small parrotlets that are often not much larger than the width of a human hand. Small species are often the hardest to spot, especially in a rainforest setting, because their coloration as well as their size helps to conceal their presence in this habitat.

Vulturine parrot

Pionopsitta vulturina

One of the most unusual of all parrots in terms of appearance, the vulturine parrot is so called because of its essentially unfeathered head, which is covered with fine, bristle-like plumage. It has been suggested that this characteristic has developed to stop the feathering becoming matted by fruit juices when these parrots feed. Young birds, distinguishable by their fully feathered heads, are believed to congregate in flocks on their own until they pair off for breeding. The call of the vulturine parrot is also very different from that of other parrots, and has a watery tone. These parrots are found in areas of lowland forest, where their presence is easily overlooked since they are quiet by nature.

Identification: Bald, blackish face with adjacent yellow area of plumage around the neck. Sexes are alike. Young birds have fully feathered greenish heads but less yellow on the neck. Like that of the adults, the base of the bill (cere) is unfeathered and very prominent.

Distribution: South of the Amazon River in north-eastern Brazil, extending in the east to the coastal zone of Brazil.
Size: 9in (23cm).
Habitat: Lowland tropical rainforest.
Nest: Unrecorded, probably in tree hollows.
Eggs: Unrecorded.
Food: Berries, other fruit, and seeds gathered in the forest canopy.

White-bellied caique

Pionites leucogaster

Most likely to be seen in small flocks, white-bellied caiques are quite bold by nature, and often tolerate a relatively close approach before flying off rapidly. Their wings make an unusual whirring sound as they become airborne, and are quite small relative to the birds' size. If disturbed, white-bellied caiques call out loudly. Their other call notes are more varied, and some have been likened to the sounds of tapirs. They sometimes associate in groups with blue-headed pionus, and can often be observed close to waterways, being less common in drier parts of their range in the south. Three distinct races of the white-bellied caique are recognized through the range of this species. They can be identified by subtle differences in color, such as the tail feathers and thighs being yellow rather than green.

Identification: White underparts and a yellow head distinguish this caique from other parrots in the region, notably the black-headed caique, which borders its northerly range. Sexes are alike. Young birds have a brown crown and nape.

Distribution: Occurs in parts of central South America, south of the Amazon from Brazil to south-eastern Peru and northern Bolivia. Has also been reported in the eastern part of Ecuador, but its occurrence there is still to be verified.
Size: 9in (23cm).
Habitat: Lowland rainforest.
Nest: Usually high up in a tree cavity.
Eggs: 2–4, white.
Food: Berries, other fruit, seeds and nuts.

Red-winged parrotlet

Blue-fronted parrotlet *Touit dilectissima*

Distribution: Panama south into northwestern South America where the species' precise range is still unclear. Extends south to near the Peruvian border.
Size: 6in (15cm).
Habitat: Wet forests, sometimes ranging up into cloud-forest areas.
Nest: Chamber located in arboreal termites' nests.
Eggs: Probably about 5, white.
Food: Berries, other fruit, blossoms, and seeds.

The parrotlets can all be recognized by their small size and rather dumpy body shape, with short, squat tails. The red-winged type, like related parrotlets, is quiet and easily overlooked in the forest canopy. Although three separate populations of these inconspicuous parrotlets have been identified, it is possible that these are not actually isolated, although this species is considered to be scarce in Central America. Red-winged parrotlets feed and roost in small groups, eating seeds as well as whole fruit. They fly low over the trees, when their high-pitched calls are most likely to be heard. Their yellow underwing coverts are also conspicuous in flight.

Identification: Mainly green, with blue feathering on the front of the head. Pronounced areas of red feathering on the sides of the wings, reduced in hens. Young birds resemble hens, but their heads are predominantly green.

Spot-winged parrotlet (*Touit stictoptera*): 7in (18cm)
Scattered distribution in the eastern Andes, from Colombia to Peru, in mature, subtropical forests. Mainly green with blackish-brown area on the wings. Sexes similar except that cocks have white, spot-like edging to some of the wing feathers.

Rusty-faced parrot (*Hapalopsittaca amazonina*): 9in (23cm)
Occurs at relatively high altitudes in the Andean cloud forests of Colombia and Venezuela. Mainly green, with yellow streaking on the sides of the heads, lacking in young birds. Sexes alike.

Short-tailed parrot (*Graydidascalus brachyurus*): 9in (23cm)
Widely distributed along the Amazon and its tributaries, from Peru, Ecuador, and Colombia in the west to French Guiana and Brazil. Predominantly green parrots with a plump appearance. Very noisy by nature. Often seen in large numbers on river islands. Sexes alike.

Purple-bellied parrot (*Triclaria malachitacea*): 11in (28cm)
Mainly southeastern Brazil. Green overall, with a distinctive purplish patch extending from lower breast. Relatively broad, long tail. Horn-colored bill. Hens lack the purplish coloring, though young birds may show traces of this patch.

Cobalt-winged parakeet

Blue-winged parakeet *Brotogeris cyanoptera*

Distribution: Western area of the Amazon Basin, from Venezuela to Bolivia.
Size: 7in (18cm).
Habitat: Forests and open areas where trees are available nearby for roosting.
Nest: Probably tree holes but may use arboreal termite mounds.
Eggs: 5, white.
Food: Fruit and seeds.

Identification: Predominantly green, with cobalt-blue flight feathers and an orange spot under the chin. Sexes alike. Young birds have grayer bills.

The seven species of the *Brotogeris* group are represented in both Central and South America. They are quite dumpy birds, all of similar size, with relatively narrow tail feathers. Green usually predominates in their plumage. They tend to be noisy, social birds by nature. Cobalt-winged parakeets are fast on the wing. Although they are sometimes seen flying across open areas and clearings, they tend to spend more time in the forest canopy than other members of the group, where their size and coloration make them relatively hard to observe. They are most likely to be encountered in lowland forests, sometimes in areas where seasonal flooding occurs.

WOODPECKERS

These birds are highly adapted to living in woodlands, and are able to hop up vertical trunks supported by their rigid, prong-like tail feathers and their powerful feet and claws. The largest member of the family, the ivory-billed woodpecker (Campephilus principalis), which measures 20in (50cm), is now believed to be extinct in southeastern U.S.A., with a tiny population surviving on Cuba.

Cream-colored woodpecker

Celeus flavus

Distribution: Colombia and French Guiana south to Bolivia and Brazil.
Size: 11in (28cm).
Habitat: Wooded areas near water, ranging from mangrove to rainforest.
Nest: Tree hollow.
Eggs: 3, white.
Food: Invertebrates and possibly some vegetable matter.

In spite of their name, some of these woodpeckers are of a more yellowish shade than others, while buffish and cinnamon-white individuals are also known. Cream-colored woodpeckers have a very distinctive call that sounds somewhat like a laugh. There is usually a close bond between members of a pair. These woodpeckers are likely to be encountered in a wide range of habitats, from mangrove swamps to savanna. They can also be found in agricultural areas, particularly coffee plantations, where they help to control insect pests.

Identification: Predominantly cream, although coloration can be quite variable, with an obvious crest. Crimson patches on the sides of the face. Wing coverts are brownish. Tail is black. Odd brown feathers may be apparent on the underparts. Hens lack the crimson plumage on the sides of the head.

Crimson-bellied woodpecker

Campephilus haematogaster

These large woodpeckers are not easy to spot, especially since they are more likely to be observed as individuals rather than as pairs or in larger groups. They are most commonly seen in the understorey, frequently quite low down on bigger trees in dense forest. They eat a variety of invertebrates, including the larvae of wood-boring beetles up to 6in (15cm) long, which they pull out from the bark using their strong, chisel-shaped bills. Crimson-bellied woodpeckers make a double rap when drumming, like related species, and have an alarm call that resembles a loud squeal. They tend to frequent relatively wet areas of montane habitat. The plumage of these woodpeckers typically appears less brightly colored when it is worn, and the white barring on the undersides of the flight feathers can be seen only in flight.

Distribution: Western Panama south to parts of Ecuador. Occurs in two apparently separate populations, with the nominate race ranging from eastern parts of Colombia south to Peru.
Size: 13in (33cm).
Habitat: Tropical forest.
Nest: Tree hollow.
Eggs: 2, white.
Food: Invertebrates.

Identification: Prominent area of red on the head. Two black stripes beneath, bordered by two yellowish-white stripes. The lower one is more extensive in hens, whose black feathering extends to the lower neck. Wings are black, rump is crimson. Underparts are crimson and black, and are blacker in the case of hens.

Magellanic woodpecker (*Campephilus magellanicus*): 15in (38cm)
Found in southern parts of South America. The cock has a bright red head and crest, with a black body and white evident on the rump. The hen, in contrast, is almost completely black, apart from a greatly reduced area of red plumage around the base of the bill, which is otherwise grayish-black. Young birds are similar to hens, but browner.

Guadeloupe woodpecker (*Melanerpes herminieri*): 11¹⁄₂in (29cm)
Restricted to the island of Guadeloupe in the southern Caribbean, though sometimes seen on Antigua. Predominantly black apart from slight reddish suffusion on the underparts, which is most apparent during the nesting period. Hens are similar, but with significantly shorter bills. Young birds duller overall.

Golden-naped woodpecker (*Melanerpes chrysauchen*): 7¹⁄₂in (19cm)
Costa Rica to Panama and northern Colombia. Distinctive golden-yellow nape and red crown, with black plumage extending from the sides of the head to the back, where there is a broad white stripe. Hens are less colorful overall. Often drums on wood with its bill.

Powerful woodpecker (*Campephilus pollens*): 14¹⁄₂in (37cm)
Andean region, from Colombia to Peru. Scarlet crest with white stripes extending from each side of the face over the wings, to create a V-shape. White back and rump. Underparts barred. Hens lack the scarlet on the head, and have darker underparts.

Black-backed three-toed woodpecker

Picoides arcticus

Ranging over a huge area, these woodpeckers are most likely to be seen where there are numerous dead pine trees, especially if the surrounding area is flooded. They often occur in groups, breeding together in close proximity where conditions are favorable. In some years, flocks may move further south than usual, occasionally crossing into the states of Nebraska, New Jersey, and Ohio in the U.S.A. This type of movement, known as an irruption, is usually the result of a shortage of food.

Distribution: Canada and northern U.S.A., from Alaska east to Newfoundland in the north and south to New York State and California.
Size: 9¹⁄₂in (24cm).
Habitat: Coniferous forest.
Nest: Tree hollow.
Eggs: 2–6, white.
Food: Mainly invertebrates, but also some vegetable matter, such as nuts.

Identification: Yellowish plumage on the head and crown, with two white stripes on each side of the face separated by an irregular, broad, black band. Wings and back are blackish, with some whitish feathering. The flanks of some birds are blacker than others, depending on the subspecies. The short inner hind toe, equivalent to the thumb, is missing, helping these birds to climb vertically. Hens are smaller with no yellow on the crown. Young birds are generally browner in color, but with more white plumage on the wings. Markings on the underparts are not as clear as those of adults.

Red-headed woodpecker

Melanerpes erythrocephalus

These woodpeckers eat a wide range of plant and animal foods, and their diet is influenced by the season. They are unusual in that they hunt not only by clambering over the bark of trees, but also by hawking insects in flight. They will even swoop down onto the ground and hop along there seeking prey. Red-headed woodpeckers also raid the nests of other birds, seizing both eggs and chicks, as well as catching mice. In northern parts of their range, these woodpeckers often migrate southward during the colder months of the year, seeking plentiful supplies of acorns and beech nuts when other foods are in short supply. They also lay down stores of food, concealing larger insects in cavities or hiding them under the bark, and returning to eat them later.

Distribution: Canada and the U.S.A., from Manitoba and southern Ontario in the north southward to Florida.
Size: 9¹⁄₂in (24cm).
Habitat: Open woodland.
Nest: Tree hollow.
Eggs: 4–10, white.
Food: Plant and animal matter.

Identification: Scarlet plumage covering the head, bordered by a narrow band of black feathering. White underparts, bluish-black coloration on the back, part of the wings, and the tail. Sexes are alike. Young birds are much browner overall, including the head.

OTHER TREE-CREEPING BIRDS

Members of this group of birds are to be found in woodland areas throughout America. Those living in the far north, where the climate can be harsh and invertebrates are often in short supply, lay down food stores to help them survive the winter period. A number of unique and localized species are also to be found on islands in the Caribbean.

Acorn woodpecker

Melanerpes formicivorus

These lively woodpeckers are typically found in oak forests, living in groups of up to 15 individuals. The colony creates special food stores, sometimes described as granaries, where they store acorns for use when food is in short supply. It can take years to build up these stores, which can involve the construction of as many as 50,000 holes in trees throughout the birds' territory. Such is their dependence on this food source that the size of the acorn crop has a direct effect on the number of woodpeckers living in the area. Food storage of this type is far more common in North American populations, since those occurring nearer the equator have a much wider range of foods available throughout the year. The nesting period also varies according to latitude, beginning in March in North America. Family groups will defend the nest site and also provide food for the chicks, which may include small lizards and similar creatures.

Identification: This species has a black area encircling the front of the face, with a white band behind which encircles the eyes. Black and white streaking is evident on the breast, with the remainder of the underparts being white. The scarlet area on the nape of the cock bird is missing in the hen. Young birds have browner upperparts, with an orange crown.

Distribution: Western North America, ranging from southern Oregon eastward to New Mexico and Texas, and south via Central America to Colombia.
Size: 9in (22$\frac{1}{2}$cm).
Habitat: Oak woodland.
Nest: Tree hollow.
Eggs: 4–6, white.
Food: Mainly acorns, with some ants.

White-striped woodcreeper

Lepidocolaptes leucogaster

As their name suggests, woodcreepers are able to climb up the bark of trees like woodpeckers, although they belong to an unrelated family. Here they hunt invertebrates, using their long, slender bills to probe into the bark. White-striped woodcreepers comb the tree in a very methodical fashion, working their way up the trunk and then flying down to the bottom of a nearby tree to work up again. Their strong feet and sharp claws enable them to climb and maintain their grip on the tree. Like woodpeckers, their tail feathers have stiffened shafts that terminate in points which dig into the bark and help to support their weight. Though they do not associate in flocks, it is not uncommon for white-striped woodcreepers to forage in the company of other related species. This can make it difficult to determine the identity of these birds in the field, especially since they may only be seen from behind.

Identification: Whitish sides to the face and throat, with a blackish stripe above the eyes. Top of the head is dark brown mottled with white, while the chest is white with black scalloping to individual feathers. Lower underparts have whitish stripes. Upper back is tawny-brown. Flight feathers, rump and relatively long tail are all rufous. Narrow, slightly down-curved bill, with a dark upper surface and paler below. Grayish feet display claws. Sexes are alike.

Distribution: Occurs in central America, where this species is restricted to the mountainous region of western Mexico.
Size: 9in (22$\frac{1}{2}$cm).
Habitat: Coniferous and oak woodlands.
Nest: Tree hollow.
Eggs: 2–3, white.
Food: Feeds exclusively on invertebrates.

Red-breasted nuthatch

Sitta canadensis

Lively and active by nature, red-breasted nuthatches are well-adapted to an arboreal lifestyle. Their small size and compact shape enable them to climb up and down tree trunks with ease, their strong toes and claws providing sufficient anchorage for them to descend head-first. Their tail feathers lack the stiff points at the tips that characterize woodpeckers, and their bills are not strong enough to bore into the trunk. However, these nuthatches are adept at pulling insects out from under the bark, and they will move along narrow branches to pluck invertebrates off leaves. The seeds of conifers help to sustain them through winter, when invertebrates are scarce. These birds have an unusual method of deterring predators from the nest hole, by smearing it with pine oil. This helps to obscure the scent of the nuthatches, whose plumage becomes heavily stained as they pass in and out of the nest.

Identification: Black cap across the top of the head, with a black line running through the eyes, separated by an intervening white stripe. White on the cheeks too. Back, wings and tail bluish-gray, with rust-colored underparts. Short, narrow blackish bill, paler below, with black legs and feet. Hens have duller plumage on the head and paler underparts. Young birds are similar to hens.

Distribution: Breeding range extends right across Canada from southeastern Alaska to Newfoundland. Winters across much of the U.S.A., sometimes as far south as northern Florida, the Gulf coast and Mexico.
Size: 4¹/₂in (11¹/₂cm).
Habitat: Coniferous and oak woodlands.
Nest: Tree hollows.
Eggs: 4–8, white with reddish-brown speckling.
Food: Invertebrates and pine nuts.

Fernandina's flicker (*Colaptes fernandinae*): 14in (35cm)
Very limited range, restricted to the Caribbean island of Cuba. Yellowish-tan overall, broken by black markings which are particularly evident on the upperparts, while the underparts tend to be lighter. Brownish sides to the face; eyes display a dark iris. Narrow, pointed black bill. Legs and feet are also blackish. Hens lack the distinctive mustache-like stripe seen in cocks.

White woodpecker (*Melanerpes candidus*): 9¹/₂in (24cm)
South America, from Surinam and French Guiana south via Brazil to parts of Bolivia, Paraguay, Argentina, and Uruguay. Also extends westward to Peru. Mainly white, with a narrow dark stripe running from behind the eye, on each side of the head, down to the wings. Wings and tail are black. There is a bright yellow patch on the hind neck, and also in the center of the belly. Hens show little striping on the head and no yellow on the hindneck. Young birds have blackish-brown upperparts, and white areas are tinged with buff.

Puerto Rican woodpecker (*Melanerpes portoricensis*): 10in (25cm)
Occurs on the Caribbean island of Puerto Rico, and on nearby Vieques, where it is more scarce. Black head and upperparts, with prominent white lores and white encircling the eyes. Lower back and rump are white, with white edging sometimes seen on adjacent areas of the wings. Underparts are reddish with buff on the flanks. Hens and young birds are similar to cocks but with less red on their underparts.

Red-breasted sapsucker

Yellow-breasted sapsucker *Sphyrapicus ruber*

True to their name, red-breasted sapsuckers feed mainly on the sap of trees, which they drill into trunks to obtain. When the young hatch, however, the adults forage more widely to feed their hungry brood, seeking insects, especially ants on the ground. A pair will often start several nest holes, and may end up using one that has been partially created already, or one used in a previous year. Both parents share the task of incubation, which lasts just under two weeks, with the young remaining in the nest a further four weeks. During this time the male usually keeps the nest clean. As fall arrives they create new sap wells, to which they regularly return over winter. Sometimes these wells trap ants, which add to their diet. They rarely eat fruit.

Distribution: Western North America, breeding as far north as southeast Alaska, down to California and Nevada. Overwinters south as far as Baja California.
Size: 9in (22¹/₂cm).
Habitat: Mainly coniferous forest.
Nest: Tree hollow.
Eggs: 3–7, white.
Food: Sap and insects.

Identification: Red head, with white area above the bill, which may extend around sides of the head. Back and wings have white wing bars. Underparts yellowish, with darker speckling. Bill is narrow and black. Sexes are alike. Young have brown heads with little red, but white over the bill.

PIGEONS, DOVES AND CUCKOOS

Flying in a woodland environment obviously presents problems, not just because of the confined space but also because it draws attention to a bird's presence, which could place it in danger. It is much better to quietly slip away from a possible predator. This is exactly what many otherwise conspicuous, and often highly terrestrial, birds such as pigeons and cuckoos do.

Key West quail dove

Geotrygon chrysia

Distribution: Occurs in the Caribbean on the Bahamas, in Hispaniola, and in Cuba. Also occurs locally on Puerto Rico.
Size: 12in (30cm).
Habitat: Forest and more open wooded terrain.
Nest: Loose platform.
Eggs: 1–2, buff.
Food: Seeds, fruit and invertebrates.

These quail doves spend most of their time on or near the ground, often frequenting densely wooded countryside, where their dark coloration makes them difficult to observe. Their calls may betray their presence, consisting of a series of low-pitched cooing notes uttered in rapid succession. They use their bills to forage among the leaf litter, eating a varied diet that includes snails and caterpillars. If disturbed, Key West quail doves will seek to walk away quietly, rather than try to fly and so betray their presence. They typically live alone, sometimes in pairs. Cocks begin to call in search of mates in January. The nesting period lasts from February to August, with pairs possibly nesting more than once. The birds sometimes conceal the nest, which is made with twigs and leaves, and sited up to 3ft (1m) off the ground in a bushy shrub or vine.

Identification: Metallic greenish area on the head, extending down the back of the neck. Prominent white banding under each eye, with reddish-brown upperparts. Underparts are pinkish-gray, becoming grayer on the abdomen. Legs and feet are reddish, and the bill is pink with a dark tip. Hens are generally duller. Young birds have brownish feathering on the underparts, and no iridescence.

Blue ground dove

Claravis pretiosa

The marked difference in color between the male and the female blue ground dove is an extreme example of sexual dimorphism within this group. Their appearance in some parts of their range, notably in Central America, is seasonal, being driven by the availability of food. These doves do not occur at high altitudes, being found mostly in the foothills of the Andes, and are most likely to be seen on the forest floor. They are quiet by nature and do not associate in flocks, so are easily overlooked. The breeding season varies with location, starting in March in Panama but usually not until September in Bolivia. The cock bird displays by bowing with his tail raised and wings quivering. The nest is a fragile structure up to 18ft (6m) off the ground. The young often leave at just two weeks of age, before they can even fly properly.

Distribution: Ranges from southeastern parts of Mexico down through Central America to Peru in western South America, and as far as Argentina on the eastern side of the continent.
Size: 9in (23cm).
Habitat: Scrub and woodland.
Nest: Platform of twigs.
Eggs: 2, white.
Food: Seeds, fruits and invertebrates.

Identification: Cock birds are very easily distinguished by their overall grayish-blue coloration, and are a darker shade of blue on the head, wings and upperparts. Variable patterning of black spotting and large black blotches on the wings, with flight feathers also black. Hens are brownish, with brown rather than black wing markings. Young birds resemble hens, but have blackish wing spots.

Pheasant cuckoo

Dromococcyx phasianellus

Distribution: Range extends from southern Mexico down through Central America as far as northern parts of Bolivia, Paraguay, and north-eastern Argentina.
Size: 14in (35cm).
Habitat: Rainforest.
Nest: Parasitic.
Eggs: White or buff, with reddish speckling.
Food: Omnivorous.

These large cuckoos are so called because they have a lifestyle similar to that of pheasants, spending much of their time on the ground. They inhabit woodland areas and plantations where there is dense cover, and will run through the undergrowth to elude pursuit. Their presence is most likely to be betrayed by their song, which sounds like a loud whistle. They often choose a prominent branch some distance off the ground to sing from, and this is where they are most likely to be observed. Like many members of their family, pheasant cuckoos do not build a nest and rear their own chicks. Instead, females lay single eggs in the nests of other birds, usually favoring domed nests that may be hanging freely. The host species varies throughout their range, but the yellow-olive flycatcher (*Tolmomyias sulphurescens cinereiceps*), found in Mexico, is typical.

Identification: Thin head with a narrow rusty crest and a pale stripe running back from the eyes. Thinner dark stripe below from the base of the bill. Chest is pale buff with darker speckling, the remainder of the underparts are white. Back and wings brown, with lighter edging on the feathers. The tail is long and broad, narrowing down its length, with paler tips to the underside of the feathers. Long, pointed bill and dark feet. Sexes alike. Young birds easily identifiable by their plain buff throat and chest.

Mountain witch dove (crested quail dove, *Geotrygon versicolor*): 12in (30cm)
Restricted to Jamaica. Unusual short grayish crest, with buffy patches below the eyes extending backward. Bluish-gray neck and underparts, with a rufous area around the vent. Back and wings mainly purplish-maroon. Flight feathers chestnut, rump and tail blackish. Hens have browner and paler underparts. Young birds display reddish-brown edging on the feathers.

Scaly-naped pigeon (*Columba squamosa*): 16in (40cm)
Widely distributed through the Caribbean, but not on Jamaica, and has not been recorded from Aruba since 1973. Reddish-purple feathering extends over the head and neck to the breast. Rest of the body is slaty-gray. Metallic coppery-red shade on the sides of the neck. Orbital skin is orangish, the bill has a red base and yellow tip. Legs and feet red. Sexes are alike. Young birds are less brightly colored overall, with rusty tones on the head and wings.

Chilean pigeon (Chilean bandtail, *Columba araucana*): 14in (35cm)
Ranges through forested areas, notably the beech forests of central and southern parts of Chile into western Argentina. Vinous-pink head, back and underparts, except for a narrow white stripe across the neck, with metallic green below. Tops of the wings are reddish-purple, the rest of the wings and rump gray. Tail also gray with a broad black band. Hens duller, with less reddish-purple on the wings. Young birds paler and grayer, with bluish-gray rump and tail.

Black-billed cuckoo

Coccyzus erythrophthalmus

Black-billed cuckoos are typically found below 3,300ft (1,100m). They are not easy to spot, being mainly solitary birds that prefer to hide in dense vegetation. Their calls are not very distinctive, resembling those of doves. Pairs sometimes nest quite close to the ground in a bush that gives good cover, or higher up in a tree fork. The diet of black-billed cuckoos varies with location, since they are opportunistic feeders. They may steal both eggs and chicks from the nests of smaller birds, as well as eating fruit and catching prey ranging from insects to lizards. In North America, these cuckoos are highly valued in farming areas due to the number of pests, especially tent caterpillars, they eat, which lessens damage to crops.

Distribution: From Alberta and Montana to the eastern coast of North America, south as far as South Carolina, Arkansas, and Texas. Migrates to western South America as far south as northern Peru, but also recorded from Paraguay.
Size: 11in (28cm).
Habitat: Various types of woodland.
Nest: Platform of sticks.
Eggs: 2–4, pale bluish-green.
Food: Omnivorous feeding habits.

Identification: Bronze-brown color on the upperparts, with underparts white. Long, narrow tail feathers that are black with white tips. Orbital skin encircling the eyes is red. The bill is black.

TANAGERS

The tanager group is comprised of approximately 240 different species, with representatives found throughout America. The largest of the tanagers, up to 11in (28cm) long, is the magpie tanager (Cissopis leveriana), so called because of its black and white plumage. Tanagers occur at a wide range of altitudes, from sea level up into the Andean region. Some North American species are migratory.

Paradise tanager

Tangara chilensis

These tanagers are rather shy by nature, and their coloration makes them hard to recognize against a dark woodland background. They are lively, restless birds with alert, curious natures. They occur in loose flocks, typically made up of 10–15 individuals, and are sometimes seen in the company of related species. Paradise tanagers usually seek out food in the upper part of the canopy, hopping along the branches there and grabbing spiders and other invertebrates as well as seeking berries and fruit.

Left: A paradise tanager on its nest. The Yuracares Native American tribe calls these birds "yeri yeri" because of the sound of their calls.

Identification: Essentially green on the sides of the face, violet-blue throat with vibrant sky-blue underparts. Rump red, with the back of the head and wings black. Sexes are alike. There is some subspecific variation, and the rump color is paler in immature birds.

Distribution: Colombia east to French Guiana and Brazil. Also present in Peru and Ecuador. Although their scientific name suggests otherwise, these tanagers are not found as far south as Chile, reaching only as far as northern Bolivia.
Size: 5in (13cm).
Habitat: Lowland areas of woodland and forest.
Nest: Cup-shaped, made of vegetation.
Eggs: 2, whitish with purple-red speckling.
Food: Fruit and invertebrates.

Beryl-spangled tanager

Tangara nigroviridis

Social by nature, beryl-spangled tanagers are usually observed either in pairs or small flocks comprised of up to 15 individuals. They move fast, rarely resting for any time on a perch. These tanagers remain relatively close to the ground when foraging. They adopt a distinctive posture with their head down when seeking spiders and similar creatures, peering under branches and leaves. Their necks are surprisingly flexible, allowing these tanagers to pluck invertebrates from relatively inaccessible sites. There is some variation between races in their bluish-green plumage.

Identification: Black plumage around the bill, extending in a band around the eyes and over the back, is separated by bluish-green plumage, which is also present on the crown. Violet hues apparent over the wings. The rump is greenish-blue, while the underparts are blackish with pronounced blue spangling. Sexes alike.

Distribution: Colombia and Venezuela south to parts of Ecuador, Peru, and Bolivia.
Size: 5in (12cm).
Habitat: Relatively open areas of forest.
Nest: Cup-shaped, made of vegetation.
Eggs: 2, creamy white to pale green, with darker speckling.
Food: Berries, other fruit, and invertebrates.

Blue-winged mountain tanager

Anisognathus flavinucha

These relatively large tanagers are the most common member of their genus in Colombia. They tend to be encountered throughout their range at lower levels than other related species, usually frequenting altitudes of 4,600–8,500ft (1,400–2,600m). They are most likely to be observed toward the tree-tops, in groups comprised of up to ten individuals. Blue-winged mountain tanagers are quiet by nature; their trilling calls are unlikely to betray their presence from any distance away. Their gape enables them to swallow some berries whole, while on other occasions they pull the skin off first.

Identification: Yellow stripe running over the crown, bordering black areas of plumage on the head. Underparts a matching shade of rich yellow. Back olive-yellow, with blue shoulder patches apparent on the wings. Color of tail and rump varies, depending on subspecies. Sexes are alike.

Distribution: Colombia and Venezuela south into Bolivia.
Size: 7¹/₂in (19cm).
Habitat: Forested areas in the Andean region.
Nest: Cup-shaped, made of vegetation.
Eggs: 2, greenish-white, speckled.
Food: Berries, other fruit, and invertebrates.

Green and gold tanager (*Tangara schrankii*): 4¹/₂in (12cm)
Colombia and Venezuela to Ecuador, Peru, Bolivia, and Brazil. Green plumage on the sides of the body and tail. The crown, underparts, and rump are golden yellow. The forehead and area surrounding the eyes are black. Hens and young birds have a green rump and black spotting on the crown.

Bay-headed tanager (*Tangara gyrola*): 4¹/₂in (12cm)
Costa Rica via Panama to Colombia, French Guiana, Brazil, Ecuador, Peru, and Bolivia. Quite variable in coloration through its wide range, but generally brown plumage on the head. Wings greenish, while underparts may vary from green to blue.

Crested ant tanager (*Habia cristata*, E): 7¹/₂in (19cm)
Confined to the western Andes of Colombia. Long, narrow, scarlet crest feathers, with scarlet throat. Upperparts reddish, with brown wings, underparts grayish. Young birds predominantly brown and have no crest. Feeds mainly on various insects, swooping down to snatch army ants on the march.

Grass-green tanager (*Chlorornis riefferii*): 8in (20cm)
Distribution extends through the Andean region, from Colombia via Peru to Bolivia. Brilliant grass-green coloration offset against chestnut-brown plumage on the sides of the face, and in the vent region. Bill and legs are red in adults. Bills of immatures are brown.

Purple honeycreeper

Cyanerpes caeruleus

Honeycreepers often move extensively through their range, with their local distribution being affected by the whereabouts of flowering trees. Their narrow, curving bills enable these birds to probe flowers to obtain nectar, but their bill shape also allows them to feed on seed pods and to seize small invertebrates. Purple honeycreepers are sufficiently agile to catch insects in flight, although they cannot hover in front of flowers as hummingbirds do. They will, however, dive down to seize spiders that try to escape off branches by dropping down on gossamer threads.

Identification: A rich shade of purple, with a black bib under the throat and black on the wings. Legs are yellow. Hens are green, with yellowish striations on the underparts. Sky-blue patches extending back from the corners of the bill and on the top of the head.

Distribution: Panama southeast via Colombia as far as French Guiana, and south to Ecuador, Peru, Bolivia and Brazil.
Size: 4in (10cm).
Habitat: Flowering trees.
Nest: Cup-shaped nest made of vegetation.
Eggs: 2, white with reddish-chocolate blotches.
Food: Nectar, berries, other fruit, and invertebrates.

NEW WORLD BLACKBIRDS

The description "New World blackbirds" reflects not only the fact that these birds are restricted to America, but also that the color black predominates in their plumage. These birds, often known as icterids, use their bills like knitting needles when constructing their intricate nests, weaving strands of plant matter together to create a remarkably stout, suspended structure.

Crested oropendola

Psarocolius decumanus

During the breeding season, the remarkable call of the male crested oropendola is heard frequently. It has been likened to the noise made by a finger repeatedly plucking the teeth of a plastic comb. These oropendolas live in colonies comprised of several cock birds, one of whom is dominant, and as many as 30 hens. The crest is used as part of the male's display, which consists of elaborate posturing as well as distinctive singing. Ordinary call notes are much shorter and harsher in tone, and are uttered by both sexes. When foraging for food, crested oropendolas frequently associate with blue jays (*Cyanocorax* species).

Identification: Mainly black, with striking blue eyes and a slight crest. Large, relatively straight, pointed white bill, which is characteristic. Chestnut-brown rump, with yellow in the tail feathers and brown undertail coverts. Hens are similar but duller, and lack a crest.

Distribution: Western Panama south via Colombia to northern Argentina and southeast Brazil.
Size: 17in (43cm) cock; hen typically 13in (33cm).
Habitat: Typically lowland wooded areas.
Nest: Suspended nest built off tree branches.
Eggs: 1–2, pale green or grayish.
Food: Mainly invertebrates.

Left: The entrance to the nest of the crested oropendola is at the top, and isolated trees are favored for nesting.

Troupial

Icterus icterus

These attractive icterids (blackbirds) are the national bird of Venezuela. They also occur naturally on the Netherlands Antilles and have been introduced to other islands in the Caribbean, notably Bonaire. It can be difficult to distinguish young birds from the adults on the basis of their plumage, but the bare area of skin surrounding the eyes is a duller shade of blue with a grayish hue in immature specimens (as pictured). They feed mainly on fruit, but also catch insects and may steal other birds' eggs. Unlike other icterids, troupials do not contruct their own nests. Instead, they take over those built by other birds, particularly rufous-fronted thornbirds (*Phacellodomus rufifrons*) and sometimes great kiskadees (*Pitangus sulphuratus*). The troupials then modify the nests by adding a new lining to meet their needs.

Identification: Black head and bill, with black on the back and on the wings, where there is also white plumage. The plumage itself is quite rough in texture here. The remainder of the body is orangish yellow in color, with a black tail. Bluish area of skin surrounds the eyes. Sexes are alike.

Distribution: Northern South America from Colombia and Venezuela to the Caribbean.
Size: 9in (23cm).
Habitat: Relatively dry woodland.
Nest: Covered (roofed) nest.
Eggs: 3, white or pale pink with dark blotches.
Food: Mainly frugivorous, but also eats invertebrates, and may rob other nests for eggs.

Orange oriole (*Icterus auratus*): 7in (19cm)
Restricted to the Yucatan peninsula in Central
America, but some birds may overwinter in
northeast Belize. Mainly orange, becoming
yellowish on rump and underparts. Narrow black
lores, with black plumage extending along sides
of the bill onto chest. Tail and wings black, with
a small white wing bar and white edging to the
flight feathers. Straight, pointed bill blackish-
gray, with gray legs and feet. Hens and young
are yellowish rather than orange, with an olive
tone on the back and a less obvious wing patch.

Montezuma oropendola (*Psarocolius
montezuma*): 19in (48cm)
Eastern Mexico to central Panama. Large,
pointed pale yellow bill, extends back above the
pale bluish eyes. Chestnut on the head,
becoming blacker on the abdomen and chestnut
again on the rump and lower underparts. Back
and wings are blackish, upper tail feathers the
same color, with yellow below. Slight trailing
crest of hair-like plumes at the back of the head.
Legs and feet gray. Hens are smaller. Young
birds duller, with entirely blackish underparts.

Black-cowled oriole (*Icterus dominicensis*):
8in (20cm)
Southeast Mexico to western Panama, also
Caribbean. Cock has a black head, chest, and
back, with blackish wings and tail, and a yellow
area at top of the wings. Rest of body yellow,
except for small brownish area on the chest. Bill
mostly black. Hens have less black on the head,
with olive-green from the crown down over the
wings. Young birds have a slight suffusion of
black on the throat, and are more lemon in color.

Northern oriole

Icterus galbula

These orioles and particularly their young
vary in appearance, which makes them hard
to identify. To add to the confusion, this
species used to be called the Baltimore
oriole, and was considered distinct from the
Bullock's oriole found in the west. New
studies suggest they are the same species,
now known as the northern oriole. The
orange eyebrows and cheeks of the cock
distinguish the western form from the
eastern. The increasing forestation of the
Great Plains enabled these birds to meet and
hybridize, to create what is in some respects
a new species. Large flocks of these
orioles migrate south in
September, and return
again in April.

Distribution: British
Columbia in Canada eastward
to Nova Scotia and across
virtually all of the U.S.A.,
except Florida and parts of
the Gulf coast. Overwinters in
Central America down to
northern South America.
Size: 8¼in (22cm).
Habitat: Deciduous
woodland.
Nest: Pendulous woven
structure.
Eggs: 4–6, grayish with
darker markings.
Food: Invertebrates and
fruit.

Identification: Breeding adult
male has a black head, with black
extending over the back and wings.
Narrow white bar above the flight
feathers, which are edged with white. Rest of
the body orange, vivid on the chest but paler
on underparts. Rump orange, with black upper
tail feathers, orange below. Narrow, pointed
grayish bill, blacker on the upper surface.
Hens have brown instead of black on the head and
upperparts. Young have olive-brown head and
upperparts, and dull underparts with variable orange.

Mountain cacique

Cacicus chrysonotus

Typically found at altitudes between 4,500–9,900ft (1,500 and 3,300m), mountain caciques
are most common in the southern part of their range, particularly in Bolivia, where they
may be found at even higher altitudes. These caciques are noisy by nature, drawing attention
to themselves with whistles and dueting as members of a group keep in contact with each
other. Flocks are small, however, and typically comprise no more than half a dozen birds.
They also forage in the company of other birds such as mountain tanagers,
often venturing to higher branches than their companions to obtain food.
Although members of a flock roost together, mountain caciques breed
in pairs rather than groups. They construct a typical woven
nest, hanging down from a branch where it will be
relatively inaccessible to potential
predators such as snakes.

Distribution: Occurs in the
Andean region of South
America, ranging from
Venezuela through Colombia,
eastern Ecuador, Peru, and
down into Bolivia.
Size: 10¼in (26cm).
Habitat: Humid montane
forest.
Nest: Pendulous woven
structure.
Eggs: Apparently unrecorded.
Food: Berries and
invertebrates.

Identification: Mainly black
with a yellow lower back and rump. Often has yellow on the wings,
depending on race. Peruvian race (*C. l. leucoramphus*) has a white collar
largely hidden by white feathering on the nape, and orange on rump. Pale
blue iris. Sexes are alike, but hens significantly smaller. Young birds are
duller black, with a weaker, horn-colored rather than mainly bluish-gray bill.

WOODLAND INSECT-CATCHERS

Insects caught on the wing feature in the diet of these birds, although hummingbirds also seek out forest flowers, which provide them with energy-rich sugar and protein-laden pollen. Hummingbirds do not occur outside America and often inhabit quite restricted areas, especially in the rainforest. In some cases the shape of the bill has evolved to enable the birds to feed on a particular type of flower.

White-tipped sicklebill hummingbird

Eutoxeres aquila

The highly distinctive, downward-curving bill of these hummingbirds enables them to draw nectar from *Heliconia* flowers. They will frequently grasp onto blossoms with their sharp claws as they probe the flowers with their beak. Their relatively subdued coloration and small size means that white-tipped sicklebills are hard to observe in woodland, especially as they are solitary by nature. They are also shy in contrast to many hummingbirds, but become quite common near their main food plant. They also hunt for small invertebrates on bark. The nest of these hummingbirds hangs down, often suspended from a palm frond, with a "tail" made of plant fibers beneath.

Identification: Characteristic sickle-shaped bill, with lower part being yellow. Glossy deep-green upperparts, and heavy black-and-white streaking on the underparts. The bronzy-green tail feathers have broad white tips. Sexes alike, but hens have slightly shorter wings compared to cocks.

Distribution: Costa Rica south to northwest Peru in the Andean region.
Size: 4$\frac{1}{2}$in (11$\frac{1}{2}$cm).
Habitat: Lower areas of forest and woodland.
Nest: Cup-shaped, made of plant fibers.
Eggs: 2, white.
Food: Nectar, pollen, and small invertebrates.

Long-tailed hermit

Phaethornis superciliosus

Distribution: Mexico south to northern Bolivia and the Amazonian region of Brazil, although distribution is not continuous through this area.
Size: 5in (13cm).
Habitat: Lower levels in forest and woodland.
Nest: Cone-shaped, made of plant fibers.
Eggs: 2, white.
Food: Nectar, pollen, and small invertebrates.

The body of these hummingbirds is tiny compared with the length of their bill, which accounts for about a third of their body length, and their long tail feathers. As is usual behavior with hummingbirds, males are highly territorial, and each establishes a small area, singing there for long periods and driving away potential rivals. The repetitive call note may be repeated up to 100 times each minute in an attempt to attract any female in the vicinity. After mating, the hen will build the nest and incubate and rear the chicks on her own. She keeps her head up when incubating, but the nest is usually concealed beneath a palm frond or similar leafy vegetation.

Left: The hen of the long-tailed hermit always incubates the eggs facing the vegetation that conceals the nest.

Identification: Dull shade of brown with bronzy-green suffusion over the back. Buff edging to the rump. Grayish-buff underparts, becoming buff on the belly, with distinctive white tips to the central tail feathers. Sexes are alike.

Tree swallow

White-bellied swallow *Tachycineta bicolor*

These swallows may be seen in huge flocks migrating to and from their breeding grounds. Nesting starts in early May in the far north of their range, with males laying claim to suitable tree holes. Nest sites are sometimes fought over, with rivals occasionally being killed in such encounters. (The incidence of these disputes is reduced in some areas thanks to the presence of alternative sites in the guise of nestboxes.) Females may also battle to obtain a mate, sometimes even driving out a sitting resident. The hen is responsible for collecting the material for the nest, which is usually made up of dry grass and pine needles, with the eggs being laid on top of a bed of feathers. Studies have revealed that during the nearly three-week period in which they remain in the nest, the nestlings are fed about every three minutes. Success is therefore dependent on the summer, and in bad weather, when invertebrates are scarce, fewer than one chick in four will survive through to fledging.

Identification: Predominantly metallic bluish-green head, extending down over the back, shoulder area, and rump, while the wings and tail are blackish. Develops a less bluish hue after the breeding season. The remainder of the body is white. Sexes alike. Young birds have brown upperparts to their bodies and often display a grayish band over the chest.

Distribution: North-central Alaska to Newfoundland south of Hudson's Bay, south to northern Louisiana and Mississippi. Winters from southern California east to the south of Virginia and down through Central America to Panama. Also in the Caribbean.
Size: 5in (12¹/₂cm).
Habitat: Breeds in wooded terrain.
Nest: Tree cavity.
Eggs: 3–8, white.
Food: Invertebrates, some berries.

Gorgeted woodstar (*Acestrura heliodor*): 2¹/₂in (6¹/₂cm)
Mountainous areas of eastern Panama south to Venezuela and northwest Ecuador. The gorgeted type is the smallest of the woodstars. Stunning pinkish gorget under the throat, lacking in hens, with white feathering on the chest. Remainder of the plumage is mainly green. The underparts of hens are cinnamon.

Wedge-billed hummingbird (*Schistes geoffroyi*): 3¹/₂in (8¹/₂cm)
Mountainous areas from Venezuela to Bolivia. Bronzy-green upperparts. White stripe extends downward from each eye, with a blackish area beneath. Short bill with a sharp point. Gorget is brilliant green with purple plumage. White band across upper chest. Hen has a duller gorget or even a white throat, depending on subspecies.

Purple-crowned fairy hummingbird (*Heliothryx barroti*): 4in (11cm)
Southeastern Mexico south to western Ecuador. Distinctive, shiny violet-purple plumage on the front of the crown, with a black stripe through the eyes. Glossy green upperparts and pure white underparts. Long tapering tail. Hen is slightly larger, with a green crown.

Hoary puffleg (*Haplophaedia lugens*): 3¹/₂in (8¹/₂cm)
Uplands of southwest Colombia and the neighboring area of northern Ecuador. Green upperparts with a coppery hue on head and rump. Grayish-black underparts. Sexes alike.

Northern royal flycatcher

Onychorhynchus mexicanus

Northern royal flycatchers rarely reveal their distinctive crowned crest, except when displaying. They do not range high into the forest canopy, and are usually seen foraging at lower levels in the company of other birds, keeping a watchful eye for invertebrates. They often hunt near forest streams, where mosquitoes and other flying insects are likely to be found. They may also be seen either singly or in pairs, hawking on the wing or darting off from a branch to catch their quarry. These birds may betray their presence by their calls, made up of a series of whistling notes. Their nests are remarkable. Built from a mass of vegetation, they hang down from a branch and measure over 36in (1m) long, affording good protection from predators. The nest chamber is located within the side of the structure.

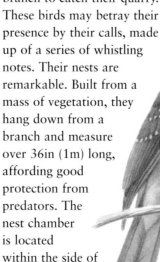

Distribution: Extends from southeastern parts of Mexico down to northwestern Peru and Bolivia, and via Venezuela to French Guiana, reaching down as far as southeastern Brazil.
Size: 7in (18cm).
Habitat: Forest, often near streams.
Nest: Hanging oval structure.
Eggs: 2, reddish-brown with darker markings.
Food: Invertebrates.

Identification: Brown head and wings, with grayer sides of the head. White throat with grayer breast. Underparts yellowish. Tail cinnamon with dark tip. Folded crest on head forms a half-circle when erect, and is red with blue edges and markings. Hens have orange in the crest. Young display dusky scalloping on chest and upperparts.

NORTHERN VISITORS

Woodland areas are rich in invertebrate life, so it is not surprising that a variety of birds seek their food there. Some have a highly specialized style of feeding, while others are opportunistic, which has helped them to spread over a wide area. Insectivorous species occurring particularly in northern areas of North America are forced to head south in the fall, in order to maintain their food supply.

Black and white warbler

Mniotilta varia

Distribution: From Canada (southern Mackenzie through central Manitoba to Newfoundland) to much of southern U.S.A. east of the Rockies. Overwinters along the Gulf coast and down through Central America into northern South America.
Size: 5in (13cm).
Habitat: Woodland.
Nest: Cup-shaped.
Eggs: 4–5, white with purple spots.
Food: Invertebrates.

With its bold patterning and a call that has been likened to a noisy wheelbarrow, the black and white warbler is relatively conspicuous. These birds arrive back in their breeding grounds during April, although they may head north before then, sometimes being spotted in more open country as well as in backyards and parks. These warblers are often better known by their traditional name of black and white creepers, due to their habit of foraging on tree trunks, probing for insects in the bark. They are surprisingly agile, being able to move both up and down the trunk. In their breeding territories, black and white warblers prefer stretches of deciduous woodland where good cover is available, since they breed on the ground. Here the pair will construct a well-disguised nest, usually close to a tree. They start to head south again from July onward. Like other wood warblers, these birds often forage as part of mixed species flocks, especially over winter.

Identification: In breeding plumage males have black feathering on the cheeks and in the vicinity of the throat, with the lower throat area becoming white over the winter. A prominent white stripe is evident above the eyes, with black and white streaking on the flanks. The lower underparts are white. Hens recognizable by their whitish cheeks, with a slight buff suffusion on the flanks. This is more apparent in young birds.

Worm-eating warbler

Helmitheros vermivorus

These warblers are difficult to observe since they frequent areas of dense undergrowth, their small size and coloration helping them to blend into their environment. Although their distribution is centered on the eastern U.S.A. they have on rare occasions been recorded in more westerly areas, even in California. Worm-eating warblers seek their food close to the ground, often on their own, although they can sometimes be found in the company of other warblers. This species is so called not because they favor earthworms but rather because they seek out caterpillars of various moths, which at this stage in their life-cycle resemble worms. Pairs return to their breeding grounds during April, and the males sing as they establish their breeding territories, often perching on a high branch, although even here they can be hard to observe. The nest is built on the ground, and is comprised mainly of dry leaves, with moss and feathers used to create a softer lining.

Distribution: Breeds in the eastern U.S.A., from southeast Iowa to New York and eastern parts of North Carolina, down as far as the central Gulf coast. Overwinters from southeastern parts of Mexico down into South America.
Size: 5¹/₂in (14cm).
Habitat: Dry woodland.
Nest: Cup-shaped.
Eggs: 4–5, white with brown spots.
Food: Invertebrates.

Identification: A black stripe extends up the sides of the crown down over the neck, with another black stripe passing through the eyes. Rest of upperparts are buff-colored. Back and wings brownish-olive. Narrow light-colored bill with pink legs and feet. Sexes alike.

Ruby-crowned kinglet

Regulus calendula

These small warblers breed in the taiga forest stretching across the far north of North America. They often search for food by hovering around the branches, darting down to seize insects such as caterpillars, and are able to balance right out at the tips of branches thanks to their small size. It is not always easy to recognize the distinctive ruby-red crown of the cock bird, since this feathering may be obscured. Ruby-crowned kinglets are very active birds, constantly on the move, and frequently flick their wings, as if something has startled them and they are about to take off. Their nest is woven with great skill and located close to the end of a branch of a spruce tree or similar conifer, where they will be relatively safe from predators. After the breeding season these small birds travel southward, arriving at their wintering grounds in September. Although sometimes sighted among mixed flocks there, they are not especially social over the winter period.

Identification: Olive-brown upperparts with a paler, whitish area encircling the eyes. Throat area pale gray, becoming yellowish on the underparts. Wings dark, with prominent white band at the top and across the wings of the cock bird. Ruby-red patch of feathering on the top of the crown. Hens lack this color, and have more dusky stripes across the wings. Young birds are more brownish on their upperparts.

Distribution: Alaska across Canada south of Hudson's Bay to Newfoundland, south to the Great Lakes and New England. Overwinters from southern U.S.A. south through Central America as far as Guatemala.
Size: 4¹/₄in (11cm).
Habitat: Forests and woodland.
Nest: Woven from plant matter.
Eggs: 5–10, creamy with fine darker speckling.
Food: Invertebrates.

Eye-ringed flatbill (*Rhynchocyclus brevirostris*): 6¹/₂in (17cm)
Southern parts of Mexico down through Central America to Ecuador. Grayish area surrounding the eyes, with a blackish border behind and a paler, grayish-whitish throat. White circle around each eye. Rest of upperparts olive-green, with blackish areas on the wings and tail. Underparts lemon, with olive markings on upper abdomen. Narrow, pointed bill, blackish above and paler below. Gray legs and feet. Sexes are alike.

Stub-tailed spadebill (White-throated spadebill, *Platyrinchus cancrominus*): 3¹/₂in (9cm)
Southeast Mexico down to northwestern Costa Rica. Rufous-brown crown, back and wings. A fawn stripe passes through the eyes and down behind the cheeks. A dark streak runs from the lores below the eyes. Throat whitish, with the underparts pale brownish. Center of the belly and undertail coverts whitish-lemon. Distinctive short, wide tail. Broad, pointed bill, dark above. Pinkish legs and feet. Male has a yellow patch on the crown, absent in the hen. Young birds have a less distinctive facial pattern.

Yellow-eyed junco (*Junco phaeonotus*): 6¹/₄in (16cm)
Southeastern Arizona and southwestern New Mexico south to Guatemala. Grayish head, with black lores highlighting the bright yellow eyes. Back and wings reddish-brown, with pale gray underparts. Mottled bluish area at the shoulders, with reddish edging to the black flight feathers. Central tail feathers are dark. Sexes are alike. Young birds have dusky rather than yellow eyes.

Dark-eyed junco

Junco hyemalis

Although these finches display variable coloration through their wide range, the fact that they breed together freely and produce fertile offspring means that they rank as one species, not four. They are widely seen, mainly in woodlands but also in other habitats when migrating. Dark-eyed juncos are mainly terrestrial in their habits, living in loose flocks that may forage widely. They are prolific when nesting, with incubation lasting just 12 days and the young fledging after a similar period. The nest is well-disguised and sited close to the ground, so that if the young are disturbed they can escape a predator by running away on their surprisingly large feet. Hens produce up to three rounds of chicks over the summer. The young feed largely on invertebrates.

Identification: Variable appearance. Eastern North American birds are mainly slaty-gray, with brownish-gray hens. In the west the Oregon junco (*J. h. thurberi*) has a black head and orange-red flanks and back, with paler brown hens. Other variants include the pink-sided type (*J. h. mearnsi*) of the central Rockies, and the white-winged type (*J. h. aikeni*), gray with white wing bars and white underparts. There are several gray-headed forms. Dark eyes in all cases. Sexes alike. Young birds have streaked patterning.

Distribution: Occurs over most of North America, breeding from Canada to Newfoundland, extending south to Mexico and Georgia in the east. Winters along the Gulf coast and into northern Mexico.
Size: 6¹/₄in (16cm).
Habitat: Woodland.
Nest: Cup of vegetation.
Eggs: 3–6, pale green to blue, with brown spots.
Food: Seeds, berries, invertebrates.

HAWAIIAN FOREST-DWELLERS

In appearance and lifestyle, native birds occurring on the Hawaiian Islands are among the most unusual to be found anywhere in the world, having developed in complete isolation from mainland species until relatively recently. However, a number of these species have, sadly, become extinct over recent years, largely as a direct result of human interference in their environment.

I'iwi

Vestiaria coccinea

Distribution: Confined to the Hawaiian Islands; this species has become extinct on Lanai, and so now occurs only on Hawaii itself, Kauai, Maui, Oahu, and Molokai.
Size: 6in (15cm).
Habitat: Woodland.
Nest: Cup-shaped, made of vegetation.
Eggs: 1–3, white with brown markings.
Food: Nectar and invertebrates.

As with many of Hawaii's birds, the common name of this honeycreeper is derived from its native name. It is most likely to be spotted around flowering plants, both native and introduced. In spite of their vivid coloration iiwis are not easy to observe; like other red forest birds, they blend very effectively with the background. Even if only briefly glimpsed, however, their downward-curving bill sets them apart from other Hawaiian birds of similar color and size. I'iwis' calls are surprisingly varied, ranging from whistles to gurgles, their most distinctive vocalizations being likened to the sound of a rusty hinge creaking open. They are also talented mimics, replicating the calls of other species such as the elepaio (*Chasiempis sandwichensis*). I'iwis are most commonly found above 2,000ft (600m), being less common on Oahu and Molokai.

Identification: Brilliant red coloration over much of the body. Wings and tail are black, with a small area of white plumage at the top of the wings. Legs and bill, which is narrow and down-curved, are also red. Young birds much duller in coloration, being yellowish-green with dark barring over their body. The plumage on the back is darker than on the underparts. Wings are black, with paler edging on some of the feathers, with the tail also black. Bills of young birds are less brightly colored than those of adults, lightening toward the tip.

Akohekohe

Crested honeycreeper *Palmeria dolei* (E)

Identification: Highly distinctive loose, bushy crest extends up between the eyes, with buff above each eye and blue beneath on the cheeks. Remainder of the head is dark, with a reddish nape. Bluish markings on the throat, with blue and brownish patterning on the underparts. Wings similarly colored on the top, with a blue band running across and blue edging to the flight feathers. Fan-shaped tail is black with a white tip, undercoverts grayish. Sexes alike. Young birds have a much shorter crest and are much duller.

Another honeycreeper that is not always easy to spot. Its rather dark overall coloration and relatively small size help to conceal its presence in the treetops where it feeds. However, the akohekohe has a very lively nature and is highly vocal, uttering a series of buzzing and whistling sounds, some not unlike a person whistling. Unfortunately this species has seriously declined in numbers. It has already vanished from Molokai, although it is not uncommon on the eastern side of East Maui, where it inhabits the upland forest areas, frequenting ohia-lehua trees in particular. Here it can sometimes be seen in flight, although sightings are made difficult by the frequent misty weather that obscures visibility in this area. From a distance, the akohekohe may be confused with the smaller apapane (*Himatione sanguinea*).

Distribution: Hawaiian Islands; now believed to be extinct on Molokai, but still survives on Maui.
Size: 7in (18cm).
Habitat: Flowering trees.
Nest: Cup-shaped, made of vegetation.
Eggs: 2, white with brown markings.
Food: Nectar and invertebrates.

Nukupuu

Hemignathus lucidus (E)

The nukupuu occurs in thick ohia forest, using its strong legs to clamber up the bark of trees. Its slender bill is used to probe for invertebrates among the moss and crevices in the bark, and it may often be seen hanging upside down looking under leaves as well. The nukupuu is already extinct on Oahu, and localized in its surviving haunts elsewhere. The Kauai race (*H. l. hanapepe*), with its distinctive white undertail coverts, is restricted to the Alakai swamp, while on Maui most sightings are likely to be on Haleakala's upper slopes. The nukupuu's presence on Hawaii itself was not confirmed until 1982. Much of the confusion surrounding its distribution there arose from its close likeness to the akiapolaau (*H. munroi*), which occurs on Hawaii too. A very detailed comparison will reveal that the akiapolaau's straight rather than slightly curved lower mandible sets it apart.

Distribution: Now restricted to Kauai, Maui, and Hawaii.
Size: 5¹/₂in (14cm).
Habitat: Forest.
Nest: Apparently unrecorded.
Eggs: Believed to be 2, white with brown markings.
Food: Mainly invertebrates.

Identification: Cock bird has a yellow head and underparts, with paler undertail coverts. The plumage on the back of the head is relatively long. Back and wings are dark olive-green. Small black area of plumage around the eyes, with the legs black too. Narrow bill is dark, with the upper part being curved and much longer than the short lower part. Hens easily distinguished by their dull olive-green plumage. Young birds resemble hens.

Ou (*Psittirostra psittacea*, E): 6¹/₂in (17cm) Hawaiian Islands, being found only in small numbers in the Alakai swamp on Kauai, and on Hawaii itself, between the Volcanoes National Park and Hamakua. Male is predominantly green with a yellow head. Bill is salmon-pink and hooked at its tip. Legs are pink. Hens can be distinguished by their green heads.

Palila (*Loxioides bailleui*, E): 7¹/₂in (19cm) Occurs only on the island of Hawaii, notably near Mauna Kea. Cock bird has a yellowish head and breast, with a narrow black area around the eyes. Rest of underparts are white. Back and rump slaty-blue, with dark yellowish-green on the wings. Bill and legs black. Hens duller, with gray merging with the yellow on the hindneck.

Maui parrotbill (*Pseudonestor xanthophrys*, E): 5¹/₂in (14cm) Restricted to Maui, on the eastern side of Haleakala. The massive, dark-colored and downward-curving upper bill of this species resembles that of a parrot. It has a bright yellow stripe above each eye. A dark olive stripe through the eyes separates the duller yellow cheeks and underparts. Dark olive-green area extends from the top of the bill over the wings. Hens less brightly colored, with smaller bills.

Akikiki (Kauai creeper, *Oreomystis bairdi*): 4¹/₂in (11cm) Occurs only on Hawaii itself. Dark gray above, with grayish-whitish underparts and darker gray flanks. Short tail feathers and short, pointed, slightly down-curving pink bill. Young birds have white areas of plumage encircling their eyes.

Bishop's oo

Moho bishopi (E)

This relatively large nectar-feeder has very distinctive, flute-like tones in its song. The bishop's oo is exceedingly difficult to spot, however, as it inhabits dense areas of rainforest and prefers the upper level of the canopy. For a period it was even regarded as being extinct, having vanished from both of the islands where it was sighted at the start of the 20th century. Then, remarkably, about 80 years after it was last recorded, the bishop's oo was rediscovered on Maui in 1981. It still survives there today, notably on the northeastern slope of Haleakala, but sadly there have been no sightings of the Molokai population since 1904. Like other honeyeaters, bishop's oos have tiny swellings on their tongue, called papillae, which act as brushes, helping them to collect flower pollen. Not surprisingly, honeyeaters are important pollinators of forest trees.

Distribution: Restricted to the Hawaiian Islands, being recorded only from Molokai and Maui.
Size: 12in (30cm).
Habitat: Dense forest.
Nest: Cup-shaped.
Eggs: 2, pinkish with dark spotting.
Food: Mainly nectar.

Identification: Predominantly blackish, with faint yellow streaking on the body and more prominent yellow areas behind the eyes and at the bend of the wing. Yellow undertail coverts. Long tail feathers, tapering to a point. Slightly down-curving bill, also tapering to a point, and black legs. Sexes are alike.

THE WOODLAND CHORUS

It is not always easy to identify birds with certainty, especially in the case of immatures coming into their adult plumage, a process that can involve several molts. There can also be regional variations in the appearance of some birds, particularly those that are widely distributed. Furthermore, distinctive color forms can crop up among normally-colored individuals. These are described as color morphs.

Mexican jay

Gray-breasted jay *Aphelocoma ultramarina*

Identification: Predominantly bluish-gray overall, differing in the depth of color through its range. Bluish-gray plumage on the head and neck, extending over the wings, with the tail also bluish. Grayish-white underparts, becoming white around the vent and on the undertail coverts. Northern birds are paler than their southerly relatives. Sexes alike. Young birds duller, typically displaying a yellowish area at the base of the bill.

Seven different races of the Mexican jay have been identified, though it is not always easy to distinguish them in the field, especially since juvenile coloration is a key factor. The length of time taken for the bills of young birds to change color varies greatly, sometimes taking up to two years. Differences in vocalizations and lifestyle have also been identified. The race *A. u. couchii*, found in southern Texas and south across the border, has a harsher call and has adopted a more territorial lifestyle than the Arizona race (*A. u. arizonae*), which lives in flocks of up to 20 birds. These flocks are usually made up of an adult pair and their young from previous years that are not yet breeding, and so are able to help the parents rear the new brood.

Distribution: Ranges from Texas, Arizona, and New Mexico in southwestern U.S.A., down through much of Mexico.
Size: 13in (33cm).
Habitat: Arid woodland.
Nest: Cup-shaped platform of sticks.
Eggs: 4–7, blue to greenish-blue.
Food: Omnivorous.

Clark's nutcracker

Nucifraga columbiana

These members of the corvid family are relatively conspicuous, often approaching campsites in search of food. Clark's nutcrackers have a varied diet, hunting small vertebrates and preying on the eggs and chicks of other birds, as well as searching rotting wood for invertebrates such as beetles. Pine nuts are also significant in their diet. They use their narrow, curved bill to prize out the seeds, sometimes wedging the pine cone in a rock crevice, which acts like a vice. Clark's nutcrackers are territorial by nature. In late summer a pair will begin to create stores of nuts and seeds. Although some of this food is consumed over winter, most of it is used to rear the chicks the following spring. If the pine crop fails, the birds are forced to abandon their territories and head elsewhere in search of food. This happens once every 15 years on average.

Identification: White crown and area around the eyes, with a white patch also evident on each wing and on the undertail coverts. Underside of the tail is also white. Wings and tail otherwise black, with the remainder of the body gray. Powerful, pointed black bill, with black legs and feet. Sexes alike. Young birds duller, with a more brownish tone to their gray plumage.

Distribution: Western North America, from southwestern Canada and western U.S.A. south to northern parts of Mexico. Sometimes irrupts into other areas from central Alaska to Texas, but uncommon in the Midwest.
Size: 12in (30cm).
Habitat: Typically montane coniferous forests.
Nest: Made of twigs and sticks.
Eggs: 2–6, green with dark brown markings.
Food: Omnivorous.

Unicolored jay (*Aphelocoma unicolor*): 14in (35½cm)
Parts of Mexico south to northern El Salvador and western Honduras, being found in cloud forest. Blue overall, with a darker blue area on sides of the head, extending below and behind the eyes. Some races are a more purplish-blue shade. Bill, legs, and feet blackish. Sexes alike. Young birds duller, with yellowish bills.

Pinyon jay (*Gymnorhinus cyanocephalus*): 11in (28cm)
Western U.S.A. south to northern Baja California. Dull blue, with whitish streaking around throat. Relatively narrow, pointed black bill. Sexes alike. Young birds are grayer in color.

Brown jay (*Cyanocorax morio*; previously *Psilorhinus morio*): 17in (44cm)
Southeastern Texas via Mexico and much of Central America to northwest Panama. Grayish-brown head, chest, and upperparts, with grayish-white underparts. Bill, legs, and feet are black. Southern individuals have white tips on inner tail feathers. Sexes alike. Young have yellowish bills.

Northern waterthrush (*Seiurus noveboracensis*): 6in (15cm)
Breeds from Alaska right across Canada except the far north, also northern U.S.A. Winters in Mexico, Ecuador and Peru. Brown upperparts, with a fawn streak from the upper bill behind each eye. Spotted throat. Underparts lemon-yellow, with darker streaking toward the vent. Undertail coverts white. Bill dark, legs and feet pinkish, bobbing as it walks. Sexes alike.

Varied thrush

Ixoreus naevius

This migratory member of the thrush family is sometimes placed within the genus *Zoothera*. It is inconspicuous, often hard to observe in the dark woods and areas near water it frequents. Varied thrushes are not shy birds, however, and have a powerful song with buzzing tones which is most often uttered in the rain. They sing most at the start of the breeding period in March, from upper branches in the forest. Varied thrushes normally feed close to the ground, foraging for invertebrates as well as eating berries. They normally nest around 15ft (4½m) off the ground. The bulky nest often includes moss. After the breeding period the thrushes leave Alaska, with many overwintering in British Columbia, while others head further south, where they may be seen in open woodland.

Identification: Bluish-gray upperparts, with a broad black stripe on the sides of the head and a prominent black band across the chest. Bright orange areas above the eyes and on the throat, upper chest, and lower underparts, the latter being mottled with gray. Orange bars also on the wings. Hens browner, with duller orange and an indistinct breastband. Young birds much duller, with brownish mottling on the throat and chest.

Distribution: Occurs in western North America, ranging from Alaska southward as far as northern parts of California.
Size: 10in (25cm).
Habitat: Coniferous forest.
Nest: Bulky and cup-shaped.
Eggs: 3–5, pale blue with dark spots.
Food: Invertebrates, some berries.

American redstart

Setophaga ruticilla

Belonging to the wood warbler rather than the thrush family, American redstarts are naturally very lively and active, almost constantly on the move seeking food, fanning open their tails and lowering their wings. Invertebrates may be hawked in flight or grabbed off bark. In parts of Latin America, where they overwinter, they are known locally as "candelita," since their jaunty nature and the coloration of cock birds combine to resemble the movements of a candle flame. Male American redstarts will sing loudly even before they gain adult plumage, which is not attained until they are over a year old. The song is most evident in spring at the start of the breeding season. The nest is built at a variable height in a suitable bush or tree, up to 75ft (23m) above the ground, and the hen incubates alone, with the eggs hatching after approximately 12 days. The young birds are reared almost entirely on invertebrates, and fledge about three weeks later.

Identification: Cock birds are very colorful, with orange patches on the wings and tail contrasting with the white plumage on the underparts and black elsewhere. Hens are a dull shade of olive-brown, with yellow rather than orange markings. Young birds resemble hens.

Distribution: Southeastern Alaska to Newfoundland, south to California in the west and South Carolina in the east. Overwinters in extreme south of the U.S.A. and via Mexico to northern South America.
Size: 6in (15cm).
Habitat: Deciduous woodland.
Nest: Cup-shaped.
Eggs: 3–5, white to bluish, with brownish spots.
Food: Invertebrates and berries.

OWLS

Owls rank among the most distinctive of all birds, thanks partly to their facial shape. Representatives of this group are very widespread in America, ranging from the coniferous forests of the far north, through the Amazon rainforest and right down to Tierra del Fuego at the southern tip of South America. Although the majority are nocturnal by nature, some will actively hunt during the daytime.

Northern saw-whet owl

Aegolius acadicus

Despite their distinctive calls, which resemble the sound of a saw being sharpened, northern saw-whet owls are hard to observe due to their small size and nocturnal nature. They are also able to fly very quietly to escape detection. This is strictly a woodland species, not found in northern coniferous areas. In southern areas it can be seen in more open, drier deciduous forest. During the day the owls rest on a branch close to a tree trunk, where their color and size make them hard to locate. They eat a variety of prey, especially rodents but also birds, invertebrates, and frogs. Pairs only come together for breeding, with the male seeking a mate by singing close to his nest hole. The young remain in the nest for a month.

Identification: Brown and white area on the face above the eyes, with white spotted area on the nape. Brown markings on the sides of the face. Underparts are white with rufous-brown markings. Wings and tail brownish with white spotting. Bill is black, irides yellow. Young birds have white eyebrows and lores, while the rest of the face is brown. Their underparts are tawny brown in color.

Distribution: Range extends across North America from British Columbia to Newfoundland, and south as far as Mexico. The race *A. a. brooksi* occurs on the Queen Charlotte Islands and *A. a. brodkorbi* in southwestern Mexico.
Size: 7$\frac{1}{2}$in (19cm).
Habitat: Mainly coniferous forest.
Nest: Tree hole.
Eggs: 3–7, white.
Food: Mainly small vertebrates.

Northern hawk owl

Surnia ulula

Distribution: Range is circumpolar, right across North America in the boreal region from southern Alaska east to Labrador. Also present in Newfoundland.
Size: 16in (40cm).
Habitat: Coniferous forest.
Nest: Tree holes.
Eggs: 5–13, white.
Food: Mainly small mammals.

These owls, occurring in the far north where day length varies significantly through the year, can be encountered at any time. Northern hawk owls are solitary by nature outside the breeding season. In late spring the male calls to attract a mate. The pair may choose from a variety of nesting sites, making use of a hole created by a woodpecker, taking over an abandoned stick nest, or simply choosing a site on top of a tree whose crown has snapped off, creating a depression. They make no attempt at nest-building themselves. The eggs are laid at two-day intervals, with the hen sitting alone and the male bringing food for her. Lemmings usually predominate in their diet, but in years when the lemming population plummets other prey, even small fish, may be caught. Breeding success is directly related to the availability of food. The young fledge at four weeks old, but it will be a further two weeks before they can fly, and they remain dependent on their parents for food for a further month.

Identification: Prominent white eyebrows and white cheeks, with whitish spotting on the dark head and wings. Broad black bars on each side of the neck. More brownish on the underparts and tail, with the underparts barred too. Eyes and bill pale yellow. Sexes are alike.

Elf owl

Micrathene whitneyi

Five different races of this small, short-tailed owl are recognized. It is the only member of its genus, and lacks ear tufts. Elf owls are nocturnal, often roosting during the day in holes created by woodpeckers, although they may also be spotted on a branch. At night they hunt from a perch, and may be drawn to the light of a campfire, swooping down unexpectedly to catch moths. Their presence may also be betrayed by their high-pitched calls, some of which sound like whistles. Pairs sometimes choose nest holes in saguaro cacti, with the female building no nest, simply laying directly on the floor of the hollow. With the exception of the isolated population in Baja California, elf owls undertake seasonal movements on the mainland, leaving the U.S.A. and overwintering in central Mexico. In spring they return north again to establish breeding territories.

Identification: Plumage varies, with brown and gray morphs identified. Upperparts brown with white spotting on the head, back and wings, creating a line across the wings. The tail is barred. Face is rufous-brown, with more prominent narrow black markings. Underparts are brownish above, becoming whiter below with fine black barring. Eyes pale yellow, with a grayish-horn bill. Head and crown grayish in young birds.

Distribution: Extends from southwestern California to central Mexico. Separate populations exist in Baja California and on Socorro Island.
Size: 5$\frac{1}{2}$in (14cm).
Habitat: Arid wooded areas.
Nest: Hollows in trees or cacti.
Eggs: 2–5, white.
Food: Mainly invertebrates.

Unspotted saw-whet owl (*Aegolius ridgwayi*): 7$\frac{1}{2}$in (19cm)
Southern parts of Mexico down to Costa Rica, Guatemala, and Panama. Whitish eyebrows and lores, paler brown face. Rufous-brown upper chest, sides of the head and upperparts, with buff underparts. Short tail. Eyes yellow, bill black. Sexes are alike. Young birds may have faint streaking on the breast.

Buff-fronted owl (*Aegolius harrisii*): 8in (20cm)
Venezuela down via Ecuador to northwest Argentina, with an apparently separate population in eastern Brazil and adjacent parts of Argentina and Paraguay. Cream-colored facial disks, with brown edging and eyebrows. Rest of the head mainly brown, with a wide yellowish-buff band around the neck and a similar line running down the wings; spotted patterning here and on the tail. Rest of upperparts brownish, with buff underparts. Sexes alike.

Boreal owl (Tengmalm's owl, *Aegolius funereus*): 11$\frac{1}{2}$in (29cm)
Circumpolar, including northern North America, ranging as far south as Oregon and New Mexico in the U.S.A. Blackish surround to the mainly white face, with white spotting on the forehead and a paler area on the back of the head. Dark throat patch. Underparts are a combination of rufous and white markings, with brown on the wings and tail, broken by white spots of variable size. Barring on the tail also. Eyes are yellow, bill pale horn-colored. Sexes are alike, but the female is larger. Young birds are similar to adults after fledging, but may be darker.

Crested owl

Lophostrix cristata

Crested owls are most likely to be seen in areas relatively close to water, at altitudes up to 4,500ft (1,500m). Their pronounced ear tufts may assist them in detecting and homing in on invertebrate prey. Small vertebrates such as rodents also feature in their diet. Pairs will roost together on a suitable branch during the daytime, often in riverine areas, relying on their plumage to conceal their presence. If disturbed they will try to hide more effectively, by stretching themselves to appear slimmer, with their ear tufts held erect. Their breeding season appears to be linked to climate, since it occurs during drier months of the year, although little is documented about their reproductive habits. The subspecies *L. c. stricklandi*, seen here, is distinguished by its unusual yellow, rather than brown, eyes.

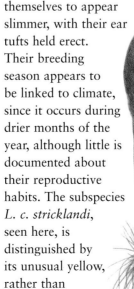

Distribution: Southern Mexico down through Central America and into northern South America, although its precise range there is unclear. Has been recorded as far south as parts of Peru, Bolivia and Brazil.
Size: 17in (43cm).
Habitat: Rainforest areas.
Nest: Tree holes.
Eggs: Not recorded.
Food: Mainly invertebrates.

Identification: White eyebrows extend to create tufts which can be raised. In the brown morph, the head and upper breast is chocolate-brown, the back and wings are paler with white spotting, and the eyes are dark. Red morph displays more even rufous color; gray morphs have brownish-gray plumage. Young tend to be whiter.

OWLS WITH VARIABLE PLUMAGE

Variation in appearance is a feature of many owls, occurring as they do in different color morphs. Such variants typically range from a reddish tone through to gray. Unlike true subspecies, these morphs occur alongside each other in the same area, even in the same nest. This diversity may have evolved to provide additional camouflage to the cryptic patterning that already characterizes these birds.

Stygian owl

Asio stygius

Stygian owls are found in highland areas, up to altitudes of 9,000ft (3,000m) or more where trees are present. They stay hidden during the daytime, roosting on a branch that allows them to get close to the trunk of a tree, keeping their ear tufts lowered unless they become frightened. They emerge to hunt under cover of darkness, flying in a distinctive manner that distinguishes them from other owls: by flapping their wings in a slow, deliberate fashion and gliding. Stygian owls are very agile in flight, however, and are able to catch bats on the wing. More typically they catch other prey, which can include birds taken from a perch. Their distinctive call is most likely to be heard at the start of the breeding season, with those of females being higher in pitch. While some pairs may nest on the ground, others often adopt tree nests abandoned by other birds.

Identification: Prominent ear tufts. Brownish facial area with white eyebrows. Upperparts predominantly brownish, with traces of white barring on the tail. White mixed with brown on the upper chest, mainly brown beneath and more buffy on the underparts. Central American birds have whiter, less buffy underparts and are grayer above. Their eyes are orange-yellow in color and the bill is black.

Distribution: Range extends from parts of Mexico through Central America to Nicaragua and Belize. Separate population in northwestern South America, another extending south to northern Argentina and southeastern Brazil. Also on Cuba, Hispaniola, and smaller neighboring islands.
Size: 18in (46cm).
Habitat: Montane forest.
Nest: Variable.
Eggs: 2, white.
Food: Mainly vertebrates.

Mottled owl

Ciccaba virgata

Mottled owls vary not only in coloration but also in size, with the largest individuals originating from the vicinity of the Lower Amazon in Brazil. They are sedentary throughout their wide area of distribution, and also nocturnal in their habits, roosting quietly on branches in secluded places during the day. The breeding season also varies according to location, often starting as early as February in northern parts of their range, but restricted to September through to November in Argentina, at the southern end of their distribution. Males are very territorial when nesting, singing from the outset to attract a mate. Mottled owls are opportunistic hunters, preferring to catch their quarry from a perch rather than on the wing. They take a wide variety of prey, with rodents featuring prominently in their diet, although reptiles and amphibians may also be caught, along with various other invertebrates.

Identification: Rounded head with no ear tufts. Coloration variable, depending on race and color morph, with some birds significantly darker than others. Generally, the head is brown, and the chest is lighter with short vertical markings, compared with the abdomen which is buff with white and brown markings. Tail heavily barred. Eyes dark brown, with a pale yellow bill.

Distribution: Exends from both coasts of Mexico down through Central America to northern parts of South America, ranging to Ecuador in the west and down to northeast Argentina and southeastern Brazil on the Atlantic coast.
Size: 14in (35cm).
Habitat: Lowland forest.
Nest: Tree hole.
Eggs: 2, white.
Food: Small vertebrates and invertebrates.

Rufous-banded owl (*Ciccaba albitarsus*; previously *Strix albitarsus*): 14in (35cm) Western South America, from Colombia and Venezuela south to Ecuador, northwest Peru, and Bolivia. Chestnut-brown facial disk, with prominent white lores and tawny and black barring on back of the head. Wings brownish, with gray and white flight feathers. Underparts are paler with white markings. Orange-yellow eyes and yellow bill. Sexes alike but hens usually larger. Young birds have a blackish mask.

Black-banded owl (*Ciccaba huhula*; previously *Strix huhula*): 14¹/₂in (36cm) Occurs over a wide area east of the Andes, south to northern Argentina and southeast Brazil. Blackish facial area, with fine white markings, and slight barring on the head. Barring more evident over the rest of the body, even on the feathering on the legs. Birds from the south are blacker than northern individuals, which have a brownish tinge to their plumage.

Mountain pygmy owl (*Glaucidium gnoma*): 6in (16cm) Southwestern U.S.A. southward, probably to the far northwest of South America. Depth of coloration varies through its range. Whitish eyebrows, with light brown plumage speckled with white spots over the head. Darker collar, and brownish wings showing fine barring and speckling. Central area of the chest down to abdomen white, with dark brown flecking on the flanks. Eyes yellow, bill pale yellow. Sexes are alike, but hens may be bigger. Young birds display even gray coloration on the crown.

Great gray owl

Strix nebulosa

These owls move quite extensively through their large range, with North American individuals even having been sighted in the vicinity of New York on occasion. Much of this movement is triggered by the availability of food, especially voles, which these owls hunt almost exclusively during the breeding season. Pairs will often take over the abandoned nests of other birds of prey such as buzzards, although they sometimes nest on the ground. The number of eggs in the clutch is directly related to the availability of food, with breeding results therefore being closely correlated with fluctuations in vole populations.

Distribution: Circumpolar, from northern Canada and Alaska south to California, Idaho and Wyoming. A separate population extends across the far north of Europe and Asia.
Size: 27in (69cm).
Habitat: Coniferous forest.
Nest: Often a platform of sticks.
Eggs: 3–6, white.
Food: Small vertebrates, especially voles.

Identification: Plumage coloration consists mainly of gray streaking and barring on a white background. The dark markings on the so-called facial disk that surrounds the eyes form concentric rings. Yellowish bill, with a blackish patch beneath. Tail is relatively long. Hens are larger in size.

Great horned owl

Bubo virginianus

These owls are not found in areas of dense forest such as the Amazon. They prefer instead to hunt in semi-open terrain, where their keen eyesight enables them to swoop down on small mammals that form the basis of their diet. They are opportunistic hunters, however, and will take a much wider range of prey, from insects and amphibians to other birds, including smaller owls. Males are quite vocal, and sing loudly to attract a mate. Pairs split up at the end of the breeding season, but may reunite again later. They breed in a wide range of locations; an unpleasant stench may give away the location of the nest site because the male may stockpile food there for the offspring.

Identification: Variable through the species' wide range. Northerly populations generally have more brown in their plumage and on the facial disk. Populations further south have a more buff tone to the feathering. Bill is grayish-black. Iris is yellow. Hens are larger than cocks.

Right: The name of these owls comes from the appearance of their so-called ear tufts.

Distribution: Alaska and Canada south over virtually the entire U.S.A. and Central America. South America from Colombia and Ecuador through Peru to Bolivia and east to Guyana; also south to Brazil and central Argentina.
Size: 22in (56cm).
Habitat: Lightly wooded areas.
Nest: Abandoned nest or on the ground.
Eggs: 2–6, white.
Food: Small vertebrates.

LARGER HUNTERS OF THE FOREST

A number of large diurnal birds of prey have adapted to life in woodlands, becoming skilled hunters in this terrain, where visibility is limited. They often range over a very wide area, and take a diverse range of prey.

Harpy eagle

Harpia harpyja

The immense power and strength of these eagles makes them fearsome predators, able to catch creatures ranging from birds such as large macaws to monkeys, sloths and even pigs. Reptiles such as iguanas and large snakes may also fall victim to these eagles. They are believed to use not just keen eyesight but also acute hearing to detect potential quarry in the forest canopy. However, they often prefer to hunt in clearings, or at areas where animals congregate, such as water sources. In the early morning, it is sometimes possible to see these magnificent eagles perched rather than flying overhead.

Identification: The female harpy eagle is much larger than the male, potentially weighing twice at much as her partner, up to 20lb (9kg). The head is grayish with a prominent, divided black crest. Upper chest is blackish, and underparts are white, aside from black-and-white barring on the tail feathers. There is fainter barring on the thighs. Wings are blackish. Young take at least five years to acquire full adult plumage. Their head and underparts are entirely white at first, changing gradually over successive molts.

Distribution: South Mexico through Central America, to Colombia and northern South America, ranging as far south as northeastern Argentina, via eastern Bolivia and Brazil.
Size: Female 41in (105cm).
Habitat: Lowland tropical forest. They rarely soar over the forest, preferring instead to fly close to the canopy.
Nest: Platform of sticks.
Eggs: 2, whitish.
Food: Vertebrates.

Black and chestnut eagle

Oroaetus isidori

These eagles are most likely to be seen at altitudes of around 6,600ft (2,000m) but they have been observed from sea level up to 11,500ft (3,500m). Relatively little is known about their habits, and they are hard to observe since they hunt mainly in the canopy, preying on quite large creatures, including monkeys, which they seize in their powerful talons. Large trees are chosen to support the weight of their nest, which can be up to 6½ft (2m) in diameter. The cock bird is responsible for feeding the single chick, and appears to concentrate on hunting squirrels for it. The young eagle spends about four months in the nest, after which time its plumage darkens over successive molts until it assumes its adult coloration at four years old.

Identification: Head, including crest feathers, back, wings, and top of the thighs are black. Lower chest and underparts are chestnut streaked with black. Tail is grayish with a black band at its tip. Iris is orange-yellow. Feet are yellow. The female can be up to 8in (20cm) larger than the male.

Distribution: Northeast Colombia and adjacent Venezuela south through Ecuador and Peru to Bolivia. Possibly no longer occurs in Argentina.
Size: Female 31½in (80cm).
Habitat: Forested areas.
Nest: Platform of sticks.
Eggs: 1, whitish with brownish spots.
Food: Other vertebrates.

Crested eagle

Morphnus guianensis

These eagles vary considerably in appearance, with pronounced differences between the light morph and the gray morph, which has a much grayer head and chest, combined with black and white barring on the underparts. Crested eagles are solitary by nature outside the breeding season. They can sometimes be spotted on a branch high up in an exposed tree, watching for prey, although with large territories to cover, sightings can be infrequent. These are birds of the lowland forest, typically seen up to 4,800ft (1,600m). They are formidable predators, taking mammals the size of woolly monkeys, as well as larger forest birds, notably guans (Cracidae). Pairs typically nest around April close to the equator; elsewhere their breeding period is unknown. They build a massive nest, with a cup-shaped depression at the center for the eggs.

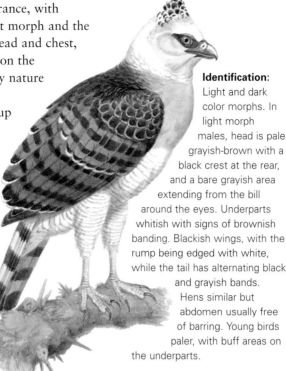

Identification: Light and dark color morphs. In light morph males, head is pale grayish-brown with a black crest at the rear, and a bare grayish area extending from the bill around the eyes. Underparts whitish with signs of brownish banding. Blackish wings, with the rump being edged with white, while the tail has alternating black and grayish bands. Hens similar but abdomen usually free of barring. Young birds paler, with buff areas on the underparts.

Distribution: Southeastern Mexico down to Panama and across South America east of the Andes, ranging down through eastern Bolivia, Paraguay and Brazil. Very occasionally sighted in northern Argentina.
Size: 35in (89cm).
Habitat: Lowland tropical forest.
Nest: Large stick nest.
Eggs: 1–2, creamy-white.
Food: Mainly mammals and birds.

Crowned solitary eagle (*Harpyhaliaetus coronatus*): 33¹/₂in (85cm)
Eastern Bolivia, western Paraguay, southern Brazil, and Argentina, also possibly Uruguay. Mainly dark gray, with a crest at the back of the head. Flight feathers and tail are darker. Tail has a broad white band and white tip. Bill mainly yellow with a dark tip. Legs and feet also yellow. Hens slightly larger. Young birds have brownish upperparts, with whitish streaking beneath.

Ornate hawk eagle (*Spizaetus ornatus*): 26in (67cm)
Southeast Mexico to Bolivia, Paraguay and north Argentina. Dark brown crest at back of the head. Sides of face and neck rufous. Throat and underparts white, brown spots and barring on lower chest and abdomen. Undertail coverts white. Barred tail with black and white markings. Wings brownish with white edging. Irides orange. Yellow bill has dark tip, feet yellow. Hens larger. Young have whiter underparts.

Black hawk eagle (*Spizaetus tyrannus*): 28in (71cm)
Central Mexico down across much of northern South America to southern Brazil and northeast Argentina. Mainly black, with crest at back of the head having white at base of feathers. Lower abdomen and undertail coverts have white barring. Long, broad tail is banded black and gray. Irides yellow, bill black, feet yellow. Hens larger. Young have more extensive white areas on the head and are browner overall.

Black and white hawk eagle

Spizastur melanoleucus

Sightings of this eagle are relatively unusual. Although distributed over a very wide area, it does not occur anywhere at high density. Large territories are essential to provide adequate hunting. Black and white hawk eagles take a wide variety of prey, from birds to opossums and probably small monkeys, also reptiles and amphibians. They hunt from high vantage points in the canopy, sometimes from fairly exposed branches. They prefer to hunt in clearings or on the edge of the forest, diving down from heights of 650ft (200m) or more, and may be heard whistling in flight. Little is known about their breeding habits, except that pairs construct a bulky platform of sticks located 120ft (40m) or more off the ground.

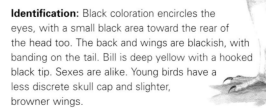

Identification: Black coloration encircles the eyes, with a small black area toward the rear of the head too. The back and wings are blackish, with banding on the tail. Bill is deep yellow with a hooked black tip. Sexes are alike. Young birds have a less discrete skull cap and slighter, browner wings.

Distribution: South Mexico through much of Central America. Isolated South American populations in Colombia, Venezuela and Peru but mostly found further east from Brazil to Bolivia and Paraguay, and in Argentina.
Size: 61in (20cm).
Habitat: Rainforest areas.
Nest: Stick nest.
Eggs: 1, white with dark brown blotches.
Food: Wide variety of prey.

OTHER HUNTERS OF THE FOREST

In addition to the larger birds of prey found in woodlands, a number of other predatory species are also encountered in this environment. They include the unusual caracaras, which are highly social by nature and feed largely on insect larvae. Other birds are more adaptable feeders, but studying these species is not always easy due to the relative inaccessibility of their habitats.

Red-throated caracara

Ibycter americanus; previously *Daptrius americanus*

Distribution: Ranges from southern Mexico through Central America to Ecuador, central Peru, and parts of northern and eastern Brazil, as far as southern Brazil.
Size: 24in (61cm).
Habitat: Rainforest.
Nest: Made of sticks.
Eggs: 2–3, whitish to buff, spotted with brown.
Food: Mainly invertebrates and some fruit.

Unusually among birds of prey, red-throated caracaras are highly social, living in established groups of up to ten individuals that all share and defend a territory. They break open small nests of wasps and bees to obtain the grubs, and remarkably escape being stung, even on their bare facial skin. It is believed that the caracaras have a natural insect-repellent on their plumage, since these normally aggressive insects do not even attempt to sting them. Occasionally, they also eat palm fruits and may even take turtle eggs. Red-throated caracaras breed infrequently, perhaps just once every five years, which may be a reflection of a stable and relatively long-lived population. Pairs may lay at a considerable height off the ground, with group members guarding the nest and gathering food for the chicks.

Identification: Mainly black on upperparts, back, wings and tail. Abdomen and undertail coverts white. Bare area of pinkish-red skin around eyes and on throat. Bill dark gray, legs and feet pink. Sexes alike. Young have more yellowish areas of exposed skin.

Collared forest falcon

Micrastur semitorquatus

Identification: Three color morphs. Black crown, with partial stripes extending down the sides of the face. Underparts and neck collar white or tawny, depending on the morph, with black back and wings. Long tail with white barring and a white tip. In dark morphs, head and underparts entirely black, except for slight white barring on the flanks. Bill black, with an area of grayish skin encircling the eyes. Legs and feet yellowish in all cases. Females larger. Upperparts of young birds more brown in color.

It is thought that collared forest falcons deliberately deceive their prey, calling close to the ground to lure other birds within reach. They are effective hunters, able to dispatch much larger species such as ocellated turkeys, guans, currassows, and other predatory birds such as mottled owls. These falcons also appear to have very acute hearing. They nest in hollows in mature trees, with the larger female defending the site against other pairs. Incubation lasts over six weeks, with chicks spending a similar interval in the nest, where they are fed increasingly by the male. They are unlikely to start hunting alone until at least six weeks after fledging. Breeding pairs usually return to the same nest every year.

Distribution: Ranges from north-central parts of Mexico through Central America to parts of Colombia, Ecuador, and Peru. Extends over much of northern South America, as far south as Bolivia, Paraguay and northern Argentina.
Size: 22in (56cm).
Habitat: Lowland rainforest.
Nest: Tree cavities.
Eggs: 2, buff to brown, with darker brown markings.
Food: Mainly vertebrates.

Bat falcon

Falco rufigularis

In spite of its name, the bat falcon is not dependent on bats for its food, since it is an adept hunter of other flying creatures, including birds and invertebrates. Occasionally, these falcons catch rodents or lizards on the ground. They can also vary their hunting strategy, watching patiently from a perch or swooping down low over the forest canopy in the hope of disturbing prey. Pairs nest in tree holes that may previously have been occupied by birds such as parrots. They become noisy and territorial at this stage, driving away other birds of prey that enter the area. The male mainly hunts alone to feed the brood.

Identification: Dark slaty-gray head, with yellow cere and skin encircling each eye. Partial white collar extends up sides of the neck, edged with a chestnut band across chest. Grayish-black wings and tail, which is barred with white and has a white tip. Thighs and undertail coverts rufous. Lower underparts blackish with white barring. Bill black, legs and feet yellowish. Hens larger. Young have black upperparts, with a buff-colored throat.

Distribution: Extends from northern Mexico down through Central America west of the Andes to Ecuador, and eastward down as far as southern Brazil and northern Argentina.
Size: 11½in (29cm).
Habitat: Forested areas.
Nest: Tree holes.
Eggs: 2–9, creamy to reddish, with dark blotches.
Food: Flying creatures.

Sharp-shinned hawk (*Accipter striatus*): 13in (34cm)
Much of North America from Alaska and Canada south to the U.S.A. as far as Panama, with birds moving south in winter. Also on various Caribbean islands. Slate-blue upperparts and barred tail with variable white-and-chestnut areas on the underparts. Females are larger.

Northern goshawk (*Accipter gentilis*): 26½in (68cm)
North America to Mexico. A separate population is present through northern Europe and Asia. Variable depth of coloration. Wings are grayish. Underparts white with grayish barring extending up around the neck. Darker area of plumage on the head and behind the eyes. Hens are larger.

Plumbeous forest falcon (*Micrastur plumbeus*): 14½in (37cm)
Southwest Colombia and northern Ecuador. Small, with dark grayish head and back. Barred underparts, with a characteristic single white band midway down the white-tipped tail feathers.

Hawaiian hawk (*Buteo solitarius*): 18in (46cm)
Restricted to the Hawaiian Islands. Endemic to Hawaii, has spread to Oahu and Maui. Brown overall, with pale rufous underparts. Females are much larger, the size difference being greater than in any other *Buteo* species. Young birds have tawny mottled plumage on the head and breast. In the pale morph, head and underparts are pale pinkish-buff, with white undertail coverts. Wings are brownish with light markings, and the tail is gray with light banding. Young pale morph birds are golden-buff.

Ridgway's hawk

Buteo ridgwayi

These hawks can be seen in a variety of different habitats, having adjusted to some degree to forest clearance, but they are still very dependent on wooded areas for hunting and nesting. The nest is large, about 20in (50cm) in diameter. It is built mostly by the male, with the hen adding material to disguise its presence. Breeding pairs fly high above the canopy to perform a conspicuous aerial courtship. The eggs take about a month to hatch, and the chicks then remain on the nest until they fledge at around three months. They are reared largely on food provided by the male. Ridgway's hawk faces an uncertain future in its native habit unless sufficient areas can be protected from deforestation. It remains most widespread in the Los Haites region of Hispaniola. Although part of the island has been set aside as a national park, policing of these boundaries remains a difficult task.

Distribution: Restricted to the Caribbean region, where it occurs on the island of Hispaniola and neighboring islets.
Size: 16in (40cm).
Habitat: Prefers undisturbed forest.
Nest: Platform of vegetation.
Eggs: 2–3, whitish with reddish blotches.
Food: Mainly vertebrates.

Identification: Grayish head, rufous underparts barred with white on chest and abdomen. Undertail coverts white. Back and wings brown, rufous-brown on the shoulders. Flight feathers dark, tail feathers dark with narrow white lines. Dull yellow bill has dark tip. Legs and feet yellow. Females duller brown above, with reddish-pink on underparts. Young are gray-brown with no rufous feathers.

GIANTS AND ODDITIES

Grassland areas are home to a surprisingly wide range of birds, including the flightless rheas, although the number of large species in South America is now significantly smaller than it was in the past. Fossil evidence has revealed how gigantic, fearsome avian carnivores roamed these plains as the age of the dinosaurs drew to a close, some 65 million years ago.

Greater rhea

Common rhea *Rhea americana*

The size of rheas prevents them from flying, but they are well equipped to defend themselves from most predators, and are able to run at speeds in excess of 37mph (60km/h). Their wings are larger than those of other flightless birds, with a claw on each so they can inflict serious injury at close quarters. Social by nature, rheas live in loose groups. When breeding, a number of hens are attracted to the male's nest and are persuaded to lay their eggs there. The eggs are golden yellow at first, changing to a whitish tone. The cock incubates the eggs and cares for the young chicks, which all hatch within a day or so of each other and start following him.

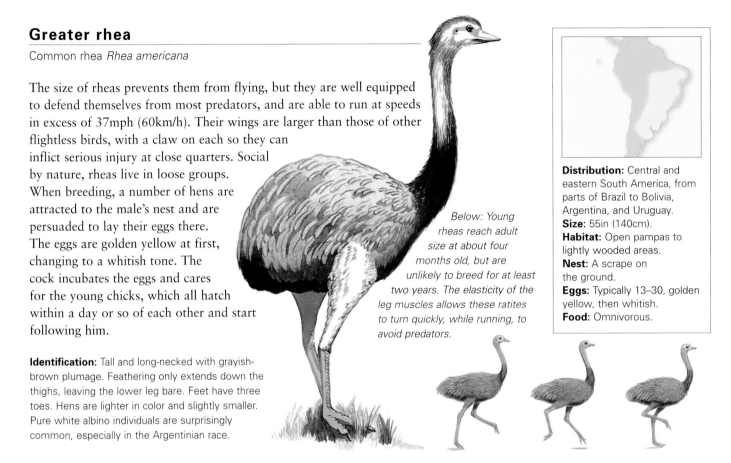

Below: Young rheas reach adult size at about four months old, but are unlikely to breed for at least two years. The elasticity of the leg muscles allows these ratites to turn quickly, while running, to avoid predators.

Distribution: Central and eastern South America, from parts of Brazil to Bolivia, Argentina, and Uruguay.
Size: 55in (140cm).
Habitat: Open pampas to lightly wooded areas.
Nest: A scrape on the ground.
Eggs: Typically 13–30, golden yellow, then whitish.
Food: Omnivorous.

Identification: Tall and long-necked with grayish-brown plumage. Feathering only extends down the thighs, leaving the lower leg bare. Feet have three toes. Hens are lighter in color and slightly smaller. Pure white albino individuals are surprisingly common, especially in the Argentinian race.

Jabiru

Jabiru mycteria

The largest flying bird in America, the jabiru has a massive bill up to 13in (33cm) long. It uses this weapon to seize and kill its prey, which include fish, small mammals, other birds, and their eggs. Jabirus are sometimes observed in groups. They are not shy, even seeking food in cultivated areas. Jabirus build a relatively large platform nest. Both the pair incubate the eggs, with chicks leaving the nest some four months after the eggs were laid. These large storks hop to aid take-off, but once airborne they fly with ease. In flight the neck is held out in a straight line, with legs trailing under the body. They are often seen circling at great heights.

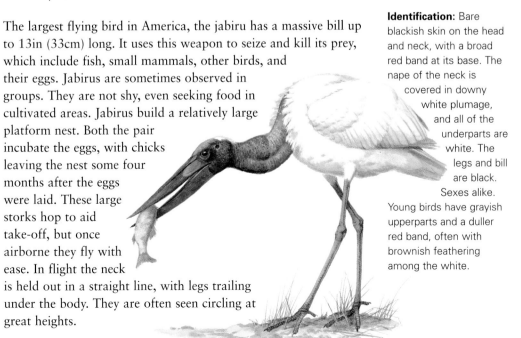

Identification: Bare blackish skin on the head and neck, with a broad red band at its base. The nape of the neck is covered in downy white plumage, and all of the underparts are white. The legs and bill are black. Sexes alike. Young birds have grayish upperparts and a duller red band, often with brownish feathering among the white.

Distribution: Ranges from southeastern Mexico down through Central America, extending as far south as northern Argentina and Uruguay in South America.
Size: 52in (132cm).
Habitat: Marshy savannas.
Nest: Platform of sticks.
Eggs: 2–4, whitish.
Food: Mainly small vertebrates.

Hawaiian goose

Nene Branta sandvicensis

Hawaiian geese are unique, partly as a result of their environment. They display relatively little webbing between their toes, reflecting the fact that they live in a dry environment, foraging for food on larva screes. Another unusual feature is that they mate on land, rather than in water. They live in flocks from June to September, with pairs subsequently nesting on their own. In the late 1700s Hawaiian geese were very numerous, with an estimated population of around 25,000, but hunting and introduced animals from cats to mongooses, which killed the geese and ate their eggs, reduced the population to near-extinction. By the early 1950s only 30 individuals remained. However, a captive-breeding program coupled with control of the predators has caused numbers of these geese to rise significantly again.

Distribution: Native range is restricted to the Hawaiian Islands, occurring on Hawaii itself and Maui. Captive-bred flocks occur in other areas, including Britain.
Size: 26in (66cm).
Habitat: Bare volcanic slopes.
Nest: Made of vegetation.
Eggs: 3–6, whitish-green.
Food: Plant matter including vegetation and berries.

Identification: Black plumage on the head, with a buff-brown area at the back. Neck is mostly white but streaked with blackish markings, with a black band encircling the base. Underparts are whitish-gray, and the area from the legs to the undertail coverts is white. Back and wings are grayish, with black and white edging to the feathers. Rump is white, with black tail feathers. Sexes are alike.

Roadrunner

Geococcyx californianus

These unusual members of the cuckoo clan are built for speed. Their common name derives from their habit of frequenting roads that attract lizards and other reptiles to bask on the heat of the tarmac early in the day to raise their body temperature. Roadrunners can run at speeds up to 23mph (37km/h), and although they can fly, they rarely take to the air. They have a distinct zygodactyl foot structure, with two toes directed forward and two behind, which may assist their balance, compared with the more usual 3:1 perching configuration. Their calls resemble the cooing of doves, and they also communicate by bill-chattering.

Distribution: Southwestern parts of the U.S.A., across from California into Mexico.
Size: 24in (61cm).
Habitat: Open country, including desert areas.
Nest: Low platform of sticks.
Eggs: 4–10, white.
Food: Insects, lizards and small snakes.

Identification: Loose, ragged, dark crest spotted with white. Streaked upper chest becoming white on the underparts. Back and wings brown with buff and whitish edging to the feathers. Powerful, sharp-tipped bill. Gray rump and long tail. Strong legs. Sexes are alike.

Antillean nighthawk (*Chordeiles gundlachii*): 10in (25cm)
Breeds in the Caribbean, including on Jamaica, Hispaniola, Cuba, the Bahamas, and the Cayman Islands, subsequently migrating to South America. Mottled tawny underparts with blackish mottled upperparts, white wing bars, and a lighter mottled stripe along the sides of the wings. Brown area below the eyes, white throat. Tiny, pointed black bill. Hens lack the white tail band of cocks.

Puna plover (*Charadrius alticola*): 7in (17cm)
Central Peru southward to northeastern Chile, western Bolivia, and as far as northwestern Argentina. White area above the bill, down onto sides of face and across underparts. Faint barring on the breast. Black stripe on the forehead, with buff-brown plumage on rest of the head. A blackish bar passes through the eyes down onto sides of the chest. Back and wings brownish. White evident on sides of the rump. Bill black. Hens have a rufous tinge on the nape. Young birds have no black markings on the head.

Rufous-bellied seedsnipe (*Attagis gayi*): 12in (30cm)
Isolated areas of Ecuador and central Peru through the Andean region down into Chile and to north-western Argentina. Heavily mottled rufous-brown overall, with black, white and brown areas on the individual feathers. Underparts are of a more pure chestnut shade. The southern population is paler overall compared with birds occurring further north. Sexes are alike.

QUAILS AND OTHER SMALL GROUND BIRDS

It is no coincidence that many of these birds have mottled upperparts, since they face danger from above, in the guise of avian predators swooping overhead. This characteristic patterning serves to break up their outline, making them hard to spot among the vegetation. They move largely on foot, which also helps to conceal their presence, and often fly only if they detect danger nearby.

Common bobwhite

Northern bobwhite *Colinus virginianus*

Taxonomists have recognized at least 22 different races of these quail, and color variation is quite marked in some cases. Differences in size are also apparent, with individuals found in southern parts of their range being smaller than those occurring in northern regions. Common bobwhites live in groups, typically numbering around a dozen birds or so. They will invade agricultural areas to forage for food, especially when crops are ripening. These birds generally prefer to seek cover on the ground, where their cryptic coloration helps to conceal them from predators, but they will fly if threatened. Populations of these quails have also been introduced well outside their normal range, not only in other parts of the U.S.A., including the northwest and on Hawaii, but also further afield in New Zealand.

Identification: There is considerable variation through the birds' wide range. Most races have a black stripe running from the bill through the eyes, with a white stripe above and a broader white area on the throat. Chestnut underparts, usually speckled with white. Wings are brownish. Hens are duller, having buff rather than white patches on the head.

Distribution: Northeastern USA southward through Mexico into western Guatemala.
Size: 10in (25cm).
Habitat: Woodland and farmland.
Nest: Scrape on the ground lined with vegetation.
Eggs: 10–15, dull white, often with blotches.
Food: Seeds and invertebrates.

Californian quail

Callipepla californica

Californian quail are highly adaptable through their range, and this characteristic has enabled breeding populations of these popular game birds to be established in locations as far apart as Hawaii, Chile, and King Island, Australia. Nesting on the ground makes Californian quail vulnerable to predators, and although the young are able to move freely as soon as they have hatched, relatively few are likely to survive long enough to breed themselves the following year. Overgrazing by farm animals can adversely affect their numbers, presumably because this reduces the food that is available to the birds. However these quail also forage in crop-growing areas, and sometimes associate in groups of up to a thousand individuals where food is plentiful.

Identification: Prominent, raised black crest that slopes forward over the bill. Top of the head is chestnut, with a white band beneath and another bordering the black area of the face. Chest is grayish, flanks are speckled. Hens lack the black and white areas, with grayish faces and smaller crests.

Distribution: Native to western North America, ranging from British Columbia in Canada southward to the warmer climates of California and Mexico.
Size: 11in (27cm).
Habitat: Semi-desert to woodland.
Nest: Grass-lined scraping on the ground.
Eggs: About 15, creamy white with brownish patches.
Food: Seeds, vegetation, and invertebrates.

Montezuma quail

Cyrtonyx montezumae

Like others of their kind, these quails are shy by nature and not easily observed unless flushed from their hiding places. They venture into woodland areas and can also be found in grassland, typically associating in small groups (described as coveys) comprised of about eight individuals, although groups of up to 25 may be observed. Montezuma quails have a varied diet, and when food is in short supply can survive on underground bulbs and tubers dug up with their powerful legs and sharp claws. As well as invertebrates, which figure prominently in their diet while breeding, they also seek out seeds and fruits. Pairs construct a domed nest up to 4in (10cm) tall, lined with leaves and grass. Both members of the pair are thought to share incubation duties. The young are able to walk on their own almost immediately after hatching, which occurs about 3^{1}/$_{2}$ weeks after egg-laying.

Identification: Males have black stripes above and below the eyes, with a black patch beneath each eye and under the throat, surrounded by white feathering. Upperparts are brownish with black mottling, possibly with a small crest on the back of the head. Depending on race, underparts may be black and white across the chest and down the flanks, with a central rufous area, or predominantly chestnut with light gray feathering broken by white spots on the flanks. Hens are less boldly marked, with no black and white markings on the face, and light rufous underparts.

Distribution: Ranges from parts of Texas, New Mexico and Arizona in the U.S.A. southward into Mexico.
Size: 9in (22cm).
Habitat: Brush and grassland.
Nest: Made of grass.
Eggs: 6–14, white, usually with darker markings.
Food: Vegetable matter and invertebrates.

Crested bobwhite quail (*Colinus cristatus*): 9in (22cm)
Panama to Colombia, Venezuela, French Guiana and northern Brazil. Appearance varies. Distinct crest, usually with a white stripe near the eyes. White speckling with thin, black borders on chestnut- or buff-colored underparts. Hens duller with a shorter crest, and no eye stripe.

Scaled quail (Blue quail, *Callipepla squamata*): 11^{1}/$_{2}$in (29cm)
Southern U.S.A. south into Mexico. Blue-scaled plumage on the breast and neck down to the browner underparts. White-edged crest on the head. Wings brownish. Hens have a smaller crest, with brown streaking on the head and throat.

Lesser prairie chicken (*Tympanuchus pallidicinctus*): 16in (41cm)
Restricted to Colorado, Kansas, Oklahoma, Texas and New Mexico. Barred brownish and white plumage. Tail has dark banding near the tip. Buffish-yellow plumage above the eyes, with inflatable orange-red air sacs on sides of head. Sexes similar, but hens lack dark tail banding.

Sharp-tailed grouse (*Tympanuchus phasianellus*): 19in (48cm)
Northern North America from Alaska across much of Canada, south into the U.S.A., where its distribution has shrunk recently. Distinguishable from other barred members of the grouse family by pointed tail feathers. Has pinkish inflatable air sacs on head. Underparts speckled. Cocks significantly larger than hens.

Greater prairie chicken

Tympanuchus cupido

The greater prairie chicken's range has declined significantly in recent years. The nominate race, called the heath hen, once had an extensive range in eastern parts of the U.S.A., but is now presumed extinct. The smaller and darker form, Attwater's prairie chicken (*T. c. attwateri*), is now extinct in southwest Louisiana and struggling to survive in Texas. This is the result of hunting and also clearance of prairie habitat. Breeding males display communally at a lek, inflating their neck sacs and uttering a far-carrying, booming call. The nest is concealed by vegetation. Egg-laying occurs from early April.

Identification: Cock has yellowish-orange areas on head. Adjacent golden air sacs are inflated as part of the display, when the dark neck feathers are also raised. The body is barred with shades of brown. Paler underparts. Short tail is blackish in cock, barred in the hen. Sides of female's head and throat are speckled, with underparts having dark markings on a white background.

Distribution: Occurs mainly to the south and west of the Great Lakes, as far south as Oklahoma, with a separate population found in the coastal area of Texas.
Size: 18^{1}/$_{2}$in (47cm).
Habitat: Prairies and associated agricultural areas.
Nest: Scrape lined with feathers.
Eggs: 5–17, olive with brown blotching.
Food: Seeds and invertebrates.

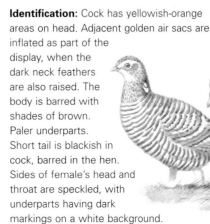

GAMEBIRDS

This group of birds also rely on their appearance to blend in with the background. The distribution of grouse extends to the frozen wastelands of the tundra zone in the far north. They are adapted to living on the ground there, molting their plumage to match the seasons. They also have feathering that extends right down over the toes to restrict heat loss and guard against frostbite.

Rock ptarmigan

Lagopus mutus

These grouse live in a region where natural cover is very scarce, and undergo a stunning transformation in appearance through the year. Their summer plumage is mottled brown, and their winter plumage is white, enabling them to merge into the snowy landscape. When snow is on the ground, they feed on buds and twigs of shrubs such as willow, which manage to grow in this treeless region. Pairs nest in the brief Arctic summer, often choosing a site protected by shrubs. The cock stays nearby while the hen incubates alone. The chicks are covered in down when they hatch and can move easily, but are not able to fly until their flight feathers have emerged fully, at about ten days old.

Identification: Mottled, brownish head with red above the eyes. Similar patterning across the body in summer, becoming white in winter. Blackish stripes on the face, lacking in hens.

Distribution: Circumpolar, extending right across the far north of North America; also present on Greenland. A similar distribution occurs in Europe and Asia.
Size: 15in (38cm).
Habitat: Tundra.
Nest: Scrape on the ground lined with vegetation.
Eggs: 6–9, creamy buff, heavily blotched and spotted with blackish-brown.
Food: Buds, leaves, berries and other plant matter.

Willow ptarmigan

Willow grouse *Lagopus lagopus*

Identification: In summer plumage, cock has brownish head and upperparts, white wings and underparts, and black tail feathers. Hens can be distinguished by the speckled appearance of their underparts. During the winter, both sexes become white overall.

Living in a very inhospitable part of the world, where the earth is permanently frozen even in the summer, these grouse rely on meagre plant growth to sustain themselves. Willow (*Salix*) is vital as a food source over winter, when the ground is blanketed with snow, while in summer, berries and even invertebrates are sought. Breeding occurs during May and June, with the eggs being laid in a scrape on the ground. Both pairs share the task of incubation, with the young hatching after about three weeks. At this stage they are especially vulnerable to predators such as the Arctic fox, and studies suggest their lifespan is unlikely to exceed two years. Their transformation into white plumage helps them to merge with the background in winter. Sometimes, if conditions get very harsh, these grouse will move much further south, having been recorded in southern Ontario and northern Minnesota.

Distribution: Range is circumpolar, extending from the Aleutian Islands, Alaska, and northwest British Columbia right across northern Canada, including Arctic islands such as Victoria, down as far as Newfoundland on the east coast.
Size: 17in (43cm).
Habitat: Arctic tundra.
Nest: Scrape on the ground.
Eggs: 2–15, yellowish with brown blotches.
Food: Willow buds and twigs.

Greater sage grouse

Centrocercus urophasianus

The distribution of these grouse is tied to their primary food source, the sagebush (*Artemisia*), especially during winter when they feed almost exclusively on this plant. They even nest under cover of sagebushes. Breeding begins in April, with males displaying on their communal display grounds (leks), inflating their air sacs. The nest is well-concealed, with a lining of sagebush leaves and grass. Incubation lasts about a month. The young are able to move independently once hatched, and are reared on invertebrates.

Identification: Cock blackish around the bill, with an orange patch above each eye and greenish display sacs. V-shape created by blackish patches broken by a whitish area on the sides of the head and upper chest, with a whitish area on the lower breast and black on the abdomen. Upperparts heavily mottled, with white speckling on the flanks. Undertail coverts black with white edging. Long, tapering tail. Mottling extends down the legs. The bill is black. Hens are smaller, lacking white on the head or breast, this area being brownish instead. Young birds resemble hens, but paler.

Distribution: Central Washington, parts of Alberta, Saskatchewan, and the Dakotas to eastern California through Nevada, Utah, and western Colorado. Formerly southern British Columbia and northern parts of Oklahoma and New Mexico.
Size: 31in (76cm).
Habitat: Areas of sagebrush.
Nest: Scrape in the ground.
Eggs: 7–15, olive-buff with a few dark spots.
Food: Mainly sagebrush.

Gunnison sage grouse (*Centrocercus minimus*): 22in (56cm)
Southeastern Utah and south-central Colorado. Cock has orange on top of the head, with a long, downward-curving black crest at the back of the head. Prominent white breast with blackish central area, marked with brown on the lower chest. Rest of underparts dark. Wings mottled brown. Tail barred with white, with narrowing feathers. Hens significantly smaller.

Chukar partridge (*Alectoris chukar*): 14in (35cm)
Southern British Columbia to Baja California and east to Colorado. Originally introduced as a game bird from Europe. Gray crown with a black stripe through each eye running down across the chest. Underparts grayish-blue, becoming fawn, with black and white barring on flanks. Brownish on the back. Cream area on the sides of the face and chest. Bill is mainly red. Hens lack the tarsal swelling of cocks, with less colorful head patterning. Young birds mainly brownish in color.

Gray partridge (Hungarian partridge, *Perdix perdix*): 12½in (32cm)
Ranges across prairies of northern U.S.A. and southern Canada. Introduced from Europe. Orangish-brown face, with a stripe extending further back. Crown, neck, and much of underparts grayish, with dark edging on the plumage. Flanks barred with brown. Wings also brown with black speckling.

White-tailed ptarmigan

Lagopus leucurus

The white-tailed is the only species of ptarmigan ranging south into the U.S.A. from Canada. It usually occurs at higher altitudes, although it descends in October to escape the worst winter weather. During summer, white-tailed ptarmigans are found close to the tree-line, where pairs establish breeding territories. The nest is concealed on the ground, and lined with feathers. Eggs are laid any time from late May until July. Hens incubate alone, with the young able to follow their parent after hatching. The population divides in winter, with males forming flocks on their own. When food is hard to find because of snow, ptarmigans feed on the buds of willow, birch and alder. Their fully feathered legs and feet afford protection from the cold.

Identification: In winter, both sexes are completely white, with males retaining a narrow red comb above the eyes. In summer, males have evident red comb with mottling on the head and upper breast, extending over the back and part of the wings, with white underparts. Hens slightly smaller and more mottled, with prominent black markings over the back, and lacking the comb. Slight variations depending on race. Young birds display barring all over the wings.

Distribution: Western North America, from Alaska through Canada into the U.S.A. in the Rocky Mountains, as far south as New Mexico. Now reestablished in the High Sierras of California.
Size: 13in (34cm).
Habitat: Tundra and mountainous areas.
Nest: Scrape on the ground.
Eggs: 5–9, cinnamon-brown with dark spots.
Food: Vegetation.

HUMMINGBIRDS AND INSECT-HUNTERS

The feeding opportunities that exist in relatively open areas of country enable birds more commonly found in the woodland, such as hummingbirds, to live successfully in this habitat. As well as flowers, which provide high-energy nectar and protein-rich pollen, there is an abundance of small invertebrates. Other birds that catch insects in flight, such as flycatchers, can also be encountered here.

Beautiful hummingbird

Calothorax pulcher

Hummingbirds as a group are restricted to the New World, with a number of species occurring in relatively open countryside, where they seek out flowers. The beautiful hummingbird feeds at a range of levels, from quite close to the ground right up into flowering trees. Like many species it has a very restricted range, which helps its identification. The speed at which beautiful hummingbirds fly and dart around makes them difficult to observe closely, especially on the wing, while their small size means they can be easily overlooked when perching. Furthermore, the brilliant colors of the male's gorget have an iridescent quality which, depending on the light, can actually make them even less conspicuous. There is no mistaking the male's display flight, however, as he soars upward to a height of perhaps 30ft (10m) before dropping back down right beside his mate. She builds the nest, and subsequently cares for their chicks on her own.

Identification: Cock has golden-green upperparts, with a black tail and wings. Underparts whitish, greener on the flanks. Area of deep rose-pink feathering with violet markings forms a gorget on the throat. Long, narrow, down-curved black bill. Hens lack the bright throat, with a buff tinge to the underparts and a pale gray streak extending from below the eyes. Tail feathers mainly black with a brown base and white tip. Young birds similar to hens.

Distribution: Occurs only in Central America, where its range is restricted to southwestern parts of Mexico.
Size: 3¹/₂in (9cm).
Habitat: Scrubland.
Nest: Small, cup-shaped.
Eggs: 2, whitish.
Food: Nectar and invertebrates.

Giant hummingbird

Patagona gigas

Identification: Bronzy to cinnamon upperparts, sometimes with a grayish tone depending on the subspecies, and long, narrow wings. Forked tail paler at the base. Relatively thick, straight bill measuring approximately 1¹/₂in (3¹/₂cm). Hens can be distinguished by the spotting on their underparts. Young birds are much grayer overall, with faint scaling on the upperparts.

As its name suggests, the giant hummingbird is the largest of over 300 species. It occurs in relatively inhospitable terrain through the Andean region, typically being found in valleys, ranging as high as 14,800ft (4,500m) in parts of Peru. Its size imposes constraints on its aerial maneuverability compared with smaller relatives, and it has a flight pattern that more closely resembles that of a swallow. Giant hummingbirds can hover when feeding, spreading their tail feathers, but often prefer to perch on the puya or cacti flowers. They can be aggressive toward other hummingbirds, chasing them away while calling loudly. The female constructs her nest in the safety of a branching cactus, although cliff faces are also used. Giant hummingbirds appear to be extending their range northward into Colombia, having established themselves in neighboring Ecuador.

Distribution: May range from the eastern Andes of Colombia southward via Ecuador, Peru and Bolivia to central parts of Chile and Argentina.
Size: 8in (20cm).
Habitat: Arid upland areas.
Nest: Small, cup-shaped.
Eggs: 2, whitish.
Food: Nectar and invertebrates.

Cassin's kingbird (*Tyrannus vociferans*):
9in (23cm)
Ranges from southwestern U.S.A. through western Mexico as far south as Guatemala. Grayish plumage on the head and upper breast, extending down the back. Prominent white area under the throat, reaching to the base of the lower bill. Lower underparts are yellowish. Wings and tail feathers are brownish, with whitish edging to the flight feathers. Pointed bill, legs and feet are all blackish. Sexes are alike.

Mexican sheartail hummingbird (*Doricha eliza;* previously *Calothorax eliza*): 4in (10cm)
Restricted to Veracruz in Mexico and the north Yucatan Peninsula. Iridescent green top to the head extends over the back, with greenish suffusion on the flanks. Throat is a metallic reddish-purple, edged with a whitish area from the eyes onto the chest and central underparts. Wings and tail feathers blackish, as is the long, narrow, slightly down-curved bill. In flight the tail feathers may be held in a V-shape, revealing orange edging. Hens are slightly smaller, with completely white underparts.

Dusky hummingbird (*Cynanthus sordidus*):
3¹/₂in (9cm)
Restricted to southwestern Mexico. A white stripe extends behind the eyes. Upperparts dull golden-green, tail feathers grayish-green. The wings are dusky gray, underparts grayish with a green suffusion on the flanks. Long, narrow bill is mainly red. Hens have paler underparts.

Rock wren

Salpinctes obsoletus

Six subspecies of this wren have been identified, although one of these, the San Benedicto rock wren (*S. o. exsul*), from the island of that name on Mexico's west coast, was wiped out by a volcanic explosion in 1952. Rock wrens are lively and easy to observe since they are naturally quite tame and conspicuous, moving from boulder to boulder in search of invertebrates, although, if danger threatens, they slip away. Their relatively loud song is especially evident during the breeding period. These wrens seek out small crevices in rocks as nest sites, creating a snug lining. They frequently build the nest on a bed of small stones that they collect themselves, for reasons that are unclear, though it may have something to do with nest sanitation. They will gather a wide variety of material to incorporate into the nest site, ranging from rabbit bones to small pieces of rusty metal.

Identification: Dark grayish-brown upperparts with black streaky markings. Chestnut-brown rump, underparts whitish-gray with fine dark streaking on the breast. Narrow, pointed grayish bill. Sexes alike. Young birds duller. Extent of black barring differs between races.

Distribution: Western North America. Breeding range extends to British Columbia; wanders widely outside the breeding period. Separate populations in parts of Mexico, Guatemala, Honduras, Nicaragua and northwestern Costa Rica.
Size: 5¹/₂in (14cm).
Habitat: Rocky areas.
Nest: Made of vegetation.
Eggs: 4–10, white with reddish-brown speckling.
Food: Invertebrates.

Fork-tailed flycatcher

Tyrannus savana

Flycatchers belong to the same genus as kingbirds, *Tyrannus*. The very long, streaming tail plumes of this species are especially conspicuous in flight. The plumes of the young birds are less than half the length of those of the adults. Fork-tailed flycatchers inhabit open savanna country, often preferring areas where there are isolated bushes rather than trees. Here they frequently perch quite close to the ground, ever-alert to feeding opportunities. Their diet consists of invertebrates. Fork-tailed flycatchers can be quite social by nature, and have occasionally been recorded in groups of more than 50 individuals, with this flocking behavior being most common outside the summer months. Although it has been suggested that these flycatchers undertake regular migrations, it now appears that they tend to be more nomadic in their habits, simply wandering from one area to another. They construct their nest from plant fibers of various types.

Identification: Black head, with white throat and underparts. The neck and back are gray, and the flight feathers are black with whitish edging. Distinctive, elongated forked tail feathers, which are longer in cock birds than in hens. Young birds recognizable by their much shorter forked tails and the dusky area on the crown.

Distribution: Ranges from southern parts of Mexico through much of Central and South America. Reaches Argentina at the most southerly point of its range.
Size: 13in (33cm).
Habitat: Savanna.
Nest: Cup-shaped, fashioned from plant fibers.
Eggs: 2–5, whitish with darker markings.
Food: Invertebrates.

PIGEONS AND DOVES

The characteristic dumpy appearance of pigeons and doves, along with their relatively subdued coloration, means that they can be quite easily identified. There is actually no strict zoological distinction between these two groups, although the term "pigeon" is usually applied to larger species, particularly members of the Columba *genus.*

Mourning dove

Carolina dove *Zenaida macroura*

These doves are so-called because of the plaintive, mournful sound of their calls. They have benefited from the provision of bird tables, particularly in the northern part of their range, and often visit gardens for the food being offered. Their powerful wings and sleek shape help these doves to fly long distances on migration, and northerly populations overwinter in Central America. In southern U.S.A., such as Florida, mourning doves are resident throughout the year. They prefer to look for food on the ground if not feeding on a bird table, and groups often wander across fields in search of seeds and other edible items. Mourning doves are now overwintering further north than they did in the past, partly as a result of more feeding opportunities from bird tables.

Identification: There is some variation in appearance through these doves' wide range, with cocks displaying pinkish buff coloration on the face, extending down to the underparts, with a dark streak just above the neck. The upper surfaces of wings and tail are brown, with several large dark spots evident on the wings. Hens are duller in coloration, being browner overall.

Distribution: Extensive range across much of North America, from southern Canada southward across the U.S.A. through Central America to Costa Rica and Panama, but distribution is affected by the season. Also occurs on the Greater Antilles in the Caribbean.
Size: 13in (34cm).
Habitat: Lightly wooded areas.
Nest: Loose pile of twigs.
Eggs: 2, white.
Food: Seeds and some invertebrates.

Black-winged dove

Metriopelia melanoptera

The male black-winged dove has a very distinctive, rather attractive chirruping call, unlike the more usual cooing calls associated with this group of birds. His call is heard more frequently during the breeding season, as he fans his tail and flicks his wings, making the white areas of plumage on these areas more visible. These doves are often sighted in association with the smaller bare-faced ground dove (*M. ceciliae*), and frequently occur in the vicinity of puya shrubs, which provide both roosting and breeding sites. Pairs may also nest in buildings, however, and sometimes even on the ground among rocky outcrops that provide them with some protection from possible predators. The nest itself is a relatively loose structure, and is usually sited quite close to the ground.

Identification: Compact body shape. Predominantly brown, aside from the black flight feathers and tail, with a white area at the shoulder that is usually hidden. There is a slight pinkish tinge on the head, and bare orangish-red skin around the eyes. Hens are duller in color and a slightly paler shade of brown. This color tends to increase in depth during the breeding period.

Distribution: Western side of South America, from Colombia and Ecuador through Peru, Chile and Argentina to Tierra del Fuego at the southern tip of the continent.
Size: 9in (23cm).
Habitat: Upland arid areas.
Nest: Platform of twigs.
Eggs: 2, white.
Food: Seeds of grasses and other plants.

Buckley's ground dove (Ecuadorian ground dove, *Columbina buckleyi*): 7in (18cm)
Northwestern Ecuador to northwestern Peru. Grayish-brown upperparts and more pinkish underparts, with grayish coloration most marked on the head. Black underwing coverts. Hen is browner, with less contrast in her plumage.

Eared dove (golden-necked dove, *Zenaida auriculata*): 11in (28cm)
Occurs over most of South America, aside from the Amazon region and Andean uplands. Very common, especially in northeastern Brazil, where migratory flocks, thought to be comprised of a million birds, can occasionally be observed. Some variation in color through the range. Two black lines behind and below the eyes, with a prominent green iridescent area behind the eyes. Wings are brownish with variable dark wing spots. Underparts are pinkish. Hens are duller in appearance.

Spot-winged pigeon (American spotted pigeon, *Columba maculosa*): 13in (33cm)
Two separate populations. One ranges from south-west Peru into western Bolivia and Argentina, distinguishable by the white edging to the gray feathers on the wings. The other, with more pronounced white areas creating the impression of spots, extends southward into southwestern Brazil, Paraguay and Uruguay. Head and underparts have a pinkish-gray tone. Hens grayer overall.

Scaled dove (*Scardafella squammata*) 8¹/₂in (22cm)
South America, with the more northerly population extending from northern Colombia to French Guinea; the other ranges from central-eastern Brazil down to northern Argentina. Grayish-brown upperparts, with black scaly edging to individual feathers over the entire body. Grayish-white forehead, a pinker tone on face and breast, becoming whitish on underparts. Hens are a duller pink. Young birds duller overall.

Gold-billed ground dove

Croaking ground dove *Columbina cruziana*

These small doves are a relatively common sight in gardens and parks, and have adapted well to changes in habitat throughout their range. They may sometimes be seen in large numbers where food is abundant, seeking seeds and other plant matter on the ground. The distinctive croaking calls uttered by cock birds are more likely to be heard during the breeding period. In common with many other pigeons and doves, the hen lays on a relatively flimsy nest. The young doves may leave the nest at just ten days old, before they are able to fly effectively, and hide in nearby vegetation.

Identification: Predominantly brownish with pinker underparts and grayish head. Bluish-gray wing coverts display variably positioned reddish-brown spots across them and a magenta stripe across the top. The bill is yellow at the base, while the tip is black. Hens are similar, but are a much more even shade of brown overall. The tail is relatively short.

Above: Both members of the pair incubate the eggs.

Distribution: Coastal region from Ecuador through Peru to northern Chile.
Size: 6in (15cm).
Habitat: Open woodland and scrub.
Nest: Loose platform of twigs.
Eggs: 2, white.
Food: Seeds of grasses and other plants.

Bare-faced ground dove

Bare-eyed ground dove *Metriopelia ceciliae*

These doves may range at altitudes up to 15,000ft (4,500m). When breeding, they will, unusually, seek out holes in cliffs or even the protection offered by buildings, rather than nesting in a tree or shrub. In the vicinity of human habitation, they often nest on houses, and forage for food in surrounding gardens. Elsewhere, they may fly quite long distances from their roosting sites in search of food. These doves are very quiet by nature, and are unlikely to betray their presence by their calls. They are also very adept at running along the ground to escape from danger.

Identification: Bright area of bare, yellowish-orange skin encircles the eyes. Back and wings are brownish with much paler, buff-colored mottling at the centers of individual feathers. Chest is pinkish-brown with brownish underparts. Hens are usually slightly duller in coloration.

Distribution: Northern Peru south into northern Chile, western Bolivia, and north-west Argentina.
Size: 6in (16cm).
Habitat: Dry, upland country.
Nest: Loose platform.
Eggs: 2, white.
Food: Seeds of grasses and other plants.

SPARROWS AND FINCHES

Adaptable feeders, these relatively small birds can be encountered in a wide range of habitats, even in areas that are relatively inhospitable such as in the high Andean region or on the tundra of the frozen north. Occasionally they can be found well outside their normal distributions. Most are relatively conspicuous, certainly outside the nesting period, when they are likely to be sighted in small flocks.

Andean siskin

Carduelis spinescens

Distribution: Occurs in the Andean region of northern South America, ranging from Venezuela and Colombia southward to northern Ecuador.
Size: 4in (10cm).
Habitat: Scrub and relatively open countryside.
Nest: Made of plant fibers of various kinds.
Eggs: 2, pale bluish white with darker markings.
Food: Seeds and also invertebrates.

These siskins have a high-pitched and attractive song, often uttered in flight. As their name asserts, they are native to the Andean region, where they are most likely to be observed at altitudes of between 5,000 and 13,500ft (1,500 to 4,100m). Here they favor scrubland and fairly open terrain. Andean siskins are sometimes hard to spot as they perch in taller trees. They are easier to observe when they venture onto the ground in search of food. These siskins may be encountered in small flocks, and sometimes forage in company with other finches, seeking *Espletia* seeds, a particular favorite. Their diet also includes insects, which provide protein. It is not uncommon among the Ecuadorian population for some birds resembling mature cocks to actually be hens. Their main area of distribution lies in the northern part of their range, and here they are quite common. It appears that these siskins are extending their range southwestward as well, with the first documented sighting of the species from northern Ecuador being made in 1982.

Identification: Has a black area extending from the bill to the top of the head. Plumage is greenish-yellow elsewhere and of a brighter hue on the underparts. Wings are black with distinct yellow markings across the flight feathers. Hens are duller in coloration, lacking the black cap, and with less yellow on the wings.

Saffron finch

Sicalis flaveola

Distribution: Much of South America, from Colombia to Argentina; also on Trinidad.
Size: 5¹/₂in (14cm).
Habitat: Lightly wooded areas.
Nest: Tree cavities.
Eggs: 4, pale blue with brownish spots.
Food: Seeds and invertebrates.

Although there are other finches with predominantly yellow plumage, the saffron finch is the most brightly colored member of the entire group, and also has one of the widest distributions. It has been introduced to various localities outside its natural range across much of South America, and is consequently seen in parts of Panama and Jamaica as well. These attractive finches can frequently be observed on the ground, foraging for food in the form of seeds and invertebrates, often in small groups or individual pairs. They are usually quite tame by nature, especially when encountered in parks and other urban areas.

Identification: Bright yellow underparts, becoming more orange at the front of the crown. Olive-brown wings and tail. Short, pointed bill. Hens have brown, streaked upperparts with whitish underparts. Young birds are also streaked, with young cocks developing a yellowish neck collar and matching chest when they first molt into adult plumage.

Grasshopper sparrow

Ammodramus savannarum

Known as grasshopper sparrows because of the way they hop over the ground in search of food, these small, rather plain-colored birds are not always easy to spot in their grassland habitat. Males are most likely to betray their presence by their song, especially at the start of the breeding season. This is the time when they are most likely to be seen in the open, trilling on a fence post or a similar exposed perch. The nesting season varies through their range, typically occurring between May and August in the Caribbean. On some islands, such as Cuba, they overwinter in large numbers, yet elsewhere (Jamaica for example) they are present throughout the year. Unfortunately, grasshopper sparrows are very susceptible to habitat disturbance, and this has led to their decline in some areas, with even overgrazing reducing their numbers.

Identification: Some races have distinctive yellow plumage at the front of each eye stripe, and a white stripe on the crown. Pronounced black streaking with chestnut edging on the crown, becoming browner on the wings. Underparts are pale brown, becoming whitish close to the vent. Sexes are alike. Young birds have streaking on the breast.

Distribution: Breeding range extends north across British Columbia, Manitoba, and New Hampshire. Winters in southern U.S.A. through Panama to western Colombia and northwestern Ecuador. Also through the Greater Antilles in the Caribbean.
Size: 5in (13cm).
Habitat: Grasslands.
Nest: Domed structure.
Eggs: 3, white with dark markings.
Food: Invertebrates and some seeds.

Hooded siskin (*Carduelis magellanica*): 5¹/₂in (14cm)
Central-southern South America, in Bolivia, Peru, Paraguay, Argentina, and Uruguay. Also a northern Andean population, from Colombia to Peru, and another in southeast Venezuela, Guyana, and northwest Brazil. Black head and yellowish chest and upper abdomen, becoming whiter below, with a green back. Hens are duller, with a grayish head and greenish underparts.

Common redpoll (*Carduelis flammea*): 5¹/₂in (14cm)
Breeds across northern North America, from Alaska to British Columbia and east to Newfoundland. Winters through southern Canada into the U.S.A. from California via Oklahoma to the Carolinas. Crimson red cap and black lores, with streaked upperparts. Pinkish chest fading to white on the streaked abdomen. White wing bars, yellowish bill. Hens lack the pink throat. Young birds lack the red cap.

Pine siskin (*Carduelis pinus*): 5in (13cm)
Breeds from southern Alaska across Canada south of Hudson's Bay to Newfoundland, and in the U.S.A. south to California and in the vicinity of the Great Lakes. Occurs widely through the U.S.A. in winter, extending south to parts of Florida, Texas, and New Mexico. Dark streaky patterning over the entire body, with solid black areas and variable patches of yellow on the wings. Variable yellow patches at the base of the tail feathers too. Narrow, pointed bill which is darker above. Sexes are alike.

Hoary redpoll

Arctic redpoll *Carduelis hornemanni*

Similar in appearance to the common redpoll (*C. flammea*), this species can easily be distinguished by its plain rump and undertail coverts. Although both redpolls occur together in some parts of their range, they do not interbreed. The distribution of the hoary redpoll extends further north, and in the treeless tundra they are forced to breed on the ground, creating a warm, cup-shaped nest lined with feathers that may be concealed among rocks or under a shrub. The chicks are reared largely on a diet of insects, which are readily available in the Arctic through the summer months, while for the remainder of the year these finches subsist primarily on seed. They are often observed in pairs or family groups, although occasionally they may be spotted in larger flocks of up to 100 individuals. Occurring so far north, it is perhaps not surprising that this redpoll has a circumpolar distribution, being also found throughout the far north of Europe and Asia.

Distribution: Breeds along the Arctic coast of North America. In winter, found over much of Canada and northern parts of the U.S.A.
Size: 5¹/₂in (14cm).
Habitat: Tundra and open country.
Nest: Cup of vegetation.
Eggs: 5–6, pale blue with light brown spots.
Food: Seeds and invertebrates.

Identification: Red patch on the crown. Pale frosty gray streaked upperparts and a prominent white wing bar, with wings otherwise appearing black. A black area surrounds the base of the stocky bill. Breeding males have pinkish chests. Hens similar but with some streaking present on the flanks.

FARMLAND BIRDS

Areas of open country have increased significantly in the recent past, with vast amounts of land being cleared for the cultivation of crops, especially in the eastern U.S.A. Natural habitats have also made way for towns and cities, while highways have cut across country. However, many birds have adapted well to these changes, and thrive in this altered environment.

Painted bunting

Passerina ciris

The cock painted bunting is popularly regarded as the most colorful of all North America's songbirds. Unfortunately, however, these relatively shy birds are not easily seen, often remaining concealed in vegetation, where their presence is more likely to be revealed by the cock's song. They have a warbling call as well as a short, harsh, warning note that is uttered at any hint of danger. The nest, too, is well hidden, and is constructed from a variety of vegetation. A pair may rear two broods in succession, and insects feature more prominently in their diet at this time. The hen builds the nest on her own and collects a variety of plant matter for this purpose, ranging from strips of bark and dead leaves to grass stems and rootlets. She chooses a well-concealed nest site, often in the fork of a tree.

Identification: Males are very colorful and unmistakable, with bluish-violet plumage on the head and a rose-red throat and underparts. The wings and back are green, with darker tail and flight feathers. Hens are drab in comparison, with green upperparts, becoming more yellowish on the underside of the body, and no bars on the wings, unlike many other finches.

Distribution: Widely distributed across the southern U.S.A. and Mexico, with populations moving south in the winter as far as Panama. Also present on Cuba.
Size: 5¹/₂in (14cm).
Habitat: Lightly wooded areas and brush.
Nest: Woven nest.
Eggs: 3–5, pale blue with darker spots.
Food: Mainly seeds, some invertebrates.

Dickcissel

Spiza americana

These finches take their unusual name from the sound of their song, which at times is repeated almost continuously from a suitable perch. Dickcissels are frequently seen in agricultural areas, often in hay fields where they can forage easily on the seeds that form the basis of their diet. When breeding, they choose a nest site close to the ground, and at ground level may hide the nest among clover or alfalfa. These finches undertake seasonal movements. On migration they sometimes form huge flocks consisting of thousands of individuals, with the birds flying in tight formation. Many spend the winter period (from October to April) in the Venezuelan llanos, although they may also congregate in agricultural areas at this time, mostly in rice fields. Dickcissels can occasionally be observed in various parts of the Caribbean, heading to and from their North American breeding grounds.

Identification: This species has a gray head with a yellow stripe above each eye leading back from the short, conical bill. A whitish area is present on the throat, with black beneath. Chest is yellowish, with white lower underparts. Back and wings are brownish with darker striations. Hens are duller, having gray underparts and lacking the prominent black area under the throat.

Distribution: Eastern North America, breeding from the vicinity of the Great Lakes and Montana down to Texas and the Gulf coast. Overwinters in parts of Central and northern South America.
Size: 7in (18cm).
Habitat: Treeless areas.
Nest: Cup-shaped.
Eggs: 4–5, pale blue.
Food: Mainly seeds.

Lark bunting

Calamospiza melanocorys

Identification: Cock in breeding condition is primarily black, with prominent white patches on the wings and a white tip to the tail. Out of color they resemble hens, which have a blackish bib and white underparts speckled with brown markings. The upperparts are brown with darker streaking, and the wings and tail are blackish.

In spite of their name, these birds are finches. The attractive song of the cock lark bunting is similar to that of a canary, making it one of the most distinctive songsters on the plains. Its accompanying display flight is equally spectacular, as it soars up and down off its perch almost vertically. This behavior is believed to have evolved because there are few trees that can be used as prominent singing sites through this region. Lark buntings live in flocks, which are often seen on the ground alongside roads, seeking seeds and invertebrates. When they do take to the wing they fly in a tight formation, wheeling together through the landscape, making it difficult for a bird of prey to target one particular individual. They breed in groups, with the nests made on the ground often hidden beneath vegetation, and the males compete with each other in song. Flocks leave the breeding grounds during late summer and head south, typically being seen in Mexico from August through to April.

Distribution: Breeds from the prairies of southern Canada to the plains of west-central U.S.A., overwintering in southern parts of the U.S.A. and Mexico.
Size: 7¹⁄₂in (19cm).
Habitat: Prairies and plains.
Nest: Scrape in the ground.
Eggs: 4–5, light blue.
Food: Seeds and invertebrates.

Pyrrhuloxia (Gray cardinal, *Cardinalis sinuatus*): 9in (23cm)
Arizona, New Mexico, and Texas, and across the U.S. border to northern Mexico. Prominent red-tipped crest, with a reddish area on the face, extending onto the chest. Rest of the head, back, and rump are grayish. Underparts lighter, with brownish areas on the wings. Tail and flight feathers reddish. Down-curved horn-colored bill. Hens lack red plumage on the face, tail and underparts, which are a brownish-gray.

Bronzed cowbird (*Molothrus aeneus*): 9in (23cm)
Breeds in Arizona, New Mexico, and Texas (leaves Arizona for winter), ranging through Central America from Mexico south to Panama. Cocks are black with a bronzy-brown on the body, and blackish wings. Red eyes, pointed blackish bill. Hens are duller, a dark gray.

Shiny cowbird (*Molothrus bonariensis*): 6¹⁄₂in (17cm)
Ranges over much of South America, from Bolivia and Paraguay south to Argentina and Uruguay, possibly also Chile. Cock birds mainly a glossy, iridescent black, with brown on the wings and a strong, pointed black bill. Hens are brownish, ranging from pale to almost black.

Bolivian blackbird (*Oreopsar bolivianus*): 9in (23cm)
Occurs in central Bolivia. Shares glossy black plumage with the shiny cowbird, but is larger in size, with a bigger, more sharply curved bill. Hens are slightly smaller than cocks. Young birds have brown primary coverts.

Horned lark

Eremophila alpestris

This is the only true member of the lark family occurring naturally in the Americas. The horned lark is primarily a terrestrial species, walking rather than hopping on the ground. If disturbed it will dart off a short distance before dropping down again. It favors open country where there is little cover. Pairs start nesting early, with hens incubating eggs in February in the northern U.S.A. This can be hazardous if the weather turns bad, since the nest may be buried by snow. Horned larks are prolific breeders, however, and soon start again, with pairs producing up to 15 chicks in a good year. Over summer pairs tend to be solitary, but in fall they come together to form quite large flocks, often with other birds.

Identification: Characteristic narrow, raised black feathers on the sides of the head create the impression of horns. Facial color varies among races, from white to yellow, with variable black markings here. Prominent black stripe across the chest. Underparts whitish with dark flecking on the flanks. Wings a variable brown. Bill and legs blackish. Hens duller with indistinct horns.

Distribution: Breeds as far north as Alaska and the Canadian Arctic, and through much of the U.S.A. as far south as Mexico. May occasionally range down to northern Colombia in South America.
Size: 7in (18cm).
Habitat: Fairly arid country.
Nest: Scrape on the ground.
Eggs: 2–5, grayish-white with brown markings.
Food: Seeds and invertebrates.

SONGBIRDS OF THE PLAINS

Some birds of the open country draw attention to themselves with their song, particularly at the start of the nesting period, as is the case with thrashers. Others with a relatively dull appearance, such as some of the New World blackbirds found here, may also undergo something of a metamorphosis, with the plumage of the males becoming more brightly colored.

Western meadowlark

Sturnella neglecta

Distribution: Breeds from British Columbia and Manitoba via Ohio and Missouri to parts of Texas and into northern Mexico. Northern populations move slightly southward in winter.
Size: 10in (25cm).
Habitat: Meadows and grassland.
Nest: Domed cup.
Eggs: 3–7, white with darker markings.
Food: Invertebrates.

Male western meadowlarks are very vocal, especially at the start of the nesting season when they are laying claim to their territories. They will choose a conspicuous site, such as a fence post, and seek not only to attract females but also to drive away rival males. In areas where their distribution overlaps with eastern meadowlarks, even eastern males are perceived as a threat and chased off, since hybridization between these two forms is not unknown. Meadowlarks, which are actually icterids or New World blackbirds, are polygamous in their breeding habits, with a single male mating with several females. Each female constructs a separate and fairly elaborate dome-shaped nest, which takes about a week, before starting to lay. The male plays no part in nest building, but will help to provide food for the young once the eggs have hatched. Western meadowlarks become more social in winter, when they may be observed in small flocks.

Identification: Brown crown extends back over the top of the head, with a brown stripe running behind the eyes. Pale brown cheeks. Back and wings brown with darker barring. A black band runs across the chest, with lores, throat, and central underparts yellow. Flanks whitish with darker spotting. Sexes alike. Young birds paler with barring rather than a band across the chest.

Bobolink

Dolichonyx oryzivorus

The bobolink's unusual name originates from the sound of the male's song, which is audible through the breeding period. Like many birds found in open country, these icterids often sing in flight. They are known locally in South America as ricebirds, due to the way they have adapted to feeding on this crop. Though found in open country in North America, bobolinks are more likely to be observed in reedy areas of marshland during their winter migration. Remarkably, despite flying such long distances, these birds travel back to the same familiar breeding grounds every spring, with the mature males arriving first. Studies of their unique song patterns have revealed not only local dialects but also that the males use different call notes to communicate with each other, compared with those that are intended to attract females. Although the majority pair individually with a female, some males have more than one partner.

Identification: Cock in breeding condition is primarily black, with pale buff on the hind neck. Prominent white wing bar, with the lower back and rump also white. Hens have a dark crown with a streak down the center, and a dark streak behind each eye. Their underparts are yellowish, with streaking on the flanks. Young birds have spotting on the throat and upper breast, with no streaking on their underparts.

Distribution: Breeds from British Columbia to Newfoundland south to northern California, Colorado, and Pennsylvania. Winters in southern South America, reaching Argentina and southern Brazil, but precise range is unclear.
Size: 7in (18cm).
Habitat: Prairies and open areas.
Nest: Cup-shaped.
Eggs: 4–7, gray with reddish-brown spotting.
Food: Seeds and invertebrates.

Red-winged blackbird

Agelaius phoeniceus

Distribution: Occurs over much of North America, breeding as far north as Alaska, and south into Central America.
Size: 9¹/₂in (24cm).
Habitat: Relatively open country.
Nest: Cup-shaped.
Eggs: 3, pale greenish blue with dark spots.
Food: Seeds and invertebrates.

Unrelated to the European blackbird, the red-winged blackbird is a member of the icterid family. It frequents marshland areas when nesting, but is seen in a much wider range of habitats during winter. In North America, red-winged blackbirds move southward for the winter period, typically traveling distances of about 440 miles (700km). Populations in Central America tend to be sedentary throughout the year, however. There is a quite marked variation in the appearance of these birds through their wide range, and it is also not uncommon for individuals to display pied markings. Both sexes sing, particularly at the start of the nesting period, and some of their call notes are different, so it is possible to tell them apart.

Identification: Only the mature male in breeding plumage displays the typical glossy black feathering and red shoulder patches with a paler buff border. Females have dark streaks running down their bodies, with more solid brownish coloration on the head, sides of the face, and over the wings.

Eastern meadowlark (*Sturnella magna*): 10in (25cm)
Southeastern Canada across eastern U.S.A. (resident through much of this area) and west to Nebraska, Arizona and Texas. Also in Mexico, ranging to northern South America. Similar to western meadowlark, with a brownish crown and a lighter central stripe, and a further stripe behind the eyes. Black band across the chest, with yellow central underparts. Flanks are whitish with dark speckling, back and wings are brownish with black barring. Yellow on face varies. Sexes are alike. Young birds are paler.

Brewer's blackbird (*Euphagus cyanocephalus*): 9in (23cm)
Southern British Columbia east to the Great Lakes and down to Baja California and western Texas. Winters south to Central Mexico, sometimes to Guatemala. Cock in breeding color is iridescent blue with a purplish hue on the head and a greenish suffusion over rest of body and wings. Eyes yellow, pointed bill black. When not breeding, may display darker brownish plumage with black barring, and blackish wings. Hens and young birds grayish-brown, with slight mottling on the back. Black wings, dark eyes.

Bendire's thrasher (*Toxostoma bendirei*): 10in (25cm)
Southwestern U.S.A. and northwestern Mexico. Mainly brown, with mottling on the breast. White tips to the long tail feathers. Undertail coverts are lighter brown. Yellow irides. Relatively long, slightly down-curved beak, with a paler lower bill. Sexes are alike.

Le Conte's thrasher

Toxostoma lecontei

Thrashers are members of the mockingbird family, and as such are talented songsters, even capable of mimicking the songs of other birds. The powerful, melodious song of these particular thrashers is most likely to be heard either at dusk or dawn, when it is most active. At this stage of the day it is easier for the birds to catch the invertebrates that form their diet. Le Conte's thrasher does not appear to be common in any part of its range. Its coloration provides effective camouflage in the sandy desert terrain, and its habits also make it inconspicuous. If disturbed, these mockingbirds generally seek to slip away undetected through the scrub, running with their long tail held upright. During the hottest parts of the day, they hide away in the shade. Their bulky nests consist mainly of twigs and are sited near to the ground, well hidden, in a cactus or shrub.

Distribution: Southwestern U.S.A. (in California, Arizona, Nevada, and Utah) and adjacent parts of Mexico, as well as Baja California and Sonora.
Size: 11in (28cm).
Habitat: Arid, open country.
Nest: Made of twigs.
Eggs: 2–4, light bluish-green with brown speckling.
Food: Invertebrates.

Identification: Distinguished from other related species by its very pale coloration, having a grayish-brown body and darker tail, with tawny undertail coverts. Dark, strongly down-curved bill, with slight streaking on the throat. Sexes alike.

INSECT-HUNTING MIGRANTS

Many New World species undertake marked seasonal movements in the course of a year. Though the focus is often on birds from inhospitable northern latitudes flying south for the winter, others in the southern hemisphere also move north toward the equator before the southern winter. Birds found close to or in the Tropics, where food supply is unaffected by the climate, remain as residents.

Groove-billed ani

Crotophaga sulcirostris

These unusual members of the cuckoo clan have a relatively slim body shape and are highly social by nature, living in groups. They even sometimes associate with the slightly larger smooth-billed ani, although they can be distinguished in flight by their more languid flight pattern, as they flap their wings and glide. Neither species is a powerful flier. Groove-billed anis have unusual breeding behavior. A number of females will lay their eggs in the same location, reflecting their highly social nature. Up to 18 eggs have therefore been recorded in a single nest. Although these birds sometimes take over open nests abandoned by other birds, they may also construct a suitably large receptacle for their eggs from sticks and other vegetation. Groups of groove-billed anis typically feed on the ground by walking along and seizing any prey that comes within reach, which may include lizards.

Identification: Dull black in color, with a distinctively shaped bill. The culmen (central ridge of the bill) is in the form of a smooth curve from the tip to the forehead. Grooves in the bill leading to the nostrils are apparent on the sides. Iris is blackish. Tail is long, with a rounded tip. Sexes similar, although hens may be slightly smaller in size.

Distribution: Southwestern U.S.A. south through Central America and Colombia, Venezuela, and French Guiana as far as northern Chile and Argentina; also present on Caribbean islands from Aruba to Trinidad.
Size: 12in (30cm).
Habitat: Scrub and pastureland.
Nest: Bowl-shaped, made of vegetation.
Eggs: 4, blue-green with chalky glaze.
Food: Mainly invertebrates.

Smooth-billed ani

Crotophaga ani

This species tends to occur in more humid areas than the groove-billed type, although they are similar in their habits. They are a common sight, partly as a result of their size and also because of their habit of perching in the open, even on fences. In cattle-ranching areas in Colombia, the anis' habit of following the herds has led to them being nicknamed *garrapateros*, meaning "tick eaters," and they are welcomed by ranchers for removing these parasites from their animals. Smooth-billed anis breed communally, like their groove-billed cousins, and can produce many eggs: 29 have been recorded in a single nest.

Identification: Dull, black plumage, with a decidedly rounded shape to the tail. Bill is black, with a distinctive smooth, raised area on the top of the upper bill close to the eyes. Sexes are similar but hens are smaller in size. Recently fledged young of this species lack the raised area on the bill, resembling groove-billed anis at this stage, although the sides of their bills are smooth.

Distribution: Southern Florida through Central America west to Ecuador and east into northern Argentina. Also present in the Caribbean.
Size: 13in (33cm).
Habitat: Brushland and open areas of country.
Nest: Large cup of vegetation.
Eggs: 4, bluish green, with chalk-like glaze.
Food: Invertebrates.

Purple martin (*Progne subis*): 8¹/₂in (22cm) North America and parts of the Caribbean, notably the Cayman Islands and Cuba, to northern South America. Cock bird is an unmistakable shade of bluish-purple overall, with black flight and tail feathers. Hens are duller, with a bluish area confined to the top of the head and the wings. Throat, breast, and flanks are brownish, as are the sides of the neck, with the lower underparts being white. Young birds resemble adult hens.

Cave swallow (*Petrochelidon fulva*): 5¹/₂in (14cm)
South-central parts of the U.S.A. down through Mexico and across many islands in the Caribbean, being permanently resident on Puerto Rico, Hispaniola, and Jamaica. Forehead reddish-brown, dark blue behind with a reddish brown collar. Reddish brown underparts too. Wings are blackish. The back is bluish with prominent white streaking, while the rump is a deep reddish-brown. Sexes are alike.

Tawny-headed swallow (*Stelgidopteryx fucata*; previously *Alopochelidon fucata*): 4¹/₂in (12¹/₂cm) Isolated populations in northern South America, notably in Venezuela and northern Brazil. Occurs widely in central South America to parts of Argentina and Uruguay. Distinctive tawny-rufous head, becoming buff on the sides of the head, extending down to the breast. Back, wings, and rump are brownish, often with paler edging. Sexes are alike. Young birds are yellowish and fawn rather than tawny.

Bank swallow

Sand martin; African sand martin; *Riparia riparia*

In the summer months, sand martins are usually observed relatively close to lakes and other stretches of water, often swooping down to catch invertebrates near the surface. They are likely to be nesting in colonies nearby, in tunnels that they excavate on suitable sandy banks. These can extend back for up to 3ft (1m), with the nesting chamber lined with grass, seaweed, or similar material. The eggs are laid on top of a soft bed of feathers. When the young birds leave the nest, they stay in groups with other chicks until their parents return to feed them, typically bringing about 60 invertebrates back on each visit. Parents recognize their offspring by their distinctive calls. If danger threatens, the repetitive alarm calls of the adult sand martins cause the young to rush back to the protection of the nest.

Identification: Predominantly brown, with white plumage on the throat, separated from the white underparts by a brown band across the breast. Long flight feathers. Small black bill. Sexes alike. Immature sand martins have shorter flight feathers and are browner than the adults.

Distribution: Throughout North America, except in the more arid regions of southwest U.S.A. Winters in South America.
Size: 4in (11cm).
Habitat: Open country, close to water.
Nest: Holes in sandbanks.
Eggs: 3–4, white.
Food: Flying invertebrates.

Northern rough-winged swallow

Stelgidopteryx serripennis

Distribution: Breeds from southern Alaska down through British Columbia, the southern prairies of Canada and across virtually the entire U.S.A. Migrates to Central America, down as far as Panama.
Size: 5in (13cm).
Habitat: Open country.
Nest: In burrows.
Eggs: 4–8, white.
Food: Invertebrates.

These swallows take their name from the tiny hooks on the feather vane of the outermost primary feather on each wing, near the shaft. These can only be seen with magnification; their purpose is unknown. Although they range over a wide area, northern rough-winged swallows are likely to be seen close to water, where they hawk insects such as midges on the wing. They also hunt prey such as caterpillars and spiders near the ground. Often seen in groups, they sometimes roost communally in holes to conserve warmth in cold weather. Pairs start to nest in May and adopt a variety of nest sites, rarely excavating their own burrows. The nest chamber is lined with available materials, from seaweed to pine needles.

Identification: Mainly brown, darker on head and wings, with long, broad flight feathers. Tail brown, underparts whitish. Thin, narrow bill. Sexes are alike. Young birds have a cinnamon tone to the upperparts.

LONG-DISTANCE TRAVELERS

A number of small birds undertake two remarkable journeys each year, flying thousands of miles up to the Arctic to breed, and then moving south again for winter. Their nesting cycle has to coincide with the brief Arctic summer, otherwise there will be no food for the young, and the adults too could starve. In summer, however, this area literally teems with insect life, providing vital food for the young.

American pipit

Anthus rubescens

Identification: Grayish upperparts, with an indistinct whitish stripe passing through each eye, becoming more brownish-gray over the back. Wings blackish. Streaking on the reddish-buff underparts, varying according to race. Rump brown, with the tail being black above. Has darker, more brownish upperparts outside the breeding period, and is more heavily streaked overall. Sexes are alike.

American pipits are active birds by nature, tending to walk rather than hop across the ground, bobbing their tails up and down regularly. Their range does not extend to northeastern parts of the U.S.A., probably because until quite recently this area was heavily forested. The males establish their territories once they reach their breeding grounds in the Arctic tundra. The nest site is carefully chosen to reduce the risk of the eggs becoming chilled: it may be partly buried, or sheltered by a rock, often apparently orientated to catch the warm rays of the sun. It is not uncommon for hens to reuse a nest which has been built previously. The hen sits alone, and the eggs hatch after about 14 days. The chicks fledge after a similar period, and are reared on invertebrates. American pipits leave their breeding grounds in early September, and head south for the winter.

Distribution: Arctic North America and western U.S.A., in parts of northern New Hampshire, California and New Mexico. Winters throughout southern U.S.A., and up to British Columbia in the west and New England in the east.
Size: 6$\frac{1}{2}$in (17cm).
Habitat: Tundra, grassland, and fields.
Nest: Cup-shaped.
Eggs: 4–5, gray with dark spots and streaks.
Food: Seeds and invertebrates.

Savannah sparrow

Passerculus sandwichensis

These widely distributed birds are as adept at running as they are flying. It is not unusual for them to escape danger by dropping down into vegetation and scampering away. Savannah sparrows can be found in a wide range of habitats, from the tundra of the far north to the grassy sand dunes of Mexico. They breed on the ground, with spiders usually featuring in the diet of the young. Various distinctive races of these sparrows are recognized; some have very limited distributions, none more so than the so-called Ipswich sparrow (*P. s. princeps*), which breeds on a tiny area of land just 20 miles (32km) long on Sable Island, Nova Scotia. It winters more widely along the east coast, including around Ipswich, Massachusetts. Another localized and distinctive form is *P. s. rostratus* from the western side of the U.S.A., which has not only developed a much broader bill but also has a quite different song pattern from all other savanna sparrows.

Identification: Varies through its range, with those from the west coast being darker than those found further east or in Alaska. Streaked appearance, with dark markings running down over the head and on the flanks. Brownish-gray to brownish-black upperparts. Underparts grayish-white. Often a yellow or whitish streak above or through the eyes, with a paler stripe on the center of the crown. Sexes are alike.

Distribution: Breeds throughout Alaska and Canada, extending south across much of the U.S.A. (except for part of the southwest) and into northern Mexico.
Size: 5$\frac{1}{2}$in (14cm).
Habitat: Grassland and open terrain.
Nest: Cup-shaped.
Eggs: 4–6, blue-green with dark speckling.
Food: Seeds and invertebrates.

Lapland longspur

Calcarius lapponicus

The nest of the Lapland longspur is set into the ground and lined with feathers, giving the hen some protection against the cold as well as helping to conceal her from predators while she is at her most vulnerable. The breeding period is short, taking advantage of the brief thaw in the tundra ice during the Arctic summer. This leads to a profusion of midges and other insects hatching in the surface meltwater, which cannot drain away because of the permanently frozen soil beneath. This abundance of insect life is available to the young Lapland longspurs once they have hatched. They grow and fledge rapidly, leaving the nest at just ten days old, and then begin to hunt themselves. Longspurs are so called because of their elongated rear claw, which may help them to maintain their balance, since they move either by walking or running instead of hopping on the ground like most birds.

Identification: Breeding males have black head and upper breast, with white behind the eyes extending down along the edge of the wings, bordered by a chestnut collar. Lower underparts white, with black streaking on the flanks. Wings a variable blackish-brown pattern. Tail black. Hens are less striking, with black-edged brown ear coverts and a black-streaked rufous collar. Black speckling on the chest. Out-of-color males resemble females, except for a broad brownish area at the back of the neck, while hens gain a brownish suffusion on the chest and flanks. Young birds have distinctive speckling on the face.

Distribution: When breeding, ranges right across the northern Arctic region of North America, overwintering mainly in southern and eastern parts of Canada and much of the U.S.A., except for the far south.
Size: 6¼in (16cm).
Habitat: Tundra and grassland.
Nest: Cup-shaped.
Eggs: 3–7, greenish buff with dark spots.
Food: Seeds and invertebrates.

Lincoln's sparrow (*Melospiza lincolnii*): 6in (15cm)
Breeds in northern and western U.S.A., moving farther south for winter. A relatively dull species, grayish-brown overall. Broad gray stripe above the eyes, with a dark gray area on the cheeks. Throat is whitish, with streaking continuing from here over the brownish breast and on the flanks, while the lower underparts are whitish. Back and wings are brownish with darker patterning. Sexes are alike. Young birds are paler.

White-crowned sparrow (*Zonotrichia leucophrys*): 7in (18cm)
Found in Central and Eastern Canada, and New England. Distinctive white crown with prominent black border, and a thinner black stripe extending back from the eyes. Sides of the face are gray, and the throat is whitish. Underparts are also gray, becoming whiter in the center of the abdomen. Wings brownish-gray with white edging; back is brown. Pointed bill is slightly orange with a dark tip. Sexes alike. Young birds have brownish heads and are duller than adults.

Vesper sparrow (*Pooecetes gramineus*): 6in (15cm)
Breeds across much of the U.S.A., wintering in the southern states. A white mustache-like streak is seen on each side of the head, with a brownish tone to the ear coverts. Upperparts buff with darker streaking, while the underparts are grayish with fine streaking on the breast and flanks. Small black area on the wing edged with white, and chestnut lesser coverts. Sexes alike.

Snow bunting

Plectrophenax nivalis

This bunting breeds closer to the North Pole than any other passerine. The cock has an attractive display flight, rising to about 30ft (10m) before starting to sing, then slowly fluttering down again. The nest is often sited among rocks that provide shelter against cold winds. The hen incubates alone for about 12 days, with the young fledging after a similar period. Outside the breeding season snow buntings are social and can be seen in flocks, usually searching for food on the ground, often in coastal areas. They are usually wary, often flying off to prevent a close approach. On the prairies they seek out seeds, berries and invertebrates to sustain them in winter.

Distribution: Circumpolar, extending through Arctic North America. Also found on Greenland. Overwinters much further south, in southern parts of Canada and northern U.S.A.
Size: 6¾in (17cm).
Habitat: Tundra and grassland.
Nest: Scrape on the ground.
Eggs: 4–6, white with reddish-brown spots.
Food: Seeds and invertebrates.

Identification: Breeding males mainly white, with black on the back, wings, and flight and tail feathers. Bill and legs black. Hens have dark brown streaking on head, buff ear coverts and brown on wings. Non-breeding males resemble hens but with a white rump and whiter wings. Young birds are grayish and streaked.

HUNTERS AND SCAVENGERS

Although both corvids and owls are most likely to be seen in wooded terrain, a number of these species inhabit more open areas of country. Their diet varies according to their environment, and in the case of owls it is possible to discover what they have eaten by examining their pellets, which are regurgitated after a meal and contain the undigested remains of their prey.

Chihuahuan raven

White-necked raven *Corvus cryptoleucus*

Distribution: Ranges from south-central U.S.A., being present in parts of Arizona, New Mexico, Colorado, Texas, and Nebraska, south to northern-central parts of Mexico.
Size: 20in (50cm).
Habitat: Arid scrubland.
Nest: Stick platform.
Eggs: 3–8, pale blue with brownish markings.
Food: Omnivorous.

This relatively small raven is closely tied to its arid habitat. It is found at lower altitudes than the common raven (*Corvus corax*), so the two species tend not to meet where their areas of distribution overlap. Chihuahuan ravens are also more social by nature than their larger cousins, and have a less guttural call. Although they are commonly seen in pairs, much larger groupings can be encountered where food is plentiful, for example around garbage dumps. They often frequent roadsides too, seeking carrion. With few trees around, pairs will build their nest wherever surroundings are suitable, using sites such as telegraph poles or the roofs of buildings. Chihuahuan ravens engage in a series of soaring and tumbling flights as part of their courtship ritual. This is the time when the white at the base of their neck feathers is most evident.

Identification: Glossy black, sometimes with a brownish tone. The feathers around the neck are often whitish at the base. Relatively long, stout bill, with very evident nasal bristles extending along two-thirds of its length. Graduated appearance of the tail is evident in flight. Sexes alike. Young birds can be recognized by their bluish irides and duller head and underparts, which are less glossy than their wings.

Burrowing owl

Athene cunicularia

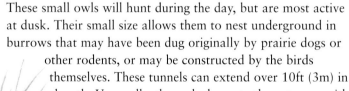

These small owls will hunt during the day, but are most active at dusk. Their small size allows them to nest underground in burrows that may have been dug originally by prairie dogs or other rodents, or may be constructed by the birds themselves. These tunnels can extend over 10ft (3m) in length. Unusually, the owls decorate the entrance with dried cattle dung, and the odor is thought to deter mammalian predators from investigating inside. Burrowing owls invariably choose an open area for the entrance to their nest site, rather than concealing it in long grass.

Distribution: North America from British Columbia east to Manitoba and south into Central America. Separate population in Florida and the Caribbean. Also occurs in South America, especially in the east from Brazil south to Tierra del Fuego.
Size: 10½in (26cm).
Habitat: Lightly wooded country.
Nest: Underground burrow.
Eggs: 5–6, white.
Food: Mainly larger invertebrates.

Identification: Brownish edging on the facial disk on the sides of the eyes, with more distinctive brownish stripes beneath the yellowish bill and white eyebrows. Chest and wings are brownish, with generally whiter underparts in the case of the North and Central American race. Burrowing owls seen in Florida and the Caribbean are a darker shade of brown. Sexes alike. Young birds are buff in color, with white underparts.

Snowy owl

Nyctea scandiaca

The plumage of these owls enables them to blend in well in the tundra region where they commonly occur. In this harsh environment, their numbers are closely related to the availability of their prey, and their population increases rapidly when lemmings are rife. Once the lemming population declines, however, so does that of the snowy owls, and breeding success is greatly reduced, so that pairs may not nest at all in some years. Adult birds are likely to be forced to abandon their usual territories at this time and have to fly south in search of other sources of food. Unusually, snowy owls are active during the daytime.

Distribution: Breeding range extends from northern Alaska across Canada. Typically overwinters in Canada, as far south as northern parts of the U.S.A.
Size: 25¹/₂in (65cm).
Habitat: Woodland, extending to the tundra.
Nest: Scrape on the ground.
Eggs: 3–11, white.
Food: Mainly lemmings but also birds, invertebrates, and fish.

Identification: Cocks are white with yellow eyes and feathering down to the claws. Hens have brown barring all over their bodies apart from their faces, which are white. Young are similar to hens.

Short-eared owl (*Asio flammeus*): 17in (43cm)
Most northerly population extends from Alaska eastward. Also present in northwest South America, across the southern part of the continent and on the Galapagos and Hawaii. Relatively small head, with slight tufts of plumage above the eyes. Variable coloration, brownish with white markings on wings. Pale-streaked chest and black feathering around the eyes. Sexes are alike.

Magellan horned owl (*Bubo magellanicus*): 18in (45cm)
Central Peru south via Bolivia, Chile, and Argentina to the tip of South America. Dark stripes evident around sides of the face, with black spotting under the bill. Yellow eyes and prominent ear tufts. Underparts whitish with black vermiculations and brown markings, paler on upper chest. Upperparts darker, with broader banding across the wings. Tail barred. Sexes are alike.

Chaco owl (*Strix chacoensis*): 14in (35cm)
Chaco region in central-southern South America, from Paraguay to Argentina. Pale whitish facial disks with darker rings. Irides brown. Underparts white with brown and buff barring, becoming buff on lower underparts. Wings similar but less white, with gray banding to flight feathers. Tail and buff-colored legs also banded. Sexes are alike. Young birds have grayish facial disks.

Barn owl

Tyto alba

These owls roost in dark environments, using buildings for this purpose in some areas. They may be seen in open country, swooping over farmland. Some individuals choose to pursue bats where these mammals are common. Males often utter harsh screeches when in flight, which serve as territorial markers, while females make a distinctive snoring sound for food at the nest. They pair for life, which can be more than 20 years. Barn owls have adapted to hunting along roadsides, but here they risk being hit by vehicles.

Distribution: Ranges from southern British Columbia across to New England and southward through Central America into South America.
Size: 15in (39cm).
Habitat: Prefers relatively open countryside.
Nest: Hollow tree or inside a building.
Eggs: 4–7, white.
Food: Voles, amphibians and invertebrates.

Identification: Very pale in color, with a whitish, heart-shaped face and underparts. In northern, central, and eastern parts of Europe, the underparts have a yellowish-orange tone. Top of the head and wings are grayish, with spots evident. Eyes are black. Males are often paler than females.

BIRDS OF PREY

Agile, aerial predators, falcons are opportunistic hunters, relying on strength and speed to overcome their prey, which frequently includes smaller birds. Caracaras, on the other hand, prefer to seek their quarry on the ground, and have benefited to a certain extent from road-building, which has provided carrion in the guise of animals and birds killed by vehicles.

Crested caracara

Common caracara *Caracara plancus*

Distribution: Occurs in southern U.S.A. south through Central America and across South America to Tierra del Fuego and the Falkland Islands.
Size: 23in (59cm).
Habitat: Prairies and relatively arid areas.
Nest: Platform of twigs.
Eggs: 2–3, white with brown markings.
Food: Meat-eater.

This predatory species has a wingspan approaching 4ft (1.2m) but tends not to fly, preferring to spend its time on the ground. Crested caracaras can move quickly on their relatively long legs, running through open country in pursuit of prey such as small rodents. They often seek out carrion in the form of road kills along highways, and when feasting on larger casualties even take precedence over vultures. However, their diet does vary according to habitat, and sometimes they will eat invertebrates. On the Falkland Islands they are considered to be a threat to newborn lambs, while in coastal areas they have learnt to harry returning seabirds into dropping their catches. Crested caracaras usually build their nest off the ground, using an untidy framework of twigs with fresh vegetation added to it. The young hatch after an incubation period of around 30 days.

Identification: Blackish cap and crest on the head, with whitish area beneath becoming barred on the back and chest. Wings and abdomen are more blackish. Bare reddish skin on the face. Neck and throat white. Dark band at the tip of the tail. Sexes alike, but hens are slightly larger in size. Young birds have brown rather than black plumage.

Long-winged harrier

Circus buffoni

These harriers have powerful wings and are believed to fly over the Andes on occasion, and regularly travel long distances when migrating. They are occasionally seen well outside what is usually regarded as their normal range, with individuals having been sighted on the Falkland Islands as well as at Tierra del Fuego. Long-winged harriers are most likely to be encountered in relatively open countryside, often in marshland and similarly wet environments.

Identification: Normal color form has a whitish area around the eyes and bill, with a further white necklace of markings beneath. Chest and wings are predominantly blackish, with white underparts. Grayish barring on the flight feathers and tail. There is also a melanistic form, in which the white plumage is replaced by black apart from on the rump. Female has brownish rather than black plumage and is significantly larger.

Distribution: South America, from southwest Colombia eastward to French Guiana, through parts of Brazil to Argentina, eastern Bolivia, and central Chile.
Size: 22in (56cm).
Habitat: Relatively open, lowland tropical areas.
Nest: Concealed on the ground in rushes.
Eggs: 2–4, whitish.
Food: Small vertebrates.

Prairie falcon

Falco mexicanus

It has been estimated that the breeding range of these falcons covers about 1.4 million square miles (3.6 million square km), but as with other predatory species the density of the birds in this area varies. Prairie falcons are opportunistic hunters, a key factor in their spread across much of North America. They prey heavily on small birds such as lark buntings, and also rodents. In arid areas greater numbers of reptiles including lizards, snakes and tortoises are caught. Prairie falcons prefer to catch their prey at or just above ground level, but also harry other birds in flight. Breeding occurs from March to July, depending on latitude. With woodland becoming scarce, these falcons have adapted to using cliff faces, laying on the rock rather than building a nest, though pairs may take over nests abandoned by other large birds.

Identification: Brown crown, with white streaking running round each side of the head above the eyes. White area behind each eye, and a dark streak running from below each eye onto the cheeks. Dark brown ear coverts, with a brown and white spotted neck and underparts. Bill pale yellow, darker at its tip. Legs and feet yellow. Sexes alike. Young birds have grayish legs and feet, with long flight feathers extending back almost as far as the tail feathers.

Distribution: British Columbia eastward through Canada around the southern part of Hudson's Bay to Newfoundland, and through western U.S.A. to northern parts of Mexico and east via Texas along the Gulf coast to Florida.
Size: 20in (51cm).
Habitat: Prairies and plains.
Nest: Often lays on a cliff ledge.
Eggs: 4–5, whitish with brownish blotches.
Food: Meat-eater.

Swainson's hawk (*Buteo swainsoni*): 22in (56cm)
From Alaska southward, mainly in the central U.S.A. Usually migrates south for the winter to southern Brazil, Argentina, and Paraguay via Central America, although some may remain in the southern U.S.A. White area from above the bill to the throat. Chest is brown and underparts are whitish with brown barring. Head and upperparts are dark. Tail is barred. Rarer reddish and black morphs occur, with these colors predominating on the underparts. Hens are larger.

Snail kite (*Rostrhamus sociabilis*): 18in (45cm)
Ranges from the Everglades of Florida south through Central America west of the Andes to Argentina. Also on Cuba. Dark gray with a white area under the tail. The bare skin from the black bill to around the eyes is reddish, becoming more colorful in the breeding season, but yellow in hens, which also have white striping under the throat. Red irises. Feeds mainly on aquatic snails.

Swallow-tailed kite (*Elanoides forficatus*): 22in (62cm)
Southeastern U.S.A., notably Florida, and into Mexico, extending to northeastern Argentina and Uruguay in South America. Head and underparts are whitish. Black on the back, with purplish and metallic green hues evident on the wings. Long flight feathers and a distinctive V-shaped tail, most apparent in flight. The bill is blackish, the eyes reddish. Sexes are alike. Young birds have shorter tails and sometimes dusky markings on their head.

White-tailed kite

Elanus leucurus

The white-tailed kite has a variable range, influenced by the availability of rodents, which form the bulk of its diet, although it also preys on small birds and invertebrates. The keen eyesight of these kites allows them to spot prey on the ground, even when hovering at heights of 30ft (10m) or more. They tend to hunt in the early morning or around dusk, when rodents are active. White-tailed kites may be seen perched on telegraph poles, though they prefer to nest in trees. Their breeding period is influenced by latitude, occurring during summer in temperate areas, with some pairs raising two broods. By the 1930s, numbers of this kite had fallen steeply in North America, but have increased again. In parts of South America, they have colonized the open terrain resulting from forest clearance, and are fairly common in cereal-growing areas.

Identification: Pale gray crown, neck, and back, with prominent black areas on shoulders, and undersides of wings in the carpal region. Black area also around each red eye. Bill blackish with yellow cere. Legs and feet yellow. Sexes alike. Young birds have grayish-brown upperparts and speckling on the breast.

Distribution: Variable, extending as far north as Nebraska, Wisconsin, and Minnesota, south through Central America and much of eastern South America, reaching parts of Chile and Argentina.
Size: 16in (41cm).
Habitat: Grassland and farmland.
Nest: Platform of sticks.
Eggs: 4–5, white with heavy brown spotting.
Food: Meat-eater.

GIANT HUNTERS

These large predatory species occur at low densities and in some cases have suffered heavy persecution. One example, the Californian condor, now ranks as one of the rarest birds in the world. Yet it is not just direct human intervention which can reduce their numbers. Being at the top of the avian food chain, they are also vulnerable to the build-up of toxic chemicals in their bodies.

Andean condor

Vultur gryphus

Andean condors are the only vultures from the New World to show clear sexual dimorphism. With a lifespan often measured in decades, and a correspondingly slow breeding cycle, pairs are only likely to rear a chick in alternate years. In spite of their strong bills, which allow them to rip open carcasses without difficulty, Andean condors are not active hunters. In coastal areas they scour seal colonies, sometimes descending in large numbers to scavenge when food is readily available.

Identification: Massive, vulture-like appearance. The bare skin on the cock's head is red, and black in the larger hen. Cock birds also display a prominent comb on the head, as well as a wattle that is absent in hens. There is a ruff of white feathering below, encircling the neck. The rest of the plumage is predominantly black aside from the grayish-white areas on the wings.

Distribution: Andean region of South America, right down this mountain range from Venezuela to Tierra del Fuego in the far south.
Size: 51in (130cm).
Habitat: Open mountainous terrain, but sometimes near sea level, where these birds seek carcasses of marine animals. Prefers to be well away from human habitation.
Nest: Caves on cliffs.
Eggs: 1, white.
Food: Carrion.

Californian condor

Gymnogyps californianus (E)

These majestic birds used to soar effortlessly on the thermals, covering huge distances in search of large carcasses in true vulture fashion, but heavy persecution brought them to the very edge of extinction. Collisions with powerlines also reduced their numbers, until the species was virtually extinct. The last remaining wild Californian condors were caught in 1987 and integrated into a highly expensive captive-breeding program, carried out at zoological collections at Los Angeles and San Diego. Five years later, the first birds bred in captivity were released back into the wild, and other releases have followed. It takes about eight years for these condors to attain sexual maturity.

Identification: Huge size, predominantly black with white areas on and under the wings. Bare, variable pinkish-orange skin on the head and neck. This entire area of bare skin is gray in young birds. Sexes alike.

Distribution: Area north of Los Angeles, California. Releases carried out around the San Joaquin Valley in California; birds are fitted with radio telemetry equipment to track their movements.
Size: 53in (134cm).
Habitat: Lightly wooded terrain.
Nest: Usually in caves.
Eggs: 1, white.
Food: Carrion.

Bald eagle

Haliaeetus leucocephalus

Distribution: From the Aleutian Islands and Alaska east across Canada and south across the U.S.A. into northern Mexico.
Size: 38in (96cm).
Habitat: Areas where there are large stretches of water.
Nest: Often huge, located in a tree or sometimes on the ground.
Eggs: 1–3, white.
Food: Vertebrates and some carrion, especially in the winter when hunting is more difficult.

The national symbol of the U.S.A., the bald eagle is a highly adaptable species, and is encountered as far north as the freezing tundra of Canada and south to the searing desert heat of Mexico. Feeding habits are diverse; these eagles tend to catch fish during the summer months, switching at other times of the year to birds as large as geese, which are seized in flight. They hunt both by sight and sound, and are drawn to areas where sea otters are feeding by recognizing their calls. The species remains far more common in the northern part of its range, where it has been subject to less habitat disturbance.

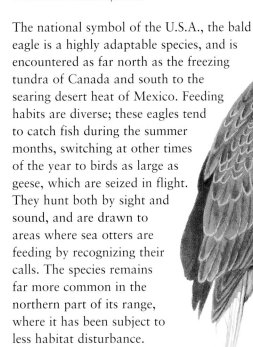

Identification: Distinctive white head and tail, yellow bill and talons. Remainder of the plumage is predominantly brown, with lighter edging to some of the feathers on the back and wings. Female is larger, and young birds have dark bills.

Above: Bald eagles may migrate more than 1,250 miles (2,000km).

Puna hawk (variable hawk, Gurney's hawk, *Buteo poecilochrous*): 24in (61cm)
Andean region from southern Colombia south to Chile and Argentina. Exists in both light and dark morphs. Light-colored cocks have whitish underparts and gray upperparts, with flight feathers blackish at the tips. The tail is white with dark speckling and a black bar. Hens have a chestnut area at the top of the wings. In the dark morph, the entire body except the tail is slate gray. In hens, the chestnut feathering extends over the upper breast, with black-and-white barring on the lower underparts.

Turkey vulture (*Cathartes aura*): 32in (81cm)
Ranges across much of the U.S.A. south via Central America to much of South America; also on islands including the Greater Antilles and the Falklands. North American population moves south in winter. Can find carcasses by scent, and feeds mainly on mammals. Bare, reddish-pink head and brownish-black plumage. Varies in size through its range. Sexes are alike.

Black-chested buzzard-eagle (*Geranoaetus melanoleucus*): 31½in (80cm)
Western side of South America, from northwest Venezuela south. Separate population in the east from Brazil to Uruguay. Slaty-gray head, chest, and upperparts. Paler gray area of fine barring on shoulders, with another on whitish undersides of the wings extending to the underparts, depending on race; otherwise these are creamy-white. Tail has pale tip. Bill yellowish with dark tip. Yellow legs and feet. Young birds brown with buff streaking on the underparts.

Golden eagle

Aquila chrysaetos

These eagles generally inhabit remote areas away from people, where they are likely to be left undisturbed. When seen in flight, the golden eagle's head looks relatively small compared to its broad tail and large, square-ended wings. Although it has some yapping call notes similar to those of a dog, calls are generally quite shrill. Its hunting skills are well adapted to its environment. In some areas, for instance, golden eagles take tortoises, dropping the reptiles from a great height in order to smash their shells before eating them; in other areas, they may prey on cats. They prefer to capture their quarry at ground level, swooping down low, rather than catching birds in the air.

Distribution: Occurs widely throughout the far north of North America, and also in western areas down into Mexico.
Size: 35in (90cm).
Habitat: Mountainous areas.
Nest: Massive cliff nest made of sticks.
Eggs: 2, white with dark markings.
Food: Mainly birds and mammals.

Identification: Brown overall, with yellowish-brown plumage on the back of the head, extending down the nape. Eagles inhabiting desert areas, such as the Middle East, tend to be slightly paler overall. Bill is yellow with a dark tip. Feet are yellow with black talons. Hens are bigger than cocks.

PIGEONS AND DOVES

Some members of this group have benefited from living in close proximity to people, although their presence is not always welcomed either in the countryside or in cities, because of the damage large flocks can cause to both crops and buildings. Their adaptable nature is further illustrated by the way their numbers can increase rapidly under favorable conditions.

Band-tailed pigeon

White-collared pigeon *Columba fasciata*

Distribution: British Columbia and western parts of the U.S.A. south through central America and western areas of South America, as far as northern Argentina.
Size: 16in (40cm).
Habitat: Woodland areas.
Nest: Platform of twigs lined with moss.
Eggs: 1, creamy white.
Food: Seeds and vegetation.

Band-tailed pigeons naturally occur in stretches of woodland, although they are now being seen with increasing frequency in suburban areas and even in towns as well. Their favored food in North America and Mexico is acorns, with seeds and vegetation also featuring prominently in their diet. However, in backyards these pigeons will eat fruits and berries, clambering around in trees rather clumsily, as well as feeding from bird tables. The Canadian population of band-tailed pigeons migrates southward at the approach of winter, as do birds from a number of U.S. states, including Arizona and Colorado. Even individuals from southwestern Texas may fly south across the border into Mexico, where the influx of northern visitors swells the resident population of pigeons dramatically at this time of year.

Identification: Appearance varies through its range. White band encircling the hind neck, with a variable metallic green area beneath. Wings are grayish. Head and underparts vary from shades of vinous pink to almost purplish-pink in South American populations. Tail feathers light gray at their tips, with a dark band near the base of the tail. Legs yellow. Sexes alike.

White-winged dove

Mesquite dove *Zenaida asiatica*

Flocks of white-winged doves often congregate in crop-growing areas around harvest time, foraging on the ground for cultivated grains. They are very adaptable by nature and can also be found in habitats ranging from semi-desert areas alongside cacti to mangrove swamps, as well as being attracted to backyards. During the breeding season in the U.S.A., pairs of white-winged doves from eastern areas breed in large colonies, while those occurring further west tend to nest individually. Subsequently, many head south for the winter, with birds from Texas, for example, flying as far as Costa Rica. Although they are often hunted, white-winged doves are still common in most areas, and the species is currently expanding its distribution in parts of the Caribbean.

Identification: So-called because of the evident white area on the leading edge of the wings when folded. Wings and tail feathers otherwise mainly brownish, with an adjacent grayer band. The head, neck and upper chest have a pinker tinge. Prominent area of bare blue skin around the eyes. Hens are duller, with less iridescence on the neck.

Distribution: Southern U.S.A. and across Mexico, except for the southeast, down to Costa Rica and Panama. Also present in the Caribbean.
Size: 12in (30cm).
Habitat: Relatively open areas, including farmland, parks and backyards.
Nest: Loose platform of twigs.
Eggs: 2, creamy-buff.
Food: Various seeds and grains.

Inca dove

Columbina inca; previously *Scardafella inca*

Identification: Brownish upperparts, with a pinker tinge to the underside of the body. Black scalloping on both wings and body. Finer scalloping on the head, which is grayer. Tail is relatively long and tapering. Rufous underwing coverts seen in flight, with a rufous bar evident when wings are closed. Hens are similar, but underparts less strongly suffused with pink.

Inca doves are typically encountered in relatively open countryside, but can often be found in urban areas throughout the year. The population is largely sedentary through its range, although sometimes these doves may be seen north of their breeding range in the U.S.A., which extends across Oklahoma, Arkansas, and Nebraska. They were first recorded there around 1870. Like many doves, pairs will breed two or three times in rapid succession when conditions are favorable, but their limited nest-building skills means that some nests will collapse, resulting in the loss of both eggs and chicks. A well-concealed site in vegetation is usually chosen, with both birds sharing incubation duties: the cock normally sits by day, while the hen takes over in late afternoon. The young grow rapidly and may leave the nest when only 12 days old, although they will not be able to fly strongly at this age.

Distribution: Southwestern U.S.A. south as far as Costa Rica. Range is extending north and south.
Size: 8¹/₂in (22cm).
Habitat: Open areas, including fields, parks and backyards.
Nest: Fragile platform of twigs and other vegetation.
Eggs: 2, white.
Food: Seeds, fruits, berries.

Long-tailed ground dove (*Uropelia campestris*): 6¹/₄in (16cm)
Two distinct populations, one from Bolivia to central Brazil, the other around the mouth of the Amazon. Gray crown with whitish-gray cheeks and bare reddish skin encircling the eyes. Nape grayish-brown, with a black and purple wing patch, edged with white. White area under the wing when seen from below, with the remaining lower surface of the wing being dark. Pale reddish-brown on chest, becoming whitish on lower underparts. Long tail tipped with white. Hens have paler pink on the underparts and an ashy-brown crown.

Ring-tailed pigeon (*Columba caribaea*): 18in (46cm)
Restricted to Jamaica. The area from the forehead to the nape is fawn-pink, with a significant area of golden-green iridescence on the hindneck. Underparts are pinkish, grayer on the flanks and near the vent. Wings grayish-brown with black flight feathers. There is a broad grayish-brown band on the tail. Hen very similar, but slightly duller overall.

Zenaida dove (pea dove, *Zenaida aurita*): 12in (30cm)
Occurs widely on Caribbean islands, also the Yucatan Peninsula in Mexico. Considered extinct in the Florida Keys. Coloration varies with race. Gray crown, with browner sides to the face and pinkish underparts. Wings grayish-brown, with large black spots. Green iridescence merging into purplish suffusion on sides of neck. Hens generally paler, with less iridescence.

Feral (rock) pigeon

Columba livia

These birds are not native to America, but were introduced from Europe, where they evolved from rock doves. This helps to explain why they often nest on narrow ledges high above sidewalks, just as their ancestors still do on windswept cliffs. Feral pigeons are common city birds, scavenging from leftovers and having virtually no fear of people. Large flocks of feral pigeons can cause serious damage to buildings, with their droppings and also by pecking away at the mortar, which provides calcium.

Identification: Dark bluish-gray head with slight green iridescence on the neck. Light gray wings with two black bars on each wing. Reddish-purple sides to the upper chest. Rest of plumage gray, with a black band at tip of the tail. Various color morphs exist, typically displaying orangish-red or white areas. Sexes are alike.

Distribution: Much of North America except the far north, through Central America and across most of South America, except for central Amazonia and extreme southern tip; also Caribbean.
Size: 14in (35cm).
Habitat: Narrow ledges of city buildings.
Nest: Loose pile of twigs.
Eggs: 2, white.
Food: Prefers seeds, but highly adaptable.

GRACKLES AND ORIOLES

Some of these conspicuous and often colorful birds are graced with an attractive song. A glimpse of yellowish-orange and black plumage, coupled with a pointed bill, is indicative of an oriole sighting. The coloration of grackles is more subdued, although they can display a striking iridescent sheen when sunlight catches their plumage, and are known to put on flamboyant displays to attract a mate.

Common grackle

Quiscalus quiscula

Identification: Variable in color, with a powerful pointed bill and long tail. The bronze form of northern and western areas has bronze feathering with a blue head, in contrast to the more purplish suffusion that characterizes the purple grackle from the Appalachian region. The southerly Florida race has a more olive-green body with a purplish head. Hens display less iridescence, especially on their underparts.

The song of the common grackle is highly distinctive, allowing individual birds to be distinguished. While singing they perform a so-called "rough out" display, in which they fluff up their plumage. This may be accompanied by dancing on the perch and flashing the eyes, which are a brilliant yellow. Males sometimes react in this way more to other males than females. In flight, they splay out their tail feathers to create a characteristic wedge shape. As fall approaches the grackles leave northern and western haunts; they only reside all year in southern areas. These can be long-lived birds, surviving to 22 years.

Distribution: Central and eastern North America, from British Colombia to south-eastern U.S.A. Occasionally sighted in Pacific states and Alaska during spring.
Size: 12½in (32cm).
Habitat: Open country, from marshland to suburban areas and parks.
Nest: Large cup-shaped structure.
Eggs: 3–7, pale green to pale rust.
Food: Seeds, invertebrates, fish, small birds.

Great-tailed grackle

Quiscalus mexicanus

The great-tailed grackle is rapidly extending its North American range in a northwesterly direction, nesting for example in Montana for the first time in 1996. It has been suggested that, at their current rate of expansion, these grackles will soon be breeding regularly in Canada. This trend is probably due to their bold, adaptable nature, especially since they thrive in areas where relatively few trees remain. Great-tailed grackles forage on the ground and will feed in large groups, particularly after nesting when pairs split up to form single-sex flocks. At the start of the breeding season males set up a territory in which several hens nest and lay, though under this system the cock does not help to incubate or rear the chicks. Perhaps not surprisingly, populations tend to have a high proportion of females, which mirrors the breeding pattern.

Identification: Cock birds are glossy black, with a purplish suffusion on the head, back and underparts. They have keel-shaped tail feathers and yellow eyes. Hens smaller and mainly brown. Young birds resemble hens, but with striped underparts.

Distribution: From Oregon south and east through Mexico (except Baja California) and into South America, eastward to Venezuela and as far south as northern Peru.
Size: 15–18in (38–46cm).
Habitat: Open areas, including suburbs.
Nest: Cup-shaped, made of twigs lined with grass.
Eggs: 3–4, blue with brownish-black markings.
Food: Seeds, invertebrates, small vertebrates.

Orchard oriole

Icterus spurius

Each year these small orioles fly long distances to and from their northern breeding grounds, often not being sighted in the far north of their range until the end of May. Some head north through Florida, while the majority fly directly across the Gulf of Mexico. Once they reach their breeding grounds pairs tend to be solitary, although they may sometimes associate with eastern kingbirds (*Tyrannus tyrannus*), which defend their nest sites vigorously. Even so, the number of orchard orioles is declining, partly, it is feared, because of nest parasitism by bronzed and brown-headed cowbirds (*Molothrus*). In some areas, over a quarter of orchard oriole nests are host to the young of these species, reducing the rate of survival of their natural offspring.
In their wintering quarters hundreds of orchard orioles may congregate together, feeding on the nectar of flowering trees and shrubs.

Identification: Mature male has a black head, back and chest, with the remainder of the body being a distinctive shade of chestnut. Hens in contrast have olive upperparts and are yellowish beneath. Young males are similar to females but with a black bib.

Distribution: South-central Canada down across much of central and eastern U.S.A. to Florida and south into Mexico. Occasionally seen in westerly U.S. states. May overwinter in South America.
Size: 7in (18cm).
Habitat: Open woodland close to water, moving into grassland and marshes.
Nest: Hanging cup of grass.
Eggs: 3–7, bluish-white with darker blotches.
Food: Fruit, insects, nectar.

Yellow oriole (*Icterus nigrogularis*): 8in (20cm) Occurs in South America, from Colombia eastward to northern Brazil. Also present on offshore islands including Trinidad and the Dutch Antilles. Predominantly yellow, with black lores and a narrow black throat bib. May have a slight orange cast to the head. Wings black with white edging to some of the feathers. Tail is black. Hens distinguishable by the slight olive cast to the yellow plumage, especially on the head and back, while young birds lack the black markings on the head.

Epaulet oriole (*Icterus cayanensis*): 7in (18cm) Ranges over much of central and eastern South America. Distinguished from other oriole species by its more subdued coloration. Cock bird has a narrow, straight bill that is mainly black, and dark brownish eyes. Plumage is black, aside from the chestnut patches or epaulets in the vicinity of the shoulder, which are not especially conspicuous. Some races have yellow patches there, and may have yellow thighs. Hen resembles the male but is generally smaller.

Hooded oriole (*Icterus cucullatus*): 8in (20cm) Ranges from California southward into Mexico and Belize. Cock bird in breeding plumage varies from yellowish-orange in northern parts of the U.S.A. through to brilliant orange in Texas, depending on race, offset against a prominent area of black on the throat. The back is black, becoming brown with black barring in winter. Hens have greenish upperparts, with the underparts having a decidedly yellow tone. White edging to the wing feathers is apparent, but not the actual bar seen in cock birds.

Spot-breasted oriole

Icterus pectoralis

The melodic, whistling song of these orioles is heard repeatedly, and though both sexes sing, the call notes of cock birds are more complex. Spot-breasted orioles may be seen in the company of other oriole species, seeking food both on the ground and from flowers. Their nest is tightly woven and secured at the tip of a branch, usually anchored around a convenient fork, making it difficult for potential predators to reach. Mimosa trees are especially favored since their spiky thorns offer added protection, though the nests may still be parasitized by cowbirds. The population in Florida, which was first recorded breeding in 1949 in the vicinity of Miami, has not spread very far in the intervening decades, occurring today in a radius of some 40 miles (64km) around the city. There are even suggestions that it has recently declined in numbers. Spot-breasted orioles have also been introduced to Cocos Island, Costa Rica.

Identification: Mainly orangish-yellow, often most fiery on the head, offset against black lores and throat. Wings black with white barring. Tail also black. Distinctive spotted patterning on the sides of the breast. Sexes alike. Young birds are olive-green over the back and lack spotted markings.

Distribution: Native to central Mexico. Separate introduced population in Florida, ranging from Brevard County southward to Dade County.
Size: 9.5in (24cm).
Habitat: Open woodland. Favors suburban gardens in Florida.
Nest: Hanging basket of grass and other vegetation, up to 20in (50cm) long.
Eggs: 3, bluish-white with dark markings.
Food: Fruits, invertebrates, and nectar.

WOODPECKERS AND WARBLERS

Both these groups of birds are at home in areas close to woodland, which is where the invertebrates that feature prominently in their diets are likely to be numerous. Though woodpeckers are traditionally regarded as bark hunters, like warblers they will also descend to the ground to seek their prey. Both groups also possess distinctive calls.

Red-bellied woodpecker

Melanerpes carolinus

Red-bellied woodpeckers have a variable diet that changes through the year. Over the summer, invertebrates are plentiful and form a high percentage of their food intake. They will also prey on vertebrates, including the nestlings of other species. In the fall, fruits of various kinds start to figure more prominently. During the winter period they sustain themselves largely on nuts and seeds, which have a high energy content, though cock birds will still spend time foraging for insects in the branches of trees (hens less so). Red-bellied woodpeckers prefer to feed off the ground, and are most likely to be sighted in deciduous trees, particularly oaks. Pairs will nest through much of the summer, often raising two or occasionally three broods of chicks. The breeding chamber is usually larger than that used for roosting.

Distribution: Eastern North America, from Ontario southward via South Dakota and southern Minnesota as far as central Texas and Florida.
Size: 9¹/₂in (24cm).
Habitat: Open woodland, parks and suburban areas.
Nest: Tree hollows.
Eggs: 3–8, white.
Food: Omnivorous.

Identification: Cocks have a red top to the head, extending to the back of the neck, whereas only the nape is red in hens. Black and white barring extends over the back and wings, and to central tail feathers. Underparts grayish-white, with reddish suffusion to center of abdomen.

Gila woodpecker

Melanerpes uropygialis

Gila woodpeckers are noisy, conspicuous and also quite aggressive by nature, particularly when close to the nest site, which may be located in a tree. Alternatively, since they occur in arid areas, it may be sited in the less conventional surroundings of a tall cactus, as high as 23ft (7m) off the ground. This affords good protection from would-be predators, but can only be occupied once the hole has dried up thoroughly and is not leaking sap. Other creatures, including small mammals and even reptiles, may subsequently take over such chambers once they have been vacated by the birds. The breeding period is usually between April and June, although a pair may sometimes nest again in July. Once fledged, the young remain with their parents until the adults begin nesting again. Their bold nature means that gila woodpeckers will readily feed on backyard bird tables, driving off other species such as European starlings (*Sturnus vulgaris*) which may otherwise seek to monopolize this food supply.

Identification: Pale grayish head and underparts, with a slightly whiter area above the bill and barring on the flanks. Black and white barring also extends down over the back and wings, and onto the tail feathers too. Cocks can be distinguished by the small red cap of plumage on the top of their head.

Distribution: Ranges from southwestern U.S.A. to Sonora. Other races occur in Baja California.
Size: 9¹/₂in (24cm).
Habitat: Scrubland and woods, extending into urban areas.
Nest: Tree hollow.
Eggs: 3–6, white.
Food: Invertebrates, seeds, and fruits.

Downy woodpecker

Picoides pubescens

Distribution: Ranges widely across much of the wooded region of North America, from southeastern Alaska to Newfoundland, and southward as far as Florida.
Size: 6½in (17cm).
Habitat: Forests, orchards, parks and backyards.
Nest: Tree hollow.
Eggs: 3–6, white.
Food: Mainly invertebrates.

Downy woodpeckers are relatively common and can be found in a variety of habitats. It is possible to attract them to backyard feeding stations by offering suet, particularly in the wintertime when other foods are likely to be scarce. They feed largely on wood-boring invertebrates, but are usually forced to seek out plant matter such as nuts through the winter. The breeding period varies across their extensive range, being later in the north, where egg-laying is unlikely to occur before May. Unusually for a woodpecker, the nest site is chosen by the female, and is almost invariably sited in a dead tree. At this time their distinctive drumming sounds can be heard echoing through the forest, as they tap on branches within their territory to keep in touch. Nesting duties are evenly shared, with pairs subsequently splitting up over the winter period to seek food and roost in tree hollows on their own.

Identification: Black on the head and ear coverts, plus a mustachial stripe with intervening white areas. Back and underparts are also white. There is a band of scalloped white markings in the vicinity of the shoulder, with spots on the black wings and inner tail feathers. Cocks have a bright red area at the back of the head.

White-breasted nuthatch (*Sitta carolinensis*): 6in (15cm)
Southwestern and eastern Canada down through much of the U.S.A., extending to Florida and Mexico. Characteristic white area on the chest, with black on back of head, and a rufous tinge to underparts. Back bluish-gray. Hens may have gray crowns, especially in the northeast.

Pileated woodpecker (*Dryocopus pileatus*): 19in (48cm)
Southern British Columbia across southern Canada to Nova Scotia, and south to the Gulf coast, Florida, northern California in the west, and Idaho and Montana in the east. More widely distributed in eastern than western U.S.A. Distinctively large. Prominent red forehead and crown, with a narrow white stripe beneath. Broad black line runs through the eyes, with a white area beneath and a broad white stripe down the neck. Wings and underparts are blackish, with white scalloping below. Hens have black rather than red mustachial stripes.

Striped woodpecker (*Picoides lignarius*): 6in (15cm)
Southern South America, in several isolated populations: west-central and southwestern Bolivia, the Andes of southern Chile, and south-west Argentina. Very small in size, with brown on the white-streaked crown, and ear coverts edged by white bands. Brown back and tail are barred with white, with brown streaking and spotting on underparts. Red or reddish-orange patch on the nape of cock birds, sometimes forming a complete band, absent in hens.

Yellow warbler

Dendroica petechia

The small resident population of yellow warblers (*D. p. gundlachi*) in Florida are of Caribbean origin, which helps to explain the distinctive green plumage on their crown. Further south, those found in coastal areas of Mexico are described as mangrove warblers, although they are simply a variety of yellow warbler. There is also wide diversity in the plumage of the young birds, which can vary from pale yellow with greener upperparts to a brown shade. Young Florida birds are easily distinguished by their gray coloration, with white underparts. Yellow warblers are popular with people seeking a natural form of pest control in their backyard, since they regularly comb the ground for invertebrates. When breeding, their nests are sometimes parasitized by cowbirds. As winter approaches, the warblers head south, to a wide area from southern Mexico down to Peru, and east to French Guiana and Brazil.

Distribution: Northern Alaska east and south across much of northern North America. Ranges down into Central America and through the Caribbean, with a tiny localized population in Florida.
Size: 5in (13cm).
Habitat: Orchards, backyards, and open woodland.
Nest: Cup of plant material in a tree fork.
Eggs: 4–5, bluish-white with darker speckling.
Food: Mainly invertebrates.

Identification: Coloration varies, especially in young birds. Yellowish, with red streaking on the underparts, and greener upperparts. Adults from northern areas greener than those found further south, while birds from Mexico often have chestnut-brown on the head.

URBAN INSECT-HUNTERS

A number of birds such as swifts and swallows have developed the ability to prey on insects in flight. Their acrobatic agility makes them exciting to observe as they twist and turn. Other insect hunters are more opportunistic, like the cowbirds, whose lifestyles have changed significantly in North America in the course of little more than a century.

Chimney swift

Chaetura pelagica

Distribution: Eastern North America. Migrates through Central America on its way to and from its South American winter quarters in Peru and northern Chile.
Size: 5in (13cm).
Habitat: Urban and agricultural areas.
Nest: Twigs held together with saliva.
Eggs: 2–7, white.
Food: Flying insects.

It is not always easy to identify swifts with certainty as they wheel far overhead in the sky, but the small and quite stocky appearance of this species can help. Chimney swifts have long wings and actively fly rather than glide, flapping their wings fast to stay airborne. When seen at close quarters their square-shaped tails have obvious spines at their tips. Being dependent on flying insects for food, the swifts are forced to head south for the winter, returning north to their breeding grounds in March and April. Just prior to migration, literally thousands of chimney swifts may congregate at favored roosts. Their habits have changed significantly due to the spread of cities in North America. Instead of the hollow trees that they would formerly have inhabited for roosting, they have switched to using chimneys, barns, and similar sites, even breeding in these surroundings.

Identification: Dark brown overall, with a paler area around the throat. Body slightly box-like in bulk, with short tail feathers and long wings. Usually seen in flight from beneath, often at a great height as they soar high. Sexes are similar.

Cliff swallow

Petrochelidon pyrrhonota

Distribution: North America and Mexico, except northern Alaska and the far northeast. Migrates via Central America to southern Brazil, Paraguay, parts of Argentina, and occasionally Chile.
Size: 5¹⁄₂in (14cm).
Habitat: Open areas near buildings.
Nest: Gourd-shaped structure of mud.
Eggs: 3–6, whitish with brown speckling.
Food: Invertebrates.

The cliff swallow has adjusted its habits to benefit from the spread of urbanization in its North American breeding grounds. In the past these swallows built their nests on cliff faces, as their name suggests, but now pairs will breed in barns, bridges and similar structures. They may even decide to use dry, hollowed gourds placed in suitable sites as artificial nests. These swallows may also nest in large colonies. The mud that forms the nest is scooped up in the swallow's bill, and, unlike in related species, is the only building material. The interior is lined with vegetation. Pairs typically take five days to build the nest. In fall the swallows head south for winter, although a few fly no further than Panama. Their return is greeted as a sign of spring.

Identification: Pale forehead, with a blue top to the head, which is encircled with chestnut plumage. Blackish area at the base of the throat. Upper chest and rump are orangish-brown, underparts otherwise whitish, with dark edging to undertail coverts. Back and wings are dark and streaked with white. Young birds have blackish heads.

Western kingbird (*Tyrannus verticalis*): 9in (22½cm)
Extends from British Columbia and Manitoba south through western U.S.A. to northern Texas and New Mexico. May be seen in eastern areas of the U.S.A. when migrating. Overwinters in Central America as far south as El Salvador. Ashy-gray head, back and upper breast, with a white area on the cheeks. Underparts yellowish. Wings and tail are a darker brown shade above, with slight scalloping on the wings. Yellow underwing coverts. Sexes are alike.

Eastern kingbird (*Tyrannus tyrannus*): 9in (22½cm)
Southern Canada across much of the U.S.A. to Florida, except for the west coast and inland in the extreme southwest. Overwinters in parts of Central and South America, from Costa Rica eastward as far as French Guiana, and parts of Peru, Bolivia, and Brazil as far as northwestern Argentina. Jet-black head, with grayer back and white scalloping on the wings. Underparts whitish, with an indistinct grayish band across the chest. Sexes are alike.

Vaux's swift (*Chaetura vauxi*): 5in (12cm)
Breeds from western North America to Venezuela in South America. Smaller in size and with higher-pitched calls than the similar chimney swift, which occurs further east in the U.S.A. Dark plumage overall, but with lighter chest plumage when seen from below. The rump is paler too. Sexes are alike.

Tropical kingbird

Olive-backed kingbird *Tyrannus melancholicus*

It is not unknown for these kingbirds to be seen across the Mexican border in the U.S.A. Pairs have been recorded breeding in parts of Arizona, while some prefer to overwinter in the relatively mild climate of California, where they can hunt for invertebrates in characteristic fashion, swooping down to catch them in flight. Tropical kingbirds are usually most conspicuous toward dusk, as they hawk night-flying insects. They are very agile on the wing, able to drop almost vertically onto a branch from above. Pairs usually build their nests high up, out on a tree limb where they will be relatively safe from predators. The olive plumage on their back may help to conceal their presence when viewed from above during the nesting period. Incubation is carried out by the female alone, and the young will fledge after approximately two weeks.

Distribution: Typically ranges from the extreme south of the U.S.A. and Mexico to Argentina, extending west of the Andes to Peru. Also occurs on Trinidad.
Size: 9½in (24cm).
Habitat: Trees, often close to water.
Nest: Cup-shaped, made of vegetation.
Eggs: 3–5, pinkish-buff with darker markings.
Food: Invertebrates.

Identification: Grayish head with a blackish eye stripe, whiter on cheeks and throat. Grayish-green on the back extends onto the chest, with rest of underparts yellow. Wings dark with scalloping on the shoulders. Coverts of underwings are yellow.

Brown-headed cowbird

Molothrus ater

Cowbirds are so-called because they traditionally followed herds of buffalo (bison) across the plains of North America, seeking the insects that were attracted to these bovids. Bison no longer thunder over the prairies, but brown-headed cowbirds have nonetheless expanded their range. This is partly due to woodland clearance, and also to the abundance of small birds that will rear the cowbirds' chicks. At nesting time, female cowbirds seek out the nests of species such as vireos. They watch and wait until the nest is complete, then deposit their own eggs before the host has laid. The young cowbirds hatch before their unfortunate nestmates, and monopolize the food supply. In some areas they are thought to have caused a great decline in the numbers of their host species.

Left: Young cowbirds grow so fast they can fledge at just nine days old.

Identification: Adult male has a characteristic brown head and metallic green-black body. Hen has grayish-brown upperparts, with paler areas around the eyes and throat. Underparts are streaked with darker markings. Young birds resemble hens but with whitish scalloping on the upperparts and more evident streaking below.

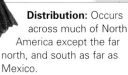

Distribution: Occurs across much of North America except the far north, and south as far as Mexico.
Size: 7½in (19cm).
Habitat: Woodland, open farmland and suburbs.
Nest: Parasitizes those of other birds.
Eggs: 10–12, white with dark speckling.
Food: Feeds on invertebrates, seeds and berries.

HUMMINGBIRDS AND JAYS

Hummingbirds feeding in backyards, either from flowers or special feeders, are one of the unique sights of America. These birds are a source of fascination as they hover in flight and feed, demonstrating their remarkable aerial agility. However, they may not always be resident throughout the year, with some species moving to warmer climes for the winter.

Ruby-throated hummingbird

Archilochus colubris

Distribution: Breeds in eastern North America, moving south to Florida and southwest to Texas through Central America to Panama for the winter. Sometimes seen in the adjoining region of the Caribbean.
Size: 3¹/₂in (9cm).
Habitat: Lightly wooded areas with flowering plants.
Nest: Cup built in trees bound with spiders' silk.
Eggs: 2, white.
Food: Nectar, pollen, sap and invertebrates.

The small size of these hummingbirds is no barrier to flying long distances, which they do back and forth to their wintering grounds each year. Cock birds usually arrive back in their breeding areas about a week before the hens are seen in May. Staying in temperate areas would mean that these birds would have difficulty finding sufficient plant nectar to sustain them through the winter. In fact, ruby-throated hummingbirds are far less specialized in their feeding habits than some members of this family, and have been recorded feeding on more than 31 different types of plant, although they display a preference for red flowers. Hens build their nest alone, binding it with the silk threads of spiders' webs, and are responsible for rearing the chicks on their own. Tiny invertebrates feature prominently in their diet at this stage.

Identification: Metallic, greenish-bronze upperparts. Has a large glossy red area of plumage under the throat. The remainder of the underparts are whitish. Hens are similar in appearance, but they have a dusky white area on their throat instead of the glossy red patch of the cocks.

Anna's hummingbird

Calypte anna

These hummingbirds are sometimes seen feeding at the holes in tree bark drilled by sapsuckers (*Sphyrapicus* species), which results in the plant's sap oozing, providing an accessible source of nutrients. At the outset of the breeding season, males become very territorial. Soon afterwards, hens begin to seek out suitable nest sites, which can include human-made structures, such as electric wires. They gather small lengths of plant fibers and bind them together with silk from spiders' webs. Lichens are used to fill in gaps between the stems, and the cup is lined with feathers. The chicks leave the nest for the first time when only 18 days old.

Identification: Mostly rose-colored head, with a bronzy-green area behind the eyes and a small white spot evident there as well. Upperparts are a shade of metallic, bronzy green, and underparts are green and whitish. Hens lack the rose-colored plumage on the head, and have a brownish throat.

Distribution: Western U.S.A., from California and offshore islands southeast to Arizona; may move to southern Oregon during the winter. Sometimes even recorded in Alaska.
Size: 4in (10cm).
Habitat: Generally woodland areas with flowers.
Nest: Cup-shaped.
Eggs: 2, white.
Food: Nectar, pollen, sap and invertebrates.

Steller's jay

Cyanocitta stelleri

Ranging over a vast area, Steller's jay has proved to be a highly adaptable species. In some areas, such as at picnic sites in the Rocky Mountains in Colorado, these jays have become very tame, accepting food from people. Elsewhere, they are much shyer. They eat a varied diet; where food is likely to be hard to find because of snow in winter, they forage for acorns in the fall, which are then stored for later use. Family groups may remain together over the winter in northern areas, and the young leave in the spring when the adult pair start to nest again. Mud is often used like cement to anchor the bulky nest of twigs together.

Identification: Dark, grayish-blue head and back, with blue underparts. Tail and wings are blue with black barring. North American variety have darker coloration and more prominent crests than those occurring further south, which have a much bluer appearance. Sexes alike.

Distribution: The largest distribution of all North American jays, extending from Alaska south through Central America to Nicaragua.
Size: 12¹⁄₂in (32cm).
Habitat: Woodland and forest.
Nest: Mound of twigs.
Eggs: 2–6, greenish or bluish with brown spotting.
Food: Omnivorous.

Black-chinned hummingbird (purple-throated hummingbird, *Archilochus alexandri*): 4in (10cm) Breeding range extends from southwest British Columbia across southern U.S.A. into Mexico. Moves further south over the winter. Black area merging into broader purple area on the sides of the face and throat. Underparts are buffy-brown, and upperparts are dull bronzy green. Hen is similar, also with a white stripe behind the eyes, and buffy-brown on the sides of the face and throat.

Broad-tailed hummingbird (*Selasphorus platycercus*): 4¹⁄₂in (11cm) Breeding range from California through Texas into southern Mexico and Guatemala. Winters entirely in Central America. Wide tail feathers. Metallic, deep reddish-purple throat and sides of the face, with buffy-brown underparts and metallic green upperparts. Hens are duller, with brown speckling on the buffy throat plumage.

Rivoli's hummingbird (magnificent hummingbird, *Eugenes fulgens*): 5in (13cm) Breeding range from southern Arizona and New Mexico in the U.S.A., with these birds wintering in Mexico. A separate population in Central America ranges as far south as western Panama. Deep purple coloration on the head, becoming blackish with a white spot behind the eyes, and a brilliant green throat. Hens have lighter brown underparts. Light green upperparts in both sexes.

Blue jay (*Cyanocitta cristata*): 12in (30cm) Found extensively in Eastern North America, down to Florida, although southerly populations tend to be smaller. Blue crest, white area on the face, edged by black feathering. Wings are blue with distinctive white markings. Black barring extends from the flight feathers to the tail. Underparts are white. Sexes are alike.

Green jay

Inca jay *Cyanocorax yncas*

These woodland birds are found in two distinct populations. Birds forming the northern population are better known as green jays, while the southerly and more social Andean races are usually described as Inca jays. One of the most unusual features of these jays is their habit of seeking out smoking areas of woodland, not only in search of small creatures that may be escaping the flames, but also to hold their wings out, allowing the smoke to permeate their plumage. This action is believed to kill off parasites such as lice that may be lurking on their bodies. Young green jays may remain with their parents and help to rear the new chicks before establishing their own territories.

Identification: Green plumage is characteristic. The northern race has a combination of blue and black plumage on the head, being green elsewhere, and underparts, including the underside of the tail, are yellowish. Iris is black. South American race has a pronounced blue crest above the bill, and pale green plumage extending right over the forehead. Iris is yellow. Sexes are alike.

Distribution: Northern population extends from Texas to Honduras, while the separate South American form ranges from Colombia to Ecuador.
Size: 10¹⁄₂in (27cm).
Habitat: Woodland and forest.
Nest: Platform of twigs and similar material.
Eggs: 3–5, grayish-lilac with dark speckling.
Food: Omnivorous.

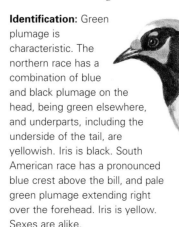

BACKYARD HUNTERS

Predators are not always welcomed in the backyard, but these birds at the top of the avian food chain are quite remarkable in the way they hunt and, in many cases, communicate with each other. Their generally bold nature helps them to thrive in the human environment, while their intelligence allows them to profit from environmental changes.

Black-billed magpie

Pica hudsonia

Distinguishable from its European relative by its calls rather than its appearance, the black-billed magpie is a common sight through much of its range. These members of the crow family are quite agile on the ground, holding their tail feathers up as they hop along. They are often blamed for the decline of songbirds because of their habit of raiding nests, taking both eggs and young chicks. These magpies also sometimes chase other birds, particularly gulls, to make them drop their food. They also eat invertebrates and fruit. Bold and garrulous by nature, a pair of black-billed magpies will not hesitate to create a commotion if their nest is threatened by a predator such as a cat. Their calls draw other magpies to the area, who then join in harrying the unfortunate feline. Their nest is a stout and usually large structure, with a protective dome of twigs.

Identification: Black head, upper breast, back, rump and tail, with a broad white patch around the abdomen. When folded, wings have a broad white stripe and dark blue areas below. Black plumage may have a green gloss. Sexes alike, but cock may have a longer tail.

Distribution: Western North America, extending from Alaska eastward to Ontario down to northeastern parts of California and northern New Mexico.
Size: 19in (48cm).
Habitat: Trees with surrounding open areas.
Nest: Dome-shaped stick pile.
Eggs: 2–8, bluish-green with darker markings.
Food: Omnivorous.

American crow

Common crow *Corvus brachyrhynchos*

Distribution: Occurs across much of North America, from British Columbia to New-foundland and south to Baja California, Colorado and central Texas.
Size: 17½in (45cm).
Habitat: Ranges widely, including into suburban areas.
Nest: Platform of sticks.
Eggs: 3–7, greenish with brown blotches.
Food: Omnivorous.

Few birds have more highly developed communication skills than these crows. It is almost impossible to approach them without being noticed, since even when feeding they have sentinels keeping a look-out for danger. They are heavily persecuted in farming areas, due to the damage that they can inflict on crops; however the benefits that they bring in foraging for potentially harmful invertebrates are frequently overlooked. American crows are highly adaptable birds, just as likely to be encountered in towns and cities as in open countryside. Noisy by nature, they tend to be much less vocal in the vicinity of their nests, which are sited in tall trees, often in public parks. The height at which they build—60ft (20m) or more off the ground—keeps them safe from most predators.

Identification: Jet-black plumage, with dark eyes and a large black bill. Sexes are alike. Calls help to distinguish this species from other crows, while the fan-shaped appearance of the tail in flight distinguishes these corvids from ravens.

American kestrel

Falco sparverius

The smallest of the North American falcons, the American kestrel can easily be overlooked unless it is hovering conspicuously along a roadside. Their remarkably keen eyesight allows these birds to spot a mouse or similar prey from as far as 90ft (30m) away. They dive down quickly to seize the unsuspecting quarry, their sharp talons ensuring a secure grip on their prey. After making a kill, the kestrel will fly up to a convenient perch with its meal, or back to the nest site if it has young. Insects such as grasshoppers are also likely to fall victim to these falcons, particularly during the summer months when they are generally more plentiful and can play a vital part in nourishing a growing brood. The vast range of these kestrels means that they need to be adaptable feeders. They have been documented in Peru as preying on both lizards and scorpions, while amphibians will also be caught on occasion.

Distribution: Extends over virtually all of America, from Alaska in the north to Tierra del Fuego at the tip of South America.
Size: 10½in (27cm).
Habitat: Open countryside and urban areas.
Nest: Typically in a hollow tree.
Eggs: 3–7, white with brown blotching.
Food: Insects and small vertebrates.

Identification: Cock has russet back barred with black, and a russet tail with a broad black subterminal bar and whitish feather tips. Top of the head is russet with adjacent grayish-blue area. Wings grayish-blue above, with black barring but much paler below, and white circular spots along the rear edge. Two distinctive vertical black stripes on the sides of the face, with an intervening whitish area and chin. Underparts paler. Hens have chestnut wings and a barred tail.

Yellow-billed magpie (*Pica nuttalli*):
16½in (42cm)
Occasionally seen as far north as Oregon, but more typically resides in the Central Valley area of California and in coastal valleys as far south as Santa Barbara County. Similar to the black-billed magpie, with a black head, back and breast. Wings and underparts have white patches. Bill is yellow, with a variable yellow patch of bare skin adjacent to the eyes. Sexes are alike.

Black-shouldered kite (*Elanus caeruleus*):
16in (41cm)
Mainly occurs through Central and South America. In North America, is sometimes seen as far north as British Columbia, hunting along highways. Grayish crown, back and wings, with prominent black patches at the shoulders. Underparts are white, enabling it to be distinguished from the Mississippi kite (*Ictinia mississippiensis*). Sexes alike. Young birds have reddish-brownish striations on their underparts, with similar suffusion on the head and neck.

Western screech owl (*Otus kennicotti*):
8½in (22cm)
Western side of North America, from northern Canada down to Mexico. Also occurs in two color morphs, although reddish individuals are decidedly uncommon outside the humid coastal northwest. The pattern of cross-barring on the plumage of this species is denser, creating an overall impression of a darker-colored bird, although depth of gray coloration varies.

Eastern screech owl

Otus asio

The red and gray morphs of these owls are equally common, sometimes even cropping up in the same nest. Habitat appears to play no part in determining coloration. Lightly wooded areas, including backyards, are favored by these birds of prey. In true owl fashion, eastern screech owls hunt at night, and despite their size are able to take relatively large quarry, including adult rats. They are opportunists, catching anything from worms to snakes and even moths, which can be seized in flight. In urban areas these owls are even known to plunge into backyard ponds at night, seizing unwary fish near the surface. The shape of their wings means that virtually no sound betrays their presence until after they have launched their deadly strike.
As with other owls, the study of the pellets regurgitated after meals has allowed ornithologists to confirm their feeding habits.

Distribution: Eastern North America, from eastern Montana and the Great Lakes down via the Gulf states to northeastern Mexico.
Size: 8½in (22cm).
Habitat: Variable, from forests to suburban areas and parks.
Nest: In a hollow tree.
Eggs: 2–8, white.
Food: Small mammals and invertebrates.

Identification: Red and gray color morphs. Widely spaced cross-barring on the underparts matches spacing of vertical stripes on a whitish ground. Yellowish-green base to the bill. Ear tufts may be raised or lowered. Lines of white spots with black edging extend diagonally across top of wings. Sexes are alike.

BLUEBIRDS AND OTHER SONGSTERS

One of the most welcome signs of spring in temperate regions is the so-called "dawn chorus," indicating the onset of the breeding period and the return of migrant songbirds. At this hour of day, when the surroundings are relatively quiet, the songs of these birds can be clearly heard in backyards and parks, making this an excellent time at which to spot them too.

Mountain bluebird

Sialia currucoides

Distribution: Western North America, wintering as far south as northern Mexico.
Size: 7in (18cm).
Habitat: Open countryside, including parkland.
Nest: Concealed cup-shaped structure.
Eggs: 4–8, whitish to pale blue.
Food: Invertebrates and berries.

The beautiful song of the mountain bluebird can be heard just before dawn, leading the Navajo people to describe them as "heralds of the rising sun." Almost immediately, when the sun appears, they become quiet again. Pairs seek shelter when they are nesting, building in hollow trees, small caves, or even on cliff faces, although they will also adopt birdhouses. Invertebrates are an important source of food for these bluebirds. However, late frosts can adversely affect the insect population, reducing the likelihood of breeding success if food is scarce when the chicks hatch. The young normally leave the nest at three weeks old, and the adult pair may rear another family before the end of summer. In the fall and through the winter berries feature more prominently in their diet, with the bluebirds venturing more regularly to birdfeeders in areas where they are resident.

Identification: Cock is blue overall, being a deeper sky-blue shade on the upperparts. Bills and legs black. Hens are brownish-gray, with white on the abdomen, and whitish scalloping seen on the wings. There may be a reddish-orange suffusion on the breast after the fall molt.

American robin

Turdus migratorius

The return of the American robin to its northern haunts is a long-awaited sign of spring. Adult cock birds usually arrive first, followed by the hens. Last to arrive are the young of the previous year, making their first flight back to the area where they were hatched. American robins are alert hunters, hopping across lawns and pausing at intervals, their head tilted slightly to one side as if listening. It is actually their keen eyesight that allows them to spot earthworms and other invertebrates in the grass. Berries also feature in their diet. Their nest is well-built, with mud serving as cement to hold the vegetation together, and carefully sited in dense vegetation to avoid the attention of predators. It is not uncommon for pale leucistic individuals to occur in this species, and even pure white albinos.

Distribution: All of North America, apart from the central far north, down as far as Mexico. Overwinters in the south of its range, including northern Guatemala, and is also seen in some Caribbean islands, such as Cuba.
Size: 10in (25cm).
Habitat: Woodlands, parks, and suburban areas.
Nest: Cup of vegetation and mud.
Eggs: 3–6, bright blue.
Food: Invertebrates and also fruit.

Identification: Cock has a blackish head, with white around the eyes and streaking under the throat. Back and wings grayish-brown, with brick red underparts and white under the vent. Hens have browner heads and orangish underparts. The underparts of young birds are speckled. Eastern birds tend to be more brightly colored than their western counterparts.

Rufous-backed robin

Rufous-backed thrush *Turdus rufopalliatus*

These relatively large robins are likely to be found in Mexico at lower altitudes than migrating American robins (*T. migratorius*). Their song is relatively similar, however, being comprised of attractive liquid call notes uttered in a relatively slow style. Rufous-backed robins are often seen throughout their range, although those reported around Oaxaca City may well be the descendants of captive individuals, rather than naturally occurring birds. The same may apply to those seen in the Distrito Federal, another part of their range where the species has not been sighted until recently. There is evidence to show that these robins regularly move northward, crossing the border into the U.S.A. where they are not normally observed; records exist not only for states such as Texas and Arizona but also for sightings further north in California during winter. Outside the breeding season, rufous-backed robins are often seen in larger groups rather than as pairs.

Identification: Grayish head, with a white throat streaked with black. Back and wing coverts reddish-brown. Wings and rump gray with reddish-brown underparts, becoming white on the lower abdomen. Sexes are alike.

Distribution: Restricted to western Mexico.
Size: 10in (25cm).
Habitat: Trees and shrubbery.
Nest: Cup-shaped.
Eggs: 2–3, whitish with reddish-brown markings.
Food: Invertebrates, berries, and fruit.

Eastern bluebird (*Sialia sialis*): 7in (18cm)
Ranges from southern Canada to the Gulf states and Arizona, extending as far south as Nicaragua. Migrates south from northern areas for the winter, occurring no farther north at this stage than southern parts of New England and southern Michigan. Blue head, wings and tail are offset against rusty red breast feathering, becoming whiter on the abdomen. Hens duller, with grayish-blue upperparts. Young birds are brown and speckled, with areas of whitish and some blue plumage.

Eastern slaty-thrush (*Turdus subalaris*): 8in (20cm)
Ranges from southern Brazil to the extreme north-east of Argentina. Typical thrush-like appearance. Grayish head and upperparts, with a slight bluish suffusion. The white throat area is heavily streaked with blackish markings, and there is a white crescent at the base of the throat. Underparts are ashy-gray, becoming paler on the abdomen. Hens are similar but have a more brownish tinge to their upperparts, with brown rather than blackish streaking on the throat. Bill is yellowish-brown, instead of the male's brighter orange-yellow shade.

Austral thrush (*Turdus falcklandii*): 10in (25cm)
Southern South America, occurring widely in Chile and southern Argentina. Also present on the Falkland Islands to the east, being the only resident thrush here. Blackish head, with olive-brown back, wings and tail. Streaked throat with white suffusion, underparts otherwise buff brown. Bill is yellow. Sexes generally alike, although hens sometimes have slightly browner heads. The mainland population has more contrast in its coloration than individuals from the Falklands, having blacker heads and paler, more yellowish-brown underparts. Young birds are recognizable in either case by their speckled plumage.

Melodious blackbird

Dives dives

Forest clearance in various parts of its range has aided the spread of the melodious blackbird over recent years. This species is often to be seen foraging for food on lawns, pausing occasionally to flick its tail feathers vertically. Although most commonly observed in pairs, much larger groups often congregate in fields. The song of the melodious blackbird is less inspired than its name suggests, consisting mainly of a series of whistles that can be loud and sharp in tone. Pairs may duet with each other on occasions. They become very territorial when breeding, with both members of the pair defending their territory. Working together, it takes these birds nearly two weeks to build their nest, using vegetation of various types and mud or cow dung to bind the fibers together. The hen is responsible for incubating the eggs on her own, although the cock will bring her food during this period. Both adult birds then forage to feed the chicks.

Distribution: Central America, ranging from Mexico south to Costa Rica.
Size: 10in (25cm).
Habitat: Open areas with woodland nearby.
Nest: Open cup in a tree.
Eggs: 3–4, blue with brown blotches.
Food: Invertebrates and berries.

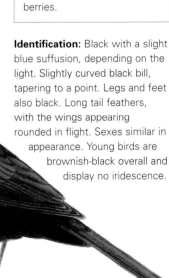

Identification: Black with a slight blue suffusion, depending on the light. Slightly curved black bill, tapering to a point. Legs and feet also black. Long tail feathers, with the wings appearing rounded in flight. Sexes similar in appearance. Young birds are brownish-black overall and display no iridescence.

NATIVE INSECT-EATERS AND INVADERS

The present-day distribution of some birds is the direct result of past human interference. The effects of this can be clearly seen in North America, where some introduced European species have now become established across virtually the entire continent. Mimics such as the catbird may even pick up the songs of these feathered invaders.

Brown thrasher

Toxostoma rufum

Distribution: This species is widely distributed in eastern parts of North America, ranging down as far as Florida and the Gulf coast. It has even been recorded in Newfoundland.
Size: 11½in (29cm).
Habitat: Woodland and hedges.
Nest: Cup-shaped.
Eggs: 2–5, being whitish to pale blue with brown speckles.
Food: Invertebrates and berries.

Thrashers are a native American group of birds. Although they are rather shy by nature, hiding away in vegetation, they will venture down to the ground to flick over leaf litter using their long bills, and snatch up any invertebrates disturbed. It has been suggested that the rhythmic movement of the bill in this context bears a resemblance to the cutting action of a scythe, and this may explain the unusual name of this species. At the outset of the breeding season it is difficult to overlook the courtship of the brown thrasher, since the cock bird takes up a prominent position to sing to his would-be mate. He perches with his head up and bill open, although any hint of danger will lead to a cessation of the song. The hen responds by offering a piece of vegetation, which probably marks the start of nest-building. Pairs work together to construct a bulky nest of plant matter, including grass, twigs, and even bark. Incubation and fledging each take about 13 days, which allows two broods of chicks to be reared during a single breeding season.

Identification: Reddish-brown upperparts, with streaking across the wings creating a scalloped appearance. Long chestnut tail feathers. Underparts marked with black streaks arranged in vertical lines running down onto the flanks; plumage is whitish in the vicinity of the throat, becoming fawn on the lower parts of the abdomen. Long, slightly down-curved black bill. Sexes are alike.

Catbird

Dumetella carolinensis

The song of these relatives of the mockingbird incorporates a sound like a cat's miaowing, which is the reason for their common name. Catbirds also possess a harsher alarm call in their vocal repertoire. They can often be heard singing after dark, especially on moonlit nights. Catbirds are quite shy by nature, and their coloration also helps them to blend into the background. Their chestnut underparts are most conspicuous during the cock's courting display, when he chases the hen in the early stages of courtship. When on the move, the catbird flicks its long tail repeatedly. Insects are a vital part of the diet of these birds, especially when they are rearing chicks, as the insects provide valuable protein. Catbirds may catch their insect prey above water, and these birds are often observed hunting in areas close to ponds and streams.

Identification: This species is slate-gray in color, with a distinctive black cap. It also has chestnut underparts, which may not be clearly visible. Sexes are alike.

Distribution: Southern Canada south and eastward across the U.S.A., as far down as Florida. Southerly winter range extends as far down as Panama and Cuba.
Size: 9in (23cm).
Habitat: Scrubland, hedgerows and backyards.
Nest: Loosely constructed cup of vegetation.
Eggs: 4–6, glossy blue-green.
Food: Fruit and insects.

Northern mockingbird (*Mimus polygottos*):
11in (28cm)
Southern Canada through the U.S.A. to southern Mexico and the Caribbean. Relatively dull, with gray upperparts, paler on the underparts. Broad white area on the wings, most apparent in flight. Sexes are alike.

Common mynah (*Acridotheres tristis*):
10in (25cm)
A member of the starling family, introduced to southern Florida. Blackish head contrasts with long, pointed yellow bill and bare yellow orbital skin around the eyes. Back is brownish. The black wings have a prominent white band across the flight feathers, also evident when the wings are closed. Undertail coverts white, with white tips to the tail feathers. Underparts otherwise brown with a slight reddish tinge. Legs are yellow, matching the bill. Sexes are alike.

Northern shrike (*Lanius excubitor*): 10in (25cm)
Widely distributed throughout North America. Ranges up to Alaska but less common in eastern areas, especially the southeast, and not present in Mexico. Gray head and back, with a thin white line running just above the eyes and a broader black stripe running through them. Underparts whitish. White banding running across the otherwise black wings. Long tail, with the central feathers being black and the shorter ones white. Stout, longish and slightly hooked black bill. Sexes are alike. Young birds display brownish markings at first.

House sparrow

Passer domesticus

A common visitor to birdfeeders and city parks, house sparrows have adapted to living close to people. They were originally brought to New York from Europe in 1850, and by 1910 had spread west to California. There are now noticeable differences within the North American population: northern individuals are larger, while those from southwestern arid areas are paler. House sparrows form loose flocks, with larger numbers gathering where food is plentiful. They spend much time on the ground, hopping along while watching for predators such as cats. It is not uncommon for them to build nests during winter, to serve as communal roosts. The bills of cock birds turn black at the start of the nesting season in spring. Several males often court a single female in what is known as a "sparrows' wedding."

Identification: Rufous-brown at the back of the head, with gray above. A black stripe runs across the eyes and a broad black bib extends down over the chest. Ear coverts and underparts are grayish, with a whiter area under the tail. Hens are browner overall with a pale stripe prominent behind each eye.

Distribution: Southern Canada southward across the U.S.A. and into Central and much of South America.
Size: 6in (15cm).
Habitat: Urban and more rural areas.
Nest: Under roofs and in tree hollows.
Eggs: 3–6, whitish with darker markings.
Food: Seeds and invertebrates.

Common starling

European starling *Sturnus vulgaris*

The common European starling is another New World invader, introduced in 1890 when a small flock of 60 starlings brought from England was set free in New York's Central Park. A further 40 were released there the following year, making the millions of starlings now present in the whole of North America direct descendants of this initial group of 100 birds. (The release came about as part of an unfulfilled plan to introduce all the birds described in the works of British playwright William Shakespeare to North America.) Small groups of starlings are often to be seen feeding in backyards, although occasionally much larger groups comprised of hundreds of birds may visit an area. In flight, European starlings are adept at avoiding predators such as hawks by weaving back and forth in close formation, to confuse a would-be attacker. Their undemanding breeding habits and belligerent nature mean that these starlings will commandeer nest holes from native species for their own use.

Distribution: Occurs widely throughout North America except the far north, just ranging south into Mexico.
Size: 8.5in (22cm).
Habitat: Near houses and buildings.
Nest: Tree hole or birdhouse.
Eggs: 2–9, white to pale blue or green.
Food: Invertebrates, berries, birdfeeder fare.

Identification: Glossy, with purplish-black plumage on the head and a greenish hue on parts of the body overlaid with spots, particularly the neck and back. Dark brown wings and tail. Hens similar, but spotting is larger and base of the tail pinkish rather than blue, as in breeding males. Young birds are duller, being brownish, and lack iridescence.

WRENS

These diminutive, rather stumpy birds are often found in residential areas, especially the aptly named house wren, which has one of the widest distributions of all birds in America, occurring virtually throughout the entire region. Other wrens have more localized distributions, benefiting from birdfeeder offerings to sustain themselves during the cold winter months.

House wren

Troglodytes aedon

The house wren appears a rather nondescript bird, but its lively, jerky movements make it instantly recognizable, even from just a brief glimpse. These wrens often frequent backyards, usually being seen among dense vegetation since they are instinctively reluctant to leave cover for long. Although wrens are small in size, they can be determined and belligerent birds, especially in defense of a chosen nest site such as a woodpecker hole in a tree, and are quite able to force the creator of the chamber to go elsewhere. They will also take occupancy of a birdhouse, particularly when sited in an area of a backyard where they feel secure. A pair will collect a jumble of vegetation such as moss and small twigs to line the interior, as well as adding feathers to make a soft pad for their eggs. House wrens are prolific breeders, frequently producing two broods of chicks during the season.

Identification: Brown upperparts, with black barring evident on the wings and tail. Underparts lighter brown, with whitish throat area. Generally indistinct pale eyebrow stripes. Narrow, relatively short bill. Sexes are alike. Young birds have a rufous rump and are a darker shade of buff on the underparts.

Distribution: Present across much of North America except the far north, extending down through Mexico and right across South America.
Size: 5in (12cm).
Habitat: Vegetation in parks and backyards.
Nest: Pile of twigs and sticks.
Eggs: 5–9, white with brown spotting.
Food: Invertebrates.

Carolina wren

Thryothorus ludovicianus

Carolina wrens are relatively easy birds to identify, due partly to their extensive white facial markings. They move with the same jerky movements as other wrens, frequenting bushes and similar dense areas of vegetation through which they can move inconspicuously. Carolina wrens are also quite noisy birds, with a song that is surprisingly loud for a bird of their size. It is uttered throughout the year, rather than just at the start of the breeding season, and sounds in part like the word "wheateater," repeated constantly. Unfortunately, young Carolina wrens often have an instinctive tendency to push northward from their southern homelands. Although in mild years they will find sufficient food to withstand the winter cold, widescale mortality occurs in these northern areas when the ground is blanketed with snow for long periods, almost wiping out the species. In due course, however, their numbers build up again, until the cycle is repeated again at some future stage.

Identification: Chestnut-brown upperparts, with black barring on the wings and tail, and white bands running across the wings. Distinctive white eye stripes, edged with black above and bordered by chestnut below. Black and white speckling on the sides of the face. Throat is white, underparts buff. Sexes are alike.

Distribution: Range extends throughout eastern U.S.A., notably in North Carolina and South Carolina.
Size: 5¹/₂in (14cm).
Habitat: Shrubbery.
Nest: Cup of vegetation.
Eggs: 4–8, whitish with brown spotting.
Food: Invertebrates feature prominently in the diet of this species, with some seeds.

Winter wren (*Troglodytes troglodytes*):
4in (10cm)
Occurs in a broad band across North America around the 50-degree line of latitude. Also extends further south into the Rocky Mountains, the Midwest, and the mountainous area of the east coast. The races found in the far north, occurring on the Aleutians and islands out in the Bering Sea, are larger than those found further south, and also have paler plumage, which helps them to retain body heat and makes them less conspicuous to predators. The longer bill may assist in gathering food. Reddish-brown back and wings with visible barring. Lighter brown underparts and a narrow eye stripe. Short tail, often held vertically, is grayish on its underside. Bill long and relatively narrow. Sexes are alike.

Bewick wren (*Thryomanes bewickii*):
5in (13cm)
This species varies in color through its range. It is common and possibly expanding in western areas of the U.S.A., although numbers in the east are thought to be falling. The grayest race (*T. b. eremophilus*) occurs in the western-central part of their distribution, having a grayish throat and underparts, with the characteristic long eye stripe extending back to the nape of the neck. Upperparts are dark gray. Nearer to the coast, these wrens display a brown suffusion to their plumage which becomes progressively darker in more northerly populations. Eastern races have rich chestnut-brown upperparts, with characteristic black markings on the wings and tail.

Canyon wren

Catherpes mexicanus

As with other wrens it is the powerful, musical song of this species that attracts attention, although it can be quite difficult to spot the songster itself, especially if partly concealed among a loose outcrop of rocks. Canyon wrens will occasionally adopt abandoned buildings as refuges. Their long, narrow bills allow them to seize invertebrates from small crevices without difficulty, their tails often bobbing up and down as they seek their quarry. Canyon wrens prefer areas around steep slopes or cliffs, whereas rock wrens (*Salpinctes obsoletus*) tend to inhabit flatter areas of countryside. For breeding they choose a site in a stone wall or a similarly inaccessible place such as a chimney. The nest is fashioned from a jumble of vegetation on a suitable ledge.

Distribution: Extends from western parts of the U.S.A. south as far as southern Mexico.
Size: 6in (15cm).
Habitat: Rocky areas.
Nest: Open cup of vegetation.
Eggs: 4–7, white with dark speckling.
Food: Invertebrates.

Identification: Black and white speckled top to the head, with a white throat and breast. Black barring on the wings and tail, with speckling on the back and underparts. Characteristic rufous underparts, with the red extending across the back, wings and tail. Sexes are alike. Long, relatively straight blackish bill. Young birds lack the white speckling of the adults.

Cactus wren

Campylorhynchus brunneicapillus

This is a surprisingly large wren that is often seen in the vicinity of cacti in its arid habitat. It builds a bulky nest of dried grass within the protective spines of these plants or in thornbushes. The nest interior is lined with fur or feathers; the entrance is to one side. Nests near the ground are concealed so they are less apparent to would-be predators. The calls of the cactus wren have a monotonous tone, consisting simply of the sound "chut" uttered repeatedly. The cactus wren does not raise its tail vertically in true wren fashion, but holds it horizontally. These birds prefer to remain near the ground, flying low and hunting for invertebrates lurking there.

Right: Cactus wrens inhabit arid areas, including scrublands and deserts.

Identification: Brown area on the top of the head extends over the nape, with a white stripe passing through the eye, and white streaking on the back. Prominent black spotting on the breast, becoming more streaked on the pale underparts. Barring is apparent on the wings and tail. Sexes are alike.

Distribution: Southwestern U.S.A. from California southward as far as central Mexico.
Size: 8½in (22cm).
Habitat: Arid areas and desert.
Nest: Large structure made of vegetation.
Eggs: 4–7, creamy white with spots.
Food: Invertebrates.

TITS, TITMICE AND CHICKADEES

These small birds are most likely to be seen in backyards during the winter months, when the absence of leaves on many trees makes them more conspicuous. They often visit bird tables and feeders during colder weather too. Members of this group are very resourceful, clearly displaying their aerobatic skills as they dart about and hang upside down to feed.

Tufted titmouse

Baelophus bicolor

Distribution: Eastern North America, from southern Ontario south to the Gulf of Mexico, although not present in southern Florida. Range appears to be expanding in some areas of Canada.
Size: 6in (15cm).
Habitat: Light, deciduous woodland.
Nest: Small tree holes and nest boxes.
Eggs: 3–8, creamy white with brown spots.
Food: Invertebrates in summer; seeds during winter.

This is the largest member of the tit family occurring in America. It is quite conspicuous through its range, thanks in part to its noisy nature. The vocal range of male tufted titmice is especially varied, and individuals are able to sing more than 15 different song patterns. Hens also sing, but not to the same extent and mainly during spring and early summer. The range of these titmice has increased northward, largely because bird-table offerings guarantee them food throughout the year. In the south, they have been recorded as hybridizing with black-crested titmice (*B. atricristatus*) in central parts of Texas. The resulting offspring have grayish crests and a pale orange band above the bill. In spite of their small size, these titmice are determined visitors to bird tables, driving off much larger species. They can be equally fierce in defending their nests.

Identification: Characteristic black band immediately above the bill, with gray crest and crown. Cheeks and underparts are whitish, with pale reddish-orange flanks. Sexes alike. Young birds are duller overall, with less contrast in their plumage.

Above: The nest cup of a titmouse, lined with soft material.

Carolina chickadee

Parus carolinensis

This species is very closely related to the black-capped chickadee (*P. atricapillus*), which occurs further north, and it is not unknown for the birds to hybridize where they overlap. Studies of their song patterns have revealed that the Carolina chickadee has a four-note call, whereas the black-capped type has a two-note whistle. Although pairs have their own territories during the summer, Carolina chickadees form larger groups in the winter months. During cold weather, they spend much longer periods roosting in tree hollows to conserve their body heat, sometimes remaining there for up to 15 hours per day. This is also the time of year when chickadees are most likely to be seen visiting bird tables in search of food.

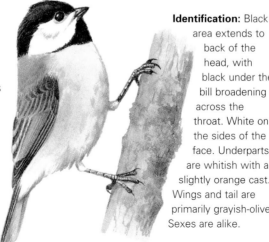

Identification: Black area extends to back of the head, with black under the bill broadening across the throat. White on the sides of the face. Underparts are whitish with a slightly orange cast. Wings and tail are primarily grayish-olive. Sexes are alike.

Distribution: Northeastern U.S.A. south to Texas and northern Florida. Occasionally recorded in Ontario, Canada.
Size: 5in (12cm).
Habitat: Light, broad-leaved woodland.
Nest: In small holes in trees, also uses nest boxes.
Eggs: 3–9, white with reddish-brown spots.
Food: Invertebrates and seeds.

Bushtit

Psaltriparus minimus

Bushtits are the smallest species of North American tit. These lively birds forage in groups of up to 40 individuals, their movements helping to disturb insects and spiders that might otherwise remain hidden. Bushtits will comb plants in this way, which makes them welcome by gardeners since they can devour unwanted infestations of pests quite rapidly. They are very agile birds, able to hang upside down from a branch when seeking food, and also have a bold nature, so it is often possible to observe them at relatively close quarters. There is a consistent difference in eye coloration between the sexes: the irises of cocks are invariably brown, whereas those of hens may vary from white through to yellow. Remarkably, this change may become apparent within a few days of the young birds fledging, since both sexes have dark eyes at first. Nesting pairs of these tits are also surprisingly tolerant of others of their own kind, to the extent that they may allow them to roost in their nest. Flocks subsequently reform once the breeding season has ended.

Identification: Three groupings exist. Those from northern areas have brownish ear coverts, brown cap, and gray upperparts, with paler, whitish underparts. Hens have grayer throats. Gray coloration extends onto the cap in the lead-colored variety. In the Central American black-eared form, cock birds have black areas on the sides of the face.

Distribution: Ranges from British Columbia in Canada south and eastward through the U.S.A. to parts of Mexico and Guatemala in Central America.
Size: 4¹/₂in (11cm).
Habitat: Scrubland.
Nest: Pendulous mass.
Eggs: 5–13, white.
Food: Mainly invertebrates. Also berries.

Bridled titmouse (*Baeolophus wollweberi*): 5in (13cm)
Southern Arizona and New Mexico south to the uplands of western Mexico. Broad grayish crest, darker at the back, with a blackish stripe running up from the bill. A blackish line runs through the eyes over cheeks, joining a prominent black area on the throat. Yellowish-gray underparts, with wings, back and tail darker gray. Bill blackish, legs and feet gray. Sexes are alike.

Black-crested titmouse (*Baeolophus atricristatus*): 6in (14¹/₂cm)
Restricted to southwestern Oklahoma and Texas. Closely related to the tufted titmouse. Pale grayish area above the bill, with black feathering and crest behind. Grayish area around the neck, extending over the back, wings and tail. Paler gray underparts, with rufous area on flanks and a whitish area around the vent. Sexes alike. Young birds have whitish forehead, with crown a darker gray than rest of upperparts.

Chestnut-backed chickadee (*Poecile rufescens*): 4¹/₂in (11¹/₂cm)
Southern coastal Alaska south via British Columbia and Montana to central California. Sooty-brown cap extends from the bill to the back of the neck, with a white area on the cheeks and a black bib on the throat. Back, flanks, and rump generally bright chestnut, with grayish-brown tail feathers. Central underparts whitish. The race *P. r. barlowi* of the coastal region of central California has grayer underparts with a little chestnut. Sexes are alike.

Plain titmouse

Oak titmouse *Baelophus inornatus;* previously *Parus inornatus*

The dull coloration of the plain titmouse helps it to blend in with its wooded habitat. Pairs maintain distinct territories throughout the year, and form life-long bonds. If one bird dies, the surviving individual may mate with a new partner. Plain titmice breed only once during the year, and the young are driven away by their parents when they are about seven weeks old, being forced to wander in search of their own territory. When feeding, these titmice will often comb branches in search of insects, although during winter acorns feature prominently in their diet—they can open these quite easily with their bill. They are also more frequent visitors to birdfeeders in winter, even picking up edible items from the ground, which are then taken to a more secluded location to be eaten. At night, plain titmice will seek out suitable roosting holes, with pairs using separate locations, although they sometimes prefer a well-hidden perch.

Distribution: Occurs in western parts of the U.S.A. extending down to Baja California and other parts of northwestern Mexico.
Size: 5in (13cm).
Habitat: Areas of oak woodland.
Nest: Old woodpecker holes, birdhouses.
Eggs: 3–9, white.
Food: Invertebrates, buds, and berries.

Identification: Differences in depth of coloration and bill size through its range. Grayish-brown overall, with a small crest at the back of the head. Underparts are a purer shade of gray than the back. Sexes alike. Formerly classified with the juniper titmouse (*B. ridgwayi*) as a single species.

SPARROWS AND TOWHEES

Although brown predominates in the coloration of these adaptable birds, there can actually be quite a variety of appearance through what is often a wide range. In spite of their relatively small size, a number of sparrows and towhees undertake extensive seasonal migrations to and from their breeding grounds during the spring and fall.

California towhee

Pipilo crissalis

The taxonomy of the towhees can be confusing. In the past, the Californian towhee and the closely related canyon towee, which occurs further west, were grouped together under the name brown towhee, although it is now clear that they are, in fact, distinct species. Even so, eight distinctive races of California towhee are recognized through its relatively small range. Pairs, which bond for life in many cases, are most likely to spotted in backyards during the breeding season, since this is when the cock bird sings loudly from a prominent perch. Even after egg-laying he continues this behavior, laying claim to their territory; any intruders will be driven away aggressively. Their nest is hidden low in vegetation, being constructed from a variety of plant material, and the hen incubates alone. Once the chicks have hatched these towhees become largely insectivorous, frequently foraging on the ground, using their feet to scratch around in the hope of discovering invertebrates hiding under leaves or other vegetation.

Identification: Predominantly brown, with the crown being a warmer shade than that of the body. The throat is buff, marked with dark spots that are largest across the upper chest. Cinnamon-brown undertail coverts. Sexes are alike. Young birds are duller with more extensive speckling on their underparts.

Distribution: Coastal western North America, from Oregon down to Baja California, extending east as far as the Cascades and Sierra Nevada Mountains.
Size: 9in (23cm).
Habitat: Chaparral, parks, and backyards.
Nest: Cup-shaped.
Eggs: 3–4, bluish-green with dark markings.
Food: Seeds and invertebrates.

Chipping sparrow

Spizella passerina

These sparrows are not easy to spot, partly because their coloration provides camouflage, but also because they hide among vegetation. Even when singing, the cock bird often chooses a fairly secluded location. The sound is distinctive, however, being essentially a monotonous "chip"-like call, which explains the species' common name. These sparrows forage mainly on the ground, although they may visit birdfeeders, especially during winter when snow blankets the ground. Each fall, chipping sparrows desert most of their North American range, migrating to southern states and further south in late September. They return to their breeding grounds in the far north the following May. The well-hidden nest is constructed from vegetation, with incubation and fledging each lasting about 12 days. This rapid breeding cycle means that in favorable conditions, they may rear two broods.

Identification: Breeding adults have a chestnut crown with white stripes beneath, and a black stripe running through the eyes. Grayish neck and underparts, with whitish throat. Wings are black and brown with whitish markings. Dark notched tail. Head coloration is brownish with darker speckling outside the nesting season.

Distribution: Most of North America south of Hudson Bay, except for central-southern U.S.A. Winters along the southern Mexican border and through Central America as far south as northern Nicaragua.
Size: 5¹/₂in (14cm).
Habitat: Parks and wooded backyards.
Nest: Cup-shaped.
Eggs: 3–5, light blue with darker markings.
Food: Seeds and invertebrates.

Lark sparrow

Chondestes grammacus

Lark sparrows have quite a musical song. In common with larks they are rather terrestrial birds, foraging on the ground not just for seeds but also invertebrates and especially grasshoppers during summer, which are used to rear their chicks. They breed on the ground or in a low bush, frequently in scrubland, where the nest can be hidden from predators, and sometimes in loose colonies. Northern populations fly south during late July and August, returning again the following spring. During the winter period they can often be seen in flocks. The range of the lark sparrow has declined over recent years. This may be due to changes in habitat, since their distribution formerly extended up the eastern seaboard to Maryland and New York. Today they are considered to be relatively scarce east of the Mississippi River.

Identification: Black stripe extending up from the bill, with a central white area dividing the chestnut coloration. White bordered with black encircles the chestnut cheek patches. Whitish underparts with very distinctive dark central breast spot. Upperparts grayish-brown with black markings. Dark brown wings and tail, showing white edging. Sexes are alike.

Distribution: Across the far south of Canada, and western and central parts of the U.S.A. Winters further south along the Mexican border and the Gulf coast to Florida.
Size: 6^1/$_2$in (17cm).
Habitat: Roadsides, farms, open country.
Nest: Cup-shaped.
Eggs: 3–5, white with dark spots.
Food: Seeds and invertebrates.

Rufous-sided towhee (Eastern towhee, *Pipilo erythrophthalmus*): 8^1/$_2$in (22cm)
Most of North America except the far north. Northern populations move south into northern Mexico in the fall. Cock bird has jet-black head, chest and back. White underparts with chestnut flanks. White area at base of primary feathers. Undertail coverts pale yellowish. Iris color varies with race: usually reddish, but whitish in Florida. Hens have brown rather than black plumage.

White-throated sparrow (*Zonotrichia albicollis*): 6^1/$_2$in (17cm)
North-central British Columbia to Newfoundland and down to New England. Winters in eastern U.S.A., also in central California, and south to northern Mexico. White throat with grayish chest and whitish underparts. May be white streaking on the head, with yellow bordered by black above the eyes. Dark brown streaks on rufous-brown wings, with white edges to some feathers. Rump brownish. Sexes are alike. Young have brown streaks on chest.

Song sparrow (*Melospiza melodia*): 6^1/$_2$in (17cm)
The Aleutians and Alaska across to Newfoundland, moving to southern Canada in winter, south to Florida and along the Gulf coast to Mexico. Thirty-nine races described, all with a dark gray stripe above the eyes and dark brownish stripe across the lower cheeks, bordering the white throat. Grayish stripe down the center of the crown, with adjacent brown plumage often streaked with black. Grayish-brown back and wings. Mainly white underparts, with brown streaking on chest. Sexes are alike. Young birds are more buff overall.

Andean sparrow

Rufous-collared sparrow *Zonotrichia capensis*

As their name suggests, Andean sparrows are most likely to be found in upland areas of South America, where they inhabit relatively open country, and are often seen in villages and towns. At least 25 different races have been identified across their wide area of distribution. The song of the cock bird also varies, although it is usually uttered from a relatively prominent position, aiding identification. Even the nesting habits of these sparrows are not consistent through their range, with those at higher altitudes producing smaller clutches, typically comprised of fewer than three eggs. This may reflect difficulties in obtaining food, or possibly indicate that the level of predation is higher in lowland areas. Breeding pairs are resident throughout the year, with the nesting period varying according to latitude. Insects feature more prominently in the diet when there are chicks to feed, with these occasionally being caught in flight.

Distribution: From Mexico down across South America to Tierra del Fuego. Most common in the Andean region but largely absent from the Amazon basin. Also on Hispaniola in the Caribbean.
Size: 5^1/$_2$in (14cm).
Habitat: Upland areas.
Nest: Cup-shaped.
Eggs: 2–5, greenish-blue with brown markings.
Food: Seeds and invertebrates.

Identification: Red-brown collar. Black crown, slight crest, gray head with black stripes. White throat with some black, pale gray underparts. Blackish wings with brown edges and white-edged barring. Young have streaked underparts and a buff nape.

SONGBIRDS

Many of these birds are a common sight, thanks to their adaptable nature. They often undertake seasonal movements southward to warmer climates in search of more favorable feeding opportunities over the winter period. Their return is keenly anticipated, however, as an indicator of the arrival of spring. Pairs will then breed perhaps twice before returning south again.

Virginian cardinal

Northern cardinal *Cardinalis cardinalis*

The range of these cardinals continues to increase both in northern and western areas, especially since the first breeding record from Canada, which dates back to 1901. This expansion probably results from bird-table offerings. The stout, conical bill of these birds is adapted to crushing seeds, although Virginian cardinals will also hunt invertebrates, particularly when they have chicks in the nest.

Distribution: From southern Ontario, Canada south through the U.S.A. to the Gulf of Mexico, and southward as far as Belize.
Size: 9in (23cm).
Habitat: Edges of woodland, parks, and backyards.
Nest: Cup-shaped, made of vegetation.
Eggs: 3-4, whitish or grayish white, with darker spots and blotches.
Food: Seeds and invertebrates.

Identification: Predominantly red, with a pointed crest. A black mask surrounds the bill extending back to the eyes and down onto the throat. Wings, back and tail are of a slightly duller shade. Hen is predominantly brown, with a slight reddish suffusion over the wings and tail. The bill in adults of both sexes is bright red, whereas that of young birds is blackish, enabling them to be distinguished from adult hens.

Scarlet tanager

Piranga olivacea

These tanagers undertake long flights each year to and from their breeding grounds. Individuals sometimes venture further afield, and are observed in more northerly and westerly areas than usual, even reaching Alaska on rare occasions. A pair of scarlet tanagers rears only one brood during the summer before returning south. These birds catch invertebrates in the undergrowth and also in flight. More unusually, scarlet tanagers rub live ants onto their plumage. This behavior, known as anting, results in formic acid being released by the ants among the feathers, which in turn drives out parasites, such as lice, from the plumage. The bright coloration of these birds is linked in part to their diet.

Identification: Mainly yellowish-olive, with underparts being more yellowish than upperparts. Cock distinguishable from the hen by having black rather than brownish wings and tail. In breeding plumage, the male has characteristic vivid scarlet plumage. Young cock birds in their first year have more orange rather than scarlet plumage.

Distribution: Migrates north to southeastern Canada and eastern U.S.A., overwintering in Central and South America, east of the Andes to Peru and Bolivia.
Size: 7in (17cm).
Habitat: Light forest and woodland.
Nest: Cup-shaped, made of stems and roots.
Eggs: 2–5, whitish to greenish blue with dark markings.
Food: Mainly invertebrates.

Blue grosbeak

Guiraca caerulea

In spite of the cock bird's distinctive plumage, the blue grosbeak is not as conspicuous as its coloration would suggest. Indeed, in poor light its feathering can appear so dark that, at a distance, it is sometimes confused with the male common cowbird (*Molothius ater*). The grosbeak's melodious song is most commonly heard early in the day, although the birds may start singing again at dusk. The song consists largely of short notes interspersed with longer trills. Cock birds usually return from their winter haunts a few days ahead of hens, frequently spending this time searching for food in groups on the ground before splitting up to nest. Pairs are likely to rear two broods of chicks over the summer period before migrating south again during September.

Identification: A dull shade of blue, with a large, grayish bill. The wings are darker, with two distinctive wing bars close to the shoulder. Hens are predominantly brownish, lighter on the underparts, and also display two buff-colored wing bars. They have some bluish feathering on the rump. Young cock birds display more widespread blue feathering among their plumage.

Distribution: Occurs widely across the U.S.A. from California in the west through to New Jersey on the east coast, and south to Costa Rica. Northern populations overwinter in Central America, ranging from Mexico to Panama.
Size: 7$\frac{1}{2}$in (19cm).
Habitat: Brush, often near water.
Nest: Cup-shaped.
Eggs: 3–4, pale blue.
Food: Seeds and invertebrates.

Lesser goldfinch (*Carduelis psaltria*): 4$\frac{1}{2}$in (11cm) Northwestern parts of the U.S.A. to parts of Mexico, including the Islas Tres Marias, occurring discontinuously down into Colombia and Venezuela and as far south as Ecuador and northern Peru. Cocks have a black crown, with remaining upperparts varying from black in the western population to green in birds occurring further east. Underparts yellow. Wings are blackish with evident white markings. Hens have a grayish-green head and duller yellow underparts, with brownish rather than black wings. Young birds similar to hens, but males display traces of black above the bill.

Black-chinned siskin (*Carduelis barbata*): 5in (13cm) Southern South America, from southern Chile down to Cape Horn. Also on the Falkland Islands. Cock has black extending from the back of the head over the crown and around the bill onto the throat. Sides of the neck and underparts yellowish. Greenish-yellow broken by darker areas on the back. Wings are black with yellow markings. Hens lack the black markings and are more greenish overall, with white area on the belly. Young birds similar to hens but display more streaking, especially on upperparts.

Summer tanager (*Piranga rubra*): 7$\frac{1}{2}$in (19$\frac{1}{2}$cm) Eastern and southern USA, reaching southern California in the west and New Jersey in the east. Winters from Mexico south to southern Peru, Bolivia and French Guiana. Cock is rosy-red overall, darker on the wings, with a prominent pale bill. Hens are generally mustard-yellow, but some display red flecking on their bodies; upperparts are grayer in western birds. Young males resemble hens, but develop a red head in their first spring.

American goldfinch

Carduelis tristis

These attractive songbirds are common throughout their range, although those in northern areas move south to warmer areas for the winter. They are often seen in larger flocks at this time, frequently in the company of related birds such as redpolls (*Acanthis* species). Their diet varies through the year, and is influenced by the availability of food. Invertebrates, which provide protein, are important for rearing chicks in the nest. Seeds are consumed through much of the year, while shoots and buds of trees such as spruce and willow will be eaten when other foods are in short supply.

Distribution: Canada southward through much of U.S.A. to northern Mexico.
Size: 5$\frac{1}{2}$in (14cm).
Habitat: Wooded or lightly wooded areas.
Nest: Cup-shaped.
Eggs: 2–7, pale blue.
Food: Seeds, other plant matter and invertebrates.

Identification: Brightly colored yellow plumage, with a black cap and black wings and tail, and white bars on the wings. Duller in winter plumage, being a more olive shade with a lless distinct black cap. Hens can be identified by their olive-yellow upperparts and more yellowish underparts, becoming brownish during winter, especially on the upperparts. The white wing barring is still apparent, enabling hens to be distinguished easily from juvenile birds.

FINCHES

Members of this group have actually benefited from human changes to the environment. Along with a greater availability of food, urban areas provide a multitude of nesting sites as people seek to attract these birds into their backyards. Although pairs may establish their own breeding territories, they usually associate in flocks for the remainder of the year.

Purple finch

Carpodacus purpureus

Occurring close to woodland areas, these finches are territorial by nature, especially during the breeding season. Males sing from favored branches, their song being very evident at this time, and they also undertake display flights to attract a partner. The nest is built on the branch of a conifer, often at a considerable height from the ground. Although some individuals remain on their breeding grounds throughout the year, others move south, where they may be sighted in small flocks. The availability of pine seeds influences their distribution during winter in particular, since in years when the crop fails these finches move to new areas in search of other food. Although their breeding range is continuous, the population splits into distinct western and eastern groups for the duration of the winter. Purple finches are quite bold and conspicuous in a garden setting, often visiting feeders, with oil-rich seeds such as sunflower being favored foods.

Identification: Cocks are rose-red over much of the body, which is especially pronounced on the head and rump. The back is red with brown streaking, while the lower underparts are whitish in the center. Hens are brownish, with whitish stripes encircling the eyes and a white area under the throat. Pale underparts heavily streaked with brown.

Distribution: Canada south of Hudson's Bay, most common in the east. Extends to southern California. Winters in the west and through much of eastern U.S.A. down along the Gulf coast, and occasionally into northern Mexico.
Size: 6in (15cm).
Habitat: Suburban areas, parks, woodland.
Nest: Cup-shaped.
Eggs: 5–6, pale bluish with dark markings.
Food: Seeds and invertebrates.

House finch

Carpodacus mexicanus

Identification: Cock has a brown cap on the head and brown ear coverts. Remainder of the head and breast are red, sometimes more orange, depending on race. Streaked white underparts, browner on the flanks. Back is streaked, with dark wing feathers typically edged with white. Hens are much duller, being streaked over their entire head and underparts.

Two separate populations of these finches occur in North America: one native to the west and the other in the east. The eastern population is descended from birds released on Long Island, near New York City, during the 1940s. There they bred successfully, but it was not until the 1960s that they began to spread more widely and become established. They appear to have benefited significantly from birdfeeders, though they also forage for berries and other items in backyards. Males have an attractive song, not unlike that of a canary. Nesting pairs are very adaptable and often breed in loose colonies, utilizing nesting baskets fixed up under the eaves of houses. They frequently raise two or more broods of chicks in rapid succession. During the fall, house finches often associate together in large flocks, and in more rural areas may be seen feeding in the fields. In spring, flocks can cause damage in orchards by pecking at the buds and flowers.

Distribution: Southwestern Canada through western parts of the U.S.A. to Texas and into Mexico. Separate population in eastern U.S.A. south of the Great Lakes. Also occurs on Hawaii.
Size: 6in (15cm).
Habitat: Open areas including cities.
Nest: Cup-shaped.
Eggs: 4–5, pale blue with black spots.
Food: Seeds and invertebrates.

Pine grosbeak

Pinicola enucleator

Identification: Cock is mainly reddish, with gray on the sides of the body and along the wings. Wings darker, with variable white edging and gray wing bars. Black forked tail. Hens are gray overall, with a yellowish head, rump and flanks, and a grayish area under the throat. Yellow color can be more russet in some cases.

As their name suggests, pine grosbeaks are closely associated with coniferous forests, though they move into deciduous woodlands in fall. Living in flocks, these finches prefer to feed off the ground, resorting to nibbling buds when seeds and fruit are scarce and snow covers the ground. In some areas, especially the western U.S.A., they are regular birdfeeder visitors. Their winter range is influenced by availability of food, with flocks sometimes moving south of their normal range when berries such as mountain ash fail. Pine grosbeaks are not very active by nature. They are also quite tame, so are fairly easy to observe. The nest is built in a tree, often close to the ground, with the young remaining there for three weeks before fledging.

Distribution: Circumpolar, being present right across northern parts of North America, and in western U.S.A. Overwinters in central parts.
Size: 9in (23cm).
Habitat: Woodland, orchards and backyards.
Nest: Bulky, cup-shaped.
Eggs: 2–5, pale bluish-green with dark blotches.
Food: Seeds, berries and invertebrates.

Lesser Antillean bullfinch (*Loxigilla noctis*): 6in (15cm)
Ranges through the Lesser Antilles, though not in the Grenadines, sometimes on Puerto Rico. Cocks are blackish, with a small red area in front of each eye, extending from the chin onto the throat. Undertail coverts may be red. Hens and cocks of the Barbadian race have brownish-olive upperparts, being grayer beneath with orange undertail coverts. Young birds resemble hens.

Hooded grosbeak (*Coccothraustes abeillei;* previously *Hesperiphona abeillei*): 7in (18cm)
Mainly Mexico, ranges into central Guatemala and northwestern El Salvador. Cock birds have black heads, wings and tail, with mainly yellow underparts and white areas on the wings. Stout bill also yellow. Hens are duller, with olive-green upperparts and grayish rather than white inner greater coverts. Young birds resemble hens, but males more yellowish on their underparts.

Rose-breasted grosbeak (*Pheucticus ludovicianus*): 8in (20cm)
Northeastern British Columbia to the Great Lakes and Canada's east coast down to Georgia. Winters in the Caribbean and Central America, south to Peru and northeast to Guyana. Cocks have a pinkish-red area on the breast bordered by white, extending onto lower underparts. Head and back jet-black, with a white wing bar and other white markings on wings. Rump white with black markings, tail black. Powerful, pale horn-colored bill. Hens have brownish streaked upperparts, with a white eye stripe and pale area under the chin. Buffy colored below, with streaked enderparts.

Evening grosbeak

Coccothraustes vespertinus

When first described in the 1820s it was believed that these birds only emerged from cover at dusk, and although this was completely incorrect they came to be known as evening grosbeaks. Their range has expanded since then. Up until the 19th century these finches were restricted to northern Canada, but suddenly, perhaps because of persistent annual food shortages, evening grosbeaks started traveling further afield to northeastern parts of the U.S.A. Ultimately, they started breeding here, and continued to spread, reaching Maryland by the 1960s, Florida and the Gulf coast a decade later. Pairs build their nest at the very end of a branch, up to 70ft (21m) off the ground, choosing a site where it will be hidden. The hen sits alone, with the chicks hatching after about two weeks. They fledge after a similar interval.

Identification: Large, thick-set finch with a powerful bill. Cocks have yellow forehead and eyebrows. Rest of head is greenish, as is the upper chest, becoming yellow on the underparts. White area on the wings, with black flight feathers and tail. Hens have a gray head and predominantly gray back, with a whitish throat and grayish-tan underparts. Young birds resemble hens.

Distribution: Southern Canada through western parts of the U.S.A. to northern Mexico. Extends eastward to Newfoundland and south to southeastern parts of the U.S.A.
Size: 8in (20cm).
Habitat: Woodland, parks and backyards.
Nest: Cup-shaped.
Eggs: 2–5, bluish-green.
Food: Seeds, berries and invertebrates.

VIREOS AND OTHER BACKYARD BIRDS

A wide variety of birds can be encountered in backyard surroundings, and they are often quite bold in this environment. Some are valuable allies for gardeners, catching invertebrates that would otherwise become pests, particularly in tropical areas. In farmland, however, they may inflict some damage on crops, especially when these are maturing.

Yucatan vireo

Vireo magister

Distribution: Caribbean coast of Mexico and on the southern part of the Yucatan Peninsula, ranging into Belize. Also on nearby Caribbean islands, including Grand Cayman.
Size: 6in (15cm).
Habitat: Scrub and mangrove.
Nest: Cup-shaped.
Eggs: 2–5, white with reddish-brown markings.
Food: Invertebrates and fruit.

Yucatan vireos may appear similar to New World warblers in size, shape and coloration. The family is widely represented in Central America, the Caribbean and adjacent parts of northern South America. The population occurring on the Caribbean island of Grand Cayman is considered sufficiently distinct to be regarded as a separate subspecies, and is known locally as "sweet Bridget" thanks to the sound of its song. The somewhat drab coloration of this species provides camouflage among the mangrove forests and scrubland it frequents. Yucatan vireos are not easy to observe among foliage, and are more often heard than seen. These vireos have an appealing song, however, that has been likened to that of a mockingbird. Invertebrates gleaned from the vegetation feature prominently in their diet, although they also seek out fruit and berries. Breeding usually occurs between April and August. The nest takes the form of a well-woven cup, secured onto a horizontal branch in a tree.

Identification: Grayish top to the head, with broad whitish stripes above the eyes and a dark line beneath running through the eyes. Back and wings olive-gray. Underparts are whitish with a buff tinge, and flanks are dusky. Relatively large blackish bill. Sexes are alike.

Bananaquit

Coereba flaveloa

Identification: Upperparts vary from dark gray to black, with a prominent white streak above the eyes. Throat is a paler shade of gray. Underparts otherwise yellowish, with white undertail coverts. White wing speculum most apparent when the wings are open. Short, dark, curved bill. Legs and feet dark grayish. Sexes are alike.

Occurring over a wide area, these common honeycreepers vary significantly in color, with some Caribbean races being completely blackish. Active and lively, bananaquits are also very bold, and some can be tamed to feed from the hand. They will even fly into homes in the Caribbean in the hope of being offered sugar. Their usual feeding method entails puncturing the bases of flowers with their sharp, narrow bill to extract nectar. This allows them to gain the sugary solution that they could not reach by probing the flower directly. They may also use their bill as a straw to suck up juice from ripe fruit. Small spiders and other invertebrates are eagerly sought, especially when feeding young chicks. Both sexes help to construct the globular-shaped suspended nest, entered near the bottom.

Distribution: Central America and the Caribbean down across much of South America, through eastern Peru, Bolivia and Paraguay to Brazil and northeastern Argentina.
Size: 4in (10cm).
Habitat: Lowlands and coastal areas.
Nest: Made of plant matter.
Eggs: 2–3, whitish with dark spots.
Food: Nectar, fruit and invertebrates.

Blue-gray tanager

Thraupis episcopus

Distribution: From Central America, reaching northwest Peru and east of the Andes to northern parts of Bolivia.
Size: 6in (16cm).
Habitat: Relatively open areas.
Nest: Made of plant matter.
Eggs: 2–3, creamy to grayish-green and spotted.
Food: Fruit and invertebrates.

Blue-gray tanagers are a common sight in many parts of their range. They are rarely observed on the ground, preferring instead to feed in the trees, sometimes even catching insects in flight. Bold by nature, they will become regular visitors to bird tables if fruit is left out for them. Pairs of blue-gray tanagers build their well-disguised nest in a tree up to 30ft (10m) off the ground. The hen sits alone, with the chicks hatching after a period of incubation lasting 14 days. Both members of the pair contribute food for the growing brood, with invertebrates featuring prominently in the diet at this time. The young leave the nest at just two weeks of age, and soon afterward the adult pair will begin nesting again, although the breeding season does vary according to locality. These tanagers are most likely to be encountered at altitudes below 5,000ft (1,500m), but they may sometimes range up to 6,500ft (2,000m).

Identification: Head and body varies from pale blue through to bluish-gray, and is lighter on the head and darker across the back. Wings and tail invariably a darker shade of blue. Shoulder area is white in individuals occurring east of the Andes, blue in those further west. Hens may have slightly olive underparts. Young birds are generally duller.

Grayish saltator (*Saltator coerulescens*): 8in (20cm)
Mexico down through lowland South America east of the Andes, also northern Colombia and Trinidad. South through central Brazil into parts of Bolivia, Paraguay, Argentina and Uruguay. Mainly grayish, with a white stripe above the eyes. White throat edged with black streaks. Grayish underparts, paler below with buff undertail coverts. Stocky grayish bill. Sexes alike.

Orange-crowned euphonia (*Euphonia saturata*): 4in (10cm)
Restricted to southwest Colombia, western Ecuador and the extreme northwest of Peru, typically under 3,000ft (1,000m). Cock has an orangish-yellow crown and underparts; rest of head, throat and body dark violet-blue. Hens have olive upperparts and yellowish underparts.

Common diuca-finch (*Diuca diuca*): 7in (18cm)
Southern Bolivia, Chile and Argentina, including Buenos Aires. Gray upperparts, with blacker wings and tail. Gray cheeks and breast, with a white throat patch. Center of the breast and belly are white. Rufous tinge on the flanks. Gray plumage of hens has a brownish suffusion.

Philadelphia vireo (*Vireo philadelphicus*): 5in (12½cm)
Breeds in southern Canada and northern U.S.A. Migrates to Central America, rarely northern Colombia. Coloration varies through its range, also brighter in fall. Grayish cap on head, with a black stripe through the eyes edged by white stripes. Upperparts greenish. Underparts yellowish, paler on the belly. Sexes are alike.

Blue-black grassquit

Volatinia jacarina

These birds are often seen in farming areas, foraging for seeds on the ground. They can also be found in towns and backyards, having adapted well to living close to humans. Blue-black grassquits are quite conspicuous despite the male's rather drab coloration, which can nevertheless have a slightly iridescent quality, depending on the light. Young birds only acquire full adult coloration at the start of their second year. When breeding, pairs tend to occupy their own territories, with nests being hidden low down among vegetation. This is the stage at which the male's distinctive buzzy song is most likely to be heard, accompanied by vertical display jumps up and down on a perch. Outside the nesting season, blue-black grassquits associate in much larger flocks of up to several hundred birds, sometimes in the company of similar species. They prefer open country, and are rarely seen in densely forested areas.

Identification: Cock birds have a glossy bluish-black appearance. When molting, their underparts are buff with evident blackish scalloping. Hens are brown overall, with whitish underparts streaked with brown. The bill in both sexes is quite narrow and slender. Young birds have buff wing bars.

Distribution: Mexico south via Panama across virtually all of northern South America, to northern Chile and central Argentina. Also present on some Caribbean islands.
Size: 4in (10cm).
Habitat: Farily open country.
Nest: Cup-shaped.
Eggs: 2–3, pale bluish with rusty markings.
Food: Seeds and invertebrates.

CLASSIFICATION

The way in which different birds are grouped is known as classification. This is not only helpful in terms of distinguishing individual species and those that are closely related, but it also enables wider assessments of relationships between larger groups to be made.

Interest in how best to group birds into distinct categories is nothing new. It dates back nearly 2,500 years to the ancient Greeks, when an early method of classification was developed by the philosopher Aristotle. He sought to group living creatures on the basis of differences in their lifestyles, rather than on the basis of anatomical distinctions, which are favored today. The first modern attempt to trace relationships between birds was made by Sir Francis Willoughby, in a book entitled *Ornithologia,* which was published in 1676. Willoughby saw the need for what was essentially an identification key that would enable readers to find an unknown bird by means of special tables devised for this purpose.

Willoughby's work concentrated solely on birds, but it was actually a Swedish botanist, Carl von Linné (also known as Linnaeus), who devised the universal system of classification that is now known as the Linnean System. Linné relied primarily on the physical similarities between living organisms as the basis for grouping them, laying the

Below: The nominate subspecies of the pearly conure (Pyrrhura lepida lepida) is identifiable by its distinctive red markings on the wing.

Above: One of the recognized subspecies of the pearly conure (Pyrrhura lepida anerythra), which differs subtley from its relative below.

foundations for the science of classification, which is now known as systematics. He refined this approach through a series of new editions of his classic work *Systema Naturae,* which was originally published in 1735 for the first time.

Linné's system operates through a series of ranks, creating what is sometimes described as a hierarchic method. Starting from a very general base, the ranks become increasingly specific, splitting into smaller groups, until, finally, individual types of birds can be identified. One advantage of this system is that when a new species is discovered, it can be fitted easily into this existing framework.

New advances

While Linnaeus and successive generations of taxonomists relied on physical similarities, the use of D.N.A. analysis is currently transforming our understanding of the natural world. By comparing sequences of the genetic material D.N.A., it is possible for ornithologists to investigate which birds share D.N.A. sequences that suggest a close relationship. This method of study is set to revolutionize taxonomy and is already leading to numerous revisions of the existing classification of birds.

How the system works

Birds, as animals, belong to the Kingdom Animalia, and, since they have backbones, are members of the phylum Chordata, which includes all vertebrates. The class Aves is the first division at which birds are separated

Above: The green plumage of the African race of ringnecked parakeet (Psittacula krameri krameri) *tends to be of a more yellowish shade, and the bill is dark.*

from other vertebrates such as mammals. Birds alone comprise this major grouping, which is subdivided into smaller categories called orders. It is then a matter of tracking an individual species down through the various ranks of classification. For example, the classificatory breakdown of the pearly conure is as follows:
Order: Psittaciformes
Family: Psittacidae
Genus: *Pyrrhura*
Species: *Pyrrhura lepida*
Subspecies: *Pyrrhura lepida lepida; Pyrrhura lepida anerythra; Pyrrhura lepida coerulescens*
If you are unsure where you are in the ranking, the way in which the names are written gives a clear indication. The names of orders end in "-formes," while family names terminate with "-idae." At or below genus level, all names are italicized, with the genus comprising one or more species. The scientific name of a species always consists of two descriptions, with the genus names being written first.

Species are the basic fundamental level in the taxonomic tree, enabling particular types of birds to be named individually. Members of a particular species generally identify with each other and do not normally interbreed with other species. However, if interbreeding does occur, the resulting offspring are known as hybrids.

At the most specific level of the taxonomic tree are subspecies: closely related forms of the same species that are nevertheless distinct enough to be identified separately. These are often defined on the basis of their size, and also because of marked differences in coloration. In the case of the pearly conure (*Pyrrhura lepida lepida*), the nominate form (meaning the first form to be recognized) can be distinguished by the repetition of the "trivial" name, *lepida*. Other races of this South American parrot boast a similar appearance to the nominate subspecies, but often with subtle differences in color on the head and wings.

It was Linné himself who devised this method of distinguishing between such closely related individuals, first describing it in 1758. His method is sometimes known as the trinomial

system, reflecting the fact that the name of the subspecies is made up of three parts.

What's in a name?

Even the choice of scientific names is not random. They give an insight into a bird's appearance or distribution, using descriptions derived from Latin. The name *flavinucha*, for example, indicates yellow plumage around the neck; the description *peruviana* in the case of the parrot-billed seed eater (*Sporophila peruviana*) indicates that the bird's habitat is in South America. In a few instances, the species' description features a person's name, for example *Calypte Anna*, popularly known as Anna's hummingbird. It was so-called in 1829 by the noted French naturalist Rene Lesson, to honor the beauty of an Italian noblewoman of the period—Anna, Duchess of Rivoli.

In order to be formally recognized as a species, an example of the bird concerned, known as the "type specimen," has to be held in a museum collection, where a detailed description of its characteristics is written up as part of the identification process.

Below: Subtle differences in color can be seen in the Indian race of ringnecked parakeet (Psittacula krameri manillensis), *which is now established in some parts of the U.S.A., most notably in the vicinity of Bakersfield, California.*

GLOSSARY

anvil: A rock or hard object against which certain species batter prey such as snails, to break the shell.

avifauna: The birds of a specified region or period of time.

breeding plumage: The often brightly colored plumage that the cock birds of some species adopt before the breeding season. Also known as summer or alternate plumage.

carpal: The area of plumage at the top of the leading edge of the wings, corresponding to the wrist.

carrion-eaters: Birds such as vultures that feed on the carcasses of dead creatures that they themselves have not killed.

cere: The fleshy area encompassing the nostrils located above the bill. Often especially prominent in parrots.

cline: A gradual change in a characteristic of a species, such as size, or the frequency of a characteristic, over a geographical area.

clumping: The way in which small birds such as the merida wren (*Cistothorus meridae*) come together and roost collectively to retain body heat.

cob: A male swan.

columbiforms: The group of birds that comprises doves and pigeons.

contour feathers: The smaller feathers covering the head and body.

corvid: A member of the Corvidae family, such as crows, ravens and jays.

coverts: The specific contour feathers covering the wings, and also present at the base of the tail.

cryptic: Refers to coloration or formation that conceals or camouflages.

culmen: The central ridge of the bill.

down: Plumage that primarily serves to conserve body heat, and has a loose texture.

eclipse plumage: A transitional plumage seen, for example, in the drakes of some species of duck, occurring after they have molted their breeding plumage; usually much duller and resembling that of a female. Also seen in some finches and other birds.

Above: White-tipped sickle hummingbird (Eutoxeres aquila).

frugivore: A species that eats mainly fruit.

irruption: An unpredictable movement of large numbers of birds, typically in search of food outside their normal range.

lek: An area where the male birds of certain species, such as the greater sage grouse (*Centrocercus urophasianus*), gather to perform their courtship displays.

lores: The area between the bill and the eyes, on each side of the face.

mantle: The plumage on the back and folded wings of certain birds when it is the same color.

melanistic: A dominance of black pigment in the plumage, such as in a particular color phase of some species.

migrant: A bird that undertakes regular seasonal movements, breeding in one location and overwintering in another.

mustachial: An area of plumage, usually a stripe, running from the bill under the eye, resembling a mustache in appearance, as seen in the Inca tern (*Larosterna inca*).

nidicolous: Refers to the chicks of species that remain in the nest for some time after hatching.

nidifugous: Describes the chicks of species that leave the nest almost immediately after hatching.

nuchal: The plumage at the nape of the neck.

orbital: The skin around the eye.

pampas: The description given to the relatively open and virtually treeless areas of grassland occurring in southern parts of the South American continent.

pectoral: Of or located on the breast.

precocial: Refers to newly hatched young that are covered with down and fully active, able to run around at this stage.

race: A geographically isolated population below the level of species, which differs slightly, typically in size or color, from other races of the same species.

racket/racquet: Enlargements at the tips of otherwise bare shafts of tail feathers, as in the blue-crowned motmot (*Momotus momota*).

raptor: A bird of prey that actively hunts its food.

ratite: Any of the large, flightless birds, such as the greater rhea (*Rhea americana*), that have a flat breastbone without the keel-like ridge of flying birds.

scapular: Of or on the shoulder.

spatule: Spoon-shaped or spatula-shaped feathers, on the wing or the tail.

speculum: A distinctive patch of color evident in the flight feathers of certain birds, particularly ducks and parrots.

syrinx: The voice organ of birds, located at the base of the trachea (windpipe).

tarsal: Refers to the area at or below the ankle in birds, as in tarsal spur.

torpidity: A state of dormancy, usually undertaken to conserve energy and combat possible starvation in the face of adverse environmental conditions.

tousling: Territorial behavior by pairs during the breeding period, in which the pair attacks the chicks of other birds, or even their own chicks, if they venture too close.

wattle: A wrinkled, fleshy, often brightly colored piece of skin that hangs from the throat or chin of certain birds, such as the long-wattled umbrellabird (*Cephalopterus penduliger*), or may be present elsewhere on the head.

zygodactyl: The 2:2 perching grip, with two toes holding the perch at the front and two at the back.

Below: Parrots have a zygodactyl perching grip.

SELECTED BIBLIOGRAPHY

Alderton, David (1992) *Parrots*, Whittet Books, London, U.K.

Brewer, David (2001) *Wrens, Dippers and Thrashers*, Christopher Helm, London, U.K.

Brudenell-Bruce, P.G.C. (1975) *The Birds of New Providence and the Bahama Islands*, Collins, London, U.K.

Bull, John & Farrand, John (1977) *The Audubon Society Field Guide to North American Birds (Eastern Region)*, Knopf, New York, U.S.A.

Byers, Clive; Olsson, Urban & Curson, Jon (1995) *Sparrows and Buntings: A Guide to the Sparrows and Buntings of North America and the World*, Pica Press, Robertsbridge, East Sussex, U.K.

Cassidy, James (ed.) (1990) *Book of North American Birds*, Reader's Digest, New York, U.S.A.

Dorst, Jean (1974) *The Life of Birds*, two vols, Weidenfeld & Nicolson, London, U.K.

Ferguson-Lees, James & Christie, David A. (2001) *Raptors of the World*, Christopher Helm, London, U.K.

Fjeldsa, Jon & Krabbe, Niels (1990) *Birds of the High Andes*, Zoological Museum, University of Copenhagen and Apollo Books, Svendborg, Denmark.

Forshaw, Joseph & Cooper, William T. (1989) *Parrots of the World*, Blandford Press, London, U.K.

Fry, C. Hilary; Fry, Kathie & Harris, Alan (1992) *Kingfishers, Bee-eaters, and Rollers*, Christopher Helm, London, U.K.

Gibbs, David; Barnes, Eustace & Cox, John (2001) *Pigeons and Doves*, Pica Press, Robertsbridge, East Sussex, U.K.

Godfrey, Earl W. (1966) *Birds of Canada*, N.M.C. Bulletin 203, National Museums of Canada, Ottawa, Canada.

Harrap, Simon & Quinn, David (1996) *Tits, Nuthatches, and Treecreepers*, Christopher Helm, London, U.K.

Hayman, Peter; Marchant, John & Prater, Tony (1986) *Shorebirds*, Christopher Helm, London, U.K.

Hilty, Steven L & Brown, William L (1986) *A Guide to the Birds of Colombia*, Princeton University Press, N.J., U.S.A.

Howell, Steve N. G. & Webb, Sophie (1995) *A Guide to the Birds of Mexico and Northern Central America*, Oxford University Press, Oxford, U.K.

Hoyo, Josep del; Elliott, Andrew & Sargatal, Jordi (series eds) (1992) *Handbook of Birds of the World*, vols 1–7, Lynx Edicions, Barcelona, Spain.

Jaramillo, Alvaro & Burke, Peter (1999) *New World Blackbirds*, Christopher Helm, London, U.K.

Johnsgard, Paul A. (1983) *The Hummingbirds of North America*, Smithsonian Institution Press, Washington D.C., U.S.A.

Land, D. (1970) *Birds of Guatemala*, Livingstone, Wynnewood, P.A., U.S.A.

Madge, Steve & Burn, Hilary (1988) *Wildfowl*, Christopher Helm, London, UK.

Madge, Steve & McGowan, Phil (2002) *Pheasants, Partridges, and Grouse*, Christopher Helm, London, U.K.

Ogilvie, Malcolm & Ogilvie, Carol (1986) *Flamingos*, Alan Sutton Publishing, Gloucester, U.K.

Peterson, Roger T. (1961) *Peterson Field Guides: Western Birds*, Houghton Mifflin Co., Boston, U.S.A.

Peterson, Roger T. (1980) *Peterson Field Guides: Eastern Birds*, Houghton Mifflin Co., Boston, U.S.A.

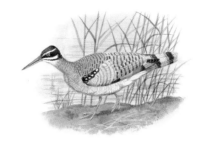

Above: Sun bittern (Eurypyga helias).

Pratt, H.D.; Bruner, P.L. & Berrett, D.G. (1987) *A Field Guide to The Birds of Hawaii and the Tropical Pacific*, Princeton University Press, Princeton, N.J., U.S.A.

Ridgely, Robert S. & Gwynee, J. (1989) *A Guide to the Birds of Panama*, Princeton University Press, Princeton, N.J., U.S.A.

Ridgely, Robert S. & Tudor, Guy (1989) *The Birds of South America*, vols 1–2, Oxford University Press, Oxford, U.K.

Ridgely, Robert S. & Greenfield, Paul J. (2001) *The Birds of Ecuador*, Christopher Helm, London, U.K.

Schauensee, Roldolphe M. de, & Phelps, William H. (1978) *A Guide to the Birds of Venezuela*, Princeton University Press, Princeton, N.J., U.S.A.

Sibley, David (2000) *The North American Bird Guide*, Pica Press, Robertsbridge, East Sussex, U.K.

Sparks, John & Soper, Tony (1987) *Penguins*, David & Charles, Devon, U.K.

Udvardy, Miklos D. F. (1977) *The Audubon Society Field Guide to North American Birds (Western Region)*, Knopf, New York, U.S.A.

PICTURE ACKNOWLEDGEMENTS

The Publishers would like to thank the following agencies for permission to reproduce their photographs in this book. Jacket credits appear on page 4.

Key: l = left, r=right, t=top, m=middle, b=bottom, E=endpaper

Dennis Avon: 43t, 246

Ardea: 2, 6tr, 7, 12tl, 12br, 14br, 15b, 19m, 19b, 20tr, 21br, 22bl, 23tl, 23b, 24b, 25tr, 25b, 26t, 26bl, 27t, 27b, 29t, 29b, 31m, 31b, 32t, 32b, 35, 36b, 37t, 37m, 38, 39t, 39m, 40, 41, 44t, 48bl, 48br, 50tl, 50b, 52t, 52b, 54f, 56b, 58, 60t, 62b, 63tr, 66tm, 66tr

NHPA: 26br, 27br, 33m

Oxford Scientific: 6b, 11, 16t, 17tl, 17ml, 18t, 18b, 21bl, 24t, 25tl, 28t, 30t, 33tr, 33b, 37b, 39b, 43b, 44m, 44b, 46t, 48t, 50tr, 54b, 56t, 60b, 62t, 63tl, 63b, 66tl

Illustrations were provided by Peter Barrett.

Additional illustrations supplied by:

Anthony Duke: 42; all location maps, 68–245

Studio Galante: 150, 151, 192, 194

Martin Knowelden: 10, 11, 12, 17tr, 19, 20, 21, 22, 28, 30, 34

Andrew Robinson: 126, 127

Below: Herring gull (Larus argentatus).

WEBSITES OF INTEREST

GENERAL CONTACTS

American Birding Association
http://www.americanbirding.org/

American Bird Conservancy
http://www.abcbirds.org/

Birding in Canada
http://www.web-nat.com/bic/

Birdnet.com
http://www.nmnh.si.edu/BIRDNET/

Bird Studies Canada
http://www.bsc-eoc.org/

Birds of National Parks
http://ice.ucdavis.edu/nps/

Birdzilla.com
http://www.birdzilla.com/

Canadian Nature Federation
http://www.cnf.ca/

Canadian Peregrine Foundation
http://www.peregrine-foundation.ca/

Canadian Wildlife Service
http://www.cws-scf.ec.gc.ca

Caribbean Species Listings
http://camacdonald.com/birding/Comparisons-Caribbean.htm

Central American Species Listings By Country
http://camacdonald.com/birding/Comparisons-CentralAm.htm

Cooper Ornithological Association
http://www.cooper.org/

Cornell Lab of Ornithology
http://birds.cornell.edu

National Parks, Forests, Wilderness areas
http://gorp.away.com/gorp/resource/main.htm

Neotropical Bird Club
http://www.neotropicalbirdclub.org

North American Bird Sounds
http://www.naturesongs.com/birds.html

North American Rare Bird Alert
http://www.narba.org/

South American Species Listings By Country
http://camacdonald.com/birding/Comparisons-SouthAmerica.htm

Surfbirds.com
http://www.surfbirds.com/

U.S. Fish & Wildlife Service
http://www.fws.gov/

U.S. STATE CONTACTS

Audubon Society chapter
http://www.audubon.org/chapter/
(Append state abbrievation at the end of this URL, e.g., for Alaska, type
http://www.audubon.org/chapter/ak

Alabama Ornithological Society
http://www.bham.net/aos/

California Bird Records Committee
http://www.wfo-cbrc.org/cbrc/index.html

Birding in Colorado
http://www.geocities.com/RainForest/Vines/1410/

Florida Ornithological Society
http://www.fosbirds.org/

Georgia Ornithological Society
http://www.gos.org/index.html

Hawaiian birds
http://www.aloha.net/~jhdenny/

The Illinois Ornithological Society
http://www.illinoisbirds.org/

Iowa Ornithologists Union
http://www.iowabirds.org/iou/iou.asp

Kansas Ornithological Society
http://www.ksbirds.org/index.html

Kentucky Ornithological Sociaty
http://www.biology.eku.edu/kos.htm

Louisiana Ornithological Society
http://losbird.org/

Maryland Ornithological Society
http://www.MDBirds.org/

Massachusetts Avian Records Committee
http://massbird.org/MARC/

Michigan Bird Records Committee
http://www.umd.umich.edu/dept/rouge_river/MBRChome.html

Minnesota Ornithologists' Union
http://biosci.cbs.umn.edu/~mou/

Nebraska Ornithologists' Union
http://rip.physics.unk.edu/NOU/

New Jersey Bird Records Committee
http://www.princeton.edu/~llarson/njrc.html

Federation of New York State Bird Clubs
http://www.fnysbc.org/

Oregon Birds Checklist
http://home.teleport.com/~skipr/birds/obrclist.htm

*Above: American goldfinch
(Carduelis tristis)*

South Dakota Bird Breeding Atlas
http://www.npsc.nbs.gov/resource/distr/birds/sdatlas/sdatlas.htm

Tennessee Ornithological Society Bird Records Committee
http://www.utm.edu/departments/artsci/biology/tbrc/tbrc.htm

Texas Ornithological Society
http://texasnaturalist.net/tos/tos.html

The Virginia Society of Ornithology
http://www.ecoventures-travel.com/vso/

Washington Ornithological Society
http://www.wos.org/

Wisconsin Society for Ornithology
http://www.uwgb.edu/birds/wso/

CANADIAN CONTACTS

Banff National Park (Alberta)
http://www.canadianrockies.net/birding.html

New Brunswick Bird Records Committee
http://personal.nbnet.nb.ca/maryspt/NBBRC

Wildlife Viewing in British Columbia
http://www.bcadventure.com/adventure/wildview/index.html

The Natural History Society of Newfoundland and Labrador
http://www.cs.mun.ca/~nhs/

Cape Breton birds (Nova Scotia)
http://www.seascape.ns.ca/~shearwater/start

Ontario Birding
http://www.web-nat.com/bic/ont/

Prince Edward Island Birding
http://www.gov.pe.ca/birds/index.php3

Bird Clubs in Quebec
http://www.coq.qc.ca/

Yukon Bird Club
http://www.yukonweb.com/community/ybc/index.html

INDEX